REPORTS
OF THE
UNITED STATES TAX COURT

July 1, 2014, to December 31, 2014

Volume 143

(Cite 143 T.C.)

SHEILA A. MURPHY
REPORTER OF DECISIONS

U.S. GOVERNMENT PRINTING OFFICE
WASHINGTON: 2014

For sale by the Superintendent of Documents, U.S. Government Publishing Office
Internet: bookstore.gpo.gov Phone: toll free (866) 512-1800; DC area (202) 512-1800
Fax: (202) 512-2104 Mail: Stop IDCC, Washington, DC 20402-0001

ISBN 978-0-16-092876-5

JUDGES OF THE UNITED STATES TAX COURT

Chief Judge

MICHAEL B. THORNTON

Judges

JOHN O. COLVIN
JAMES S. HALPERN
MAURICE B. FOLEY
JUAN F. VASQUEZ
JOSEPH H. GALE
L. PAIGE MARVEL [1]
JOSEPH ROBERT GOEKE
MARK V. HOLMES
DAVID GUSTAFSON
ELIZABETH CREWSON PARIS
RICHARD T. MORRISON
KATHLEEN KERRIGAN
RONALD L. BUCH
ALBERT G. LAUBER
JOSEPH W. NEGA
CARY DOUGLAS PUGH [2]
TAMARA W. ASHFORD [3]

Senior Judges recalled to perform judicial duties under the provisions of section 7447 of the Internal Revenue Code:

HOWARD A. DAWSON, JR.
HERBERT L. CHABOT
MARY ANN COHEN
STEPHEN J. SWIFT [4]
JULIAN I. JACOBS
JOEL GERBER
THOMAS B. WELLS
ROBERT P. RUWE
LAURENCE J. WHALEN
CAROLYN P. CHIECHI
DAVID LARO
HARRY A. HAINES
ROBERT A. WHERRY, JR.

Special Trial Judges

PETER J. PANUTHOS, *Chief Special Trial Judge*

ROBERT N. ARMEN, JR.
LEWIS R. CARLUZZO
JOHN F. DEAN [5]
DANIEL A. GUY, JR.

ROBERT R. DI TROLIO, *Clerk*

[1] Judge Marvel was reappointed and took the oath of office on December 3, 2014.
[2] Judge Pugh took the oath of office on December 16, 2014.
[3] Judge Ashford took the oath of office on December 19, 2014.
[4] Judge Swift was recalled on December 14, 2014.
[5] Special Trial Judge Dean retired on July 20, 2014.

TABLE OF CASES

REPORTS

OF THE

UNITED STATES TAX COURT

GUARDIAN INDUSTRIES CORP., PETITIONER *v.* COMMISSIONER OF INTERNAL REVENUE, RESPONDENT

Docket No. 20755–12. Filed July 17, 2014.

I.R.C. section 162(f) denies a deduction for "any fine or similar penalty paid to a government for the violation of any law." Section 1.162–21(a), Income Tax Regs., provides that the term "government" includes a "corporation or other entity serving as an agency or instrumentality" of a domestic or foreign government. In 2008 P, a U.S. corporation, paid a fine to the Commission of the European Community (Commission) for participating in a price-fixing cartel that violated the competition provisions of European Community (EC) law. P subsequently claimed a deduction for this payment on its 2008 Federal income tax return. R disallowed the claimed deduction under I.R.C. section 162(f), contending that the Commission is an instrumentality of the government of a foreign country within the meaning of section 1.162–21(a), Income Tax Regs.

1. *Held*: The phrase "government of a foreign country," as used in section 1.162–21(a), Income Tax Regs., may refer both to the government of a single foreign country and to the governments of two or more foreign countries.

2. *Held, further*, the Commission is an entity serving as an instrumentality of the EC member states within the meaning of section 1.162–21(a)(2) and (3), Income Tax Regs.

3. *Held, further*, P's claimed deduction for the fine paid to the Commission was properly disallowed under I.R.C. section 162(f).

Allen Duane Webber, *Jaclyn J. Pampel*, *Summer M. Austin*, and *Katie M. Marcusse*, for petitioner.

Dennis M. Kelly, *Heather L. Lampert*, and *Robert M. Morrison*, for respondent.

OPINION

LAUBER, *Judge*: Following an examination of petitioner's Federal income tax returns for 2005–08, the Internal Revenue Service (IRS or respondent) determined tax deficiencies and accuracy-related penalties under section 6662(a).[1] After concessions, the remaining substantive issue concerns the deductibility of a €20 million payment that petitioner made in 2008 to the Commission of the European Community (Commission).[2] The IRS disallowed a deduction for this payment under section 162(f), which provides that "[n]o deduction shall be allowed * * * for any fine or similar penalty paid to a government for the violation of any law." The parties have filed cross-motions for partial summary judgment on this point.

Petitioner does not dispute that the €20 million payment was a "fine or similar penalty" or that this payment was made "for the violation of * * * [a] law." The question the parties have submitted for resolution by summary judgment is whether the payment was made "to a government." The answer depends on whether the European Community (EC), and specifically the Commission, is an "agency or instrumentality" of "[t]he government of a foreign country" within the meaning of section 1.162–21(a), Income Tax Regs.

We hold that the term "government of a foreign country" as used in this regulation can refer to a single government or to multiple governments and thus embraces the governments of the EC member states. We further hold that the EC, and specifically the Commission, is an "instrumentality" of the EC member states considered individually and collectively. We believe these holdings to be consistent with a recent opinion of the U.S. Court of Appeals for the Second Circuit, which holds that the EC is an "agency or instrumentality of a foreign state" for purposes of the Foreign Sovereign Immunities Act (FSIA), 28 U.S.C. sec. 1603(b) (2006). *See European Cmty. v. RJR Nabisco, Inc.*, 764 F.3d 129 (2d Cir. 2014), *vacating* 814 F. Supp. 2d 189 (E.D.N.Y. 2011). Concluding as we do that the €20 million fine was non-

[1] Unless otherwise indicated, all statutory references are to the Internal Revenue Code in effect for the tax years in issue, and all Rule references are to the Tax Court Rules of Practice and Procedure. We round all monetary amounts to the nearest dollar.

[2] The parties filed a stipulation of settled issues resolving the other substantive issue, concerning petitioner's subpart F foreign base company services income. Upon disposition of the pending motions, the only outstanding matters will be the accuracy-related penalties and computational adjustments.

deductible under section 162(f) because it was paid to an "instrumentality" of the "government of a foreign country," we will grant respondent's motion for partial summary judgment and deny petitioner's motion.

Background

The following facts are not in dispute and are derived principally from the pleadings, the stipulation of facts, and the related exhibits. At the time petitioner filed its petition, its principal place of business was in Michigan. [3]

The EC was established in 1958 pursuant to the Treaty Establishing the European Economic Community (EC Treaty). [4] The EC was created to accomplish common objectives that could not be efficiently achieved by individual action of the member states. The European Union (EU) came into existence in 1993 with the Treaty on European Union. During 2008 the EC had 27 member states and was one of several entities collectively constituting the EU, with a separate legal personhood distinct from the EU. [5]

[3] The parties submitted an extensive stipulation of facts with attached exhibits that deals comprehensively with relevant aspects of EC law. Where necessary, we have consulted resources outside the stipulation to provide a fuller picture. *See* Rule 146 ("The Court's determination [of foreign law] shall be treated as a ruling on a question of law."); *Greene v. Commissioner*, 85 T.C. 1024, 1026 n.3 (1985) (determining that the Court is not bound by the stipulations of the parties as to matters of law); *Curtis v. Beatrice Foods Co.*, 481 F. Supp. 1275, 1285 (S.D.N.Y. 1980) ("[F]ederal judges may reject even the uncontradicted conclusions of an expert witness and reach their own decisions on the basis of independent examination of foreign legal authorities."), *aff'd without published opinion*, 633 F.2d 203 (2d Cir. 1980).

[4] We cite the consolidated version of the Treaty on European Union and of the Treaty Establishing the European Community, C 321 E/1.

[5] In 2009 the Lisbon Treaty incorporated the EC, along with other European bodies, into the EU. *See* Treaty of Lisbon Amending the Treaty on European Union and the Treaty Establishing the European Community, Dec. 13, 2007, 2007 O.J. (C 306). The EC continued to operate as it had previously, but after 2009 it was no longer an independent entity. *See* Brian F. Havel & Gabriel S. Sanchez, "Restoring Global Aviation's 'Cosmopolitan Mentalité,'" 29 B.U. Int'l L.J. 1, 3 n.2 (2011) ("While some scholars have labored in the past to keep the European Union conceptually separate from the European Community, with the former referring to a geographic and political territory and the latter designating a source of law

Continued

Under the EC Treaty, shared objectives were to be implemented by the EC acting alone, by the EC and the member states sharing competences, or by the EC's undertaking to support, coordinate, or supplement actions of the individual member states. The EC Treaty defines the EC's areas of authority and limits its powers to act outside those areas. *See* EC Treaty art. 5. As relevant to this Opinion, the institutional framework created to implement the goals of the EC consists of the Parliament, the Council, and the Commission, along with the Court of Justice and the Court of Auditors. *Id.* art. 7.

The Parliament, a semi-legislative body, consists of representatives directly elected by the citizens of the member states. The Council is a legislative body composed of government ministers from each member state who are authorized to commit their respective governments. *Id.* art. 203. The Council exercises, jointly with the Parliament, legislative and budgetary functions. *See id.* arts. 161, 202. However, the Council and the Parliament generally exercise their decision-making power only upon the basis of a proposal from the Commission.

The Commission functions in effect as the EC's executive branch. It consists of a President from one member state, who is nominated by the Council and approved by the Parliament, and a commissioner from each other member state. The latter must be approved by the Parliament and by the Council, which appoints each Commission member to a five-year term. *Id.* art. 214. Commission members are required to be completely independent in the performance of their duties, which means that they must act solely on behalf of the EC and not on behalf of any individual member state or the government thereof. Individual Commission members can be removed only for cause, by the Court of Justice upon proper application by the Council or the Commission. *See id.* art. 216.

To further economic unity and the goal of a well-regulated common market, the EC Treaty tasks the Commission with enforcing rules governing competition and free trade. These include rules that bar price-fixing, abusive market positions, and mergers that violate competition mandates. *See id.* arts.

and policy, * * * [the Lisbon Treaty] abolished this distinction.").

81, 82, 85. As in effect during 2008,[6] EC Treaty article 81 restricted (among other things) actions that directly or indirectly fixed the purchase or selling prices of goods. On application of a member state or on its own initiative, the Commission was authorized to investigate cases of suspected infringement of article 81; propose measures to bring the infringement to an end; and, if the infringement continued, record the infringement in a decision. *Id.* art. 85. A Commission decision addressing competition or free trade violations is binding upon all those to whom it is addressed. EC Treaty art. 249.

During 2008 the relationship between the Commission and the competition authorities of the member states was governed by a regulation enacted by the Council in 2002. *See* Regulation No. 1/2003, 2003 O.J. (L 1) 1. Under this regulation, responsibility for enforcing EC competition rules, previously exercised by the Commission alone, was shared between the Commission and national authorities. National authorities and national courts were thenceforth required to apply EC Treaty articles 81 and 82 in individual cases. Regulation 1/2003 arts. 3, 5, 6. They were also empowered to impose liability on infringing parties and decree remedies based on EC as well as national law, provided the application of national law did not prejudice the uniform application of EC rules governing competition.

Regulation 1/2003 requires the Commission and national authorities to apply EC competition law in "close cooperation." *Id.* art. 11(1). To achieve this goal, the regulation established the European Competition Network (ECN), consisting of the Commission and national competition agencies. Participants in the ECN were encouraged to pool experience, share information, conduct joint investigations, and allocate resources in an efficient manner.[7]

---

[6] After 2008 articles 81 and 82 were replaced by articles 101 and 102. Treaty on the Functioning of the European Union, 2008 O.J. (C 115) 47.

[7] An EC Notice issued in 2004 explained the objectives of the ECN. *See* Commission Notice on Cooperation within the Network of Competition Authorities, 2004 O.J. (C 101) 43:

> Together the * * * [national authorities] and the Commission form a network of public authorities: they act in the public interest and cooperate closely in order to protect competition. The network is a forum for

Continued

The Commission is authorized to conduct necessary inspections, with the aid of national authorities, by entering places of business, examining books and records, and sealing business premises. *Id.* art. 20. Businesses are required to submit to these inspections. If a business opposes an inspection, the relevant member state is required to provide the Commission with any needed assistance, including the assistance of the state's police power.

Although Regulation 1/2003 permits national authorities to bring infringement actions, the Commission has a right of first refusal to commence its own proceeding. A national authority must inform the Commission in writing before taking any formal steps toward conducting its own investigation. If the Commission does not act at that time, the relevant national authority, before issuing any decision concerning infringement, must inform the Commission of the impending decision. The Commission again has the option (rarely exercised at this juncture) to commence a proceeding of its own. The Commission's initiation of proceedings relieves national authorities of their competence to apply EC competition rules to the matter. Once the Commission issues a decision, national authorities and courts are barred from taking any action inconsistent with its decision. *Id.* arts. 3, 11, 16.

After beginning a proceeding, the Commission continues to share information with relevant national authorities and may consult in a collaborative manner with the Council or the Parliament.[8] Before recording a decision finding infringement, the Commission confers with the Advisory Committee on Restrictive Practices and Dominant Positions, composed of representatives of national authorities of the member states.

---

discussion and cooperation in the application and enforcement of EC competition policy. It provides a framework for the cooperation of European competition authorities in cases where Articles 81 and 82 of the Treaty are applied and is the basis for the creation and maintenance of a common competition culture in Europe.

[8] "[T]he Commission would be foolish to ignore the inter-institutional context within which all European policy is made. It should come as no surprise to find, therefore, that the Commission has often encouraged parliamentary and Council involvement where formally none was necessary." Michelle Cini & Lee McGowan, Competition Policy in the European Union 44 (2009).

Member states, through this committee, may have their opinions heard, but they cannot override the Commission's decision or dictate the final outcome.

Commission decisions are ultimately enforced by national authorities. EC Treaty art. 256. National authorities are required to enforce Commission decisions with no formality other than verification of the decision's authenticity, without modifying the decision or limiting its scope. *Ibid.* Following this verification, the Commission can proceed to seek enforcement of its decision, in accordance with the law of the member state, by bringing the matter before the relevant national tribunal.

This case arises from an investigation that the Commission conducted of Guardian Industries Corp. (Guardian) and its wholly owned Luxembourg subsidiary, Guardian Europe S.à.r.l. (Guardian Europe). Guardian and Guardian Europe manufactured and sold float glass, fabricated-glass products, fiberglass insulation, and other building materials to customers in Europe and elsewhere. In 2004 a group of glass producers and suppliers approached petitioner with a view to discussing and agreeing on prices and price increases for glass products. The Commission suspected that these companies were fixing prices of their products and initiated an investigation into this suspected anticompetitive behavior.

In November 2007 the Commission concluded its investigation and issued a decision determining that Guardian and Guardian Europe had participated in a cartel that infringed the competition provisions of EC Treaty article 81 by fixing prices. In December 2007 the Commission notified Guardian and Guardian Europe of its decision and advised that they were jointly and severally liable for a fine of €148 million. In March 2008 petitioner paid the Commission €20 million; Guardian Europe paid the Commission €91 million; and the two companies provided the Commission a guaranty covering the remaining €37 million. Neither the payment by Guardian Europe nor the guaranty is at issue here.

Guardian timely filed its Federal income tax return for 2008. On its return Guardian deducted the payment it made to the Commission, which was $30,260,000 when converted to dollars at the relevant exchange rate. Following an examination, the IRS sent petitioner a notice of deficiency disallowing this deduction under section 162(f).

Discussion

I. *Summary Judgment Standard*

The purpose of summary judgment is to expedite litigation and avoid unnecessary and expensive trials. *See FPL Grp., Inc. & Subs. v. Commissioner*, 116 T.C. 73, 74 (2001). We may grant summary judgment when there is no genuine dispute of material fact and a decision may be rendered as a matter of law. Rule 121(b); *Elec. Arts, Inc. v. Commissioner*, 118 T.C. 226, 238 (2002). The parties agree on all questions of basic fact and have expressed that consensus by filing cross-motions for partial summary judgment. We conclude that the question presented is appropriate for summary adjudication.

II. *Governing Statutory Framework*

Section 162(a) permits taxpayers to deduct "all the ordinary and necessary expenses paid or incurred during the taxable year in carrying on any trade or business." Section 162(f) excepts from this general rule "any fine or similar penalty paid to a government for the violation of any law." The parties have stipulated that Guardian's payment to the Commission constitutes a "fine or similar penalty paid * * * for the violation of [a] law."[9] The parties disagree as to whether the payment was made "to a government."

The Treasury regulations provide that no deduction shall be allowed for a fine or penalty paid to:

> (1) The government of the United States, a State, a territory or possession of the United States, the District of Columbia, or the Commonwealth of Puerto Rico;
>
> (2) The government of a foreign country; or
>
> (3) A political subdivision of, or corporation or other entity serving as an agency or instrumentality of, any of the above.
>
> [Sec. 1.162–21(a), Income Tax Regs.]

---

[9] Petitioner stipulated that "[i]f the Commission was an 'agency or instrumentality' of the government of a foreign country within the meaning of Treasury Regulation section 1.162–21(a), Guardian was not entitled to deduct the Payment under section 162(a)." Petitioner informed the Court that it "does not agree, in substance, that the Payment constituted the payment of a 'fine or penalty.'" But it agreed that it would not contest the Commissioner's determination that the payment should be so characterized.

Petitioner does not challenge the validity of this regulation.

Respondent agrees that the Commission is neither "[t]he government of a foreign country" nor "[a] political subdivision" thereof. Accordingly, the question for decision is whether the Commission is an "entity serving as an agency or instrumentality" of "[t]he government of a foreign country" within the meaning of this regulation. The parties have not brought to our attention, and we have not discovered, any prior authority that addresses this question directly. [10]

A. *"Government of a Foreign Country"*

The Commission is required to act on behalf of the EC and its member states collectively, and it is forbidden to act in the exclusive interest of any single government. Before we examine whether the Commission is an "agency or instrumentality," therefore, we must answer the threshold question whether the term "government of a foreign country," as used in section 1.162–21(a), Income Tax Regs., embraces the plural as well as the singular.

As a general matter of statutory interpretation, "unless the context indicates otherwise—words importing the singular include and apply to several persons, parties, or things." 1 U.S.C. sec. 1 (2006). This canon of construction is fully applicable in Federal tax cases. *See* sec. 7701(p)(1) (referring to 1 U.S.C. sec. 1 for "[s]ingular as including plural"). This Court and other courts have invoked this principle in numerous contexts analogous to that here.

In *Estate of Shamberg v. Commissioner*, 3 T.C. 131 (1944), *aff'd*, 144 F.2d 998 (2d Cir. 1944), the question was whether interest paid on bonds issued by the Port of New York Authority, a joint agency of the States of New York and New

[10] In his final summary judgment brief, respondent contends for the first time that his interpretation of the regulation is entitled to deference under *Bowles v. Seminole Rock & Sand Co.*, 325 U.S. 410, 414 (1945). We need not decide whether respondent timely advanced his deference argument or whether we would defer to litigating positions that do not derive their support from regulations, rulings, or longstanding administrative practice. *See Bowen v. Georgetown Univ. Hosp.*, 488 U.S. 204, 212 (1988); *Garnett v. Commissioner*, 132 T.C. 368, 381 (2009) (citing *Gen. Dynamics Corp. & Subs. v. Commissioner*, 108 T.C. 107, 120–121 (1997)). As explained more fully below, we are able to decide this case in respondent's favor without according any deference to his interpretation of section 1.162–21(a), Income Tax Regs.

Jersey, was exempt from tax under a statute that excluded from gross income interest on "the obligations of a State, Territory, or any political subdivision thereof." *Id.* at 134 (citing section 22(b)(4) of Revenue Acts of 1936 and 1938). After concluding that the Port Authority exercised sovereign powers, the Court addressed "the final objection that * * * [it] is not a political subdivision of 'a' state but of two states, and hence falls outside the exemption." *Id.* at 145. We rejected this argument: "[T]he answer, as we see it, is that the Port Authority is the political subdivision of a state—the State of New York—and also the political subdivision of another State—the State of New Jersey." *Ibid.* The Court of Appeals for the Second Circuit, in an opinion by Judge Augustus Hand, affirmed this conclusion. *See Estate of Shamberg*, 144 F.2d at 1006 ("The argument that the exemption does not apply to the Authority because two states, rather than one, created the agency is far from persuasive.").

In *RJR Nabisco*, 764 F.3d at 143–144 (citing 28 U.S.C. sec. 1603(b)), the Court of Appeals held that the EC constitutes "an organ of a foreign state" and is thus an "agency or instrumentality of a foreign state" for FSIA purposes. As Judge Leval put it: "There is no logic to the proposition that an entity that serves as an organ of one foreign state cannot also serve as the organ of another." *Id.* at 147. Citing 1 U.S.C. sec. 1, the court found no indication in the FSIA "that the phrase 'a foreign state' must be interpreted to exclude an organ that serves as an agency of several states." *Ibid.*; *accord, e.g.*, *In re Aircrash Disaster Near Roselawn, Ind.*, 96 F.3d 932, 938–939 (7th Cir. 1996) (holding that an entity created by multiple governments is an "agency or instrumentality" under FSIA); *Mangattu v. M/V Ibn Hayyan*, 35 F.3d 205, 208 (5th Cir. 1994) (same); *In re EAL Corp.*, No. 93–cv578 (SLR), 1994 WL 828320 (D. Del. Aug. 3, 1994) (entity created by 15 European nations and responsible for European air traffic control was an instrumentality of "a foreign state" under FSIA); *LeDonne v. Gulf Air, Inc.*, 700 F. Supp. 1400, 1406 (E.D. Va. 1988) (corporation created by treaty among four nations was an instrumentality of "a foreign state" under FSIA).

We are instructed to apply the singular-includes-the-plural canon of construction "unless the context indicates otherwise." 1 U.S.C. sec. 1; *see Metallics Recycling Co. v. Commis-*

sioner, 79 T.C. 730, 738 (1982) ("[W]hether the rule of 1 U.S.C. sec. 1 is to be applied * * * depends upon congressional intent in enacting the * * * [statute.]"), *aff'd*, 732 F.2d 523 (6th Cir. 1984). We discern nothing in section 162(f) or the congressional intent underlying its enactment that would render this canon of construction inapplicable here.

Congress enacted section 162(f) to preclude tax deductions for civil penalties imposed for violation of U.S. or foreign law. *See Hawronsky v. Commissioner*, 105 T.C. 94, 97 (1995), *aff'd without published opinion*, 98 F.3d 1338 (5th Cir. 1996). Petitioner has stipulated that the €20 million fine was imposed for violation of EC law. Under EC law, both the Commission and EC national authorities could investigate and sanction violations of EC Treaty articles 81 and 82. Had the Commission not proceeded against Guardian, an EC member state could have initiated a substantially identical infringement proceeding and could have imposed the same liability upon petitioner, for the same conduct, based on the same EC law. It would be an odd result, and a result plainly contrary to the statute's purpose, if a penalty imposed by one member state would be nondeductible under section 162(f), whereas the same penalty imposed by multiple member states, or an entity acting on their behalf, would qualify for deduction.[11]

Like the District Court in *LeDonne*, 700 F. Supp. at 1406, we decline to construe section 162(f) and the regulations interpreting it by employing an "unnecessary literalism that runs counter to * * * [their] purpose and ignores the well-established international practice of states acting jointly through treaty-created entities for public or sovereign purposes." We conclude that the phrase "government of a foreign country," as used in section 1.162–21(a), Income Tax Regs., may refer both to the government of a single foreign country

[11] Indeed, it is not clear to what extent petitioner disputes the application of the singular-includes-the-plural canon of construction. In its final reply brief, petitioner agrees that "[t]he Commission is not automatically disqualified as an 'agency or instrumentality' of 'the government of a foreign country' solely because the European Community was formed by more than one Member State." Petitioner hypothesizes, for example, that "an agency or instrumentality of the Latvian Government could also serve as an agency or instrumentality of the Estonian Government," provided that the entity qualified as an "agency or instrumentality" under petitioner's proposed test.

and to the governments of two or more foreign countries. As applied here, the term embraces the governments of the EC member states acting individually or collectively. *Cf. RJR Nabisco*, 764 F.3d at 144 ("The European Community was formed by its member nations to serve on their collective behalf * * *. We see no reason why it is not properly described as an organ of each nation."). The remaining question, and the chief focus of the parties' dispute, is whether the Commission is an "entity serving as an agency or instrumentality" of the EC member states. We turn now to that question.

B. *"Agency or Instrumentality"*

Because the terms "agency" and "instrumentality" as used in section 1.162–21(a)(3), Income Tax Regs., are not defined in the statute, the regulations, or the legislative history, we employ the standard tools of construction to discern their meaning. Regulations are interpreted in the same manner as statutes. *See Austin v. Commissioner*, 141 T.C. 551, 563 (2013) (citing *Black & Decker Corp. v. Commissioner*, 986 F.2d 60, 65 (4th Cir. 1993), *aff'g* T.C. Memo. 1991–557). In determining "the plain meaning of the statute, the court must look to the particular statutory language at issue, as well as the language and design of the statute as a whole." *K Mart Corp. v. Cartier, Inc.*, 486 U.S. 281, 291 (1988); *Norfolk Energy, Inc. v. Hodel*, 898 F.2d 1435, 1442 (9th Cir. 1990). When a statute is ambiguous, a court must find the interpretation that "can most fairly be said to be embedded in the statute, in the sense of being most harmonious with its scheme and with the general purposes that Congress manifested." *NLRB v. Lion Oil Co.*, 352 U.S. 282, 297 (1957).

1. *"Plain Meaning" Proposed by Guardian*

Our initial inquiry is whether the language of the regulation is so plain as to permit only one reasonable interpretation of the phrase "agency or instrumentality." *See, e.g., Robinson v. Shell Oil Co.*, 519 U.S. 337, 340 (1997). Petitioner's central argument hinges on its submission that this phrase does have a plain meaning. According to Guardian, "[t]he common sense reading of the term 'agency or instrumentality' in the context of the applicable regulatory language, and as informed by applicable dictionary definitions, demonstrates that such term encompasses only entities that act as divisions or subsidiary branches of a government." Under Guardian's proposed test, an entity qualifies as an "agency or instrumentality" of a foreign government only if it: (1) is controlled by that government; (2) acts exclusively on behalf of that government; and (3) is subordinate to that government. The Commission would not pass this test.

We do not agree that the phrase "agency or instrumentality" has an unambiguous plain meaning. A term is ambiguous if it is "capable of being understood in two or more possible senses or ways." *Chickasaw Nation v. United States*, 534 U.S. 84, 90 (2001). "Agency" and "instrumentality" are terms of considerable breadth, and they are susceptible of different meanings in different contexts. Although Guardian offered dictionary definitions showing that "agency or instrumentality" can refer to an administrative division of a government, both words are commonly used in other, less specific, senses. For example, "agency" is defined as "[t]he means or mode of acting; instrumentality"; and "instrumentality" is defined as "[a] means; an agency." American Heritage Dictionary 32, 910 (5th ed. 2011). Black's Law Dictionary 870 (9th ed. 2009) defines an "instrumentality" as "[a] thing used to achieve an end or purpose" and as "[a] means or agency through which a function of another entity is accomplished." *See RJR Nabisco*, 764 F.3d at 144 (although some definitions "characterize an organ as subordinate to a larger entity," the fact that a word "is sometimes used to refer to a smaller part of a larger whole does not mean that the word can serve only in that fashion").

Judicial precedent is hostile to the notion that the terms "agency" and "instrumentality" have an unambiguous plain meaning that dictionaries can illuminate. We have discovered at least five distinct tests that courts have employed to determine, in various contexts, whether an entity is an "agency" or "instrumentality" of government. *See Fed. Reserve Bank of St. Louis v. Metrocentre Improvement Dist. #1*, 657 F.2d 183, 185 (8th Cir. 1981) (whether entity is an "agency or instrumentality" for purposes of intergovernmental tax immunity), *aff'd*, 455 U.S. 995 (1982); *Michigan v. United States*, 40 F.3d 817, 829 (6th Cir. 1994) (same); *Filler v. Hanvit Bank*, 378 F.3d 213, 217 (2d Cir. 2004) (whether entity is an "agency or instrumentality" for FSIA purposes); *Soucie v. David*, 448 F.2d 1067, 1075 (D.C. Cir. 1971) (whether entity is an "agency" for APA purposes); *Groves v. United States*, 533 F.2d 1376, 1383 (5th Cir. 1976) (whether entity is an "agency" for purposes of section 911(a)(1) exclusion for foreign earned income). Indeed, an entity can be an "agency" or "instrumentality" of government for one purpose but not another. *Compare Gradall v. United States*, 329 F.2d 960, 964 (Ct. Cl. 1963) (American Red Cross is an "instrumentality" of the United States), *with* Rev. Rul. 60–36, 1960–1 C.B. 279 (American Red Cross is not an "agency" of the United States for purposes of excluding foreign income from taxation under former section 911). None of these courts found the term "agency" or "instrumentality" to have a plain meaning, and none of them relied on dictionary definitions as a reliable guide to discerning the proper interpretation of these words in context. Petitioner has cited no case in which a court has done so.[12]

Moreover, we find little merit in the definition that petitioner proposes to capture the plain meaning of these terms. If we adopted Guardian's definition of "agency or instrumentality," these words in the regulation would become superfluous. According to Guardian, an entity qualifies as an "agency or instrumentality" only if it acts as a division or subsidiary branch of a government to which it is subordinate and by which it is controlled. Under this definition, an "agency or instrumentality" equates to a "political subdivision." *See, e.g.*, *Garb v. Republic of Poland*, 440 F.3d 579, 596 n.21 (2d Cir. 2006) ("political subdivision" includes all governmental units beneath the central government, including local governments).

It is a well-accepted canon of construction that a statute ought to be construed so that no clause, sentence, or word is

---

[12] Petitioner cites two cases in which courts determined the meaning of instrumentality by applying the canon of construction noscitur a sociis. *See Edison v. Douberly*, 604 F.3d 1307, 1309 (11th Cir. 2010); *Green v. City of New York*, 465 F.3d 65, 79 (2d Cir. 2006). These cases are inapposite; the noscitur a sociis canon cannot properly be applied to interpret the regulation at issue. *See infra* pp. 15–16. In any event, these cases show the error of petitioner's submission that the phrase "agency or instrumentality" has an unambiguous plain meaning: "Only if an attempt to discern the plain meaning fails because the statute is ambiguous, do we resort to canons of construction." *Green*, 465 F.3d at 78.

rendered superfluous, void, or insignificant. *See Duncan v. Walker*, 533 U.S. 167, 174 (2001). The regulation at issue explicitly refers in the disjunctive to "a political subdivision," on the one hand, and to "an agency or instrumentality" on the other. *See* sec. 1.162–21(a)(3), Income Tax Regs. (disallowing deduction for fine paid to "a political subdivision of, or a corporation or other entity serving as an agency or instrumentality of, any of the above"). By equating "agency or instrumentality" with "political subdivision," petitioner would deprive "agency or instrumentality" of any independent meaning. We decline to adopt an interpretation of the regulation that renders a substantial portion of it meaningless. *See Filler*, 378 F.3d at 219–220 (rejecting plaintiffs' proposed construction of FSIA under antisurplusage canon because it would equate "foreign state" with "political subdivision," whereas statute repeatedly employs those terms in the disjunctive).

Petitioner tries to support its proposed definition of "agency or instrumentality" by relying on the canon of construction noscitur a sociis—a Latin phrase meaning "it is known by its associates." This canon of construction "hold[s] that the meaning of an unclear word or phrase should be determined by the words immediately surrounding it." Black's Law Dictionary 1160–1161. While noscitur a sociis is most commonly applied to lists of three or more terms, it may apply "when two or more words are grouped together." 2A Norman J. Singer & J.D. Shambie Singer, Sutherland Statutory Construction, sec. 47:16, at 359 (7th ed. 2014). Because "political subdivision" appears in the same clause as "agency or instrumentality," petitioner argues that the latter phrase should be given a limiting construction that essentially equates it to the former.

This argument is unconvincing for two reasons. First, noscitur a sociis is properly applied to limit the scope of a potentially broad statutory term, not to render that term altogether superfluous. For example, in *Jarecki v. G.D. Searle & Co.*, 367 U.S. 303, 307 (1961), the Supreme Court employed noscitur a sociis to interpret the term "discovery" as used in section 456(a)(2)(B) of the 1939 Code, which imposed tax on "[i]ncome resulting from exploration, discovery, or prospecting." Whereas "discovery" is a broad term that in other contexts can include geographical and scientific discoveries, the Court held that its association with "exploration" and "prospecting" suggested that the term, as used in this statute, had the narrower meaning of "discovery of mineral resources." *G.D. Searle & Co.*, 367 U.S. at 307. This application of noscitur a sociis did not deprive "discovery" of independent meaning; it simply limited the scope of the term to one type of discovery. By contrast, petitioner's application of this canon would equate "agency or instrumentality" with "political subdivision" and thus render the former phrase superfluous.

Second, noscitur a sociis is typically applied to a series of coequal terms that are in a syntactically equivalent position. *See, e.g.*, *G.D. Searle & Co.*, 367 U.S. at 307 (applying this canon to "income resulting from exploration, discovery, or prospecting"); *Green v. City of New York*, 465 F.3d 65, 78–79 (2d Cir. 2006) (applying this canon to "any department, agency, special purpose district, or other instrumentality of a State"). Here, we do not have a series or list of three coequal terms. Rather, the regulation defines "government" to include "[a] political subdivision of, or corporation or other entity serving as an agency or instrumentality of, any of the above." Sec. 1.162–21(a)(3), Income Tax Regs. This is not a series to which noscitur a sociis is properly applied, because the syntax tells us to expect two distinct sets, not three coequal members of the same set.[13]

In sum, we conclude that paragraph (a)(3) of the regulation does not have a plain meaning, and we reject the specific "plain meaning" definition that Guardian proposes. Because we determine the phrase "agency or instrumentality" as used in this regulation to be ambiguous, we must look beyond the plain meaning and find the interpretation that makes the most sense given the context in which this phrase appears. *See Lion Oil Co.*, 352 U.S. at 297.

---

[13] For example, assume a regulation that defined a "disqualified person" to include "a family member of, or a business partner or associate of," an individual. The noscitur a sociis canon might properly be applied to give similar scope to the terms "business partner" and "associate." However, this canon could not properly be applied to equate "business partner or associate" with "family member." Similarly here, noscitur a sociis may reasonably be applied to give similar scope to the terms "agency" and "instrumentality." But this canon cannot properly be applied to equate "agency or instrumentality" with "political subdivision."

2. *A Functional Approach*

Courts tasked with ascertaining whether a particular entity is an "agency" or "instrumentality" of government have found it difficult to rely on dictionary definitions. Because "it [is] clear that any general definition can be of only limited utility to a court confronted with one of the myriad organizational arrangements for getting the business of the government done," courts have generally adopted a "more functional" approach to this question. *Wash. Research Project, Inc. v. HEW*, 504 F.2d 238, 245–246 (D.C. Cir. 1974) (determining whether "initial review group" performing peer review on proposals for government grants was an "agency" for Freedom of Information Act purposes). "The unavoidable fact," as Judge McGowan explained, "is that each new arrangement must be examined anew and in its own context." *Id.* at 246. Our task is to determine the appropriate test to use in deciding whether the Commission should be regarded as an "agency or instrumentality" of the EC member states, given the context in which it operates and the legislative purpose underlying section 162(f).

We addressed a similar question in *Estate of Shamberg*, where we held that the Port of New York Authority, a joint agency of New York and New Jersey, was a "political subdivision" for purposes of the tax exemption for interest paid on State and local bonds. *See supra* pp. 9–10. The Port Authority was a "[m]utual endeavor * * * approved by the legislatures of the two states and Congress," designed to assure cooperation in the development of the Port of New York. *Estate of Shamberg*, 3 T.C. at 132. It was constituted by the proper authorities of each State "for the purpose of carrying out some of its public functions," *id.* at 141, and it was "engaged in the performance of a sovereign function of each of the states of New York and New Jersey," *id.* at 143–144 (quoting *Case v. Commissioner*, 34 B.T.A. 1229, 1247 (1936), *aff'd*, 92 F.2d 999 (2d Cir. 1937)). We deemed it immaterial that the Port Authority lacked certain sovereign powers, such as the power to tax. *See ibid.* And we concluded that it need not necessarily exercise "an 'essential' governmental function." *Id.* at 137. Rather, we held that the Port Authority was a "political subdivision" of New York and New Jersey and that the interest paid on its bonds was exempt from Federal income tax, because it had been "delegated the right to exercise part of the sovereign power of the State." [14]

The courts have applied a similar analysis in holding that Federal Reserve banks constitute "instrumentalities" of the United States for purposes of immunity from State and local taxation. For example, in *Metrocentre Improvement Dist. #1*, the Court of Appeals for the Eighth Circuit cited Supreme Court precedent for the proposition that "a governmental instrumentality is one that performs an important governmental function." 657 F.2d at 185 (citing *Fed. Land Bank v. Bismark Lumber Co.*, 314 U.S. 95, 102 (1941), and *Fed. Land Bank v. Priddy*, 295 U.S. 229, 231 (1935)). Applying this test, the court held that the bank was an instrumentality of the Federal Government because it conducted "important governmental functions regarding the issuance of currency * * * [and] general fiscal duties of the United States." *Ibid.* The court reached this conclusion notwithstanding the "great independence" from political authority that Federal Reserve banks enjoy in performing their duties. *Id.* at 185 n.2. This test, like the test we adopted in *Estate of Shamberg*, focuses not on whether the government has plenary control over the entity, but on whether the entity exercises sovereign powers and discharges an important governmental function. *See, e.g.*, *United States v. Michigan*, 851 F.2d 803, 806 (6th Cir. 1988).

In a variety of contexts, courts have stated that "[t]he authority to act with the sanction of government behind it determines whether or not a governmental agency exists." *Lassiter v. Guy F. Atkinson Co.*, 176 F.2d 984, 991 (9th Cir. 1949). [15] Whether an entity has "the authority to act with the

---

[14] We noted in *Estate of Shamberg* that the Port Authority would also constitute a "political subdivision" under the test adopted in *Little v. Williams*, 231 U.S. 335, 341 (1913), which held that a levee district endowed with taxing powers was a "political subdivision" where it was "a subordinate agency of the state exercising a power of the state." *See Estate of Shamberg*, 3 T.C. at 142. However, the principal basis for this Court's holding was that the Port Authority had been "delegated the right to exercise part of the sovereign power of the State." *Id.* at 141–142.

[15] *See, e.g.*, *United States v. Herman*, 589 F.2d 1191, 1210 (3d Cir. 1978) (whether entity was an "agency" for APA purposes); *Bell v. Commissioner*, 278 F.2d 100, 103 (4th Cir. 1960) (whether entity was an "agency" for purposes of foreign earned income exclusion), *aff'g* 30 T.C. 559 (1958); *Kam Koon Wan v. Black*, 188 F.2d 558, 561 (9th Cir. 1951) (whether military governor of Hawaii was an "agency of the United States" for purposes of

sanction of government behind it" seems especially relevant in the context of section 162(f). The power to impose fines and penalties is an essential attribute of sovereignty. Thus, in determining whether an entity is "an agency or instrumentality" for purposes of section 162(f), it is important to ascertain not only whether the entity has been delegated power to impose fines, but also whether it has the authority of government behind it when it seeks to collect the fine or otherwise enforce its decision. The real sting from imposition of a fine or penalty follows from the ability to collect it.

We conclude that an entity should be regarded as an "agency or instrumentality" for purposes of section 162(f) if it has been delegated the right to exercise part of the sovereign power of a government or governments; if it performs an important governmental function; and if it has the authority to act with the sanction of government behind it. This functional test is "most harmonious with * * * [the statutory] scheme and with the general purposes that Congress manifested" when acting to disallow tax deductions for payments determined to violate public policy. *See Lion Oil Co.*, 352 U.S. at 297.

3. *Application to the Commission*

The member states created the EC to establish "a common market and an economic and monetary union" and "to promote throughout the Community a harmonious, balanced and sustainable development of economic activities." EC Treaty art. 2. "The management of a common currency and the maintenance of economic stability are quintessential national purposes." *RJR Nabisco*, 764 F.3d at 145. The EC and the Commission perform an array of important government functions, including the regulation of commerce, the issuance of currency, and overseeing the fiscal affairs of the EC member states. *See Metrocentre Improvement Dist. #1*, 657 F.2d at 185.

The Commission acts as the executive branch of the EC. Because a proposal from the Commission is a prerequisite for

---

Portal-to-Portal Act of 1947); *McKinney v. Caldera*, 141 F. Supp. 2d 25, 32 (D.D.C. 2001) (same); *Ellsworth Bottling Co. v. United States*, 408 F. Supp. 280, 282 (W.D. Okla. 1975) (same).

most actions by the Council and the Parliament, the Commission performs important government functions in every field in which the EC operates. In particular, the member states conferred upon the EC and the Commission the authority to enforce laws regarding free trade and competition. The enforcement of competition laws and the implementation of competition policy—whether by the Commission in Europe or the Federal Trade Commission in the United States—constitute important government functions.[16]

The member states and the Commission share authority for enforcing EC competition law, and national authorities are required to apply EC competition law in their own courts. But once the Commission initiates proceedings, the member states are barred from bringing their own actions. This makes it clear that the Commission has been "delegated the right to exercise part of the sovereign power" of the EC member states. *See Estate of Shamberg*, 3 T.C. at 142.

The power to impose civil and criminal penalties for violation of law is an essential attribute of sovereignty. The Commission and national authorities are authorized to impose the same types of penalties, under the same EC law, for the same types of anticompetitive behavior. Petitioner has stipulated that the €20 million penalty at issue was imposed "for violation of law." Because the Commission has been delegated final authority to impose penalties for violation of law, it clearly exercises sovereign power.

The Commission likewise has "[t]he authority to act with the sanction of government behind it." *Lassiter*, 176 F.2d at 991. When conducting investigations, the Commission is authorized to enter places of business, examine books and records, and seal business premises. Regulation 1/2003 art. 20. If a business opposes an inspection, the member state must provide the Commission with any needed assistance, including the assistance of the state's police power. When the

[16] The United States recognizes the EC's sovereign authority over antitrust matters. In enacting the International Antitrust Enforcement Assistance Act of 1994, Pub. L. No. 103–438, 108 Stat. 4597 (current version at 15 U.S.C. secs. 6201–6212 (2006)), Congress provided that a "regional economic integration organization" such as the EC may act as the antitrust authority for its member states. *See* 15 U.S.C. sec. 6211(9); H.R. Rept. No. 103–772, at 14 (1994), 1994 U.S.C.C.A.N. 3647, 3654.

Commission enters a decision, that decision must be enforced by national authorities; no formality is required other than verification of its authenticity. The Commission has the authority "to act with the sanction of government behind it" because it can impose penalties for violation of EC law, and these decisions must be enforced by the governments of all EC member states.

We conclude that the Commission is an "entity serving as an agency or instrumentality" of the EC member states within the meaning of section 1.162–21(a)(3), Income Tax Regs., and specifically that it serves as an "instrumentality" of the EC member states, because it exercises part of the sovereign power of the EC member states, performs important government functions, and has authority to act with the sanction of those governments behind it. We believe this conclusion to be consistent not only with judicial precedent in analogous areas of law, but also with the legislative purpose underlying section 162(f). Congress enacted this provision to prevent taxpayers from deducting fines or penalties paid for violation of U.S. or foreign law. The €20 million penalty at issue here was imposed and paid for violation of EC law. Given the context and statutory purpose, it makes no difference that the penalty was paid to the Commission on behalf of EC member states collectively rather than to the government of an EC member state individually.[17]

4. *Petitioner's Arguments*

Guardian concedes that the €20 million penalty would be nondeductible under section 162(f) if it had been paid (for example) to the Government of France, a political subdivision of the Government of France, or a competition agency subordinate to the Government of France. In urging the

---

[17] The District Court in *In re EAL Corp.*, No. 93–cv578 (SLR), 1994 WL 828320 at *4, reached a similar conclusion in a related context:

> Eurocontrol is charged with the regulation and governance of aviation and air traffic in its [fifteen European] Member States. * * * [But for the creation of Eurocontrol], each of Eurocontrol's Member States likely would maintain its own FAA-equivalent to perform the duties presently performed by Eurocontrol within the borders of that nation. It is beyond dispute that each such entity would be an 'agency or instrumentality of a foreign state' within the meaning of the FSIA. Formation of Eurocontrol by these sovereigns should not change this result. * * *

opposite result here, petitioner relies chiefly on the fact that the Commission is not controlled by, or subordinate to, the government of any individual EC member state. We have already rejected petitioner's proposed definition of "agency or instrumentality" as a matter of textual interpretation. *See supra* pp. 12–16. We likewise find it to be unsupported by judicial precedent or common sense.

Petitioner's central argument is that an agency or instrumentality must be *below* a government. This argument might have appeal if we were considering whether an entity is an "agency or instrumentality" of a single known government. Guardian cites cases, for example, addressing whether a territory or possession of the United States constitutes "an agency thereof" for purposes of the foreign earned income exclusion under section 911(a) and (b)(1)(B)(ii).[18] Because an entity serving as an "agency or instrumentality" of a single government will almost invariably be subordinate to that government, these courts logically employed a "control" test.

Petitioner's approach has less appeal when one is considering the status of an entity as an "agency or instrumentality" of multiple governments. When sovereign states enter into a treaty to accomplish shared goals, it is rare that any signatory nation exercises unilateral control over the entities thus created. Typically, signatories voluntarily restrict their authority to act unilaterally, as the EC member states have done, in favor of a collective regulatory scheme that they believe will serve their long-term interests. The fact that the Commission is not subordinate to, or subject to the control of, any individual member state thus has little relevance in deciding whether it is an "agency or instrumentality" of the member states collectively.

The precedents dealing with entities created by multiple sovereigns supports this commonsense conclusion. In *Estate of Shamberg*, for example, neither New York nor New Jersey could exercise unilateral control over the Port Authority, since its power was exercised by 12 commissioners, half of

[18] *See Payne v. United States*, 980 F.2d 148 (2d Cir. 1992) (Panama Canal Commission was an "agency of the United States"). *Compare Groves v. United States*, 533 F.2d 1376 (5th Cir. 1976) (Trust Territory of the Pacific Islands is an "agency of the United States"), *with McComish v. Commissioner*, 580 F.2d 1323 (9th Cir. 1978) (Trust Territory of the Pacific Islands is not an "agency of the United States"), *rev'g* 64 T.C. 909 (1975).

whom were appointed by the Governor of each State. This Court nevertheless held the Port Authority to be a "political subdivision" of New York and of New Jersey. 3 T.C. at 146. In *LeDonne*, 700 F. Supp. at 1406, the defendant was a corporation created by a treaty among four Persian Gulf nations. No government could exercise unilateral control over the corporation because it was "owned equally by [the] four foreign states, not one which has a majority of its shares." *Ibid.* The court nevertheless held that the airline was an "agency or instrumentality of a foreign state" for FSIA purposes. *Ibid.* And in *In re EAL Corp.*, 1994 WL 828320, at *4, the court held that an entity created by 15 nations to operate the European air traffic control system was an "agency or instrumentality of a foreign state" under the FSIA, even though it was not subordinate to, or subject to the unilateral control of, any single nation.[19]

Petitioner notes correctly that the Commission, far from being subject to control by individual member states, can act in a manner contrary to a member state's wishes and interest. The Commission, for example, may investigate and fine a company resident in a member state—as it did here with respect to Guardian Europe, a Luxembourg company—over objection from that state. Petitioner also notes correctly that while member states under the EC Treaty have ultimate control over the EC and the Commission, they cannot control the day-to-day operations of either entity or dictate its conclusions concerning any particular matter.

Neither of these observations undermines the status of the Commission as an "instrumentality" of the member states. No nation joined the EC expecting that every issue would be decided in its favor. European nations joined the union because they believed that the long-term strategic benefits of membership would outweigh short-term tactical losses. In order for the Commission to constitute an "instrumentality" of the 27 member states, it is not necessary that each nation

[19] As noted earlier, petitioner agrees in theory that an entity can be an "agency or instrumentality" of government even though it has been formed by more than one sovereign. *See supra* note 11. However, petitioner asserts that this could be true only if that entity is controlled by, is subordinate to, and acts on behalf of each government considered separately. Petitioner cites no example of such an entity, and it is hard to understand how such an entity could function efficaciously in the real world.

benefit equally from, or be entirely happy with, every decision the Commission makes.

Nor is the status of the Commission as an "instrumentality" of the EC member states undermined by the relative independence they have given it. The particular form that an entity assumes is not determinative as to whether it is an "agency" or "instrumentality" of government. *See Inland Waterways Corp. v. Young*, 309 U.S. 517, 523 (1940) ("[T]he form which Government takes * * * is wholly immaterial."); *Lassiter*, 176 F.2d at 991. The U.S. Congress has endowed various regulatory agencies with considerable independence by providing (for example) that their members can be removed only for cause and by staggering their terms so as not to coincide with election cycles. *See, e.g.*, *Humphrey's Ex'r v. United States*, 295 U.S. 602 (1935). The possession of such independence does not deprive the Federal Trade Commission, the Federal Reserve Board, or the National Labor Relations Board of its status as an "instrumentalit[y] of the United States." We see no reason why a different analysis should apply to the Commission. The level of independence that member states have chosen to give to the Commission should have no relevance in deciding whether the penalties it imposes can escape the bar on tax deductibility that Congress enacted in section 162(f). *Cf. RJR Nabisco*, 764 F.3d at 145 (EC constitutes an "organ" of the EC member states for FSIA purposes even though member states do not "micromanage every aspect of * * * [its] activities"); *Michigan v. United States*, 40 F.3d 817, 828 (6th Cir. 1994) (education trust constituted a public agency for purposes of intergovernmental tax immunity even though the trust was "functionally independent" of the State and "fiscally independent").

Finally, petitioner contends that the test we have adopted proves too much. According to Guardian, if the Commission is recognized as an "agency or instrumentality" of government for purposes of section 162(f), the same conclusion would follow for "thousands of additional treaty-based entities and international organizations." Guardian notes that Congress has considered, but decided against, amending section 162(f) to provide that amounts paid to certain nongovernmental entities would be treated as paid "to a government."[20] Unless we adopt its narrow definition of "agency or instrumentality," Guardian contends, we would unjustifiably expand the scope of section 162(f) to include payments to this larger group.

Petitioner has provided no reason to believe that the nongovernmental entities it hypothesizes resemble the Commission in respects that are salient for purposes of our analysis. Petitioner has provided no evidence, for example, that such entities have been delegated sovereign powers to impose penalties, backed by the sanction of government, for violation of law. Absent such evidence, these entities could not qualify under this Opinion as instrumentalities of a foreign government for purposes of section 162(f). And we see little relevance in the fact that Congress has not amended section 162(f) to cover amounts paid to nongovernmental entities. Our holding is that Guardian's €20 million fine was paid to a governmental entity, and is thus covered by section 162(f) as it exists, because the Commission is an "entity serving as an agency or instrumentality" of a foreign government within the meaning of section 1.162–21(a), Income Tax Regs.

C. *The Filler Test*

The courts have crafted various tests for determining whether an entity constitutes an agency or instrumentality of government for purposes of different statutory regimes. In *Filler*, the Court of Appeals for the Second Circuit enunciated a five-part test for making this determination for FSIA purposes. In *RJR Nabisco*, 764 F.3d at 144–147, the court applied the *Filler* factors to the EC and ruled that it is an "organ" of a foreign government and thus "an agency or instrumentality of a foreign government" within the meaning of 28 U.S.C. sec. 1603(b).

Although both parties discuss the *Filler* test, neither urges that we adopt it for purposes of resolving the tax question presented here. In the interest of completeness, we will nevertheless consider how this case might be decided under that approach. Applying the *Filler* test in the section 162(f) context, we would reach the same result that the Court of

[20] *See* S. 506, 111th Cong., sec. 309 (2009); H.R. 2136, 110th Cong., sec. 309 (2007); S. 681, 110th Cong., sec. 309 (2007); S. 1890, 109th Cong., sec. 2 (2005); S. 936, 108th Cong., sec. 2 (2003).

Appeals reached in the FSIA context. *See RJR Nabisco*, 764 F.3d at 144–147. This result is consistent with our analysis above.

Under the FSIA, an entity qualifies for immunity from suit in U.S. courts if it is "an agency or instrumentality of a foreign state." One way in which an entity can qualify as an "agency or instrumentality" is if it constitutes "an organ of a foreign state or political subdivision thereof." 28 U.S.C. sec. 1603(a), (b)(2). In *Filler*, 378 F.3d at 217, the court noted that "there is no specific test for 'organ' status under the FSIA," but it mentioned five factors as relevant:

> (1) whether the foreign state created the entity for a national purpose;
> (2) whether the foreign state actively supervises the entity;
> (3) whether the foreign state requires the hiring of public employees and pays their salaries;
> (4) whether the entity holds exclusive rights to some right in the [foreign] country; and
> (5) how the entity is treated under foreign state law.

A court balances these factors without particular emphasis on any given factor and without requiring that every factor weigh in favor of a particular outcome. *See RJR Nabisco*, 764 F.3d at 144 ("[T]hese factors invite a balancing process [such] that an entity can be an organ even if not all of the factors are satisfied."); *Kelly v. Syria Shell Petroleum Dev. B.V.*, 213 F.3d 841, 847 (5th Cir. 2000) (while the five factors "provide a helpful framework, we will not apply them mechanically or require that all five support an organ-determination").

The first factor is whether a foreign state or foreign states "created the entity for a national purpose." This inquiry closely resembles the inquiry we have made as to whether the Commission "performs an important government function." The Court of Appeals in *RJR Nabisco*, 764 F.3d at 145, deemed it "beyond doubt" that the member states founded the EC "for a 'national purpose.'" The first *Filler* factor, which we believe to be the most important for purposes of section 162(f), thus furnishes strong support for the conclusion that the Commission is an "agency or instrumentality" of the EC member states.

The second factor is whether a foreign state "actively supervises the entity," *e.g.*, whether it regulates the entity or directs its appointments or official acts. *See Peninsula Asset Mgmt. (Cayman) Ltd. v. Hankook Tire Co.*, 476 F.3d 140, 143

(2d Cir. 2007). The Court of Appeals in *RJR Nabisco*, 764 F.3d at 145, resolved this factor in favor of the EC, concluding that the member states' supervision of the Council "enables * * * [them] to supervise the [EC's] most significant policy decisions." Although the member states do not control the details of the Commission's regulatory activity or dictate its appointments, we reach a similar conclusion here.

Respondent admits, and we agree, that the Commission, like the EC, operated with a significant degree of autonomy; that the Commission and its members were required to act independently of their member states; and that the Parliament was not directly answerable to the governments of the member states. The Council, the body most closely controlled by the member states, lacked direct authority to appoint or remove members of the Commission. On the other hand, the member states did nominate the Commission's members and exercised ultimate control over it, defining its areas of authority and limiting its power to act outside those areas. EC Treaty art. 5. The Commission's only source of authority was the EC Treaty, which the member states retained power to amend. The fact that the relevant treaties were amended five times between 1987 and 2007 evidences the reality of that control.[21]

The member states did exercise some influence over Commission decisions in the competition area. The member states coordinated and cooperated with the Commission through the European Competition Network regarding investigations and decisions. This cooperation included pooling experience, conducting joint investigations, sharing information, and allocating cases and resources. During the course of investigations, the Commission often consulted in a collaborative manner with the Council and the Parliament. Before recording infringement in a decision, the Commission was

[21] Significant amendments to the treaties include the following: (a) the Single European Act, June 29, 1987, 1987 O.J. (L 169) 1; (b) the TEU, also known as the Treaty of Maastricht, in 1993; (c) the EC Treaty, also known as the Treaty of Amsterdam, in 1997; (d) the Treaty of Nice amending the Treaty on European Union, the Treaties establishing the European Communities and certain related acts, Feb. 26, 2001, 2001 O.J. (C 80) 1; and (e) the Treaty of Lisbon amending the Treaty on European Union and the Treaty establishing the European Community, Dec. 13, 2007, 2007 O.J. (C 306) 1.

required to confer with the Advisory Committee on Restrictive Practices and Dominant Positions, which was composed of representatives of national authorities of the member states. Thus, although the Commission could record an infringement contrary to the request of a member state, the member states had influence over its decisionmaking process.

For reasons adequate to themselves, the member states have chosen to exercise their supervisory authority over the EC and the Commission through a consultative and collaborative, rather than an autocratic, process. In the competition arena, this supervision is "active" in the sense that the Commission consults regularly with numerous organs of the EC and numerous representatives of the member states, all of whom have the ability to influence its decisions. Cognizant that the second *Filler* factor "does not require the foreign state to micro manage every aspect of the organ's activities," *RJR Nabisco*, 2014 WL 1613878, at *13, we conclude that the "active supervision" factor slightly favors the Commission or is neutral here.

The third factor is whether "the foreign state requires the hiring of public employees and pays their salaries." The Court of Appeals in *RJR Nabisco* concluded that EC officials are "public employees" in that they exercise "'powers conferred by public law and duties designed to safeguard the general interests of the state.'" *RJR Nabisco*, 764 F.3d at 145 (quoting *RJR Nabisco*, 814 F. Supp. 2d at 205). Similarly, the member states "indirectly pay the salaries" of EC officials, since they pay into the EC's general fund, from which those salaries are paid. *Ibid.* RJR Nabisco nevertheless argued that this factor disfavored "organ" status because the EC literally employs these individuals; it, not the member states, sets their salaries and cuts their paychecks.

The Court of Appeals concluded that the formal arrangements used to pay diplomatic salaries are "of small importance at best," *id.* at 146, and we agree with that conclusion. If we were considering whether the Commission were an "agency or instrumentality" of a single foreign government, whether that government formally employed its officers might be a salient factor. *Cf. Glencore, Ltd. v. Chase Manhattan Bank, N.A.*, No. 92–civ6214, 1998 WL 74294, at *3 (S.D.N.Y. Feb. 20, 1998) (concluding that bank officials employed by the government of India were "public employees" under the FSIA). But these formal employment details seem insignificant in the present context, where we are considering whether a penalty imposed by an entity created by multiple sovereigns qualifies for a tax deduction. The salient fact is that Commission officials are public employees who exercise powers conferred by public law, including the power to impose penalties backed by the sanction of government. Like the Court of Appeals in *RJR Nabisco*, we regard the third *Filler* factor as basically neutral here and in any event as a factor that should be given little weight.

The fourth factor is whether the entity "holds exclusive rights to some right in the foreign country." The Court of Appeals in *RJR Nabisco*, 764 F.3d at 146, concluded that the EC holds "the exclusive right to exercise a number of significant governmental powers" in the EC member states, including the right to "authorize the issue of banknotes within the Community" and "to conclude the Multilateral Agreements on Trade in Goods." With respect to competition law specifically, the Commission has the right to conduct investigations of anticompetitive behavior within member states and to record an infringement for competition violations. This factor favors finding that the EC is an "instrumentality" of the member states.

The fifth factor considers "how the entity is treated under foreign state law." In *RJR Nabisco*, 764 F.3d at 146, the member states advised the District Court that they consider the European Community to be a governmental entity, and the U.S. Department of State "advised that it accepts this representation." On this basis, the Court of Appeals concluded that the EC "appears to satisfy this factor." The fact that "the member states have ceded portions of their governmental authority to the * * * [EC] to be exercised by it in their stead and on their collective behalf seems to confirm its status as an organ and agency of the member states." *Ibid.*

Petitioner argues that the member states do not regard the Commission as an "agency or instrumentality" below them but as a supranational body that is in some sense above them. The Court of Appeals answered this argument succinctly:

> This argument * * * depends on the proposition that a governmental entity created by a collectivity of governments * * * cannot be at once a supranational entity and an organ or agency of the actors that created

> it. It appears to us that both descriptions are accurate, and the fact that the * * * [EC] functions as a supranational governmental entity does not negate its also being an organ and agency of its member states, which continue to exist as sovereign nations, notwithstanding having delegated some of their governmental powers to the supranational agency they created. [*Id.* at 146–147.]

We agree with this analysis and conclude that the fifth *Filler* factor supports the conclusion that the Commission, as the executive branch of the EC, is an "agency or instrumentality" of its member states.

On balance, we believe that three of the *Filler* factors strongly support the Commission's status as an "agency or instrumentality" of the EC member states and that the other two factors slightly favor the Commission, are neutral, or deserve little weight in the section 162(f) setting. Cognizant that these factors should not be applied "mechanically," *Kelly*, 213 F.3d at 847, but rather in a manner sensitive to the context, we conclude that the Commission constitutes an "agency or instrumentality" of the EC member states both under the *Filler* test and under the framework we have adopted. Because Guardian's €20 million fine was paid to an "agency or instrumentality" of a "foreign government" within the meaning of section 1.162–21(a), Income Tax Regs., that payment was nondeductible for Federal income tax purposes by virtue of section 162(f). We will therefore grant respondent's motion for partial summary judgment and deny petitioner's motion.

An appropriate order will be issued.

RENALD EICHLER, PETITIONER *v.* COMMISSIONER OF INTERNAL REVENUE, RESPONDENT

Docket No. 725–12L. Filed July 23, 2014.

After R assessed trust fund recovery penalties against him, P requested a partial pay installment agreement. Before P's request had been input into the IRS computer system or acted upon, R sent P Letters CP 90, Final Notice—Notice of Intent to Levy and Notice of Your Right to a Hearing. P timely requested a collection due process (CDP) hearing, renewing his request for an installment agreement and asserting that the Letters CP 90 should be withdrawn as invalid pursuant to I.R.C. sec. 6331(k)(2), which prohibits the IRS from making a levy while an offer for an installment agreement is pending. During the CDP hearing R's settlement officer conditioned acceptance of an installment agreement on P's making an $8,520 downpayment. P declined this proposal as resulting in economic hardship. R's final determination sustained the proposed levy on the ground that P had declined R's proposed installment agreement; it rejected P's request that the Letters CP 90 be withdrawn as invalid. *Held*: I.R.C. sec. 6331(k)(2) did not preclude R from issuing the Letters CP 90 after P submitted his offer for an installment agreement. *Held, further*, R's determination not to rescind the Letters CP 90 was not an abuse of discretion under relevant provisions of the Internal Revenue Manual. *Held, further*, because the record does not allow for meaningful review of R's determination regarding the appropriateness of the $8,520 downpayment as a condition of an installment agreement, this case will be remanded for further proceedings.

Mark Harrington Westlake, for petitioner.
John R. Bampfield, for respondent.

OPINION

THORNTON, *Chief Judge*: Petitioner seeks review pursuant to section 6330(d) of respondent's determination sustaining a proposed levy. [1] This case is before us on the parties' cross-motions for summary judgment.

Background

The record reveals or the parties do not dispute the following.

When he filed his petition, petitioner lived in Tennessee. On December 20, 2010, respondent assessed against him these section 6672 trust fund recovery penalties: $89,760 for the fourth quarter of 2008, $82,725 for the first quarter of 2009, and $16,889 for the second quarter of 2009.

By letter dated April 11, 2011, petitioner's representative, Mark Harrington Westlake, sent to the Internal Revenue Service's (IRS) Service Center in Atlanta, Georgia, a letter requesting, among other things, a "partial payment install-

[1] Unless otherwise indicated, all section references are to the Internal Revenue Code in effect at all relevant times, and all Rule references are to the Tax Court Rules of Practice and Procedure. All monetary amounts are rounded to the nearest dollar.

ment agreement" of $350 per month for the three quarters previously mentioned as well as the fourth quarter of 2007. This letter was accompanied by a completed and signed Form 433–A, Collection Information Statement for Wage Earners and Self-Employed Individuals, and supporting financial documentation.

On April 28, 2011, respondent received petitioner's request.[2] Pursuant to Internal Revenue Manual (IRM) pt. 5.14.1.3 (Mar. 4, 2011), the IRS Collection Division is required to input certain codes—"TC 971 AC 043" for installment agreement requests not immediately approved and "TC 971 AC 063" for requests immediately approved—into the IRS computer system within 24 hours of receiving an installment agreement request if it meets certain requirements. Although petitioner's request met these requirements, the IRS Collection Division failed to input any code until June 6, 2011, when the "TC 971 AC 043" code was input.

In the meantime, on May 9, 2011, respondent had sent to petitioner three Letters CP 90, Final Notice—Notice of Intent to Levy and Notice of Your Right to a Hearing (notices of intent to levy), with respect to petitioner's unpaid trust fund recovery penalties for the last quarter of 2008 and first two quarters of 2009.[3]

On May 13, 2011, the IRS Service Center in Atlanta, Georgia, sent petitioner a letter in response to the installment agreement request, stating:

> We have not resolved this matter because we haven't completed all the processing necessary for a complete response. However, we will contact you again within 45 days with our reply. You don't need to do anything further now on this matter.
>
> * * * * * * *
>
> We've delayed sending you further notices while we research this matter. If you receive or have received additional notices * * *, please contact us.

---

[2] The record does not show why petitioner's April 11, 2011, letter took 17 days to reach respondent.

[3] The notices of intent to levy referenced Publication 594, The IRS Collection Process. Publication 594 explains, among other things, that the IRS is prohibited from levying against a taxpayer's property while an installment agreement request "is being considered".

This May 13, 2011, letter erroneously stated that it was in reference to petitioner's 2008 Federal income tax rather than the trust fund recovery penalties at issue in this case.

On June 1, 2011, the Office of Appeals (Appeals) received a timely Form 12153, Request for a Collection Due Process or Equivalent Hearing, from petitioner indicating the following reason for his request:

> I previously submitted Form 433–A with supporting documentation and a request for an installment agreement. (Copy attached) The Final Notice (CP 90) was issued prematurely. I request that the Final Notice be withdrawn and that the installment payment agreement I requested be implemented. In the alternative I REQUEST AN IN PERSON HEARING IN NASHVILLE, TN.

By cover letter accompanying the Form 12153 petitioner asserted that the notices of intent to levy should be withdrawn pursuant to section 6331(k) and IRM pt. 5.11.1.2.2.8 (Jan. 1, 2006).

On September 1, 2011, an IRS settlement officer, Suzanne Magee (SO Magee), notified petitioner that she was in receipt of his request for an Appeals hearing and that she had scheduled an in-person conference for October 4, 2011.

On September 26, 2011, Mr. Westlake sent SO Magee a letter asserting that petitioner's installment agreement request had been submitted and was pending when the notices of intent to levy had been issued. Mr. Westlake requested that the notices be rescinded. He also stated:

> Please note that since the prior Form 433–A was submitted the taxpayers have become obligated for two additional court ordered payments on judgments. Moreover, they continue to receive dunning notices from many of the unsecured creditors shown on the exhibit to the Form 433–A. I am hopeful that my correspondence to those creditors will persuade them that filing further lawsuits will be futile.
>
> Dr. Renald Eichler is 76 years of age and Dr. Priscilla Eichler is 71 years of age.
>
> They have lived in their home since 1971. The current indebtedness against the home, i.e., $720,000 was incurred in an effort to prop up the non-profit educational corporation for which both of them worked. Those efforts were unsuccessful. The non-profit corporation itself lost its assets in foreclosure. I believe that it may have attempted a reorganization before it closed.
>
> We had originally requested a partial payment installment agreement in the amount of $350 per month. However, the taxpayers' financial situa-

tion has deteriorated and accordingly, we are now requesting that the accounts be designated "Currently Not Collectible."

Mr. Westlake also submitted with the letter a completed Form 433–A and supporting financial documentation. The Form 433–A reflected total gross monthly income of $5,464, of which $3,079 was attributable to petitioner and $2,385 was attributable to his wife.[4] The Form 433–A reported monthly expenses of $5,573, including the following:

Expense	*Amount*
Food, clothing, & misc.	$985
Housing and utilities	3,500
Vehicle operating costs	488
Health insurance—Humana	112
Out-of-pocket healthcare costs	288
Court-ordered payments	200
Taxes (income and FICA)	212

The Form 433–A also reported debts of approximately $260,000 "on credit cards and store accounts and judgments."

On October 4, 2011, SO Magee conducted an in-person conference with petitioner, petitioner's wife, and Mr. Westlake. At the hearing Mr. Westlake once again argued that the notices of intent to levy had been issued prematurely because petitioner had submitted an installment agreement offer that was pending when the notices were issued. SO Magee determined that the issuance of the notices of intent to levy was not premature and that these notices should not be rescinded. After discussing potential collection alternatives, SO Magee requested additional supporting documentation.

On October 17, 2011, petitioner provided the requested supporting documentation to SO Magee. By cover letter Mr. Westlake renewed his objection that the notices of intent to levy had been issued prematurely and that they should be rescinded. He also requested a $25-per-month installment agreement as a collection alternative to the proposed levy.

On October 19, 2011, after reviewing petitioner's documentation, SO Magee phoned Mr. Westlake and left him a voicemail message, requesting certain bank statements to substantiate some of petitioner's expenses and indicating that the notices of intent to levy would not be rescinded.

[4] Petitioner's wife is not a party to this proceeding.

On October 26, 2012, Mr. Westlake provided the requested bank statements to SO Magee. A joint bank account petitioner shared with his wife showed a balance of $15,214 as of October 20, 2011. Mr. Westlake again renewed his request for a $25-per-month installment agreement and rescission of the notices of intent to levy.

SO Magee reviewed petitioner's Form 433–A and supporting financial documentation. She concluded that an appropriate collection alternative would be an installment agreement of $25 per month for one year increasing to $734 per month in November 2012, provided that petitioner also submitted with his installment agreement a downpayment of $8,520.

On October 28, 2011, SO Magee called Mr. Westlake to confirm receipt of the additional financial documentation. She also communicated to Mr. Westlake her proposed installment agreement collection alternative to the proposed levy.

By letter dated November 8, 2011, Mr. Westlake agreed to SO Magee's proposal that petitioner pay $25 per month, increasing to $734 per month in November 2012. He disagreed, however, that petitioner should be required to make an $8,520 downpayment, stating: "Please refer to my prior correspondence explaining that $15,000 had originally been borrowed from family members. I have since confirmed that the funds were loaned to Mrs. Eichler by her sister. Repayment of that loan would fully deplete the savings account." He also indicated that if SO Magee was "unable or unwilling to accept the proposed $25 per month installment agreement with an automatic twelve month increase, but without the initial $8,520 payment and with the rescission of the [notices of intent to levy] * * *, please issue your final determination".

On December 8, 2011, Appeals issued to petitioner a Notice of Determination Concerning Collection Action(s) Under Section 6320 and/or 6330 (notice). In the notice Appeals sustained the proposed levy. The notice stated that "under current procedures" the notice of intent to levy "is deemed valid and will not be rescinded even when there is a pending installment agreement." The notice also stated: "Based on the financial information provided during the hearing process Appeals determined the appropriate collection resolution to be an installment agreement with down payment of $8,520 then $25 per month for 12 months to increase to $734 per month thereafter. The down payment is your percentage share of a joint savings account with your wife."

Discussion

A. *Summary Judgment Standard*

Summary judgment is intended to expedite litigation and avoid unnecessary and expensive trials. *Fla. Peach Corp. v. Commissioner*, 90 T.C. 678, 681 (1988). Summary judgment may be granted where there is no genuine dispute as to any material fact and a decision may be rendered as a matter of law. Rule 121(b). The moving party bears the burden of showing that there is no genuine dispute as to any material fact, and factual inferences will be read in a manner most favorable to the party opposing summary judgment. *See id.*; *Sundstrand Corp. v. Commissioner*, 98 T.C. 518, 520 (1992), *aff'd*, 17 F.3d 965 (7th Cir. 1994).

B. *Statutory Framework*

Section 6331(a) provides that if any person liable to pay any tax neglects or refuses to pay such tax within 10 days after notice and demand for payment, then the Secretary is authorized to collect such tax by levy upon that person's property. Section 6330(a) requires the Secretary to send written notice to the person of that person's right to request an Appeals hearing before a levy is made. If an Appeals hearing is requested, the Appeals officer must, at the hearing, verify that the requirements of any applicable law or administrative procedure have been met. Sec. 6330(b)(1), (c)(1). Section 6330(c)(2) prescribes the matters that a person may raise at the Appeals hearing, including spousal defenses, challenges to the appropriateness of the Commissioner's intended collection action, and possible alternative means of collection, including offers-in-compromise (OIC) and installment agreements. The existence or amount of the underlying tax liability may also be contested, but only if the person did not receive a notice of deficiency or did not otherwise have an opportunity to dispute the tax liability. Sec. 6330(c)(2)(B); *see also Sego v. Commissioner*, 114 T.C. 604, 609 (2000).

C. *Standard of Review*

Petitioner has not challenged his underlying tax liabilities. We review respondent's determination for abuse of discretion, asking whether it was arbitrary, capricious, or without sound basis in fact or law. *See, e.g., Murphy v. Commissioner*, 125 T.C. 301, 320 (2005), *aff'd*, 469 F.3d 27 (1st Cir. 2006); *Sego v. Commissioner*, 114 T.C. at 610.

D. *Whether Respondent's Determination Not To Rescind the Notices of Intent To Levy Was an Abuse of Discretion*

Petitioner argues that respondent abused his discretion in refusing to rescind the notices of intent to levy. He argues that section 6331(k)(2) precludes the IRS from issuing a notice of intent to levy while an installment agreement offer is pending.

Although section 6331(a) grants the Secretary authority to levy upon a taxpayer's property or rights to property, various subsections of section 6331 prohibit the Secretary from levying under certain circumstances. *See* sec. 6331(f), (g), (i), (j), (k). Section 6331(k)(2) provides:

> (2) INSTALLMENT AGREEMENTS.—No levy may be made under subsection (a) on the property or rights to property of any person with respect to any unpaid tax—
>
> (A) during the period that an offer by such person for an installment agreement under section 6159 for payment of such unpaid tax is pending with the Secretary; and
>
> (B) if such offer is rejected by the Secretary, during the 30 days thereafter (and, if an appeal of such rejection is filed within such 30 days, during the period that such appeal is pending) * * *

By its terms this statute bars the IRS, while a taxpayer's offer for an agreement request is pending, from making a levy; it does not bar the IRS from issuing notices of intent to levy.[5] *Accord United States v. Austin*, No. 09–10405–RWZ,

[5] The notice of determination does not expressly reflect any determination as to whether petitioner's installment agreement offer was in fact "pending" when the IRS issued the notices of intent to levy. Rather, the notice of determination proceeds upon the premise that a notice of intent to levy is valid and will not be rescinded "even when there is a pending installment agreement." In this proceeding respondent argues for the first time that the installment agreement was not pending when the notices of intent were issued. In support of this argument, respondent points to the May 13, 2011, letter from the IRS Service Center in Atlanta which stated

Continued

2010 WL 1711294, at *3 n.2 (D. Mass. Apr. 26, 2010), *aff'd*, 526 Fed. Appx. 2 (1st Cir. 2013); *Politte v. United States*, No. 07CV1950 JLS (CAB), 2009 WL 3166924, at *5 (S.D. Cal. Aug. 6, 2009); *see also Living Care Alts. of Utica, Inc. v. United States*, 411 F.3d 621, 629 (6th Cir. 2005) (holding that section 6331(f) and (j), which provides, similarly to section 6331(k), that "no levy may be made" before the IRS has taken certain actions, do not bar the IRS from issuing notices of intent to levy before taking these actions); *Medlock v. United States*, 325 F. Supp. 2d 1064, 1079 (C.D. Cal. 2003) (same).[6] The regulations expressly provide that while levy is prohibited "[t]he IRS may take actions other than levy to protect the interests of the Government". Sec. 301.6331–4(b)(1), Proced. & Admin. Regs. A notice of intent to levy is an action other than a levy to protect the interests of the Government; unlike a levy, it is merely preliminary to a collection action, rather than a collection action barred by section 6331(k)(2). *See Politte*, 2009 WL 3166924, at *5.

---

that "we haven't completed all the processing necessary for a complete response". It is unclear from the record to what extent this delay in processing petitioner's installment agreement offer was attributable to the IRS' failure to input the offer into its computer system until June 6, 2011. In any event, because we decide the issue of the effect of sec. 6331(k)(2) in respondent's favor even if we assume, as apparently did Appeals, that petitioner's offer was pending when the IRS issued the notices of intent to levy, it is unnecessary to consider respondent's argument raised for the first time in this proceeding. *Cf. Antioco v. Commissioner*, T.C. Memo. 2013–35 (declining to uphold a notice of determination on grounds other than those relied upon in the notice (citing *SEC v. Chenery Corp.*, 332 U.S. 194 (1947), and *SEC v. Chenery Corp.*, 318 U.S. 80 (1943))); *Jones v. Commissioner*, T.C. Memo. 2012–274 (same); *Salahuddin v. Commissioner*, T.C. Memo. 2012–141 (same).

[6] We are mindful that in *Tucker v. Commissioner*, T.C. Memo. 2011–67 (upholding Appeals' rejection of an OIC), *aff'd*, 676 F.3d 1129 (D.C. Cir. 2012), in the "Background" section of the opinion, a footnote indicated that the IRS had withdrawn a notice of intent to levy that it had issued after the taxpayer had submitted an OIC. By way of explanation, the footnote stated: "Section 6331(k)(1) provides for a restraint on levy while an OIC is pending, and the issuance of the notice of levy violated that restriction." *Id.*, slip op. at 8 n.6. This dictum, however, did not represent a holding or a predicate to any holding in *Tucker*, as made explicit in the same footnote: "The issuance of that first levy notice (and its subsequent withdrawal) was not part of the CDP hearing or determination and is not part of the CDP appeal at issue here." *Id.* Accordingly, the dictum in *Tucker* concerning sec. 6331(k)(1) does not control this case.

Accordingly, under the regulations, consistent with the plain language of the statute, the IRS was not prohibited from issuing the notices of intent to levy after petitioner submitted his offer for an installment agreement.

Petitioner also argues that respondent should have rescinded the notices of intent to levy pursuant to IRM pt. 5.11.1.2.2.8 and IRM pt. 5.14.1.3. In the first instance we observe that provisions of the IRM do not carry the force and effect of law or confer rights on taxpayers. *See, e.g, Fargo v. Commissioner*, 447 F.3d 706, 713 (9th Cir. 2006), *aff'g* T.C. Memo. 2004–13. In any event, we conclude that respondent did not abuse his discretion in applying these provisions.

IRM pt. 5.11.1.2.2.8 appears in the part of the IRM that provides information and guidance to revenue officers in the collection process. It directs the IRS Collection Division to rescind notices of intent to levy in certain circumstances, one of which is when a notice of intent to levy is issued while levy action is prohibited and the taxpayer timely requests an Appeals hearing. By contrast, IRM pt. 8.22.2.2.2.2(5) (Dec. 14, 2010) states that Appeals should not rescind a notice of intent to levy that was issued during the pendency of an installment agreement, even where levy is prohibited. Petitioner argues that these two provisions are inconsistent and that we should treat IRM pt. 5.11.1.2.2.8 as controlling. We disagree. The IRM is not necessarily inconsistent in directing the Collection Division and Appeals to take different actions. SO Magee did not abuse her discretion in following the IRM provisions directed to and applicable to Appeals, of which she was a part.

In sum, we hold that respondent did not abuse his discretion in declining to rescind the notices of intent to levy.

E. *Respondent's Determination Requiring Petitioner To Make an $8,520 Downpayment as a Condition of His Installment Agreement*

Petitioner also argues that respondent abused his discretion in determining that petitioner should make an $8,520 downpayment as a condition of his installment agreement.[7]

[7] Petitioner does not take issue with SO Magee's determination requiring installment payments of $25 per month for one year followed by payments

Continued

Petitioner argues that having to make the $8,520 down payment would cause economic hardship for him and his wife.

Section 6159 authorizes the Secretary to enter into an installment agreement upon determining that the proposed installment agreement would facilitate full or partial collection of the tax liability. Recognizing that the Secretary has the discretion to accept or reject any proposed installment agreement, *see* sec. 301.6159–1(c)(1)(i), Proced. & Admin. Regs., the Court gives due deference to the Secretary's determination, *see Marascalco v. Commissioner*, T.C. Memo. 2010–130, *aff'd*, 420 Fed. Appx. 423 (5th Cir. 2011).

The IRM describes procedures the IRS uses in determining whether a proposed installment agreement facilitates the collection of an unpaid tax liability. These procedures require taxpayers to liquidate assets in order to qualify for an installment agreement in the absence of special circumstances such as old age, ill health, or economic hardship. *See* IRM pt. 5.14.1.4(5) and (6) (June 1, 2010).

During petitioner's Appeals hearing Mr. Westlake asserted repeatedly that petitioner and his wife were elderly and had limited financial resources and that making the $8,520 downpayment would pose an undue economic hardship for them. Additionally, Mr. Westlake asserted that the funds in the joint bank account did not actually belong to petitioner. We find no indication in the record that SO Magee expressly considered these issues.

Because the record does not allow for meaningful review in this regard, and there is a genuine dispute of material fact, we will deny the parties' cross-motions for summary judgment and remand this case for Appeals to clarify the basis for SO Magee's determination with regard to the appropriateness of requiring the disputed downpayment in the light of the concerns petitioner raised. *See Hoyle v. Commissioner*, 131 T.C. 197, 204–205 (2008). Upon remand Appeals shall consider any new collection alternative that petitioner may wish to propose, taking into account any changed circumstances and other relevant factors.

---

of $734 per month thereafter.

To reflect the foregoing,

An appropriate order will be issued.

RERI HOLDINGS I, LLC, HAROLD LEVINE, TAX MATTERS PARTNER, PETITIONER *v.* COMMISSIONER OF INTERNAL REVENUE, RESPONDENT

Docket No. 9324–08. Filed August 11, 2014.

LLC1 contributed a successor member interest in a second LLC (LLC2) to University. R moves for partial summary judgment that (1) the actuarial tables under I.R.C. sec. 7520 do not apply to value the successor member interest and (2) TMP failed to substantiate the value of the successor member interest with a qualified appraisal as defined in sec. 1.170A–13(c)(3), Income Tax Regs. *Held*: *Pierre v. Commissioner*, 133 T.C. 24 (2009), followed; LLC2, a disregarded entity, is not disregarded in determining value of the successor member interest in LLC2 that LLC1 contributed to University. *Held, further*, *Estate of Gribauskas v. Commissioner*, 116 T.C. 142 (2001), *rev'd and remanded*, 342 F.3d 85 (2d Cir. 2003), distinguished on ground that successor member interest involved right to receive a capital asset in the future and not a stream of fixed payments. *Held, further*, we will deny R's motion.

Randall Gregory Dick and *Rebekah E. Schechtman*, for petitioner.

Travis Vance III, *Kristen I. Nygren*, *John M. Altman*, and *Leon St. Laurent*, for respondent.

OPINION

HALPERN, *Judge*: This is a partnership-level action brought in response to a notice of final partnership administrative adjustment. The action involves RERI Holdings I, LLC (RERI). On its 2003 income tax return RERI reported a charitable contribution of property worth $33,019,000. Respondent determined that RERI overstated the value of the contribution by $29,119,000. He also determined that, on account of the overstatement, he would apply an accuracy-related penalty to any resulting underpayment of income tax. Petitioner assigned error to respondent's determinations. Respondent answered, supporting his determination that RERI had overstated the value of the contribution with the allegation that the transaction giving rise to RERI's charitable contribution "is a sham for tax purposes or lacks economic substance, and therefore the transaction should be disregarded for federal tax purposes and the deduction disallowed in its entirety."

The case is presently before us on respondent's motion for partial summary judgment (motion). Respondent moves for partial summary adjudication in his favor that (1) the actuarial tables under section 7520[1] do not apply to value the future (remainder) interest in property that RERI contributed to the University of Michigan (University) in 2003 and (2) RERI failed to substantiate the value of its contribution with a qualified appraisal. Petitioner objects. We will deny the motion.

Background

Previously in this case we disposed by order of a motion by respondent for partial summary judgment[2] and by Memorandum Opinion and order of a motion by petitioner for partial summary judgment. *RERI Holdings I, LLC v. Commissioner*, T.C. Memo. 2014–99 (rejecting petitioner's claim that, as a matter of law, the doctrines of "sham" and "lack of economic substance" are inapplicable to the determination of whether a taxpayer's charitable contribution is allowed under section 170). In doing so we relied on certain facts that we believed are not in dispute. We shall, therefore, with minor modifications and additions as relevant to the motion, again rely on those facts. The facts we rely on are as follows.

---

[1] Unless otherwise indicated, all section references are to the Internal Revenue Code in effect for 2003, and all Rule references are to the Tax Court Rules of Practice and Procedure.

[2] Respondent moved for partial summary adjudication in his favor that, if the valuation tables provided for in sec. 7520 are to be used in valuing the charitable contribution in issue, the value of the real property underlying the contribution must be reduced by (1) depreciation and (2) the entire amount of the indebtedness encumbering the underlying property. By order dated May 5, 2011 (order), we granted that motion with respect to respondent's first prayer and denied it with respect to his second prayer, which we treated as asking for judgment that the charitable contribution had to be reduced by the amount of the indebtedness. We denied the motion on the ground that there was a genuine dispute as to a material fact. *See* Rule 121(b).

RERI

RERI was formed as a Delaware limited liability company on March 4, 2002. It was dissolved on May 11, 2004. RERI is classified as a partnership for Federal income tax purposes. For 2003, RERI filed a Form 1065, U.S. Return of Partnership Income (return).

The Charitable Contribution

RERI reported on the return as a charitable contribution its transfer to the Regents of the University of what RERI described on the return as "100% of the remainder estate in the membership interest in RS Hawthorne Holdings, LLC" (Holdings). Holdings, RERI reported, "owns all of the membership interest of a ['single purpose, single member'] Delaware limited liability company". That Delaware LLC is RS Hawthorne, LLC (Hawthorne), which RERI described on the return as owning "the fee simple absolute in a parcel of land improved as a AT&T web hosting facility located at 2301 West 120th Street, Hawthorne, California" (Hawthorne property).

Red Sea Tech I, Inc.

The Hawthorne property had come to be owned by Hawthorne on February 6, 2002, pursuant to Hawthorne's execution of a real estate contract that Hawthorne had received from Red Sea Tech I, Inc. (Red Sea). Hawthorne purchased the Hawthorne property from InterGate LAII, LLC (Intergate), for $42,350,000. To fund that purchase, Hawthorne borrowed $43,671,739 from Branch Banking & Trust Co. (BB&T), signing a promissory note (promissory note or note) and securing its repayment obligation by, among other things, a deed of trust (mortgage) and an "Absolute Assignment of Rents and Lease". The promissory note called for payments in installments (including interest) over a period of 14 years and 3 months (February 15, 2002–May 15, 2016), with the final payment, due May 15, 2016, constituting a "balloon" payment of $11.8 million. AT&T occupied the Hawthorne property pursuant to a triple net lease between it and Intergate. That lease had commenced on December 1, 2000, and was for a term of 15½ years, until May 31, 2016, with AT&T having three renewal options of 5 years each.

The Temporal Interests

Initially, Red Sea was the sole member of Holdings. On February 7, 2002, Red Sea created two temporal interests in its membership interest in Holdings (Holdings membership interest or, sometimes, Holdings)—a possessory term of years member interest (TOYS interest) and a future, successor member interest (SMI). The TOYS interest commenced in February 2002 and is to run almost 18 years, through December 31, 2020. The SMI becomes possessory on January 1, 2021, on termination of the TOYS interest.

Sale to RJS

RJS Realty Corp. (RJS) is a Delaware corporation. On February 7, 2002, RJS purchased the SMI for $1,610,000. By the agreement of sale (assignment agreement), among other things, Red Sea agreed to prohibit Holdings or Hawthorne from encumbering the Hawthorne property without the consent of RJS. Red Sea also agreed to prohibit the transfer of any interest in the Hawthorne property or the creation of any "lien or encumbrance" on the property that would "materially adversely affect" its value. The assignment agreement limits Red Sea's (and any successor in interest's) liability for breach of the agreement. An assignee's recourse for breach of the agreement is limited to the interest (the TOYS interest) retained by Red Sea. The assignment agreement provides that it "shall be interpreted and construed in a manner consistent with the common law of estates in property of the State of New York and the statutory scheme of future interests and estates in property of the State of New York that is set forth in the New York Estates, Powers and Trust Law as in effect on the date hereof".

RERI's Purchase

On March 25, 2002, RJS sold the SMI to RERI for $2,950,000, RERI paying $1,880,000 in cash and executing a nonrecourse promissory note for the balance.

The Gift Agreement

On August 27, 2003, RERI's principal investor, Stephen M. Ross, pledged that he would make a gift of $4 million (later increased to $5 million) to the University for the benefit of its Department of Athletics (gift agreement).

Under the gift agreement, Mr. Ross pledged and agreed "to transfer, or to have transferred" the SMI to the University no later than December 31, 2003. Upon receiving the SMI, the University was to hold it at a nominal value of $1 and credit Mr. Ross' pledge in the amount of $1. The University agreed to hold the SMI for a minimum of two years, "after which the University shall sell" the SMI and credit Mr. Ross' account "to a value equal to the net proceeds received by the University" for the SMI. RERI's donation of the SMI to the University was completed on the same day as the gift agreement, August 27, 2003. Consistent with the gift agreement, the agreement embodying RERI's donation of the SMI to the University required the University to hold the SMI "for a period of two years". (We shall hereafter refer to the University's obligations—first, to hold the SMI for a minimum of two years and, then, to sell it—as the two-year hold-sell requirement.)

Appraisal of the Hawthorne Property

In September 2003, RERI retained Howard C. Gelbtuch of Greenwich Realty Advisors to appraise a hypothetical remainder interest in the Hawthorne property. Mr. Gelbtuch concluded that the fair market value of "the leased fee interest in the * * * [Hawthorne] property as of August 28, 2003, is US $55,000,000", and that the "investment value" of a hypothetical remainder interest in that property vesting on January 1, 2021, was $32,935,000.[3] Mr. Gelbtuch determined that value by multiplying his valuation of the underlying leased fee interest by an actuarial factor taken from the tables promulgated under sections 2031 and 7520. *See* sec. 20.2031–7(d)(1), Estate Tax Regs. (2003); sec. 1.7520–1(a)(1), Income Tax Regs. (2003).[4] In his appraisal report, Mr. Gelbtuch states that he was "advised that the applicable Remainder Interest Actuarial Factor as provided in Section 7520 of the Internal Revenue Code of 1986 for the month of

[3] The appraisal and professional fees were calculated as $84,000, for a total reported charitable contribution by the partnership of $33,019,000.

[4] Mr. Gelbtuch was asked to and did, in fact, appraise a hypothetical remainder interest in the Hawthorne property, not the SMI.

contribution is .598793705.” Mr. Gelbtuch appraised the leased fee interest assuming that it was “free and clear of any and all liens or encumbrances”.

Sale of the SMI

On or about December 23, 2005, after the expiration of the required two-year holding period, and after obtaining its own appraisal of the remainder interest in the Hawthorne property as of July 20, 2005, which valued that interest at $6.5 million (on the basis of a “Reversion Value” of the Hawthorne property after 15 years), the University sold the SMI to HRK Real Estate Holdings, LLC (HRK), a Delaware LLC indirectly owned by petitioner and one of his associates, for $1,940,000.[5]

HRK had pre-sold the SMI to a third-party individual for $3 million on or about December 20, 2005. On December 26, 2006, that third party donated the SMI to another charitable organization and claimed a charitable contribution deduction of $29,930,000 in connection therewith, again on the basis of an appraisal by Mr. Gelbtuch of a hypothetical remainder interest in the Hawthorne property.

Discussion

I. *Summary Judgment*

Pursuant to Rule 121(a), “[e]ither party may move, with or without supporting affidavits or declarations, for a summary adjudication in the moving party’s favor upon all or any part of the legal issues in controversy.” A summary judgment is appropriate “if the pleadings, answers to interrogatories, depositions, admissions, and any other acceptable materials, together with the affidavits or declarations, if any, show that there is no genuine dispute as to any material fact and that a decision may be rendered as a matter of law.” Rule 121(b).

[5] As a result of petitioner’s donation of the SMI to the University and other donations of similar successor member interests in other LLCs arranged by Mr. Ross, the University derived sale proceeds of $4,276,604, which it credited to Mr. Ross’ $5 million pledge. Respondent alleges that, in at least some of those cases, the amounts realized by the University on its sales of the donated successor remainder member interests were far less than the appraisal thereof for which the donor, presumably, claimed a sec. 170 deduction.

A summary judgment may be made upon part of the legal issues in controversy. *See id.* In response to a motion for summary judgment, an adverse party may not rest upon mere allegations or denials of the moving party's pleading but "must set forth specific facts showing that there is a genuine dispute for trial." Rule 121(d).

II. *Application of the Actuarial Tables Under Section 7520 in Valuing the SMI*

A. *Applicable Law*

Section 170(a)(1) allows a deduction for "any charitable contribution * * * made within the taxable year * * * only if verified under regulations prescribed by the Secretary." Section 1.170A–1(c)(1), Income Tax Regs., generally provides that the amount of a contribution "made in property other than money * * * is the fair market value of the property at the time of the contribution". Section 1.170A–1(c)(2), Income Tax Regs., provides that "fair market value is the price at which the property would change hands between a willing buyer and a willing seller, neither being under any compulsion to buy or sell and both having reasonable knowledge of relevant facts."

In most cases, the willing buyer-willing seller standard is not applied directly to annuities, life estates, terms of years, remainders, reversions and similar partial interests in property. In general, those interests are valued by determining the fair market value of the underlying property and dividing the value among the several interests in the property on the basis of their present values. In pertinent part, section 7520(a) provides with respect to remainder interests:

> SEC. 7520(a). GENERAL RULE.—For purposes of this title, [i.e., title 26 U.S.C., the Internal Revenue Code] the value of any * * * remainder * * * interest shall be determined—
>
> (1) under tables prescribed by the Secretary, and
>
> (2) by using an interest rate (rounded to the nearest 2/10ths of 1 percent) equal to 120 percent of the Federal midterm rate in effect under section 1274(d)(1) for the month in which the valuation date falls.
>
> If an income * * * tax charitable contribution is allowable for any part of the property transferred, the taxpayer may elect to use such Federal midterm rate for either of the 2 months preceding the month in which the valuation date falls for purposes of paragraph (2). * * *

Section 1.7520–1(a)(1), Income Tax Regs.,[6] applicable to remainder interests, provides: "Except as otherwise provided in this section and in § 1.7520–3 (relating to exceptions to the use of prescribed tables under certain circumstances), in the case of certain transactions after April 30, 1989, subject to the income tax, the fair market value of * * * remainders * * * is their present value determined under this section." Section 1.7520–1(c), Income Tax Regs., generally provides that "present value" is to be computed by using tables (section 7520 tables) reflecting the section 7520 interest rate component and, if necessary, the mortality component described in the section 7520 regulations. See also section 1.7520–2(a)(1), Income Tax Regs., which provides: "Valuation.—Except as otherwise provided in this section and in § 1.7520–3 * * * the fair market value of * * * remainders * * * for which an income tax charitable deduction is allowable is the present value of such interests determined under § 1.7520–1."

Section 1.7520–3(b)(1)(i)(C), Income Tax Regs., describes an "ordinary remainder or reversionary interest" as "the right to receive an interest in property at the end of one or more measuring lives or some other defined period." The regulation provides that such an interest may be present-valued using a "standard section 7520 remainder factor" as defined therein. *Id.*

Section 1.7520–3(b)(1)(ii), Income Tax Regs., describes a "restricted beneficial interest", in part, as a remainder interest "that is subject to a contingency, power, or other restriction, whether the restriction is provided for by the terms of the * * * governing instrument or is caused by other circumstances." That regulation further provides: "In general, a standard section 7520 * * * remainder factor may not be used to value a restricted beneficial interest." *Id.* It provides, however, that "a special section 7520 * * * remainder factor may be used to value a restricted beneficial interest under some circumstances", citing an example in section 1.7520–3(b)(4), Income Tax Regs., that is not germane to this case.[7] *Id.*

---

[6] The regulations cited and discussed herein are those that were in effect for 2003, the year in issue.

[7] As discussed *infra* pp. 63–64, respondent alleges that the SMI was a

If neither the section 7520 tables nor a special section 7520 factor is applicable to determining the value of a remainder interest, then the fair market value of the remainder interest is determined without regard for section 7520 on the basis of all of the facts and circumstances. *See* sec. 1.7520–3(b)(1)(iii), Income Tax Regs.

Section 1.7520–3(b)(2), Income Tax Regs., is entitled "Provisions of governing instrument and other limitations on source of payment." Section 1.7520–3(b)(2)(iii), Income Tax Regs., provides with respect to remainder and reversionary interests:

> (iii) Remainder and reversionary interests. A standard section 7520 remainder interest factor for an ordinary remainder or reversionary interest may not be used to determine the present value of a remainder or reversionary interest (whether in trust or otherwise) unless, consistent with the preservation and protection that the law of trusts would provide for a person who is unqualifiedly designated as the remainder beneficiary of a trust for a similar duration, the effect of the administrative and dispositive provisions for the interest or interests that precede the remainder or reversionary interest is to assure that the property will be adequately preserved and protected (e.g., from erosion, invasion, depletion, or damage) until the remainder or reversionary interest takes effect in possession and enjoyment. This degree of preservation and protection is provided only if it was the transferor's intent, as manifested by the provisions of the arrangement and the surrounding circumstances, that the entire disposition provide the remainder or reversionary beneficiary with an undiminished interest in the property transferred at the time of the termination of the prior interest.

See also section 1.7520–3(b)(2)(ii)(A), Income Tax Regs., which, in addressing the requirements of a "governing instrument" with respect to "[i]ncome and similar interests",

---

restricted beneficial interest precluding Mr. Gelbtuch's use of the sec. 7520 tables. Respondent appears to treat that preclusion as mandated by and synonymous with the statement in sec. 1.7520–3(b)(1)(ii), Income Tax Regs., that "[i]n general, a standard section 7520 * * * remainder factor may not be used to value a restricted beneficial interest." Petitioner does not allege the right to file on RERI's behalf a ruling request under sec. 1.7520–1(c), Income Tax Regs., seeking from respondent a "special section 7520 * * * remainder factor" in order to value the SMI. *See* sec. 1.7520–3(b)(1)(ii), Income Tax Regs. Nor do the parties discuss the possible use of such a factor herein in lieu of the "standard" sec. 7520 factor or what that might mean in arriving at a value of the SMI. Therefore, we will address the issue as framed by the parties: whether petitioner is entitled to use the sec. 7520 tables (i.e., a "standard" sec. 7520 remainder factor) in valuing the SMI.

provides that the income beneficiary's interest is adequately protected (i.e., is an ordinary beneficial interest subject to valuation using a "standard section 7520 income factor") "only if it was the transferor's intent, as manifested by the provisions of the governing instrument and the surrounding circumstances, that the trust provide an income interest for the income beneficiary during the specified period of time that is *consistent with the value of the trust corpus and with its preservation*." (Emphasis added.)

The wasting nature of depreciable and depletable real property is reflected in a special rule requiring that, in determining the value of a remainder interest in real property for purposes of section 170 (allowing an income tax deduction for any charitable contribution), depreciation and depletion be taken into account. Section 170(f)(4) provides: "For purposes of this section, in determining the value of a remainder interest in real property, depreciation (computed on the straight line method) and depletion of such property shall be taken into account, and such value shall be discounted at a rate of 6 percent per annum, except that the Secretary may prescribe a different rate."

B. *Whether on the Authority of Pierre v. Commissioner We Should Disregard the Check-the-Box Regulations in the Context of a Valuation for Purposes of Section 170, and, if So, Whether That Disregard Necessarily Invalidates Mr. Gelbtuch's Valuation as a Valuation of the SMI Because He Improperly Applied the Section 7520 Tables to the Hawthorne Property Rather Than to the Value of the Holdings Membership Interest*

1. *The Parties' Arguments*

Respondent argues that Mr. Gelbtuch improperly appraised a hypothetical remainder interest in the Hawthorne property rather than the SMI that RERI did, in fact, donate to the University. He argues that, assuming the section 7520 tables are applicable to value the SMI, the section 7520 remainder interest factor should have been applied "to the fair market value of Holdings, a recognized legal entity formed under Delaware law, rather than [to] the market value of the Hawthorne Property."

Petitioner defends Mr. Gelbtuch's application of the section 7520 tables to the fair market value of the Hawthorne property on the ground that both Holdings and its wholly owned subsidiary, Hawthorne, which owned the Hawthorne property, were LLCs wholly owned by Red Sea and, therefore, were "disregarded entities" pursuant to section 301.7701–3(b)(1)(ii), Proced. & Admin. Regs. Petitioner argues that our Opinion in *Pierre v. Commissioner*, 133 T.C. 24 (2009), in which we held that an LLC constituting a disregarded entity under the foregoing regulation may not be disregarded for purposes of valuing the gift of an interest therein, is applicable only for Federal gift tax purposes, not for purposes of determining the income tax deduction for a charitable contribution of an interest in a disregarded LLC, the sole asset of which is an interest in real estate. Respondent rejects petitioner's reliance on the check-the-box regulations to disregard Holdings and Hawthorne, noting that, although this Court "considered * * * [the] issue in the context of the federal gift tax provisions, the Tax Court's rationale in *Pierre* is equally applicable to the instant case."

Petitioner, recognizing that *Pierre* involved gifts and valuations of fractional interests in an LLC, posits that "had 100% of the Pierre LLC interests been transferred to one person the Court in *Pierre* would have agreed that no discounts were appropriate"; i.e., that the transferred LLC interests and the underlying assets represented thereby would be of equal value. In further support of that argument, petitioner notes that "respondent fails to discuss how one would go about valuing the interests transferred since the 100% owner of the LLC could collapse the structure, terminating the LLC", again suggesting that the SMI and the remainder interest in the Hawthorne property were of equal value. Similarly, in defending the Gelbtuch appraisal as a "qualified appraisal" under section 1.170A–13(c)(3), Income Tax Regs., petitioner questions how an appraisal of the SMI "would produce a different result as the underlying asset would still have to be valued", and he further notes: "[w]hile respondent argues the wrong property was * * * valued, * * * [he] does not suggest how else the value of the * * * [SMI] would be determined." Thus, petitioner suggests that, even if Mr. Gelbtuch did apply the section 7520 tables to a fair market valuation of the wrong property, that impropriety was of no economic consequence and, therefore, should be ignored.

2. *Analysis*

a. *Applicability of Pierre*

In *Pierre*, the LLC, wholly owned by the individual donor of the fractional interests therein, was validly formed under New York law. We determined that, even though the LLC was a disregarded entity under the check-the-box regulations, that designation did not control the valuation of the fractional LLC interests transferred by the donor taxpayer for Federal gift tax purposes. In holding that the gifts were of fractional interests in the LLC rather than of pro rata shares of the LLC's underlying assets, we noted that, under New York law, the taxpayer "did not have a property interest in the underlying assets of" the LLC and that "Federal law could not create a property right in those assets." *Pierre v. Commissioner*, 133 T.C. at 29–30. We further noted that the question of how the transfer of an ownership interest in an LLC should be valued for Federal gift tax purposes "is not the question addressed by the check-the-box regulations". *Id.* at 35.

We also find significant Judge Cohen's admonition in her concurring opinion (joined by 8 of the other 9 Judges joining in the 10-Judge majority opinion), that "[w]here the property transferred is an interest in a single-member LLC * * * validly created and recognized under State law, the willing buyer cannot be expected to disregard that LLC." *Id.* at 37.

We were faced in *Pierre*, as we are faced here, with identifying the appropriate property against which to apply the customary willing seller and willing buyer standard (here, as a first step in applying the section 7520 tables). The customary willing seller and willing buyer standard is described in substantially identical language both for valuing charitable contributions of property for income tax purposes and for valuing gifts of property for gift tax purposes. *Compare* sec. 1.170A–1(c)(2), Income Tax Regs., *with* sec. 25.2512–1, Gift Tax Regs. *See* sec. 20.2031–1(b), Estate Tax Regs. (same definition for estate tax valuations). And it is only on account of a charitable contribution deduction provided for in the gift tax statute that gifts to charity are not included in the amount of taxable gifts. *See* sec. 2522. We see no reason to identify the property to be valued for income tax purposes (and subject to a charitable contribution deduction) differently from the property to be valued for gift tax purposes (and subject to a charitable contribution deduction).[8]

Thus, we agree with respondent that, on the rationale of *Pierre*, for purposes of determining the value of RERI's charitable contribution to the University, the property RERI transferred to the University was the SMI. We also agree with respondent that, on the face of it, Mr. Gelbtuch did not determine the value of the SMI; rather, on the face of it, by applying the section 7520 tables to the value of the Hawthorne property, he determined the value of a hypothetical remainder interest in that property. The question is whether the latter value may serve as an acceptable substitute for the former value.

b. *Whether Mr. Gelbtuch's Application of the Section 7520 Tables to the Value of the Hawthorne Property Necessarily Invalidates Mr. Gelbtuch's Valuation as a Valuation of the SMI*

On the basis of the rationale of *Pierre*, the property that RERI transferred to the University was the SMI, and it thus would have been no error for Mr. Gelbtuch to have determined the value of the Holdings membership interest and to have applied the section 7520 tables to that value to determine the value of the SMI. That, however, does not nec-

---

[8] Nevertheless, the value of a remainder interest in real property contributed to a qualified charitable organization may be greater for gift tax or estate tax purposes than it is for income tax purposes. Unlike sec. 170(f), neither the gift tax nor the estate tax provisions contain an express requirement that depreciation or depletion be taken into account in determining the value of a remainder interest in real property. Apparently, the Commissioner takes that omission to be intentional. *See* Rev. Rul. 76–473, 1976–2 C.B. 306 (gift tax value of charitable remainder interest in personal residence following 20-year possessory interest determined without taking into consideration depreciation for period before charity's possession. "The value of the charitable remainder interest is higher for gift tax purposes than for income tax purposes."); *see also Nat'l Bank of Commerce in Memphis v. United States*, 422 F.2d 1074, 1076 (6th Cir. 1970) (estate tax deduction for transfer of charitable remainder computed simply by multiplying current asset value by factor from tables); *Estate of Bachman v. Commissioner*, T.C. Memo. 1975–186 (to same effect).

essarily mean that RERI fatally erred in determining the value of the SMI by having Mr. Gelbtuch determine the value of a hypothetical remainder interest in the Hawthorne property. *Pierre* involved transfers of present interests in a single-member LLC to two trusts, which interests, because of discounts for lack of marketability and control, were argued to be worth less than the donees' pro rata shares of the assets of the LLC. Petitioner points out that RERI transferred to the University a future interest in Holdings that, when it becomes a present (possessory) interest at the termination of the TOYS interest, will encompass 100% of the membership interest in Holdings. Therefore, petitioner argues, there is not necessarily any difference between the value of the property owned by Holdings indirectly (the Hawthorne property) and the value of the property (Holdings) to which Mr. Gelbtuch should have applied the section 7520 tables in determining the value of the SMI. It follows, petitioner suggests, that, absent restrictions applicable to one and not the other, *see* discussion *infra*, there is no difference between the value of Holdings and the value of the leased fee interest in the Hawthorne property that was, in effect, Holdings' sole asset. If so, petitioner continues, then Mr. Gelbtuch's valuation of the latter, in effect, would have constituted a valuation of the former, so that the section 7520 tables could properly be applied to the latter in arriving at a value for the SMI. In response to petitioner's suggestion, respondent admits that, "[i]n normal course, there exists a unity of interest between a single-member entity and the assets owned by such entity."[9] But he argues that Red Sea's split of Holdings into the TOYS interest and the SMI gave rise to "'a multiple ownership structure' unlike where one party owned 100 percent."

It is true that Red Sea did divide the Holdings membership interest into a present (TOYS) interest and a future (SMI) interest; it is also true that, applying the section 7520 tables to determine the present value of each, neither value is equal to the combined value of the two interests. Pursuant to sec-

[9] In support of that statement, respondent states: "*See e.g.*, *Pierre* at 43 (Halpern, dissenting) citing 18 C.J.S., *Corporations*, at § 4 (2007) and *Smart v. Int'l Bd. of Elec. Workers, Local 702*, 315 F.3d 721, 723 (7th Cir. 2002) regarding the rule of unity which exists amongst a sole proprietor and such entrepreneur's business."

tion 7520 and its implementing regulations, the method for determining the value of an ordinary income interest or an ordinary remainder interest (or, in some cases, an income or a remainder interest constituting a restricted beneficial interest) is to determine the fair market value of the property out of which the two interests were created and to divide that value among the two interests on the basis of their present values. *See* sec. 1.7520–1(a)(1), Income Tax Regs. For a remainder interest following a term of years interest, the section 7520 tables reflect only interest rate and timing variables. *See* sec. 1.7520–1(c), Income Tax Regs. But, if those section 7520 tables do apply to value the SMI, they fully reflect Congress' and the Secretary's concerns that the SMI represents less than the 100% of the Holdings membership interest. And if it can be assumed that (1) the Hawthorne property and Holdings are of equal value and (2) no restrictions burden the SMI, then nothing may be lost in allowing the Hawthorne property to substitute for the Holdings membership interest in applying the section 7520 tables to determine the value of the SMI.[10]

There is an unresolved issue of fact concerning whether the value of a hypothetical remainder interest in the Hawthorne property can stand proxy for the SMI. That issue involves the two-year hold-sell requirement imposed on the University with respect to its possession of the SMI. Does that requirement cause the SMI to be a restricted beneficial interest for which a standard section 7520 remainder factor may not be applied to determine fair market value, *see* sec. 1.7520–3(b)(1)(ii), Income Tax Regs., or, if not, does it at

---

[10] We note in passing that, in valuing the Hawthorne property, Mr. Gelbtuch assumed that it was unencumbered by any indebtedness. Our intuition is that any valuation of Holdings (a holding company) would reflect Hawthorne's net asset value (i.e., the value of its assets less the value of its liabilities), thus taking into account the liability represented by the promissory note and the mortgage. In that event, Mr. Gelbtuch's valuation of the Hawthorne property on the assumption that it was "free and clear of any and all liens or encumbrances" could not be considered a substitute for a valuation of Holdings, and, hence, his valuation of a hypothetical remainder interest in the Hawthorne property (applying the sec. 7520 tables to the debt-free value of that property), could not be considered a substitute for a valuation of the SMI. It is incumbent on the parties to address that issue at the appropriate time. In the order, *see supra* note 2, we did not address that specific issue.

least reduce the value of the SMI below that of a hypothetical remainder interest in the Hawthorne property? We discuss the restricted beneficial interest issue *infra* pp. 63–71.

If we determine the fact issue adversely to petitioner, we would agree with respondent that Mr. Gelbtuch's application of the section 7520 tables to the fair market value of the Hawthorne property necessarily resulted in a valuation (of a hypothetical remainder interest therein) that may not substitute for a valuation of the SMI.[11] If, on the other hand, we are persuaded that an appraisal of a hypothetical remainder interest in the Hawthorne property can substitute for an appraisal of the SMI, we would be inclined to apply the often invoked principle of "[n]o harm; no foul", *see, e.g.*, *King v. Nat'l Human Res. Comm., Inc.*, 218 F.3d 719, 724 (7th Cir. 2000), and reject respondent's argument that we must, as a matter of law, disregard Mr. Gelbtuch's appraisal because he improperly applied the section 7520 tables to the fair market value of the Hawthorne property rather than to the fair market value of Holdings. It would be premature to apply that principle herein, however, because there exist unresolved questions of both law and fact.

C. *Whether the Regulations Preclude Application of the Section 7520 Tables To Value the SMI*

1. *Introduction*

The SMI is a remainder interest in Holdings, and its fair market value is its present value determined by applying the section 7520 tables only if (1) the SMI is an ordinary remainder interest and the provisions of section 1.7520–3(b)(2)(iii), Income Tax Regs. (requiring that preservation and protection of the underlying property (the Holdings membership interest) is assured), are satisfied or (2) the SMI is a restricted beneficial interest for which a standard section 7520 remainder factor may be used. *See* sec. 1.7520–3(b)(1)(ii), Income Tax Regs.

[11] The same would be true should we ultimately determine that Mr. Gelbtuch's appraisal cannot substitute for a valuation of the SMI because of his failure to take the mortgage into account.

2. *Summary of the Parties' Arguments*

Respondent's principal argument is that section 1.7520–3(b)(2)(iii), Income Tax Regs., precludes application of the section 7520 tables to determine the value of the SMI. Respondent argues that, because the holder of the SMI does not "enjoy the same protections as would be afforded to a trust remainderman", there is no assurance that such holder "will receive the Hawthorne Property in its original form." Respondent worries about devaluation of the Holdings membership interest because of depreciation of the Hawthorne property, its sale, or additional or unpaid mortgage indebtedness. Therefore, respondent argues, whether the SMI constitutes an ordinary remainder interest or not, the preservation and protection requirements of section 1.7520–3(b)(2)(iii), Income Tax Regs., preclude application of the section 7520 tables.

Additionally, respondent argues that, because of the two-year hold-sell requirement, the SMI is a restricted beneficial interest within the meaning of section 1.7520–3(b)(1)(ii), Income Tax Regs., to which the section 7520 tables cannot be applied.

Petitioner argues that the SMI follows a term of years interest (i.e., the TOYS interest) and is therefore an ordinary remainder interest within the meaning of section 1.7520–3(b)(1)(i)(C), Income Tax Regs. Petitioner rejects respondent's reading of section 1.7520–3(b)(2)(iii), Income Tax Regs., arguing that "the regulation basically provides * * * consistent with the laws of trusts, * * * [that] the trustee * * * must protect against waste." He further argues that "the regulation simply provides that the interest of the property [e.g., a remainder interest] as opposed to its value, be undiminished", and that it is only "concerned with the initial beneficiary having the power to utilize the assets of the trust so that there is a real possibility that there will be nothing or little left for a remainderman." Petitioner also "discerns" from the regulatory language "that the interest being discussed is a remainder interest in a trust and not a remainder interest in real property." Petitioner argues that the SMI holder's right to protect its interest arises under contract and property law, not trust law (i.e., the SMI holder is not the remainder beneficiary of a trust), and that, in any event, the SMI is adequately protected by the severe limitations in the Red Sea-RJS assignment agreement on the right of the TOYS interest to encumber the Hawthorne property. He thinks that respondent overstates the possibility of a devaluation of the Holdings membership interest, arguing that depreciation does not preclude the use of the section 7520 tables and that respondent's concern that the remainder will be diminished in value is "so remote as to be negligible."

Lastly, petitioner disputes respondent's argument that the two-year hold-sell requirement renders the SMI a restricted beneficial interest to which the section 7520 tables are inapplicable. Rather, petitioner argues, a restriction on the right to dispose of an interest in property is not the type of restriction contemplated in the regulation, section 1.7520–3(b)(1)(ii), Income Tax Regs., defining the term "restricted beneficial interest."

3. *Analysis*

a. *Introduction*

We may summarily dispose of petitioner's argument that the preservation and protection requirements found in section 1.7520–3(b)(2)(iii), Income Tax Regs., apply only with respect to property held in trust. They do not. The parenthetical in the first sentence of the regulation makes that quite clear: "A standard section 7520 remainder interest factor for an ordinary remainder * * * interest may not be used to determine the present value of a remainder * * * interest (*whether in trust or otherwise*) unless". *Id.* (emphasis added).

Therefore, for respondent to prevail on his claim that the section 7520 tables are inapplicable in determining the fair market value of the SMI, he must show either (1) that the SMI is an ordinary remainder interest for which the preservation and protection requirements of section 1.7520–3(b)(2)(iii), Income Tax Regs., are not satisfied or (2) that the SMI is a restricted beneficial interest whose value may not be determined by application of a standard section 7520 remainder factor.

b. *Preservation and Protection of the Property*

i. *Risk of Hawthorne's Encumbering or Selling the Hawthorne Property*

Respondent argues that, because Hawthorne may encumber or sell the Hawthorne property, there is no assurance that the value of the Holdings membership interest will be preserved and protected until the holder of the SMI comes into possession of that interest. *See* sec. 1.7520–3(b)(2)(iii), Income Tax Regs. As stated *supra* in our background discussion, by the assignment agreement, Red Sea agreed to prohibit Holdings or Hawthorne from encumbering the Hawthorne property without the consent of RJS, the initial transferee of the SMI under that agreement. By that agreement, Red Sea also agreed to prohibit the transfer of any interest in the Hawthorne property or the creation of any "lien or encumbrance" on that property that would "materially adversely affect" its value. Respondent argues that, in the event the Hawthorne property is either sold or encumbered in violation of the assignment agreement,[12] RJS and, subsequently, RERI and the University, as owners of the SMI, would have the right, under that agreement, only "to receive, as damages, the very interest promised", i.e., the SMI. Thus, respondent concludes, "the successor member interest holder is afforded substantially less protection than that of a trust remainderman", in violation of the principal requirement for the use of a "standard section 7520 remainder interest factor" under section 1.7520–3(b)(2)(iii), Income Tax Regs. Petitioner responds that the risks that the SMI might be diminished by any such action are remote possibilities that, pursuant to regulations under section 170, are not to be taken into account in valuing a charitable contribution. *See* sec. 1.170A–1(e), Income Tax Regs. (possibility that charitable transfer will not become effective disregarded if, on the date of the gift, that possibility "is so remote as to be negligible"). Therefore, petitioner argues the assignment agree-

[12] Both petitioner and respondent refer to the possibility that the owner of the TOYS interest might encumber the Hawthorne property. In fact, it would appear that Hawthorne, the owner of the property, would be the only person who could encumber the property. That is the occurrence actually contemplated (and prohibited without RJS' consent) by the parties to the assignment agreement.

ment does not lack assurance that the Holdings membership interest will be adequately preserved and protected.

Respondent has not shown that either Red Sea, Holdings, or Hawthorne intends a sale of the Hawthorne property. Moreover, the property into possession of which the SMI holder will come is the Holdings membership interest, *not* the Hawthorne property. Holdings' assets (whether held directly or indirectly) may change without necessarily putting into jeopardy the SMI holder's rights to future possession and enjoyment of a valuable Holdings membership interest. Similarly, respondent has not shown any intent to encumber the Hawthorne property in violation of the assignment agreement, except, perhaps, in connection with a refinancing or restructuring of the balloon payment. That possibility is acknowledged by petitioner should AT&T not exercise its option to renew its lease in May 2016, when the initial lease term is to expire and the $11.8 million balloon payment becomes due. But even in that event, it is not clear that such a refinancing would entail an additional, burdensome encumbrance on the Hawthorne property as a new mortgage would, presumably, replace the existing mortgage on the Hawthorne property and, therefore, not cause any diminution of the property's fair market value. Moreover, even if the Hawthorne property were otherwise encumbered, that would not necessarily put into jeopardy the SMI holder's rights to future possession and enjoyment of the Holdings membership interest.

Respondent has not made his case that the risk of Hawthorne's selling or encumbering the Hawthorne property jeopardizes the SMI holder's rights to future possession and enjoyment of the Holdings membership interest so as to preclude use of a standard section 7520 remainder interest factor to determine the present value of the SMI. *See* sec. 1.7520–3(b)(2)(iii), Income Tax Regs.[13] At best, respondent

[13] We note in passing that, in discussing the limitation-on-liability provision of the assignment agreement, which respondent claims jeopardizes the SMI holder's future interest in the Holdings membership interest, respondent may have confused the TOYS interest and the SMI. That provision (paragraph C of the covenants portion of the assignment agreement) provides that, in the event of an assignor's (Red Sea's or one of its successor's) breach of the agreement, the assignee's (RJS' or one of its successor's, e.g., RERI's or the University's) recourse is limited to the assignor's "Retained

has identified a dispute as to a material issue of fact; i.e., Hawthorne's (and others') intentions.

ii. *Risk of Nonpayment of the Promissory Note and Foreclosure*

The parties differ sharply as to whether the possibility that Hawthorne will be unable to make the $11.8 million balloon payment on the May 15, 2016, due date poses a sufficient risk of foreclosure and sale of the Hawthorne property to warrant a conclusion that the Holdings membership interest value will not be adequately preserved and protected for the benefit of the SMI. If there is sufficient risk of foreclosure, that would foreclose use of a standard remainder interest factor to determine the present value of the SMI. *See* sec. 1.7520–3(b)(2)(iii), Income Tax Regs. Petitioner views the risk as a remote contingency to be disregarded.

The record shows that the Hawthorne property is Hawthorne's only asset and that the AT&T lease is its only source of income. The promissory note calls for a final, $11.8 million balloon payment on May 15, 2016. By the end of May 2016 (the conclusion of the first term of the AT&T lease), Hawthorne should have received sufficient payments under the AT&T lease to have made all installment payments called for by the note and to have accumulated a surplus (assuming no distributions) of approximately $5.7 million. That would leave $6.1 million to be raised to make the balloon payment.

Petitioner views as remote the possibility of default on the balloon payment. Specifically, petitioner states:

> Petitioner submits that at the time of the donation it was expected that AT&T would exercise its option to renew the lease and thus the balloon payment paid. Defaulting on the final payment due on the loan was as remote as Hawthorne defaulting on the underlying mortgage. It can also be anticipated that at the time of the donation the balloon payment would be refinanced or restructured or the premises leased to another party if AT&T did not exercise its option.

Interest" (i.e., the TOYS interest) in Holdings. Respondent's claim is that the limitation-on-liability provision "only permits the successor member interest holder to receive, as damages, the very interest promised", i.e., the SMI. That is not the case. The SMI holder could receive as damages all of the TOYS interest, which, when united with the SMI, represents complete ownership of Holdings.

In response to those arguments, respondent continues to maintain that "there is a possibility that the balloon payment would not get paid, thus resulting in foreclosure or acquisition of the Hawthorne Property", in which event, "the SMI holder would possess a worthless membership interest in * * * [Holdings]." Respondent further argues that there is no evidence that the loan would be refinanced or even could be refinanced "due to the provisions petitioner relies upon to argue that encumbrances are not permitted", respondent's assumption apparently being that the parties would interpret such a replacement financing as the type of encumbrance that is prohibited by the Red Sea-RJS Assignment Agreement.

The foregoing arguments by both parties are based entirely on speculation. Respondent, whose motion it is we are considering, has not convinced us that Hawthorne, as obligor on the promissory note, would not be able to raise the more than $6 million needed to make the $11.8 million balloon payment on May 15, 2016. Nor has respondent convinced us that the risk of refinancing the remaining debt presents anything other than a conventional commercial risk that has little effect on the safety of Holdings as a long-term investment. Moreover, given Hawthorne's expected payment of a substantial amount of principal (close to $32 million) before the due date of the balloon payment, what equity will Hawthorne have in the Hawthorne property, a portion of which might be recouped on a forced sale of the Hawthorne property to safeguard Holdings' (and the SMI's) value? Indeed, how will the value of the SMI interest be affected by the fact that principal payments under the promissory note are to be paid from rental income that, but for the assignment of rents to BB&T, it would seem should be distributed to the TOYS interest holder?[14] The only "fact" before us is the certainty

---

[14] In response to respondent's prior motion for partial summary judgment, *see supra* note 2, petitioner stated that the mortgage would "be fully amortized by * * * the owner of the TOY[S] Interest". 1 Joseph Rasch & Robert F. Dolan, N.Y. Law & Practice of Real Property, sec. 6:27 (2d ed.) ("Payment of principal of mortgage") states in pertinent part:

> A life tenant is under no obligation to pay the principal of a mortgage encumbering the property; this must be paid by the remainderman. If the life tenant does pay it, he may recover such payment from the remainderman.[9]

that the lease payments will be insufficient (by more than $6 million) to enable Hawthorne to make that payment. And although, as petitioner argues, it was "expected" or "anticipated" at the time of RERI's gift of the SMI that there would be a refinancing, a lease extension, or a new lease, any one of which could have generated the funds needed to make the balloon payment, expectation and anticipation are not synonymous with certainty. Therefore, we find that the parties' dispute as to whether the risk of Hawthorne's defaulting on the $11.8 million balloon payment is the type of contingency that would jeopardize the value of Holdings and, thus, the value of the SMI, in contravention of section 1.7520–3(b)(2)(iii), Income Tax Regs., constitutes a dispute as to a material fact, which precludes summary adjudication that the risk of nonpayment of the balloon payment on the promissory note warrants a conclusion that Holdings' value will not be adequately preserved and protected for the benefit of the SMI.

c. *Restricted Beneficial Interest*

i. *The Parties' Arguments*

Respondent summarizes his position with respect to the impact of the two-year hold-sell requirement as follows:

> As a result of the "hold-sell" restrictions imposed by the Gift Agreement and the * * * [Assignment Agreement], the successor member interest was a restricted beneficial interest for purposes of section 7520. Furthermore, the consequence of these restrictions dictated that the University would never become the owner of the underlying Hawthorne Property or enjoy the benefits and burdens of * * * [owning that property].

Respondent concludes: "Since there was no intention to transfer an interest, which would be unrestricted prior to the expiration of the prior TOYS interest, the section 7520 tables may not be used."

In rebuttal to respondent's arguments, petitioner cites our conclusion in *Estate of Gribauskas v. Commissioner*, 116 T.C. 142, 165 (2001) (*Estate of Gribauskas I*), *rev'd and remanded*, 342 F.3d 85 (2d Cir. 2003) (*Estate of Gribauskas II*), involving the value of nonassignable future installments of lottery winnings, that "a restriction within the meaning of * * * [section 20.7520–3(b)(1)(ii), Estate Tax Regs.] is one

[FN9]*Collins v McKenna* (1921) 116 Misc 72, 189 NYS 433.

which jeopardizes receipt of the payment stream, not one which merely impacts on the ability of the payee to dispose of his or her right thereto." Petitioner also notes that we further stated in *Estate of Gribauskas I* that "the cases addressing attempts to avoid use of the [section 7520] tables * * * [generally] required a factual showing that renders unrealistic and unreasonable the return or mortality assumptions underlying the tables." *Id.* at 161. Petitioner states: "Not only is the * * * [SMI] not a restricted beneficial interest for purposes of section 7520, but such a determination is clearly factual and cannot be determined as a matter of law as sought by respondent."

Petitioner also relies upon two U.S. Courts of Appeals cases that hold that restrictions on the marketability of an income stream constituting an interest in property are not the type of restriction that would render the section 7520 tables inapplicable in valuing the property interest. In *Cook v. Commissioner*, 349 F.3d 850, 854 (5th Cir. 2003), *aff'g* T.C. Memo. 2001–170, the Court of Appeals stated: "In enacting § 7520(a)(1) and requiring valuation by the tables, Congress displayed a preference for convenience and certainty over accuracy in the individual case." The Court of Appeals reiterated that statement in *Anthony v. United States*, 520 F.3d 374, 377 (5th Cir. 2008). In petitioner's view, the two-year hold requirement does not furnish a reason to abandon the judicial preference for valuing partial interests in property under the section 7520 tables.

Lastly, petitioner argues that the gift agreement embodying the sell requirement has no bearing on the issue because it did not affect the University's rights with respect to the property "as * * * [the University] would still own and control * * * [the SMI] regardless of whether * * * [it] adhered to the gift agreement."

ii. *Analysis*

(a) *The Two-Year Hold-Sell Requirement*

We find fault with both parties' analyses of the impact of the two-year hold-sell requirement.

Our principal problem with respondent's argument is his apparent assumption that no restricted beneficial interest may be valued using the section 7520 tables. Section 1.7520–

3(b)(1)(ii), Income Tax Regs., provides that "[*i*]*n general*, a standard section 7520 * * * remainder factor may not be used to value a restricted beneficial interest." (Emphasis added.) The two-year hold-sell requirement is undeniably a restriction on the University's rights with respect to its ownership of the SMI. But that fact, in and of itself, does not provide a sufficient basis to conclude that the SMI is a restricted beneficial interest for which a standard section 7520 remainder factor may not be used to determine value. Respondent's position also ignores the admonition, uniformly expressed in the caselaw dealing with the application of the section 7520 tables, that those tables must be used "unless it is shown that the result is so unrealistic and unreasonable that either some modification in the prescribed method should be made, or complete departure from the method should be taken, and a more reasonable and realistic means of determining value is available" (unrealistic and unreasonable fair market value standard). *Weller v. Commissioner*, 38 T.C. 790, 803 (1962) (citations omitted). To the same effect, see *Anthony*, 520 F.3d at 383; *Cook v. Commissioner*, 349 F.3d at 854; *Estate of Gribauskas II*, 342 F.3d at 87; *Shackleford v. United States*, 262 F.3d 1028, 1031 (9th Cir. 2001). Therefore, we reject respondent's premise that any restriction applicable to a remainder interest is, per se, a restriction that renders the interest a restricted beneficial interest for which use of the section 7520 tables is unavailable.

Petitioner agrees that application of the section 7520 tables is conditioned on nonviolation of the unrealistic and unreasonable fair market value standard. But he relies on our statements in *Estate of Gribauskas I*, 116 T.C. at 165, that a restriction on alienation is not a restriction covered by section 1.7520–3(b)(1)(ii), Income Tax Regs., defining a restricted beneficial interest. Petitioner also relies on *Anthony* and *Cook*, which reach the same result. Petitioner's argument overlooks two important facts. First, all three of the cited cases involve the valuation of a present right to a stream of income and not the valuation of a right to future possession of corpus. That distinction was drawn by the Court of Appeals in *Cook v. Commissioner*, 349 F.3d at 856, where it stated: "We agree that the right to alienate is necessary to value a capital asset; however, we think it unreasonable to apply a non-marketability discount when the asset to be valued is the right, independent of market forces, to receive a certain amount of money annually for a certain term." Second, our decision in *Estate of Gribauskas I* was reversed by *Estate of Gribauskas II*, which held that a restriction on marketability may constitute a restriction that prevents application of the section 7520 tables in valuing an interest in property if it results in a violation of the unrealistic and unreasonable fair market value standard.[15]

We are not bound, pursuant to the doctrine of *Golsen v. Commissioner*, 54 T.C. 742 (1970), *aff'd*, 445 F.2d 985 (10th Cir. 1971), to follow *Estate of Gribauskas II* because RERI, whose principal place of business was in New York, was dissolved in 2004. Therefore, it had no principal place of business when it filed its petition in 2008. As a result, the court to which, barring a written stipulation to the contrary, an appeal of this case would lie would be the Court of Appeals for the D.C. (not the Second) Circuit. *See* sec. 7482(b); *Peat Oil & Gas Assocs. v. Commissioner*, T.C. Memo. 1993–130, 1993 WL 95592, at *6. That court has not as yet addressed the material restriction on the transferability issue.

Nor are we bound by the doctrine of stare decisis to follow our holding in *Estate of Gribauskas I* in this case. *Estate of Gribauskas I* involved a promised stream of fixed payments and is thus distinguishable from the valuation problem here before us, the present value of the right to receive a capital asset in the future. And while that capital asset may itself represent nothing more than the expectation of a future income stream, we generally rely on market prices to determine the value of capital assets such as shares of stock because the value of such assets is not readily ascertainable absent a transfer from buyer to seller. *See Cook v. Commissioner*, 349 F.3d at 856.

We conclude that the impact of both the restriction on alienation (i.e., the two-year hold requirement) and the two-year sell requirement is a restriction that must be measured against the unrealistic and unreasonable fair market value

---

[15] In so holding, the Court of Appeals for the Second Circuit followed the Court of Appeals for the Ninth Circuit in *Shackleford v. United States*, 262 F.3d 1028 (9th Cir. 2001), which reached that result. *See Estate of Gribauskas v. Commissioner*, 342 F.3d 85, 89 (2d Cir. 2003), *rev'g and remanding* 116 T.C. 142 (2001).

standard. It is true, as petitioner argues, that the latter requirement is found only in the gift agreement and not in the assignment agreement. But, as a signatory to both agreements, the University was bound by both, and it is quite possible to interpret the two-year hold-sell requirement in the gift agreement as, in effect, a condition of Mr. Ross' $5 million pledge to the University thereunder. Disputes under the gift agreement were to be governed by Michigan law, and the assignment agreement was to be construed in accordance with Delaware law. Neither party has addressed Mr. Ross' rights under Michigan and Delaware law in the event the University were to violate the two-year hold-sell requirement. Thus, there remains a question of fact [16] as to whether that requirement constituted a meaningful restriction relating to the SMI because the University's violation thereof would have justified Mr. Ross' reneging on all or a portion of his pledge, thereby reducing the value of the SMI in the University's hands. [17]

Neither party has presented evidence with respect to the impact, if any, of the two-year hold-sell requirement on the fair market value of the SMI. [18] Therefore, the impact

[16] *See, e.g., Moulton v. Commissioner*, T.C. Memo. 2009–38, 2009 WL 416010, at *5 (holding that the characterization of a claim under applicable State law, in that case, for purposes of determining the applicability of the sec. 104(a)(2) exclusion from income of damages for physical injury, is a question of fact).

[17] In that regard, we note that, before the University's sale of the SMI to HRK for $1,940,000, Mr. Ross had threatened to treat his pledge as offset by the full amount of HRK's offer of that amount if the University were to reject it and, later, sell the SMI for less.

[18] Even if the University's violation of the two-year hold-sell requirement would have had adverse economic consequences to the University, it is not clear that that violation would have had any impact on the actual value of the SMI (which is the relevant inquiry herein), as the violation would have been irrelevant to the purchaser of the SMI from the University. Conversely, if the University felt bound to abide by the requirement (as, apparently, it did), respondent argues that the "consequence" of the two-year hold-sell restriction "dictated that the University would never become the owner of the underlying Hawthorne Property or enjoy the benefits and burdens of * * * [owning it]." But respondent furnishes no evidence that that fact would have adversely affected the SMI's value. Moreover, it is arguable that the two-year hold restriction did not adversely affect value because, at the time of sale, the purchaser from the University would have been two years closer to possession than was the University when it ac-

Continued

on the SMI's value of the two-year hold-sell restriction also presents issues of material fact.

(b) *Whether Use of the Section 7520 Tables Would Violate the Unrealistic and Unreasonable Fair Market Value Standard*

In *Estate of Gribauskas II*, 342 F.3d at 88, the Court of Appeals for the Second Circuit noted the Commissioner's agreement that the taxpayer's valuation of the income stream in that case (lottery winnings in the form of an annuity), which was more than $900,000 below the value prescribed by the section 7520 tables ($2,603,661.02 versus $3,528,058.22), accurately reflected the market discount attributable to the restrictions on transferability of the income stream. The court stated that, under those circumstances, "application of the tables would clearly 'produce a substantially unrealistic and unreasonable result'". *Id.* (quoting *O'Reilly v. Commissioner*, 973 F.2d 1403, 1408 (8th Cir. 1992), *rev'g* 95 T.C. 646 (1990)). On that basis, the court held that "valuing the winnings pursuant to the tables was erroneous." *Id.* In *Anthony*, 520 F.3d at 384, the Court of Appeals for the Fifth Circuit ignored a roughly 50% disparity between the taxpayer's expert valuation of a lottery winnings annuity and the value derived pursuant to the section 7520 tables in sustaining the latter valuation. But that determination was based upon its prior determination, following its holding in *Cook*, that such large valuation disparities, if they result from marketability or transferability restrictions, are to be ignored, a position that the Courts of Appeals for both the Second and Ninth Circuits have rejected, and that the Court of Appeals for the Fifth Circuit itself has indicated should not be followed in determining the application of the section 7520 tables to a capital asset rather than an annuity.

In this case, sales of the SMI and an appraisal commissioned by the University (University appraisal) all indicate that the actual fair market value of the SMI, within a timeframe stretching from approximately 18 months before

---

quired the SMI, a fact that might have enhanced its value; and the two-year sell restriction would not have been a factor in the negotiations between the University and any prospective purchaser because the latter would not have been restricted by it.

RERI's August 27, 2003, gift of the SMI to the University to 2 years and 4 months thereafter, was substantially less than Mr. Gelbtuch's $32,935,000 valuation of the hypothetical remainder interest in the Hawthorne property using the section 7520 tables.

The relevant sales (and valuation) of the SMI are as follows:

(1) February 7, 2002: Red Sea's sale of the SMI to RJS for $1,610,000.

(2) March 25, 2002: RJS' sale of the SMI to RERI for $2,950,000.

(3) July 20, 2005: the University appraisal determining the value of a remainder interest in the Hawthorne property to be $6.5 million.

(4) On or about December 23, 2005: the University's sale of the SMI to HRK for $1,940,000.

(5) December 26, 2005: purported sale of the SMI by HRK to an unidentified purchaser for $3 million.

All four of the foregoing sales were for amounts substantially below Mr. Gelbtuch's appraised value of a hypothetical remainder interest in the Hawthorne property, determined using the section 7520 tables. The sales were for amounts ranging from approximately 5% to 9% of Mr. Gelbtuch's $32,935,000 appraisal, and the University appraisal was for an amount approximately 20% of that appraisal. Even with allowances for market fluctuations during the approximately 3-year, 10-month period of the foregoing transactions, the huge disparity between the SMI's fair market value as determined by actual sales and an independent valuation and its value based on Mr. Gelbtuch's appraisal is prima facie violative of the unrealistic and unreasonable fair market value standard.[19] Moreover, the reason for the disparity is of no

[19] With regard to the presence of significant market fluctuations, we note that Mr. Gelbtuch made a second appraisal of the Hawthorne property and a hypothetical remainder interest therein as of December 26, 2006, in which he concluded that the fair market value of the property was $64,185,000 and that of the hypothetical remainder interest (per the sec. 7520 tables) was $29,930,000. That reflects an increase in the property's appraised value and a decrease (due to application of a lower discount rate) in the hypothetical remainder interest's value, as compared with Mr. Gelbtuch's appraisal (as of August 28, 2003), in which he found those values to be $55,000,000 and $32,935,000, respectively (using a remainder

Continued

consequence. If the end result is a disparity of the foregoing magnitude between actual fair market value and value derived by applying the section 7520 tables, the tables are inapplicable under the unrealistic and unreasonable fair market value standard.

Neither party has directly addressed this issue of actual versus derived (per the section 7520 tables) value. Respondent cites caselaw acknowledging the relevance of the unrealistic and unreasonable fair market value standard. Petitioner attempts to refute respondent's argument for non-application of the section 7520 tables on the ground that each of the risks and contingencies identified by respondent is either remote (and, therefore, to be disregarded) or irrelevant. We find nothing in the record before us that definitively explains the foregoing large disparity in values. It may be attributable to one or more of the restrictions or contingencies discussed *supra*, but, for the reasons stated, that determination must await the resolution of unresolved issues of fact. Also, it may be attributable to the fact, discussed *supra*, that, compared to the application of the section 7520 tables to Holdings' (based on Hawthorne's) net asset value to determine the value of the SMI, the application of the section 7520 tables to the value of the Hawthorne property without taking into account the burden of the mortgage on that property produces a value for a hypothetical remainder interest in the Hawthorne property that is not reflective of the value of the SMI. If so, adjustment would have to be made for that liability or the value of a hypothetical remainder interest in the Hawthorne property would have to be rejected as a substitute for the value of the SMI. It also may reflect the fact that the foregoing sales of the SMI were not intended to be

---

factor of 0.598793705 to calculate the value of the hypothetical remainder interest). For the later appraisal, Mr. Gelbtuch was "advised that the applicable Remainder Interest Discount Rate as provided in Section 7520 of the Internal Revenue Code of 1986 for the month of contribution is 5.6 percent." Petitioner has not reconciled for us the use of a smaller factor to calculate the value of a remainder that was less distant. In any event, the two appraisals do not differ significantly as regards the valuation of the remainder interest, and the lower appraisal is still some $27 to $28 million higher that the amounts for which the SMI was twice sold on or about the "as of" appraisal date.

truly reflective of the SMI's fair market value on the dates of sale.[20]

In any event, the issue of whether the disparity between the SMI's value based upon the University appraisal and the sales of the SMI both before and after its contribution to the University, and its value based upon the Gelbtuch appraisal using the section 7520 tables results in a violation of the unrealistic and unreasonable fair market value standard is also an unresolved issue of material fact.

4. *Conclusion*

Because there remain genuine disputes as to material facts, we will deny the motion to the extent that respondent asks us to rule that the section 7520 tables do not apply to value the SMI.

III. *Whether the Gelbtuch Appraisal Was a Qualified Appraisal*

A. *Applicable Law*

As noted *supra*, section 170(a)(1) allows a charitable contribution deduction, but only if the contribution is "verified under regulations prescribed by the Secretary." The Deficit Reduction Act of 1984 (DEFRA), Pub. L. No. 98–369, sec. 155, 98 Stat. at 691, ordered the Secretary to prescribe regulations under section 170(a)(1) requiring a taxpayer claiming a deduction for a contribution of property worth more than $5,000 to "obtain [and retain] a qualified appraisal for the property contributed", attach an "appraisal summary" to the return reporting the deduction, and "include on such return such additional information * * * as the Secretary may prescribe in such regulations." *See* DEFRA sec. 155(a)(1).

[20] RERI's contribution of the SMI to the University resulted in a claimed deduction far in excess of RERI's investment therein. That contribution was followed by the University's sale of the SMI to HRK and HRK's resale of it, which was followed, ultimately, by the last purchaser's contribution of the SMI to another charitable organization, again allegedly resulting in a large deduction in excess of either HRK's or the donor's investment. That chain of events suggests the presence of a scheme to generate large deductions, through application of the sec. 7520 tables, for multiple charitable contributions of the same asset, in which each of the donors made a small investment. Such a scheme at least suggests tax shelter aspects that the parties may want to address at trial and on brief.

DEFRA defines a "qualified appraisal" as one prepared by a "qualified appraiser" that includes:

> (A) a description of the property appraised,
> (B) the fair market value of such property on the date of contribution and the specific basis for the valuation,
> (C) a statement that such appraisal was prepared for income tax purposes,
> (D) the qualifications of the qualified appraiser,
> (E) the signature and TIN of such appraiser, and
> (F) such additional information as the Secretary prescribes in such regulations.
> [*Id.* para. (4), 98 Stat. at 692.]

In response to that directive, the Secretary issued section 1.170A–13(c), Income Tax Regs. (sometimes, DEFRA regulations),[21] applicable to charitable contributions of property in excess of $5,000 by certain taxpayers, including individuals and partnerships, after December 31, 1984.

Section 1.170A–13(c)(1)(i), Income Tax Regs., provides, in pertinent part: "No deduction under section 170 shall be allowed * * * [for a covered contribution] unless the substantiation requirements described in paragraph (c)(2) of this section are met." Paragraph (c)(2)(i)(A) requires the donor-taxpayer to "[o]btain a qualified appraisal (as defined in paragraph (c)(3) of this section) for * * * [the] property contributed." Paragraph (c)(3)(i) describes a "qualified appraisal", in pertinent part, as "an appraisal document that * * * [i]ncludes the information required by paragraph (c)(3)(ii) of this section". Paragraph (c)(3)(ii) lists among the items of information that a qualified appraisal "shall include":

> (A) A description of the property in sufficient detail for a person who is not generally familiar with the type of property to ascertain that the property that was appraised is the property that was (or will be) contributed;
>
> * * * * * * *

[21] The DEFRA regulations govern this case. Congress largely codified those regulations in 2004 by enacting sec. 170(f)(11) as part of the American Jobs Creation Act of 2004 (AJCA), Pub. L. No. 108–357, sec. 883(a), 118 Stat. at 1631. That provision, which, unlike the DEFRA regulations, contains a "reasonable cause" exception for failure to comply with its terms, applies to contributions made after June 3, 2004. *See* AJCA sec. 883(b), 118 Stat. at 1632. Therefore, it does not apply to the 2003 contribution at issue herein.

(D) The terms of any agreement or understanding entered into (or expected to be entered into) by or on behalf of the donor or donee that relates to the use, sale, or other disposition of the property contributed, including, for example, the terms of any agreement or understanding that—

(1) Restricts temporarily or permanently a donee's right to use or dispose of the donated property,

(2) Reserves to, or confers upon, anyone (other than a donee organization or an organization participating with a donee organization in cooperative fundraising) any right to the income from the contributed property or to the possession of the property, including the right to vote donated securities, to acquire the property by purchase or otherwise, or to designate the person having such income, possession, or right to acquire, * * *

* * * * * * *

(I) The appraised fair market value (within the meaning of § 1.170A–1(c)(2)) of the property on the date (or expected date) of contribution;

(J) The method of valuation used to determine the fair market value, such as the income approach, the market-data approach, and the replacement-cost-less-depreciation approach; and

(K) The specific basis for the valuation, such as specific comparable sales transactions or statistical sampling, including a justification for using sampling and an explanation of the sampling procedure employed.

Under certain circumstances, "substantial compliance" with the requirements for a qualified appraisal will be sufficient to consider an appraisal qualified within the meaning of DEFRA sec. 155(a)(1) and (4) and section 1.170A–13(c)(3), Income Tax Regs. See *Bond v. Commissioner*, 100 T.C. 32, 41–42 (1993), in which we determined that the taxpayers' failure "to obtain and attach to their return a separate written appraisal containing the information specified in respondent's regulations" constituted a violation of "procedural or directory" requirements as apposed to mandatory requirements that go to "the essence of the thing to be done" and, therefore, are "a precondition to an effective election." We held that, where all of the procedural defects concerning the appraisal and the appraiser were corrected either on the Form 8283, Noncash Charitable Contributions (the appraisal summary attached to the return),[22] or at or near the

[22] See also *Simmons v. Commissioner*, T.C. Memo. 2009–208, 2009 WL 2950610, at *7–*8, *aff'd*, 646 F.3d 6 (D.C. Cir. 2011), wherein we determined that defects in the appraisal could be cured by the Form 8283 attached to the return.

commencement of the audit, the taxpayers "substantially complied with section 1.170–13A, Income Tax Regs., and are entitled to the charitable deduction claimed." *Id.* at 41–42. Compare *Hewitt v. Commissioner*, 109 T.C. 258 (1997), *aff'd without published opinion*, 166 F.3d 332 (4th Cir. 1998), in which we declined to extend *Bond* to circumstances in which the taxpayers neither obtained an appraisal nor attached an appraisal summary to their return. See also *Estate of Evenchik v. Commissioner*, T.C. Memo. 2013–34, in which we found that an appraisal did not constitute a qualified appraisal of the contributed property (72% of the stock of a corporation) because it was an appraisal of the assets of the corporation, not of the contributed shares. In *Estate of Evenchik*, we relied upon our decision in *Smith v. Commissioner*, T.C. Memo. 2007–368, 2007 WL 4410771, *aff'd*, 364 Fed. Appx. 317 (9th Cir. 2009), which involved charitable contributions of fractional interests in a family limited partnership (FLP), supported by an appraisal of the FLP's sole underlying asset, shares in a closely held, family-owned C corporation. In *Smith v. Commissioner*, 2007 WL 4410771, at *20, we held that that and other violations of the reporting requirements in the DEFRA regulations resulted in the taxpayers' "failure to substantially comply or otherwise provide respondent with sufficient information to accomplish the statutory purpose" of enabling the Commissioner to "understand and monitor the claimed contributions".

B. *The Parties' Arguments*

Respondent argues that, because Mr. Gelbtuch appraised the wrong property, his appraisal "does not present a method of valuation of the property contributed * * * [and] also fails to contain a specific basis for a method of valuation for the actual property conveyed to the University" in violation of section 1.170A–13(c)(3)(ii)(J) and (K), Income Tax Regs. Respondent further argues that, by submitting an appraisal that "does not describe the property transferred to the University", the Gelbtuch appraisal also violates the property description requirement of section 1.170A–13(c)(3)(ii)(A), Income Tax Regs., citing *Smith* and *Estate of Evenchik*.

Respondent also argues that, by failing to mention the two-year hold-sell requirement, the Gelbtuch appraisal violates the requirement in section 1.170A–13(c)(3)(ii)(D)(1), Income

Tax Regs., that a qualified appraisal include "[t]he terms of any agreement or understanding * * * by or on behalf of the donor or donee that * * * [r]estricts temporarily or permanently a donee's right to use or dispose of the donated property". In support of that argument, respondent cites our opinion in *Rothman v. Commissioner*, T.C. Memo. 2012–163, 2012 WL 2094306, *vacated in part on reconsideration*, T.C. Memo. 2012–218, 2012 WL 3101513, wherein we held that the taxpayers' appraisal of a historic preservation facade easement was not a qualified appraisal because, among other reasons, the appraisal did not adequately describe how, if at all, the restrictions on the taxpayer-homeowners' use of their home, resulting from their donation of the easement, "affected the fair market value of the encumbered subject property." *Id.*, 2012 WL 2094306, at *11.

Respondent also points to other perceived deficiencies in the Gelbtuch appraisal: its failure to take into account (1) AT&T's right to "remove the improvements made to the Hawthorne property should it elect not to exercise the five year options" and (2) the "mortgage and depreciation on the Hawthorne property". Respondent apparently views those disclosure omissions as additional failures to disclose restrictions on the use or disposition of the property in violation of section 1.170A–13(c)(3)(ii)(D)(1), Income Tax Regs. In connection with Mr. Gelbtuch's failure to address the potential impact of the mortgage on the value of the Hawthorne property, respondent cites our opinion in *Rothman*, wherein we suggest that an appraisal's failure to reveal the existence and terms of a mortgage on the donated property may, by itself, 2012 WL 3101513, at *4, or in conjunction with other defects, 2012 WL 2094306, at *14, render an appraisal unqualified under the DEFRA regulations.

In addition, respondent points to the Gelbtuch appraisal's determination of the SMI's "investment value" rather than its fair market value as a violation of section 1.170A–13(c)(3)(ii)(I), Income Tax Regs., which requires that the appraisal "shall include * * * the appraised fair market value * * * of the property on the date * * * of contribution".

Lastly, respondent argues that the Gelbtuch appraisal is not a qualified appraisal because it grossly overvalues a hypothetical remainder interest in the Hawthorne property.

In response to respondent's argument that the Gelbtuch appraisal fails to constitute a qualified appraisal because it values the wrong property interest, petitioner argues: "Regardless of whether *Pierre* applies [to prevent looking through Holdings (and Hawthorne) to its sole, income-producing asset, the Hawthorne property], the only way to value a single member LLC is by valuing the underlying assets." He distinguishes *Smith* and *Estate of Evenchik* on the ground that both involved contributions of partial interests in the entities (in *Smith*, an FLP, in *Estate of Evenchik*, a corporation) owning the underlying assets that were actually appraised.[23]

Petitioner also argues that Mr. Gelbtuch's failure to mention the gift agreement containing the two-year hold-sell requirement does not warrant a conclusion that the Gelbtuch appraisal failed to substantially comply with the requirements for a qualified appraisal. He bases that argument on the fact that petitioner gave the gift agreement to the agent at the beginning of the audit and that respondent "had sufficient information to determine whether an audit was necessary as intended by the purpose of the regulations." Petitioner also repeats his argument, made in defending the application of the section 7520 tables herein, that, because the two-year hold-sell requirement set forth in the gift agreement was not a condition of the donation, i.e., it did not interfere with the University's ownership of or right to sell the SMI at any time, "there was no articulated or perceived consequences to any violation of the agreement. Regardless of subsequent events, Ross was still obligated to give $5 million to the University."

In response to respondent's argument that Mr. Gelbtuch's failure to mention either the mortgage or AT&T's right to remove improvements violated the requirement in section

---

[23] Petitioner attempts to further distinguish *Estate of Evenchik v. Commissioner*, T.C. Memo. 2013–34, on the ground that, in this case but not in *Estate of Evenchik*, the donated asset (i.e., the SMI) "was accurately described on [F]orm 8283 as required by the regulations and supplied the necessary information to allow the Commissioner to assess the donation and whether an audit was necessary." That is not a valid distinction, since, in *Estate of Evenchik*, we specifically found that the Form 8283 *did* describe the donated property: "15,534.67 shares Chateau Apartments, Inc. common stock". *Id.* at *4.

1.170A–13(c)(3)(ii)(D)(1), Income Tax Regs., that a qualified appraisal disclose "the terms of any agreement or understanding * * * [restricting] a donee's right to use or dispose of the donated property", petitioner argues that (1) AT&T had no right to remove improvements and (2) even if it did, neither that right nor the mortgage arose out of "any agreement or understanding entered into * * * by or on behalf of the donor or donee" as required by the foregoing regulation.

Petitioner also disputes respondent's argument that the Gelbtuch appraisal is fatally flawed because it fails to compute the SMI's fair market value, but instead computes the "investment value" of a remainder interest in the Hawthorne property. Petitioner points out that, in the case of a remainder interest in real property (in petitioner's view, the asset properly valued pursuant to the "check-the-box" regulations), pursuant to section 170(f)(4), section 1.170A–12(c), Income Tax Regs., and section 25.2512–5(d), Gift Tax Regs., fair market value is "present value" as determined under the section 7520 tables. *See* sec. 25.2512–5(d)(2)(ii), Gift Tax Regs.[24]

C. *Analysis*

1. *Appraisal of the Wrong Property*

We agree with petitioner that both *Estate of Evenchik* and *Smith*, upon which respondent places principal reliance, are distinguishable. As petitioner points out, both cases concerned contributions of partial interests in entities holding

[24] At the conclusion of his response to the motion, petitioner concedes that, if we find *Pierre v. Commissioner*, 133 T.C. 24 (2009), applicable to this case, a new appraisal (of the SMI) would be required. It would appear, however, that a new appraisal at this or any future time could not constitute a qualified appraisal, which, pursuant to sec. 1.170A–13(c)(3)(iv)(B), Income Tax Regs., must have been "received by the donor before the due date (including extensions) of * * * [RERI's 2003 return]". *See also Jorgenson v. Commissioner*, T.C. Memo. 2000–38, 2000 WL 134332, at *4, *8 (failure to obtain a qualified appraisal before the return due date was not cured by submission to the IRS of letters drafted by two appraisers after the return was filed). As discussed *infra*, however, if petitioner is able to persuade us that there is no difference in value between the SMI and a hypothetical remainder interest in the Hawthorne property and that the latter was properly appraised, we would conclude that the Gelbtuch appraisal constituted a qualified appraisal despite our determination that *Pierre* requires an appraisal of the former.

the property that was actually appraised. In *Smith*, the contributions were of minority interests in three FLPs (and were, therefore, presumably subject to minority and, perhaps, marketability discounts) and, in *Estate of Evenchik*, the taxpayer contributed a 72% interest in a corporation, the value of which 72% interest, the parties stipulated, was only 65% of the value reported. *Estate of Evenchik v. Commissioner*, at *5 n.3. In this case, petitioner transferred a future interest (the SMI) in Holdings, whose sole asset was (indirectly) the Hawthorne property. Disregarding for the moment Hawthorne's liabilities, whether the section 7520 tables are applied to the value of Holdings to determine the value of the SMI or are applied to the value of the Hawthorne property to determine the value of a hypothetical remainder interest therein at the end of a term equal to the duration of the SMI, the resulting values should be equal. Moreover, any confusion respondent might have had regarding the property actually donated to the University was eliminated by the Form 8283 attached to RERI's 2003 return, which identified the SMI as the property contributed and clarified Holdings' indirect interest, through Hawthorne, of 100% ownership of the Hawthorne property. In the circumstances of this case, we attach more weight to the Form 8283 than we did in *Estate of Evenchik*, where the Form 8283 also identified the actual property contributed, which, as noted *supra*, was not equal in value to the appraised property. Assuming the evidence in this case demonstrates that the SMI and the remainder interest in the Hawthorne property were of equal value, we would find that the inclusion, in the Form 8283, of the missing information required to be included in the appraisal by section 1.170A–13(c)(3)(ii)(A), Income Tax Regs., i.e., a description of the property actually donated to the University, constituted substantial compliance with that provision. We believe that result is consistent with the requirement, embodied in DEFRA, that a qualified appraisal provide sufficient return information in support of the claimed valuation so as "to enable respondent to deal more effectively with the prevalent use of overvaluations", which we have described as DEFRA's principal objective. *See Hewitt v. Commissioner*, 109 T.C. at 265. See also *Simmons v. Commissioner*, T.C. Memo. 2009–208, 2009 WL 2950610, at *8, *aff'd*, 646 F.3d 6 (D.C. Cir. 2011), wherein we determined that information included in the Form 8283 was sufficient to cure the appraisal's omissions of required information.

We find that Mr. Gelbtuch's appraisal of the hypothetical remainder interest in the Hawthorne property, rather than of the SMI, does not, in and of itself, prevent his appraisal from constituting a qualified appraisal under section 1.170A–13(c)(3), Income Tax Regs. Rather, the issue of whether that appraisal constitutes a qualified appraisal turns on whether we may reasonably conclude that its failure to take into account restrictions and encumbrances applicable to either the SMI or the Hawthorne property that are cited by respondent rendered it an unacceptable alternative to a direct appraisal of the SMI.

2. *The Appraisal's Failure To Consider the Two-Year Hold-Sell Requirement*

The two-year hold-sell requirement is a restriction on the disposition of the SMI, not of the hypothetical remainder interest in the Hawthorne property. As such, it creates two potential problems for petitioner. First, it may mean that the section 7520 tables, applied by Mr. Gelbtuch to determine the value of a hypothetical remainder interest in the Hawthorne property, may not be applicable to determine the fair market value of the SMI. *See* sec. 1.7520–3(b)(1)(ii), Income Tax Regs. ("In general, standard section 7520 * * * remainder factor may not be used to value a restricted beneficial interest."). In that case, the Gelbtuch appraisal would be irrelevant. Second, on its face, the appraisal's failure to mention the restriction may disqualify the appraisal as a substitute for an actual appraisal of the SMI because the omission constitutes a violation of the directive in section 1.170A–13(c)(3)(ii)(D)(1), Income Tax Regs., that the appraisal inform as to "[t]he terms of any agreement or understanding entered into * * * by or on behalf of the donor or donee that * * * [r]estricts temporarily * * * a donee's right to * * * dispose of the donated property".

We have determined *supra* that Mr. Ross' right to renege on all or part of his $5 million pledge to the University, should it violate the two-year hold-sell requirement, raises an unresolved issue of State law and, therefore, an issue of material fact as to the economic impact on the University had it violated that requirement. We also have determined that there are additional issues of material fact concerning the adverse impact, if any, on the value of the SMI in the University's hands should it either violate or, alternatively, observe the two-year hold-sell requirement. Those unresolved factual inquiries are relevant because we conclude that an appraisal's failure to take into account the terms of a restriction described in section 1.170A–13(c)(3)(ii)(D)(1), Income Tax Regs., does not automatically result in the failure of that appraisal to constitute a qualified appraisal. We find it implicit in that provision that such a result is justified only if the omission relates to a restriction that reasonably can be said to have some adverse impact on the value of the donated asset. Otherwise, as we stated in the context of considering whether the section 7520 tables may apply herein, it is a case of no harm, no foul, and the omission may be disregarded.[25]

3. *The Appraisal's Failure To Consider AT&T's Right of Removal on Lease Termination*

The lease agreement between Intergate and AT&T provides that,

> upon the expiration or termination of this Lease, all improvements and additions to the Premises except * * * [cabling and wiring included within the scope of AT&T's work, its alterations from all interstitial/ceiling plenum areas, furniture, equipment and personal property, and back-up generators and associated equipment] shall be deemed property of Landlord and shall not be removed by Tenant from the Premises.

All or most of the "improvements" that AT&T has a right to remove would appear to be either personal property or easily removable fixtures, which also constitute or are akin to personal property, rather than significant improvements to the premises. Thus, it appears that AT&T's right of removal is quite limited and probably of little or no effect on the value of the Hawthorne property. The relevant point, however, is that the parties' dispute regarding the impact of AT&T's right of removal on the Hawthorne property's value raises an issue as to whether the Gelbtuch appraisal overvalued the

[25] Our conclusion in that regard is consistent with our determination herein that an appraisal of the "wrong" property might not be fatal to the appraisal's status as a qualified appraisal if the "wrong" property is shown to have (or potentially have) a value no different from that of the donated property.

Hawthorne property, not an issue as to whether it constituted a qualified appraisal. Mr. Gelbtuch's failure to assess the valuation impact, if any, of AT&T's right of removal does not violate any of the requirements of section 1.170A–13(c)(3), Income Tax Regs., for a qualified appraisal. We disagree with respondent's argument that the Gelbtuch appraisal's failure to disclose AT&T's limited right of removal constituted a failure to disclose "significant terms and conditions affecting the use and disposition of * * * [the SMI]" in violation of section 1.170A–13(c)(3)(ii)(D)(1), Income Tax Regs. It does not seem possible that AT&T's removal of what is largely, if not exclusively, personal property would, in any way, interfere with the subsequent use or disposition of the building. Most importantly, however, we agree with petitioner that AT&T's right of removal, being a term of the lease between Intergate and AT&T, did not constitute a term of an "agreement * * * entered into * * * by or on behalf of the donor or donee" as required by the foregoing regulation. Therefore, the impact of AT&T's right of removal is not germane to the qualified appraisal issue.

4. *The Appraisal's Failure To Consider the Mortgage or Depreciation on the Hawthorne Property*

Mr. Gelbtuch's failure to consider the mortgage on the Hawthorne property in his appraisal thereof also does not constitute an omission of "[t]he terms of * * * [an] agreement * * * entered into * * * by or on behalf of the donor or donee", as required by section 1.170A–13(c)(3)(ii)(D)(1), Income Tax Regs. Rather it was part of the deed of trust executed by Hawthorne (the borrower), Commonwealth Land Title Insurance Co., and BB&T (the lender), which secured the loan that financed Hawthorne's purchase of the Hawthorne property. Therefore, that failure, like Mr. Gelbtuch's failure to consider AT&T's right of removal, relates to the accuracy of the Gelbtuch appraisal. It is not germane to the issue of whether it was a qualified appraisal under the DEFRA regulations.

Similarly, Mr. Gelbtuch's failure to discuss the potential impact of depreciation on the Hawthorne property is not an omission covered by the foregoing regulation. Therefore, it too is not germane to the qualified appraisal issue.[26]

5. *Mr. Gelbtuch's Finding of "Investment Value" Rather Than Fair Market Value*

In his appraisal, Mr. Gelbtuch does refer to the value he assigns to the hypothetical remainder interest in the Hawthorne property as its "investment value", for which he provides the following dictionary definition: "The specific value of an investment to a particular investor or class of investors based on individual investment requirements; distinguished from market value, which is impersonal and detached." As defined by Mr. Gelbtuch, the term "investment value" appears to be unrelated to the value that he actually derives for the hypothetical remainder interest in the Hawthorne property. We agree with petitioner that Mr. Gelbtuch's method for valuing a hypothetical remainder interest in the Hawthorne property was in accordance with section 170(f)(4), section 1.170A–12(c), Income Tax Regs., and section 25.2512–5(d)(2)(ii), Gift Tax Regs., to the extent that, when read together, those provisions require that the valuation of a remainder interest in real property be made by applying the section 7520 tables to the fair market value of the property.[27] That Mr. Gelbtuch mislabeled his valuation of a hypothetical remainder interest as its "investment value" is of no consequence.[28]

Moreover, as in the case of Mr. Gelbtuch's failure to discuss the mortgage, depreciation of the Hawthorne property, or AT&T's right of removal, an allegedly improper valuation of the donated property is not something that would result in Mr. Gelbtuch's appraisal's not constituting a qualified appraisal under the DEFRA regulations.

---

[26] Respondent does not argue nor do we find that a failure to discuss depreciation constitutes a failure to discuss "the physical condition of the property", in violation of sec. 1.170A–13(c)(3)(ii)(B), Income Tax Regs.

[27] Mr. Gelbtuch did not take into account depreciation in valuing the hypothetical remainder in the Hawthorne property, which, like his failure to consider the mortgage, goes to the accuracy of his appraisal.

[28] What's in a name? that which we call a rose

By any other name would smell as sweet; * * * [William Shakespeare, Romeo and Juliet, act 2, sc. 2.]

6. *Alleged Gross Overvaluation of the Hypothetical Remainder Interest in the Hawthorne Property*

Respondent argues that Mr. Gelbtuch grossly overvalued the hypothetical remainder interest in the Hawthorne property (apparently assuming, for the sake of argument, that it may be considered a proxy for the SMI) in the light of the much smaller amounts paid for the SMI in a series of sales thereof both shortly before and after RERI's donation of it to the University. Once again, respondent's argument is inapposite as it goes to the accuracy of Mr. Gelbtuch's appraisal, not to its status as a qualified appraisal under the DEFRA regulations.

D. *Conclusion*

Respondent's arguments in support of his motion for partial summary judgment that the Gelbtuch appraisal fails to satisfy the DEFRA regulations' definition of (and, therefore, does not constitute) a qualified appraisal are either inapposite or involve unresolved disputes of material fact. Therefore, we will deny the motion to the extent respondent asks us to rule that petitioner failed to substantiate the value of the SMI with a qualified appraisal.

An appropriate order will be issued denying respondent's motion for partial summary judgment.

JOHN C. BEDROSIAN AND JUDITH D. BEDROSIAN, PETITIONERS *v.* COMMISSIONER OF INTERNAL REVENUE, RESPONDENT

Docket No. 12341–05. Filed August 13, 2014.

Ps invested in a Son-of-BOSS transaction through a partnership that was subject to the Tax Equity and Fiscal Responsibility Act of 1982 (TEFRA), Pub. L. No. 97–248, 96 Stat. 324. R issued an FPAA with respect to the partnership; R included with the FPAA a notice under I.R.C. sec. 6223(e), informing Ps of their right to opt out of the TEFRA proceeding. The FPAA was properly mailed, but Ps claim that they did not receive it within the time in which to file a timely petition. Ps filed an untimely petition, which the Court dismissed; the Court of Appeals for the Ninth Circuit upheld the dismissal. R also issued a notice of deficiency (NOD) that duplicated the adjustments in the FPAA and included additional adjustments. Ps filed a timely petition with respect to the NOD. Ps moved for summary judgment asking that we determine that we have jurisdiction over all of the items in the NOD, including those that were included in the previously issued FPAA. *Held*: The partnership items did not convert to nonpartnership items under I.R.C. sec. 6223(e)(2) because the partnership proceeding was ongoing at the time the IRS mailed the FPAA. *Held, further*, the partnership items did not convert to nonpartnership items under I.R.C. sec. 6223(e)(3) because filing a petition with respect to an NOD is not substantial compliance with procedures for opting out of a TEFRA proceeding. *Held, further*, the Secretary did not reasonably determine under I.R.C. sec. 6231(g)(2) that TEFRA did not apply to the partnership. *Held, further*, we are bound by the Court of Appeals for the Ninth Circuit's prior holding that we lack jurisdiction over the partnership items in the NOD.

Richard E. Hodge and *Steve Mather*, for petitioners.

Melanie R. Urban and *Janet Reiners Balboni*, for respondent.

OPINION

BUCH, *Judge*: This case combines a system for examining and litigating partnership controversies that differs from typical deficiency procedures with missteps by both the agency charged with administering this system and petitioners' representatives. The confluence of these missteps ultimately deprives us of jurisdiction over the partnership items set forth in the notice of deficiency that underlies this matter—a result mandated by both the statutory scheme and controlling precedent of the Court of Appeals for the Ninth Circuit, to which this case is appealable. But first, some background.

Background

I. *The Transaction*

The underlying transaction in this case is what has come to be known as a Son-of-BOSS transaction, with this variant using foreign currency options. *See generally Kligfeld Holdings v. Commissioner*, 128 T.C. 192 (2007); Notice 2000–44, 2000–2 C.B. 255. The Bedrosians created two entities, JCB Stone Canyon Investments, LLC (LLC), and Stone Canyon Investors, Inc. (S corporation), which in turn formed a third entity, Stone Canyon Partners (Stone Canyon). On October 16, 2000, the Bedrosians timely filed Form 1040, U.S. Individual Income Tax Return, for 1999 in which they claimed large flowthrough losses stemming from the transaction through their interests in the LLC and the S corporation.

Because Stone Canyon had flowthrough entities as its partners, the small partnership exception of section 6231(a)(1)(B)(i) [1] did not apply, and Stone Canyon was subject to the unified audit and litigation procedures of sections 6221–6234, commonly referred to as TEFRA. [2] These procedures affect not only the audit and litigation of a passthrough entity, but also the preparation of a passthrough entity's return.

The same day that the Bedrosians filed their return, Stone Canyon timely filed Form 1065, U.S. Partnership Return of Income, for 1999. On line 4 of Schedule B, Other Information, Stone Canyon answered "no" to the question "Is this partnership subject to the consolidated audit procedures of sections 6221 through 6233? If 'Yes,' see Designation of Tax Matters Partner below". Notwithstanding the "no" answer on line 4, Stone Canyon designated the LLC as its tax matters partner (TMP). Stone Canyon attached to its Form 1065 a Schedule K–1, Partner's Share of Income, Credits, Deductions, etc., identifying the LLC as being an "INDIVIDUAL" in response to the question "What type of entity is this partner?", even though the name of the partner was the LLC name. Stone Canyon identified the S corporation as an "S CORPORATION" in response to the same question on a second Schedule K–1.

II. *The Audit*

The parties have spilled a great amount of ink on the subject of what transpired during the audit, most of which is irrelevant to the ultimate conclusions in this case. Nonetheless, we summarize what transpired to provide context.

---

[1] All section references are to the Internal Revenue Code (Code) in effect for the years at issue, and all Rule references are to the Tax Court Rules of Practice and Procedure, unless otherwise indicated.

[2] TEFRA is shorthand for the Tax Equity and Fiscal Responsibility Act of 1982, Pub. L. No. 97–248, sec. 1(a), 96 Stat. at 324.

In September 2003 Revenue Agent Harold Jung mailed Mr. Bedrosian a letter informing him that the Internal Revenue Service (IRS) had selected his Form 1040 for 1999 for audit. In the letter Revenue Agent Jung requested that Mr. Bedrosian consent to extend the period of limitations, which was set to expire in less than two months, on an enclosed Form 872, Consent to Extend the Time to Assess Tax. On September 10, 2003, the Bedrosians submitted to the IRS Form 2848, Power of Attorney and Declaration of Representative, designating Richard E. Hodge, an attorney, and Linda Olson, a certified public accountant, as their representatives with respect to the examination of their Form 1040 for 1999.[3] Revenue Agent Jung did not request a Form 2848 with respect to Stone Canyon, the S corporation, or the LLC.

The Bedrosians submitted to the IRS the completed Form 872, in which they agreed to extend the period of limitations for assessment of their individual income tax for 1999 to August 31, 2004. Revenue Agent Jung did not request a form extending the period of limitations for assessment of tax attributable to partnership items and affected items of Stone Canyon for 1999. The parties agree that the Form 872 was ineffective to extend the period of limitations for assessment of tax attributable to partnership items and affected items of Stone Canyon for 1999.[4]

The next month, for reasons unexplained in the record, the administrative files with respect to the audit were transferred from Revenue Agent Jung to Revenue Agent Deborah Smyth. By that time, the period set forth in section 6229(a), which is the minimum period within which to assess tax attributable to partnership items and affected items for Stone Canyon's 1999 tax year, had expired.[5] Revenue Agent Smyth was well aware of that fact. And while she believed after reviewing the administrative files that Stone Canyon was subject to the TEFRA procedures, she continued con-

---

[3] Notwithstanding being included on the Form 2848, it appears from the record that Mr. Hodge did not have any involvement in the audit.

[4] *See* sec. 6229(b)(3); *Ginsburg v. Commissioner*, 127 T.C. 75 (2006).

[5] *See Rhone-Poulenc Surfactants & Specialties L.P. v. Commissioner*, 114 T.C. 533 (2000). Stone Canyon's Form 1065 for 1999 was filed on October 16, 2000. The period described in sec. 6229(a) would have expired on October 16, 2003.

ducting the Stone Canyon audit by examining the Bedrosians' Form 1040 for 1999.

She also examined the Bedrosians' Form 1040 for 2000, which was filed on October 15, 2001. On their Form 1040 for 2000 the Bedrosians claimed a comparatively small net operating loss carryover from 1999 and a deduction for legal, accounting, consulting, and advisory fees (collectively, transaction fees).

At Revenue Agent Smyth's request the Bedrosians submitted to the IRS a second Form 872 for 1999, in which they agreed to further extend the period of limitations for assessment from August 31, 2004, to April 30, 2005. Also at Revenue Agent Smyth's request, the Bedrosians submitted to the IRS Form 872–I, Consent to Extend the Time to Assess Tax As Well As Tax Attributable to Items of a Partnership, for 2000 in which they agreed to extend the period of limitations for assessment of their income tax, including tax attributable to partnership items and affected items of Stone Canyon, to April 30, 2005.

In May 2004 Revenue Agent Smyth mailed a letter to Ms. Olson (with copies to the Bedrosians) offering the Bedrosians the opportunity to participate in a settlement. They chose not to participate. In November 2004 Revenue Agent Smyth mailed Ms. Olson a letter (with copies to the Bedrosians) acknowledging the Bedrosians' choice and requesting that they provide additional information with respect to the transaction. Enclosed with the letter was the IRS' fourth information document request. The letter stated: "Once we receive the information, we will provide you with Form 4549–A, Income Tax Examination Changes (Audit Report), which will show the tax deficiency, any applicable penalties, and interest you owe. If you wish to agree to the determination, you will sign and return Form 870 (Waiver)."

Revenue Agent Smyth later participated in a conference call with IRS Office of Chief Counsel attorneys and the IRS Son-of-BOSS TEFRA coordinator to discuss "how to proceed with this case in order to disallow the net operating loss carryforward deductions claimed on Petitioners' Form 1040 for the 2000 tax year, in view of * * * [her] determination that the limitations period for issuing a notice of final partnership administrative adjustment (FPAA) for the 1999 tax year had expired." The TEFRA coordinator advised Revenue

Agent Smyth that the IRS should issue an FPAA for 1999 in order to disallow the NOL carryforward deduction for 2000. Revenue Agent Smyth's understanding of the TEFRA coordinator's advice was "not that the Service would issue an FPAA for the 1999 tax year *instead of* the notice of deficiency * * * for the 1999 and 2000 tax years * * * [but] that the Service would issue an FPAA *in addition to* the notice of deficiency for the 1999 and 2000 tax years."

Revenue Agent Smyth called Ms. Olson and informed her that the IRS would soon issue a notice of beginning of administrative proceeding (NBAP) for 1999. Ms. Olson inquired as to why the IRS would issue an NBAP with respect to Stone Canyon for 1999 when Revenue Agent Smyth was in the process of issuing audit reports with respect to the Bedrosians' Form 1040 for that same year. Revenue Agent Smyth responded that "the NBAP was procedural and that the TEFRA examination would be 'opened and shut'."

On February 2, 2005, Revenue Agent Smyth mailed separate copies of the NBAP to Mr. Bedrosian as the sole managing member of the LLC and to him in his individual capacity. Revenue Agent Smyth did not mail a copy of the NBAP to Mr. Hodge or to Ms. Olson, presumably because the IRS did not request and did not have a power of attorney on file authorizing either of them to represent Stone Canyon, the S corporation, or the LLC. Also on February 2, Revenue Agent Smyth mailed Ms. Olson a letter stating in relevant part: "As promised, enclosed are copies of the proposed audit reports for the Bedrosians for their 1999 through 2002 tax years * * *. Besides using these for reference purposes, I would suggest that they also be checked for accuracy—given the large number of inter-related adjustments created by exam changes."[6] Revenue Agent Smyth enclosed in the letter Forms 4549–A for 1999 through 2002.

A few days later, Revenue Agent Smyth began drafting both an FPAA for Stone Canyon and a notice of deficiency for the Bedrosians. She completed the drafting of both the FPAA and the notice of deficiency the following day.

[6] It appears that Revenue Agent Smyth reviewed the Bedrosians' Forms 1040 for 2001 and 2002 for the limited purpose of making carryover adjustments arising from the adjustments for 1999 and 2000.

A series of correspondence followed. On February 15, 2005, Revenue Agent Smyth mailed Ms. Olson Forms 870, Waiver of Restrictions on Assessment and Collection of Deficiency in Tax and Acceptance of Overassessment, and corrected Forms 4549–A for 1999 and 2000; these related to the examination of the Bedrosians. On February 18, 2005, Ms. Olson mailed Revenue Agent Smyth a letter informing her that the Bedrosians had received the NBAPs and had forwarded them to her; the NBAPs related to the examination of Stone Canyon. Ms. Olson further informed Revenue Agent Smyth of a new address for Stone Canyon, the S corporation, and the LLC. In fact, those entities were not yet receiving mail at that new address. In the last paragraph of the letter, Ms. Olson wrote: "You mentioned that these administrative proceedings would basically be opened and shut. Are there * * * any more documents that need to be reviewed other than the closing of the proceedings? If so then I may need to prepare [p]ower of [a]ttorneys for each of them." Revenue Agent Smyth never responded to Ms. Olson's letter dated February 18, 2005, which her office received on February 22. However, Revenue Agent Smyth continued communicating with Ms. Olson regarding the Bedrosians' audit. On March 29, 2005, Revenue Agent Smyth mailed Ms. Olson a letter (with copies to the Bedrosians) stating in relevant part:

> Enclosed you will find Form 4549–A, *Income Tax Examination Changes* (Audit Report) which shows the tax deficiency, any applicable penalties, and interest; explanations for the adjustments are provided on Form 886–A, *Explanation of Items*. To agree to the tax, penalties, and interest, you may sign the enclosed Form 870 (Waiver) and return to me at the above address. * * *
>
> If you do not agree with the tax, penalties, and interest shown on the Audit Report, a statutory notice of deficiency will be sent to you.

Then on March 30, 2005, Revenue Agent Smyth closed her case file with instructions to the IRS' processing unit to issue the notice of deficiency to the Bedrosians.

On April 8, 2005 (62 days after mailing the NBAPs), the IRS mailed a total of 14 copies of the FPAA for 1999 to three different addresses on file for the Bedrosians, Stone Canyon, the S corporation, and the LLC. The IRS did not mail a copy of the FPAA to Mr. Hodge or to Ms. Olson. In the FPAA the IRS made partnership-level adjustments the effect of which was to disallow the losses stemming from the transaction.

The IRS enclosed with the FPAA a notice under section 6223(e) labeled "Untimely Notice Letter—TEFRA Proceeding is Ongoing" informing the recipient that the IRS had failed to issue an NBAP within the time required (at least 120 days before the FPAA) and that the recipient could elect under section 6223(e)(3)(B) to opt out of the TEFRA proceeding. The IRS also enclosed with the FPAA Form 870–PT, Agreement for Partnership Items and Partnership Level Determinations as to Penalties, Additions to Tax, and Additional Amounts, and Form 4605–A, Examination Changes—Partnerships, Fiduciaries, Small Business Corporations, and Domestic International Sales Corporations, for 1999.

Eleven days later, on April 19, 2005, the IRS mailed the Bedrosians the notice of deficiency (with a copy to Ms. Olson) for 1999 and 2000 (2005 notice). In the 2005 notice the IRS made partner-level adjustments disallowing the flowthrough losses on the Bedrosians' Form 1040 for 1999. Because the Bedrosians owned 100% of the interest in Stone Canyon through their interests in the LLC and the S corporation, the adjustments in the FPAA and those in the notice of deficiency resulted in the disallowance of the same losses, the former at the partnership level and the latter at the partner level. The IRS made some additional adjustments in the 2005 notice, including computational adjustments and adjustments disallowing the NOL carryover and the transaction fees for 2000. The IRS determined deficiencies, additions to tax, and penalties with respect to the Bedrosians' Federal income tax for 1999 and 2000 as follows:

Year	*Deficiency*	*Addition to tax sec. 6651(a)(1)*	*Penalty sec. 6662(a)*
1999	$3,498,882	$134,781	$1,392,553
2000	12,137	-0-	4,855

III. *Litigation History*

On July 5, 2005, the Bedrosians timely filed a petition disputing the adjustments in the 2005 notice. Respondent answered. On August 30, 2005, the Bedrosians remitted $4,269,819 to the IRS. They designated the remittance to cover the 1999 and 2000 deficiencies and estimated interest on those deficiencies. The IRS treated the remittance as a payment.

On June 30, 2006, almost a year after the Bedrosians had filed their petition, respondent moved to dismiss this case for lack of jurisdiction on the ground that the 2005 notice was invalid in that it consisted entirely of adjustments to partnership items or affected items. Respondent now claims that he has "consistently taken the position that * * * [the] Partnership is subject to the TEFRA provisions of the Code."[7] We held that we do not have jurisdiction over the adjustments to partnership items or affected items that were listed in the notice of deficiency but that we do have jurisdiction over the disallowance of the deductions for transaction fees for 2000. *Bedrosian v. Commissioner*, T.C. Memo. 2007–375 (2005 notice case). The parties agreed that all of the adjustments for 1999 were partnership items or affected items. *See id.*, slip op. at 7. We granted respondent's motion to dismiss insofar as it related to the adjustments for 1999 and the NOL carryover for 2000 and denied the motion insofar as it related to the transaction fees.[8]

On September 5, 2006, the IRS issued an affected items notice of deficiency to the Bedrosians (2006 notice). On November 30, 2006, the Bedrosians filed a timely petition in response to the 2006 notice. We held that we lacked jurisdiction over that case, however, because the deficiencies had been paid and assessed before the issuance of the 2006 notice. *Bedrosian v. Commissioner*, T.C. Memo. 2007–376 (2006 notice case), *aff'd*, 358 Fed. Appx. 868 (9th Cir. 2009). In other words, there was no deficiency.

On May 1, 2007, the LLC, as the TMP of Stone Canyon, filed an untimely petition in response to the FPAA. Both parties filed motions to dismiss, with the TMP alleging that the

[7] If, at the time the petition was filed, respondent believed that Stone Canyon was subject to the TEFRA procedures, he should not have waited almost a year to file a motion to dismiss for lack of jurisdiction. *See* Internal Revenue Manual (IRM) pt. 35.3.2.1(3) (Sept. 21, 2012) ("A jurisdictional defect should be raised in a motion to dismiss for lack of jurisdiction as soon as the jurisdictional defect is discovered and any evidence needed to support such a motion is acquired. Field attorneys should avoid waiting to raise such defects in the answer, stipulation or motion under T.C. Rule 122 in order to ensure a prompt resolution of the case and to avoid unnecessary work for the Tax Court."). A similar provision was in effect at the time the petition was filed.

[8] At that time neither party raised, nor did we consider, the possible application of sec. 6223(e) or 6231(g).

FPAA was invalid because it was not mailed to the proper address and respondent alleging that the petition was untimely. We granted respondent's motion to dismiss the FPAA case for lack of jurisdiction. We held that the FPAA was valid and that the petition was untimely. *Stone Canyon Partners v. Commissioner*, T.C. Memo. 2007–377 (FPAA case), *aff'd sub nom. Bedrosian v. Commissioner*, 358 Fed. Appx. 868 (9th Cir. 2009).

The respective petitioners appealed the orders of dismissal for lack of jurisdiction in the 2006 notice case and the FPAA case and attempted to appeal the order in this 2005 notice case to the Court of Appeals for the Ninth Circuit. The Court of Appeals affirmed the dismissals in the 2006 notice case and the FPAA case. *Bedrosian v. Commissioner*, 358 Fed. Appx. at 869–871. To the extent the Bedrosians sought to appeal the holding in this case, the Court of Appeals dismissed the appeal for lack of jurisdiction on the ground that we had dismissed this case only in part and that there was no final judgment from which an appeal could properly be taken. *Id.* at 870. Notwithstanding that it dismissed the appeal, however, the Court of Appeals remarked about our jurisdiction in this case: "But both parties concede that the 2005 notice of deficiency was invalid because it was issued while partnership proceedings were pending. No assessment could possibly deprive the Tax Court of jurisdiction over that particular deficiency, because the Tax Court never had jurisdiction over 'such deficiency' in the first place." *Id.* We interpret this statement as meaning that the 2005 notice was invalid only insofar as it covered partnership items.

On February 2, 2010, the Bedrosians filed a motion for leave to file an amended petition in this case and lodged an amended petition raising a new theory, that "[t]he interests of justice require a finding that Petitioners' be deemed to have elected that the partnership items of * * * [the Partnership] be converted to nonpartnership items on or before April 19, 2005". On June 1, 2010, respondent filed an objection to the Bedrosians' motion.

In June 2010 this case was assigned to a Special Trial Judge pursuant to section 7443A and Rules 180 and 183. Because leave to amend a pleading shall be freely given, Rule 41, the Bedrosians' motion was granted, thus allowing the amendment.

Next the Bedrosians filed a motion for summary judgment arguing (1) that the Court has jurisdiction over all of the adjustments in the 2005 notice of deficiency and (2) that the adjustments for 1999 are barred by the statute of limitations. Along with the motion, the Bedrosians filed a memorandum of points and authorities in which they argued that the adjustments in the 2005 notice that relate to partnership items were converted to nonpartnership items because, they assert, the partnership items for 1999 were converted to nonpartnership items by operation of section 6223(e)(2) and the partnership items for 2000 (and alternatively for 1999) were converted to nonpartnership items through a deemed election under section 6223(e)(3) that was made by filing the petition in this case. The Bedrosians' motion for summary judgment did not address the transaction fees for 2000, which we previously held were neither partnership nor affected items. *Bedrosian v. Commissioner*, T.C. Memo. 2007–375. Respondent filed an objection to the Bedrosians' motion for summary judgment to which the Bedrosians replied.

The Special Trial Judge filed and served on the parties recommended findings of fact and conclusions of law (proposed report) pursuant to Rules 182(e) and 183. The proposed report concludes that "the petition is sufficient to effect an election of nonpartnership item treatment." The proposed report does not address the Bedrosians' statute of limitations argument. Pursuant to Rule 183(c), respondent filed objections to the proposed report and the Bedrosians filed a response to respondent's objections. In accordance with Rule 183(c), this case was then assigned to a Judge of this Court.

While considering the issues addressed in the proposed report, the Court ordered the parties to file additional memoranda regarding the potential applicability of section 6231(g)(2). Under Rule 183(d), "[t]he Judge to whom the case is assigned may adopt the Special Trial Judge's recommended findings of fact and conclusions of law, or may modify or reject them in whole or in part, or may direct the filing of additional briefs, or may receive further evidence, or may direct oral argument, or may recommit the recommended findings of fact and conclusions of law with instructions." *See also Rawls Trading, L.P. v. Commissioner*, 138 T.C. 271, 284 (2012) ("[W]e are under an affirmative duty to investigate the extent of our subject matter jurisdiction."). More specifically, the Court inquired whether respondent reasonably determined that TEFRA did not apply to Stone Canyon for the years at issue. In short, section 6231(g)(2) provides that the TEFRA procedures do not apply to a partnership if the Secretary reasonably but erroneously determines, on the basis of the partnership's return, that the partnership is not subject to TEFRA. If section 6231(g)(2) applies, then a partnership that should be subject to TEFRA will instead be subject to the deficiency procedures of subchapter B of chapter 63 of the Code (i.e., the normal deficiency procedures).

The parties filed opening and answering briefs addressing their positions as to whether section 6231(g)(2) applies under the facts of this case. Respondent argues that section 6231(g)(2) does not apply because the IRS did not determine that Stone Canyon was not subject to TEFRA and that, if the IRS had made such a determination, the determination would not have been reasonable. In contrast, the Bedrosians argue that section 6231(g)(2) applies because the IRS determined that the normal deficiency procedures applied, and that the IRS' determination was reasonable.[9]

This briefing turned into a sideshow. Respondent admitted to making erroneous statements on the record regarding what happened during the course of the examination, and the Bedrosians went on the offensive. In their answering brief, the Bedrosians accused respondent of taking "deliberately false and fraudulent actions and * * * [making] false and fraudulent representations to the Court since the outset of this case." Respondent subsequently filed a response to the Bedrosians' allegations of fraud, in which respondent "apologize[d] to the Court and to Petitioners' Counsel for not clearly identifying and explaining the ostensible conflict between the Memorandum Brief and respondent's prior representations." The Bedrosians then filed a reply to respondent's response to the allegations of fraud, in which they contend that the "implausibility and incongruity of respondent's

[9] Notably, it appears that the Bedrosians' position regarding sec. 6231(g) would, in effect, undermine their statute of limitations argument. The effect of sec. 6231(g)(2) is to render the whole of the TEFRA provisions inapplicable to the partnership at issue. As a result, sec. 6229(b)(3), the linchpin of the Bedrosians' statute of limitations argument, would be inapplicable.

statements and actions with respect to respondent's current position, combined with respondent's previous misrepresentations, make the current version of the 'facts' impossible to believe." Ultimately, this sideshow has no bearing on this case.

Discussion

I. *Summary Judgment*

Summary judgment may be granted where the pleadings and other materials show that there is no genuine dispute as to any material fact and that a decision may be rendered as a matter of law. Rule 121(b); *Sundstrand Corp. v. Commissioner*, 98 T.C. 518, 520 (1992), *aff'd*, 17 F.3d 965 (7th Cir. 1994). The burden is on the moving party (in this case, the Bedrosians) to demonstrate that there is no genuine dispute as to any material fact and that they are entitled to judgment as a matter of law. *FPL Grp., Inc. & Subs. v. Commissioner*, 116 T.C. 73, 74–75 (2001). In considering a motion for summary judgment, evidence is viewed in the light most favorable to the nonmoving party. *Bond v. Commissioner*, 100 T.C. 32, 36 (1993). The nonmoving party may not rest upon the mere allegations or denials of his or her pleading but must set forth specific facts showing there is a genuine dispute for trial. *Sundstrand Corp. v. Commissioner*, 98 T.C. at 520.

II. *Conversion Under Section 6223(e)*

The Bedrosians' motion for summary judgment focuses on section 6223(e). Section 6223(e) provides alternate rules for when the IRS fails to issue certain notices within certain time constraints. More specifically, the IRS is required to issue an NBAP at least 120 days before it issues an FPAA. Sec. 6223(d)(1). The failure to allow sufficient time between the NBAP and the FPAA does not invalidate either notice. *Starlight Mine v. Commissioner*, T.C. Memo. 1991–59 n.3 ("Petitioners also contend that the FPAA was invalid because not all the notice partners were sent copies of the FPAA. However, see section 6223(e) for a notice partner's rights in such a situation; there is no provision therein for invalidating an FPAA sent to the TMP."). Instead, the failure gives rise to statutory rights under section 6223(e). The specific remedy afforded to the taxpayer differs depending on whether the proceeding is ongoing at the time the IRS mails notice to the taxpayer. *Compare* sec. 6223(e)(2), *with id.* para. (3).

A. *Section 6223(e)(2)—Proceedings Finished*

The Bedrosians first argue that their partnership items converted to nonpartnership items by operation of law under section 6223(e)(2). Section 6223(e)(2) applies if, at the time the IRS mails notice to the taxpayer, the TEFRA proceeding has concluded. The Code specifically defines what it means for the proceeding to have concluded: either (i) the period within which to have filed a petition with respect to an FPAA must have expired with no petition's having been filed or (ii) a decision with respect to an FPAA proceeding that was actually brought must have become final. Only if one of those events has occurred will a partner's items be deemed converted to nonpartnership items unless the partner opts to be bound by the TEFRA proceeding. Sec. 6223(e)(2).

Factually, neither of those events had occurred at the time notice was mailed to the partners of Stone Canyon. The IRS mailed the NBAP and the FPAA 62 days apart, and at the time that either was mailed, the TEFRA proceeding was ongoing. Therefore, section 6223(e)(2) simply could not apply. The Bedrosians argue, however, that we should read a third test for the conclusion of a partnership proceeding into section 6223(e)(2)—that the period of limitations for assessment has expired.

There is no support for this argument in the statute; moreover, it is logically unworkable. The Code is explicit regarding what causes a conversion under section 6223(e)(2), and there is no mention of a period of limitations. Moreover, the expiration of the period of limitations does not cause a conversion of partnership items to nonpartnership items under the other TEFRA provisions relating to the conversion of partnership items found in section 6231(b) and (c).

To the extent the Bedrosians ask us to read such a rule into the statute, we cannot do so. Congress writes the laws; we do not. And such a rule would make little sense. The period of limitations for one partner may be very different from that for another. If one partner is an unidentified partner, then section 6229(e) would hold open that partner's period of limitations until at least one year after that partner is properly identified, which may be longer than the periods of limitations of other partners.[10] Likewise, because section 6229 operates only as a minimum period of limitations, if one partner had a substantial omission of income on his personal return, then that partner's period of limitations would be held open beyond those of the other partners. *See generally Rhone-Poulenc Surfactants & Specialties, L.P. v. Commissioner*, 114 T.C. at 533. Moreover, section 6226(d)(1) explicitly provides that the time and place for a partner to raise an affirmative defense relating to the period of limitations is in the TEFRA proceeding. Treating the expiration of the period of limitations as an automatic conversion would conflict with this provision. The rule the Bedrosians advocate would simply be unworkable.

In short, we agree with the proposed report's discussion of section 6229(e)(2) both for the reasons stated in it and those stated above.

B. *Section 6223(e)(3)—Proceedings Still Going On*

The Bedrosians' alternative argument is that they made a timely election to have their partnership items converted to nonpartnership items under section 6223(e)(3). Like section 6223(e)(2), discussed above, section 6223(e)(3) applies when the IRS issues an NBAP or an FPAA outside of the timeframe required by section 6223(d). In this case, the IRS issued the NBAP with respect to Stone Canyon less than 120 days before the FPAA, so this first hurdle is met. In contrast to section 6223(e)(2), section 6223(e)(3) applies only if the TEFRA proceeding is ongoing at the time the IRS issues the notice. Again, as discussed above, the notices were mailed to the partners 62 days apart. When the NBAP was mailed, the FPAA had not yet been issued, so the period within which to petition for a review of the FPAA had not yet begun to run. And because the FPAA was mailed simultaneously to the TMP and to the Bedrosians, at the time the FPAA was mailed the period within which to file a petition from that

[10] Indeed, the unidentified partner rule may well apply to the Bedrosians in this case. The Bedrosians are not identified on the face of the partnership return, and there is nothing in the record to indicate that their identifying information was provided in accordance with the regulations under sec. 6223. *See Taylor v. Commissioner*, T.C. Memo. 1992–219. However, we need not decide this question.

FPAA had just begun. It certainly had not lapsed. Thus, the TEFRA proceeding was ongoing, so this hurdle is likewise met. In such a situation, a taxpayer has the same options as under section 6223(e)(2), but the manner of electing is reversed. Specifically, if a partner makes a timely election, the partner may opt out of the TEFRA proceeding by having his items converted to nonpartnership items. Sec. 6223(e)(3)(B). In the absence of an election, however, the partner remains bound by the TEFRA proceeding. Sec. 6223(e)(3) ("the partner shall be a party to the proceeding unless such partner elects").

The question for the Court is whether the Bedrosians made the election. The proposed report finds that such an election was made under the doctrine of substantial compliance; we conclude otherwise as a matter of law. We give due regard to the findings of fact in the proposed report, *see* Rule 183(d), and indeed, we take no issue with those findings of fact. It is in the application of the law to those facts where we find error.

To opt out of the TEFRA proceeding under section 6223(e), the electing partner must make an election as follows:

> (2) *Time and manner of making election.* The election shall be made by filing a statement with the Internal Revenue Service office mailing the notice regarding the proceeding within 45 days after the date on which that notice was mailed.
>
> (3) *Contents of statement.* The statement shall—
>
> (i) Be clearly identified as an election under section 6223(e)(2) or (3),
>
> (ii) Specify the election being made (that is, application of final partnership administrative adjustment, court decision, consistent settlement agreement, or nonpartnership item treatment),
>
> (iii) Identify the partner making the election and the partnership by name, address, and taxpayer identification number,
>
> (iv) Specify the partnership taxable year to which the election relates, and
>
> (v) Be signed by the partner making the election.
>
> [Sec. 301.6223(e)–2T, Temporary Proced. & Admin. Regs., 52 Fed. Reg. 6785 (Mar. 5, 1987).]

The Bedrosians focus on their petition as their purported election under this regulation. The petition, however, did not satisfy the criteria for making an election under section 6223(e)(3).

We begin with the fact that the petition was not filed within the time for making an election under section

301.6223(e)–2T, Temporary Proced. & Admin. Regs., *supra*. The regulation requires that the election be made within 45 days after the date on which the notice is mailed. Although it is unclear whether the "notice" refers to the NBAP or the FPAA, because the FPAA is the later notice in this case, we will presume the FPAA is the operative notice.[11] The petition was filed on July 5, 2005, 88 days after the mailing of the FPAA.

The petition also was not filed with the proper office for making an election under section 6223(e). The regulation requires that the election be filed with the office that issued the notice (we will presume "notice" refers to the FPAA). The petition was not filed with the office that issued the FPAA; indeed, it was not filed with the IRS at all. The petition was filed with this Court.

The petition also does not clearly indicate that it was an election under section 6223(e)(3). In fact, the original petition filed in this case did not indicate that the Bedrosians intended to make an election of any kind; this position was first raised by the amended petition, lodged 1,761 days after the IRS mailed the FPAA, which stated that the Bedrosians should "be deemed to have elected that the partnership items of Stone Canyon Partners be converted to nonpartnership items". Moreover, because the Bedrosians did not know of their eligibility to make an election and did not contemplate that they were making such an election, it is unsurprising that the original petition did not specify the nature of the election that was being made (in this case, nonpartnership item treatment).

Some of the requirements for making an election under section 6223(e) might, arguably, be satisfied by the petition. It identified the partner and the partnership, although it did not contain the partnership address or taxpayer identification number. The petition mentioned the years at issue in the deficiency case, which are the same years that would have been the subject of an election. And although not signed

[11] The current regulation clarifies that the FPAA is the operative notice, but that regulation became effective on October 4, 2001, for partnership years beginning after that date. *See* sec. 301.6223(e)–2(e), Proced. & Admin. Regs. A temporary regulation was effective for the partnership years at issue, and the IRS took the same position even before the final regulations. Field Service Advisory 1993, 1993 WL 1469668.

by the partner making the election, the petition was signed by counsel for that partner.

The Bedrosians argue that it would be "untenable" to hold them to the requirements of making a proper election because they had not received actual notice within the 45-day period within which to make such an election. This amounts to rearguing the *Stone Canyon Partners* case that we already decided and that the Court of Appeals for the Ninth Circuit already affirmed. *Stone Canyon Partners v. Commissioner*, T.C. Memo. 2007–377. Actual notice is not the standard; the standard is whether the IRS met the requirements for sending proper notice. We already held that it did, and the Court of Appeals already affirmed our decision in that case.

Recognizing that the Bedrosians did not make a proper election, the proposed report turns to the doctrine of substantial compliance, correctly setting forth the standard. The proposed report states:

> The substantial compliance doctrine is a narrow equitable doctrine that courts use to avoid taxpayer hardship if the taxpayer establishes that he or she intended to comply with a provision, did everything reasonably possible to comply with the provision, but did not comply with the provision because of a failure to meet the provision's specific requirements. [Proposed report at 13–14 (citing *Samueli v. Commissioner*, 132 T.C. 336, 345 (2009), *Sawyer v. Cnty. of Sonoma*, 719 F.2d 1001, 1007–1008 (9th Cir. 1983), and *Fischer Indus., Inc. v. Commissioner*, 87 T.C. 116, 122 (1986), *aff'd*, 843 F.2d 224 (6th Cir. 1988)).]

The proposed report correctly notes that the manner in which the election is made is regulatory, not statutory, and thus strict compliance is not required. *Id.* at 14–15. In doing so, however, the proposed report states that "the Court has found that the documents submitted in lieu of a formal election must 'evidence an affirmative intent on taxpayer's part to make the required election and be bound thereby.'" *Id.* at 17 (quoting *Fischer Indus., Inc. & Subs. v. Commissioner*, 87 T.C. at 122). But the proposed report does not address this affirmative intent requirement in its substantial compliance analysis.

The Bedrosians did not have the affirmative intent to make the required election; they had not received the FPAA or the notice under section 6223(e). Presumably they did not even know that such an election was available to them at the time. Indeed, elsewhere the proposed report acknowledges as much, stating that "petitioners raise a new theory [in their amended petition] that there was a constructive or deemed election converting all partnership items for 1999 and 2000 into nonpartnership items." If an election under section 6223(e) was a new theory in 2010 when the amended petition was filed, then it could not have been the Bedrosians' "affirmative intent" in 2005 when they filed their initial petition.

The proposed report thoroughly strings together examples of substantial compliance, yet it does not address the common thread of intent. In the cited cases, the people who successfully invoked the doctrine of substantial compliance intended to make an election. Indeed, the first such case cited by the proposed report is *Samueli v. Commissioner*, 132 T.C. 336, which involved a failed attempt to invoke substantial compliance, but even there the taxpayers were able to show intent. That TEFRA-related case involved a situation in which the taxpayers alleged that, when they filed an amended individual income tax return, they really intended to file an administrative adjustment request under section 6227. Their argument failed because "[t]he requisite intent needed to be present contemporaneously with the filing of the partner AAR, not later when petitioners believed it to be more advantageous to have had that intent initially." *Id.* at 345–346. Likewise here; the intent to make an election under section 6223(e) needed to be present at the time the purported election was made, not 1,761 days later and with the benefit of hindsight.

Another case cited in the proposed report also focused on intent, but phrased the standard a bit more expansively. In *Fischer Indus., Inc.*, the Court articulated the standard as one that is governed by intent, stating:

> "We have examined the cases as to what constitutes a statement of election under various provisions of the Internal Revenue Code and have found that, absent a formal election, a submitted return and its attached schedules must evidence an affirmative intent on taxpayer's part to make the required election and be bound thereby. Failure to manifest such intent has repeatedly resulted in taxpayer's alleged election being rejected." * * * [*Fischer Indus., Inc. v. Commissioner*, 87 T.C. at 122 (quoting *Atl. Veneer Corp. v. Commissioner*, 85 T.C. 1075, 1082–1083 (1985), *aff'd*, 812 F.2d 158 (4th Cir. 1987)); citations omitted.]

In that case, the Court noted that an election can, in some situations be made on an amended return, stating that "if the circumstances necessitating an election arise after the filing of an original return, [the election can be made] as soon as practicable on an amended return." *Id.* In the case before us, the purported election does not appear on a return but on the petition filed in this Court. If we were to apply the standard from *Fischer* in this case, we would ask whether the Bedrosians' intent to elect out of TEFRA appeared on either the original petition filed in this case or "as soon as practicable on an amended" petition. Again, no such intent appears on the original petition. The Bedrosians first raised the notion of an election under section 6223(e) at least 33 months after they became aware of the FPAA.[12] In the interim, Stone Canyon and the Bedrosians had lost jurisdictional arguments in both this Court and in the Court of Appeals for the Ninth Circuit. This was not "as soon as practicable"; this was with the benefit of hindsight. And an attempt to benefit from hindsight weighs against a finding of substantial compliance. *Taylor v. Commissioner*, 67 T.C. 1071, 1077–1078 (1977).

Even if we look past the lack of intent, there is a lack of substantial compliance in the manner the election was made. The proposed report cites various cases that found substantial compliance where a taxpayer made a footfault in making an election. Such footfaults include making the election with the wrong IRS office, *Hewlett-Packard Co. v. Commissioner*, 67 T.C. 736, 748 (1977), omitting information, *Sperapani v. Commissioner*, 42 T.C. 308, 330–333 (1964), or making an untimely election, *Estate of Chamberlain v. Commissioner*, T.C. Memo. 1999–181, *aff'd*, 9 Fed. Appx. 713 (9th Cir. 2001). In the various examples of substantial compliance cited in the proposed report, however, the taxpayers made isolated footfaults. A taxpayer may well have intended to make an election, but as a result of an error or omission the taxpayer did not fully comply with the requirements to make an election. In such a situation a taxpayer might be deemed to have substantially complied. But aggregating footfaults

[12] The 33 months is calculated from the time the petition was filed in this Court with respect to the Stone Canyon FPAA until the date the amended petition was lodged.

eventually moves away from compliance, beyond substantial compliance, and all the way to noncompliance. The Bedrosians did not submit the supposed election to the proper IRS office, did not include the necessary information, *and* did not make an election in the time allowed. This cannot be said to be substantial compliance.

The proposed report concludes that "[f]ailing to treat the petition as an election where a reasonable fix can be made under the circumstances would lead to a harsh result which is well out of proportion to the omission. Without such a fix, petitioners would be denied their day in Court." Proposed report at 18 (citations omitted). The Bedrosians' day in court to challenge partnership items was available to them by filing a timely petition from the FPAA. If they did not receive notice, it was by operation of the last known address rule as implemented through TEFRA. While the result might be unfortunate, this is the way the TEFRA rules operate in this case. And the Bedrosians have already challenged whether the TEFRA notice was effective and lost, in both this Court and the Court of Appeals for the Ninth Circuit. It is not for us to create a remedy where none exists.

In sum, we conclude that the Bedrosians did not intend to make an election under section 6223(e)(3). Even if we look past their lack of intent, we conclude that their petition did not substantially comply with the requirements to make such an election. In so concluding, we do not disturb the findings of fact in the proposed report.

III. *Application of Section 6231(g)(2)*

In an effort to explore options that even the parties had not considered, the Court ordered the parties to submit memoranda on the question of whether section 6231(g)(2) might apply in this case. Under section 6231(g)(2), the TEFRA provisions do not apply to a partnership if the Secretary reasonably determines, on the basis of the face of the partnership return, that TEFRA does not apply.

A. *Application of TEFRA*

In prior cases we have described the TEFRA procedures as "distressingly complex and confusing". *See, e.g., Tigers Eye Trading, LLC v. Commissioner*, 138 T.C. 67, 92 (2012); *Rhone-Poulenc Surfactants & Specialties, L.P. v. Commis-*

sioner, 114 T.C. at 539–540. It can even be complex and confusing to determine whether a partnership is subject to TEFRA.

The TEFRA provisions begin with the presumption that TEFRA applies to any entity that is required to file a partnership return. Sec. 6231(a)(1)(A). But there is an exception for small partnerships. A small partnership is any partnership having 10 or fewer partners each of whom is an individual (other than a nonresident alien), a C corporation, or an estate of a deceased partner. Sec. 6231(a)(1)(B)(i). Implicit in this exception, a partnership will not be considered to be a small partnership if any partner during the taxable year is a "pass-thru partner". *Id.*; *Brennan v. Commissioner*, T.C. Memo. 2012–187, 2012 WL 2740897, at *3; sec. 301.6231(a)(1)–1(a)(2), Proced. & Admin. Regs. A "pass-thru partner" is a partnership, estate, trust, S corporation, nominee, or other similar person through whom other persons hold an interest in the partnership, and includes disregarded entities such as single-member LLCs. *See 6611, Ltd. v. Commissioner*, T.C. Memo. 2013–49, at *62 n.29; *Tigers Eye Trading, LLC v. Commissioner*, T.C. Memo. 2009–121, 2009 WL 1475159, at *11; Rev. Rul. 2004–88, 2004–2 C.B. 165.

Stone Canyon was subject to TEFRA. Both partners of Stone Canyon were passthrough partners; as a result it did not qualify as a small partnership and was subject to the TEFRA procedures. Yet until the IRS issued its notices, and perhaps afterward, there was apparent confusion over whether TEFRA applied to the adjustments at issue.

B. *Section 6231(g)*

Congress was aware of the problem of determining whether TEFRA applies, and it enacted section 6231(g) as part of the Taxpayer Relief Act of 1997, Pub. L. No. 105–34, sec. 1232(a), 111 Stat. at 1023, in an attempt to address the problem. Section 6231(g) provides:

> SEC. 6231(g). PARTNERSHIP RETURN TO BE DETERMINATIVE OF WHETHER SUBCHAPTER APPLIES.—
>
> (1) DETERMINATION THAT SUBCHAPTER APPLIES.—If, on the basis of a partnership return for a taxable year, the Secretary reasonably determines that this subchapter applies to such partnership for such year but such determination is erroneous, then the provisions of this

subchapter are hereby extended to such partnership (and its items) for such taxable year and to partners of such partnership.

(2) DETERMINATION THAT SUBCHAPTER DOES NOT APPLY.—If, on the basis of a partnership return for a taxable year, the Secretary reasonably determines that this subchapter does not apply to such partnership for such year but such determination is erroneous, then the provisions of this subchapter shall not apply to such partnership (and its items) for such taxable year or to partners of such partnership.

This provision was intended as a relief provision for the IRS in situations in which the IRS has difficulty determining whether a partnership is subject to TEFRA. The House Ways and Means Committee report makes this clear, stating, in part:

Reasons for Change

The IRS often finds it difficult to determine whether to follow the TEFRA partnership procedures or the regular deficiency procedures. * * * [T]he IRS might inadvertently apply the wrong procedures and possibly jeopardize any assessment. Permitting the IRS to rely on a partnership's return would simplify the IRS' task.

Explanation of Provision

The bill permits the IRS to apply the TEFRA audit procedures if, based on the partnership's return for the year, the IRS reasonably determines that those procedures should apply. Similarly, the provision permits the IRS to apply the normal deficiency procedures if, based on the partnership's return for the year, the IRS reasonably determines that those procedures should apply.

[H.R. Rept. No. 105–148, at 587–588 (1997), 1997–4 C.B. (Vol. 1) 319, 909–910.]

As the committee report makes clear, Congress' goal in enacting section 6231(g) was to simplify the IRS' task of choosing between the TEFRA procedures and the normal deficiency procedures by permitting the IRS to rely on a partnership's return. Paragraph (1) of section 6231(g) extends the TEFRA procedures to a non-TEFRA partnership where the IRS reasonably but erroneously determines that those procedures apply. Paragraph (2) of section 6231(g) operates to make the provisions of TEFRA inapplicable to a TEFRA partnership where the IRS reasonably but erroneously determines that TEFRA does not apply. By providing these alternatives, it is clear that Congress intended that the IRS would make one of two mutually exclusive determinations with respect to a partnership on the basis of the partnership's return: either TEFRA applies or it does not.

C. *Section 6231(g)(2)*

The parties agree that Stone Canyon is properly subject to TEFRA. As previously stated, section 6231(g)(1) operates to bring a non-TEFRA partnership within the scope of TEFRA; that section is clearly not applicable here. Section 6231(g)(2) has the opposite effect. It operates to take a TEFRA partnership outside the scope of TEFRA by making the provisions of TEFRA inapplicable to the partnership. The parties disagree whether section 6231(g)(2) applies here.

Section 6231(g)(2) applies to a partnership for a taxable year if three elements are met: (1) the IRS determined on the basis of the partnership's return that the TEFRA procedures did not apply to the partnership for that year; (2) the determination was reasonable; and (3) the determination turned out to be erroneous. This third element is not at issue. The parties agree that Stone Canyon is subject to TEFRA. Thus it follows that if the IRS had determined on the basis of the Stone Canyon return that TEFRA does not apply, then that determination would have been erroneous.

The parties dispute the first two elements of section 6231(g)(2). The Bedrosians argue that the "IRS Clearly Determined that the Normal Deficiency Procedures Applied in Our Case" and that "there is ample evidence of the reasonableness" of that determination. Respondent argues that the IRS "did not determine by reference to the Partnership return that the normal deficiency procedures apply in this instance" and that "any determination that [the] TEFRA procedures did not apply to the Partnership would have been unreasonable as [a] matter of law." We address each of these elements in turn.

1. *A Determination That TEFRA Does Not Apply*

The first element of section 6231(g)(2) is met in this case if, on the basis of Stone Canyon's 1999 return, the IRS determined that the TEFRA procedures did not apply. Neither the statute nor the committee report provides any guidance as to the meaning of the phrase "on the basis of a partnership return" or as to when the IRS is to make its determination. However, both the TEFRA and non-TEFRA provisions provide a clear indication of when the IRS has made a determination—the notice that concludes the examination. In a

TEFRA case this is the notice of final partnership administrative adjustment; in a deficiency case this is the notice of deficiency.

We have made clear, back to the earliest days of TEFRA litigation, that the FPAA is the IRS' determination. In *Clovis I v. Commissioner*, 88 T.C. 980, 982 (1987), we wrote:

> The FPAA is to the litigation of partnership items and affected items pursuant to the partnership audit and litigation provisions of section 6221 et seq., what the statutory notice of deficiency is to tax controversies before this Court that involve respondent's determination of a deficiency, i.e., it is the notice to affected taxpayers that respondent has made a final administrative determination for particular tax years. * * *

Inherent in the determination of partnership items is the determination that TEFRA applies to the partnership in which those items arose; if TEFRA did not apply there would be no FPAA and no partnership items.

In contrast, one might argue that the IRS determined at some earlier time that TEFRA did not apply. Undoubtedly, the IRS initially treated the examination underlying this case as though it was not a TEFRA examination. The Form 1040 was assigned to Revenue Agent Jung for examination. Shortly thereafter, the IRS requested that the Bedrosians extend their period of limitations, not that attributable to items of Stone Canyon. The Bedrosians provided a power of attorney with respect to their personal tax matters, not those of Stone Canyon. *See* sec. 301.6223(c)–1(e)(2), Proced. & Admin. Regs. (providing specific requirements for furnishing a power of attorney with respect to TEFRA proceedings); Internal Revenue Manual (IRM) pt. 8.19.6.5(2) (June 1, 2007) ("For a Form 2848 to cover both partnership items and nonpartnership items, the partner should state in the power of attorney that authority for both matters is granted to the representative."). The IRS then communicated with the Bedrosians' representative about the examination, including providing proposed audit changes that related to items originating in the partnership. But none of this amounts to a determination. These events are part of the give-and-take of an ongoing examination.

To look to the actions within an ongoing exam to find a "determination" would be an unworkable rule raising any number of problems. This would arguably permit anyone to look behind the final notice (either FPAA or notice of deficiency) to try to argue that the IRS had, at some earlier time, determined that the opposite procedure applies. Looking behind the notice is disfavored. *See Greenberg's Express, Inc. v. Commissioner*, 62 T.C. 324, 327–328 (1974) ("As a general rule, this Court will not look behind a deficiency notice to examine the evidence used or the propriety of respondent's motives or of the administrative policy or procedure involved in making his determinations."). In making that inquiry, the Court would look to some undefined standard for what constituted such a determination. Moreover, it would leave open the question of which IRS employees have the authority to make such a determination. Section 6231(g) rests that power with the Secretary, but we can find no specific delegation of this authority.

In contrast, notices that conclude an audit, an FPAA or a notice of deficiency, have long been understood as determinations. *Clovis I v. Commissioner*, 88 T.C. at 982. The IRS has delegated the authority to issue them. *See, e.g.*, Delegation Orders 4–8 (authority to issue a notice of deficiency) and 4–19 (authority to issue an FPAA). And the notices have the benefit of providing a clear demarcation of when a determination was made.

In this case, however, the IRS issued both notices: the IRS issued an FPAA for Stone Canyon on April 8, 2005, and a notice of deficiency to the Bedrosians making the same adjustments (plus additional adjustments) 11 days later. We believe the earlier notice controls.

Neither section 6231(g) nor the committee report explicitly addresses the possibility that the IRS might audit a partnership using both procedures. When Congress enacted the TEFRA procedures, it intended the normal deficiency procedures and the TEFRA procedures to be separate and distinct procedures, with the former governing nonpartnership items and the latter governing partnership items. Even the IRM describes the two procedures as "mutually exclusive". *See* IRM pt. 4.31.2.1.1(1) (June 1, 2004) ("[T]he TEFRA partnership rules and the deficiency procedures are mutually exclusive."). Nonetheless, the IRS occasionally follows both procedures in practice to protect the Government's interests when it is unsure which of the procedures applies. *See id.* pt. 4.31.2.1.8(1) (June 20, 2013) ("These key cases are controlled as both TEFRA and nonTEFRA. This is done when it is unclear whether a key case is TEFRA or nonTEFRA to protect the government's interest.").

By implication, however, section 6231(g) makes it clear that only one determination can be made for the partnership. In other areas within TEFRA, a single partner can be removed from a TEFRA proceeding such that adjustments are made with respect to one partner while all other partners are bound by the TEFRA proceeding. *See, e.g.*, secs. 6227(d)(1), (3), 6231(c)(2). In contrast, section 6231(g) addresses partnershipwide, not partner-specific, determinations. Both section 6231(g)(1) and (2) make this clear: if paragraph (1) applies, "then the provisions of this subchapter are hereby extended *to such partnership*", and if paragraph (2) applies, "then the provisions of this subchapter shall not apply *to such partnership*." (Emphasis added.) There is nothing in section 6231(g) to indicate that Congress intended to allow the IRS to determine that TEFRA applies to one partner in a partnership while simultaneously determining that it does not apply to another partner in the same partnership. Thus, we conclude that the IRS must make a single determination for the partnership.

In this instance, the IRS determined that TEFRA applies to the partnership. The FPAA was the first notice issued and clearly indicated that the IRS was taking the position that TEFRA applied to Stone Canyon. Because section 6231(g) requires a single, partnershipwide determination, the IRS could not thereafter determine that TEFRA did not apply to that same partnership. And, under the facts of this case, a determination that TEFRA did not apply to Stone Canyon would not have been reasonable.

2. *Reasonableness*

If the IRS had determined that TEFRA does not apply to Stone Canyon, that determination would not have been reasonable.

For section 6231(g)(2) to apply, the IRS must reasonably determine that the partnership at issue is not subject to TEFRA. The Code does not define what is reasonable for purposes of section 6231(g)(1) or (2). There is no indication that Congress intended the term "reasonable" to have any specific meaning, and so we give it its ordinary meaning. *See Crane v. Commissioner*, 331 U.S. 1, 6 (1947); *Keene v. Commissioner*, 121 T.C. 8, 14 (2003).

In determining the ordinary meaning of words, it is appropriate to consult dictionaries. *See Nat'l Muffler Dealers Ass'n, Inc. v. United States*, 440 U.S. 472, 480 n.10 (1979); *Rome I, Ltd. v. Commissioner*, 96 T.C. 697, 704 (1991). The Random House College Dictionary 1100 (rev. ed. 1980) defines the term "reasonable" as: (1) "agreeable to or in accord with reason or sound judgment; logical"; (2) "not exceeding the limit prescribed by reason; not excessive"; (3) "moderate in price; not expensive"; (4) "endowed with reason"; and (5) "capable of rational behavior, decision, etc.". Webster's II New Riverside University Dictionary 980 (1984) similarly defines the term as: (1) "[c]apable of reasoning"; (2) "[g]overned by or in accordance with reason or sound thinking"; (3) "[w]ithin the bounds of common sense"; and (4) "[n]ot extreme or excessive".

These definitions are not inconsistent with the use of the term "reasonable" elsewhere in the Code. The use of that term that is the most analogous to the current situation can be found in the phrase "reasonable basis" when referring to the standard of reporting. *See, e.g.*, secs. 6662(d)(2)(B), 6676, 6694(a)(2)(B); *see also* 31 C.F.R. sec. 10.34(a) (2011) (setting forth the Circular 230 ethical standards regarding tax return preparation). Determining whether TEFRA applies to a particular partnership involves the application of the law (specifically, section 6231(a)(1)) to a set of facts (specifically, the information shown on the face of a partnership return). The reasonable basis standard of reporting involves the same type of inquiry. For that purpose, reasonable basis is defined as

> a relatively high standard of tax reporting, that is, significantly higher than not frivolous or not patently improper. The reasonable basis standard is not satisfied by a return position that is merely arguable or that is merely a colorable claim. If a return position is reasonably based on one or more of the authorities set forth in § 1.6662-4(d)(3)(iii) (taking into account the relevance and persuasiveness of the authorities, and subsequent developments), the return position will generally satisfy the reasonable basis standard even though it may not satisfy the substantial authority standard as defined in § 1.6662–4 (d)(2). * * * [Sec. 1.6662–3(b)(3), Income Tax Regs.]

Against this backdrop, we analyze whether a determination based on the Stone Canyon partnership return that TEFRA does not apply to Stone Canyon would have been reasonable. Stone Canyon's Form 1065 for 1999 contained conflicting and necessarily erroneous information. On one hand, Stone Canyon expressly reported that it was not subject to the TEFRA procedures by answering "no" to the question on line 4 of Schedule B, which asks: "Is this partnership subject to the consolidated audit procedures of sections 6221 through 6233? If 'Yes,' see Designation of Tax Matters Partner below". Yet Stone Canyon designated a TMP.

Notwithstanding these inconsistencies, the Schedules K–1 that were included with and are part of the partnership return make it clear that the partnership must have been subject to TEFRA as a matter of law. One of the Schedules K–1 listed an LLC as one of the members of Stone Canyon but then identified the LLC as an individual. Another Schedule K–1 listed an S corporation as one of the members of Stone Canyon and identified it as an S corporation. The presence of any passthrough partner precludes the application of the small partnership exception of section 6231(a)(1)(B) and renders the partnership subject to TEFRA as a matter of law. Relying on the face of the partnership return, the only reasonable conclusion is that TEFRA applies to Stone Canyon.

The Bedrosians even acknowledged this point in one of the memoranda that they filed before the Court raised the issue of section 6231(g)(2). They stated: "It was clear from the Stone Canyon Partners' partnership returns that partners in Stone Canyon Partners were themselves pass-through entities. This makes Stone Canyon Partners subject to the TEFRA procedures *automatically*." Memorandum of Points and Authorities in Support of Petitioners' Motion for Summary Judgment, at 15 (Nov. 30, 2010).

Because it would have been unreasonable to determine that TEFRA does not apply to Stone Canyon, we find that section 6231(g)(2) does not apply.

IV. *Law of the Case*

As discussed above, we conclude that no election was made under section 6223(e)(2) to opt out of the TEFRA proceedings regarding Stone Canyon. We also conclude that the IRS did not determine that TEFRA did not apply to Stone Canyon (and if it made such a determination, it would have been unreasonable). In addition to these reasons, we must rule against the Bedrosians because we are bound by what the Court of Appeals for the Ninth Circuit has already decided in this case.

We previously held that we lack jurisdiction over the partnership items that were included in the notice of deficiency at issue here, which, in essence, the Bedrosians ask us to reconsider. But the Court of Appeals already agreed with this Court's determination that the notice of deficiency was invalid as to the partnership items. As the Court of Appeals put it: "[T]he Tax Court never had jurisdiction over 'such deficiency' in the first place." *Bedrosian v. Commissioner*, 358 Fed. Appx. at 870. The phrase "such deficiency" refers to the partnership items that the IRS included in the notice of deficiency; however, we still had jurisdiction over the nonpartnership items for 2000 (i.e., the transaction fees). As a result, the Court of Appeals dismissed the Bedrosians' appeal from our decision in T.C. Memo. 2007–375 because "there is no final judgment as to all claims." The Court of Appeals remanded the case for further proceedings concerning the taxable year 2000, and we received the mandate on February 1, 2010.

The "law of the case" doctrine "posits that when a court decides upon a rule of law, that decision should continue to govern the same issues in subsequent stages in the same case." *Arizona v. California*, 460 U.S. 605, 618 (1983). It has been recognized and repeatedly applied by this Court and by the Court of Appeals for the Ninth Circuit, *see, e.g.*, *United States v. Alexander*, 106 F.3d 874 (9th Cir. 1997); *Herrington v. Cnty. of Sonoma*, 12 F.3d 901 (9th Cir. 1993); *Pollei v. Commissioner*, 94 T.C. 595 (1990); *Dixon v. Commissioner*, T.C. Memo. 2006–190, and precludes reconsideration of an issue that has been decided in this case, *Thomas v. Bible*, 983 F.2d 152, 154 (9th Cir. 1993). The issues that a lower court is precluded from reconsidering "include those that were decided by the appellate court expressly or by necessary implication." *Pollei v. Commissioner*, 94 T.C. at 601 (citing *In re Beverly Hills Bancorp*, 752 F.2d 1334 (9th Cir. 1984)).

Following either the section 6223(e) approach advocated by the Bedrosians or the section 6231(g)(2) approach would require that we reconsider our prior opinion in T.C. Memo. 2007–375 wherein we held that we lack jurisdiction over the very same items over which the Bedrosians now ask us to find jurisdiction. Doing so would violate the law of the case. Following the section 6223(e) approach would have us find jurisdiction over the partnership items in the 2005 notice of deficiency; the Court of Appeals for the Ninth Circuit has already held that we do not have jurisdiction over those items. Following the section 6231(g)(2) approach would render the FPAA and the *Stone Canyon Partners* proceeding a nullity; the Court of Appeals already upheld the validity of the notice that underlay that proceeding and affirmed our decision in that case. The law of the case doctrine precludes us from reconsidering these rulings.

It is worth noting that the Bedrosians raised their allegations regarding the IRS' muddled handling of this case in the *Stone Canyon Partners* FPAA case. They alleged two affirmative defenses to the adjustments in the FPAA. The first defense was that the FPAA was invalid because it was not mailed to the last known address. Their second affirmative defense was as follows:

> The Commissioner failed to properly conduct a partnership-level proceeding * * * and issued a Notice of Deficiency proposing adjustments to partners' returns less than one month after issuing the FPAA, in violation of law. As a result, even if the FPAA had been timely received, the premature issuance of the Notice of Deficiency proposing adjustments based on the FPAA would have misled the partnership and its partners into concluding that the procedures for obtaining judicial review of the Notice of Deficiency superseded and obviated the procedures for obtaining judicial review of the FPAA. Therefore, any purported adjustments made by Commissioner in the FPAA are of no force and effect * * *.

In this passage, the Bedrosians clearly alleged that the IRS "failed to properly conduct a partnership-level proceeding"; that the FPAA was "of no force and effect"; that the notice of deficiency issued to them individually could reasonably be construed as the method the IRS had selected to resolve the 1999 partnership items; and that the notice of deficiency issued to them individually "superseded and obviated" the FPAA. Although the Bedrosians did not frame their argument using the terminology of section 6231(g)(2), their factual allegations are essentially the same factual allegations that they now advance to support their contention that this case should be governed by individual deficiency procedures. For whatever reason, the Bedrosians abandoned this theory and argued the last known address issue, which was rejected both by this Court and by the Court of Appeals for the Ninth Circuit. They cannot now collaterally attack what has become a final decision.

Conclusion

The Bedrosians cannot use this deficiency proceeding to make a collateral attack because of the final decision in *Stone Canyon Partners* or the opinion of the Court of Appeals in their prior appeal in this case. Their arguments regarding sections 6223(e) and 6231(g) amount to just that. Moreover, their arguments fail on the merits. The Bedrosians' partnership items did not automatically convert under section 6231(e)(2), and they neither made an election under section 6223(e)(3) nor substantially complied with the procedures for making such an election. Regarding section 6231(g)(2), the IRS determined that TEFRA applied to Stone Canyon, as evidenced by the Stone Canyon FPAA. If the IRS had determined that TEFRA did not apply to Stone Canyon, that determination would not have been reasonable because Stone Canyon had passthrough partners, which preclude it from falling within the small partnership exception.

To reflect the foregoing,

An appropriate order will be issued.

Reviewed by the Court.

HALPERN, GALE, HOLMES, KERRIGAN, LAUBER, and NEGA, *JJ.*, agree with this opinion of the Court.

KROUPA, *J.*,[13] concurs in the result only.

GUSTAFSON and MORRISON, *JJ.*, did not participate in the consideration of this opinion.

---

[13] Judge Kroupa retired on June 16, 2014.

HALPERN, *J.*, concurring: I have joined the majority's opinion and write separately only to address Judge Vasquez' complaint that we have denied the Bedrosians their day in court. I do not believe that to be the case. Judge Vasquez is the author of our Memorandum Opinion *Stone Canyon Partners v. Commissioner*, T.C. Memo. 2007–377, 2007 WL 4526512, *aff'd*, 358 Fed. Appx. 868 (9th Cir. 2009). In that case, we disposed of two competing motions to dismiss for lack of jurisdiction. One was made by JCB Stone Canyon Investments LLC (LLC), as tax matters partner (TMP) of Stone Canyon Partners. The grounds for that motion were that the Commissioner had failed to issue a valid notice of final partnership administrative adjustment (FPAA) since he had addressed no copy to a proper address. The Commissioner's competing motion was on the grounds that the petition was untimely. We denied the TMP's motion and granted the Commissioner's motion.

In its untimely filed petition, the TMP stated that the adjustments proposed in the FPAA were "the same adjustments" proposed in the notice of deficiency on which this case is based. The TMP assigned error to the FPAA and raised two affirmative defenses: one, that the FPAA was not mailed to the proper address, and, two, as noted by the majority, *see* op. Ct. p. 113, that the Commissioner's muddled handling of the case deprived the FPAA of any vitality. Only the first affirmative defense was advanced as a ground for the TMP's motion.

We first addressed the TMP's motion. It argued that the FPAA was invalid "because it was never mailed to the appropriate address, and as a result petitioner did not receive notice as required pursuant to the Code." We reviewed the rules governing the proper address for an FPAA and noted: "As is the case with a statutory notice of deficiency, the validity of a properly mailed FPAA is not contingent upon actual receipt by either the tax matters partner or a notice partner." *Stone Canyon Partners v. Commissioner*, 2007 WL 4526512, at *3. We then turned to determining whether any of the 14 FPAAs the Commissioner mailed to three different addresses were sufficient. The FPAAs were addressed variously to "Stone Canyon Partners, c/o John Bedrosian", "JCB Stone Canyon Investments, LLC, c/o John Bedrosian", "Stone Canyon Investors, Inc., c/o John Bedrosian", "John

Bedrosian", and "Judith Bedrosian". We stated not once but twice: "By mailing FPAAs to multiple addressees at multiple addresses, respondent made a good faith effort to notify all affected parties of the partnership adjustments, thus satisfying the notice requirement of sec. 6223(a)." *Id.*, 2007 WL 4526512, at *4. With respect to one of the addresses, to which FPAAs addressed directly to the Bedrosians were sent, we stated: "[That] address was a proper address to which respondent could mail the FPAAs to the Bedrosians as individuals and as indirect partners of * * * [LLC] and * * * [Stone Canyon Investors, Inc.]."

On the basis of our finding that the section 6223(a) notice requirements were satisfied, we denied the TMP's motion and granted the Commissioner's motion that the petition filed almost two years after the FPAAs were mailed was untimely and, thus, invalid. *See id.* at *5. The Court of Appeals acknowledged the Bedrosians' assertion that they did not receive the FPAA at any address. *Bedrosian v. Commissioner*, 358 Fed. Appx. at 869. It held, however: "Because we determine that the IRS validly mailed the FPAA to the Bedrosians, we affirm the Tax Court's dismissal for lack of jurisdiction of their untimely petition." *Id.*

Because the Commissioner sent them an FPAA, the Bedrosians were "notice partners". *See* sec. 6231(a)(8). Consequently, upon the failure of the TMP to file a petition in response to the FPAA, either of them could have done so. *See* sec. 6226(b). Their opportunity for a day in court to contest the FPAA—which the TMP (effectively, the Bedrosians) in the petition conceded presented "the same adjustments" proposed in the notice of deficiency on which this case is based—expired 150 days after the FPAA was issued. *See id.* They failed to meet that deadline. As one court has aptly put it in response to a due process challenge to a period of limitations:

> While it is undeniably true that access to the courts and an opportunity to be heard are fundamental aspects of procedural due process, it is equally clear that the bar imposed by a validly enacted and reasonable statute of limitations does not deprive a suitor of his day in court in derogation of that clause.[5] * * * [First fn. ref. omitted.]
>
> [5]As one court has stated:
>
> Statutes of limitation have been part of the law of every civilized nation from time immemorial. Since each sovereignty may organize its judicial tribunals according to its own notions of policy, it has been rec-

ognized since the early days of this republic that statutes of limitation are within the sovereign power of each state to enact. Such statutes, having the effect of denying any judicial remedy for the enforcement of an otherwise valid claim, are justified on grounds of policy and as statutes of repose "designed to protect the citizens from stale and vexatious claims and to make an end to the possibility of litigation after the lapse of a reasonable time." *Guaranty Trust Co. of New York v. United States*, 304 U.S. 126, 58 S. Ct. 785, 82 L. Ed. 1224 (1937). The legislative body, in enacting such legislation, may weigh the conflicting interests between one person's right to enforce an otherwise valid claim and another person's right to be confronted with any claim against him before the lapse of time has likely rendered unavailable or difficult the matter of obtaining or presenting proof. Any balance of these conflicting interests which is not arbitrary or capricious is within the legislative authority and not subject to constitutional attack for lack of due process. *Hargraves v. Brackett Stripping Machine Co.*, 317 F. Supp. 676, 682–83 (E.D. Tenn. 1970). * * *

[*Saffioti v. Wilson*, 392 F. Supp. 1335, 1339 (S.D.N.Y. 1975).]

Indeed, the very argument that the Bedrosians make here concerning the Commissioner's muddled handling of the case, the TMP raised in assigning error to the FPAA. Judge Vasquez' penultimate paragraph in his report in *Stone Canyon Partners v. Commissioner*, 2007 WL 4526512, at *5, reads as follows: "In reaching all of our holdings herein, we have considered all arguments made by the parties, and, to the extent not mentioned above, we find them to be irrelevant or without merit." While it is not clear whether he intended that bit of boilerplate to refer to arguments other than those made in support of the motions, the TMP's affirmative defense certainly raised the issue in the case.

Petitioners have had their opportunity for a day in court. Whether they actually received the FPAA is beside the point. All Congress required is that it be mailed to them at a proper address. Judge Vasquez found that it was. *Stone Canyon Partners* is a partnership-level case, and, for that reason, the partners do not, upon failure to file a petition in response to the FPAA, have the opportunity to sue for a refund, as they would if the case were a deficiency case. *See* sec. 7422(h); *see also, e.g., McCann v. United States*, 105 Fed. Cl. 120, 122 (2012), *aff'd*, 2012 WL 6839761 (Fed. Cir. Nov. 27, 2012). That is a legislative choice that we have no authority to mitigate.

GALE, HOLMES, BUCH, LAUBER, and NEGA, *JJ.*, agree with this concurring opinion.

GOEKE, *J.*, concurring: I agree with the majority's reasoning on the merits of petitioners' arguments and accordingly concur in the judgment. I write separately to critique its law of the case doctrine analysis and to discuss the implications of petitioners' failure to timely challenge the Stone Canyon FPAA.

The majority concludes that we may not find that we have jurisdiction over the partnership items in the 2005 notice of deficiency, "because we are bound by what the Court of Appeals for the Ninth Circuit has already decided in this case." *See* op. Ct. p. 112. The majority goes on to state:

> We previously held that we lack jurisdiction over the partnership items that were included in the notice of deficiency at issue here, which, in essence, the Bedrosians ask us to reconsider. But the Court of Appeals already agreed with this Court's determination that the notice of deficiency was invalid as to the partnership items. As the Court of Appeals put it: "[T]he Tax Court never had jurisdiction over 'such deficiency' in the first place." * * * [*See id.*]

I do not agree that we are bound by the quoted statement.

The law of the case doctrine "ordinarily precludes a court from re-examining an issue previously decided by the same court, or a higher appellate court, in the same case." *Moore v. James H. Matthews & Co.*, 682 F.2d 830, 833 (9th Cir. 1982). "A significant corollary to the doctrine is that dicta have no preclusive effect." *Milgard Tempering, Inc. v. Selas Corp. of Am.*, 902 F.2d 703, 715 (9th Cir. 1990) (citing *Ducey v. United States*, 830 F.2d 1071, 1072 (9th Cir. 1987).

I acknowledge that the Court of Appeals for the Ninth Circuit apparently agreed with our initial decision that we lacked jurisdiction over the partnership items in the 2005 notice of deficiency, but it appears that the statement the majority quotes was dictum. On appeal the Court of Appeals considered three Tax Court opinions: (1) its dismissal for lack of jurisdiction of the Bedrosians' untimely petition challenging the 2005 FPAA; (2) its partial dismissal of the Bedrosians' petition challenging the 2005 notice of deficiency; and (3) its dismissal for lack of jurisdiction of the Bedrosians' petition challenging the 2006 affected items notice of deficiency. The Court of Appeals affirmed opinions (1) and (3) but held that it did not have jurisdiction to review opinion

(2), because it was not a "final decision".[1] *See Bedrosian v. Commissioner*, 358 Fed. Appx. 868, 870 (9th Cir. 2009), *aff'g* T.C. Memo. 2007–376.

The case before us concerns our jurisdiction over the partnership items in the 2005 notice of deficiency (opinion (2) above). The statement the majority quotes appears in the Court of Appeals' analysis of our dismissal of the Bedrosians' petition challenging the 2006 affected items notice (opinion (3) above). The Court of Appeals concluded it could not review opinion (2) but in its analysis of opinion (3) suggested that it agreed with opinion (2). It is not clear whether the Court of Appeals' statement about opinion (2) was necessary to its holding on opinion (3). Consequently, it is unclear whether the statement precludes us from reconsidering our jurisdiction in this case.

The law of the case doctrine typically precludes a court from reexamining an issue it previously decided in the same case. *See Moore*, 682 F.2d at 833. We previously opined that we had no jurisdiction over the partnership items in the 2005 notice of deficiency. Consequently, the law of the case doctrine already binds us on the basis of our own opinion. I find it unnecessary and incorrect to determine whether it also binds us on the basis of the Court of Appeals' opinion.

Additionally, I find it worth noting that the Court of Appeals' affirmation of our dismissal of the separate Stone Canyon partnership case (holding that the FPAA was valid and that the petition filed in response to the FPAA was untimely) necessarily means that the partnership proceedings were complete as to partnership items and that the Commissioner was free to proceed to make assessments or determinations regarding affected items. The partnership item adjustments determined in the FPAA became final when the time for filing a petition expired. *See* sec. 6225. And our dismissal of the partnership proceeding for lack of a timely filed petition prevents us in a partner-level proceeding from upsetting the FPAA adjustments. *See* sec. 6226(h) (providing that if a petition challenging the adjustments in an FPAA is dismissed, "the decision of the court

[1] The Court of Appeals found that because we had only partially dismissed the Bedrosians' petition challenging the 2005 notice of deficiency, their appeal was interlocutory.

dismissing the action shall be considered as its decision that the * * * [FPAA] is correct").

As we stated in *Tigers Eye Trading, LLC v. Commissioner*, 138 T.C. 67, 89 (2012):

> Under the TEFRA procedures all partnership items, the proper allocation of those partnership items among the partners, and the applicability of any penalty, addition to tax, or additional amount that relates to an adjustment to a partnership item are determined in a single partnership-level proceeding. Sec. 6226. The determinations of partnership items in partnership-level proceedings are binding on the partners and may not be challenged in subsequent partner-level proceedings. *See* secs. 6230(c)(4), 7422(h).

PARIS, *J.*, agrees with this concurring opinion.

VASQUEZ, *J.*, dissenting: Our society has a longstanding and "'deep-rooted historic tradition that everyone should have his own day in court.'" *Richards v. Jefferson Cnty., Ala.*, 517 U.S. 793, 798 (1996) (quoting 18 Charles Alan Wright et al., Federal Practice and Procedure, sec. 4449, p. 417 (1981)). "The opportunity to be heard is an essential requisite of due process of law in judicial proceedings." *Id.* at 797 n.4. This Court "has consistently and zealously guarded a taxpayer's right to his day in court, whenever there was a bona fide dispute between him and the Commissioner of Internal Revenue." *Petersen v. Commissioner*, T.C. Memo. 1977–4, 1977 Tax Ct. Memo LEXIS 439, at *6. We have recognized the importance not only to the affected taxpayer, but also to the public's confidence in the tax collection system that the opportunity for judicial review of bona fide disputes be protected. *Id.*

The opinion of the Court departs from these deeply ingrained principles by denying the Bedrosians their day in court.[1] I believe the result reached by the opinion of the Court is not only inconsistent with the interests of justice but is also the product of an erroneous view of the governing law.

The opinion of the Court devotes the bulk of its energy to arguing that sections 6223(e) and 6231(g)(2), two highly com-

---

[1] This Court previously held that we have jurisdiction over the transaction fees for 2000, *see Bedrosian v. Commissioner*, T.C. Memo. 2007–375, and the opinion of the Court does not disturb this holding.

plicated provisions within TEFRA, do not apply in this case. *See* op. Ct. pp. 95–111. The opinion of the Court then goes on to conclude, seemingly irrespective of its prior discussion, that this Court must rule against the Bedrosians under the "law of the case" doctrine. *See id.* pp. 111–114. I respectfully disagree. I will first explain why the reliance of the opinion of the Court on the "law of the case" doctrine is misplaced. I will then show how section 6231(g)(2) operates to confer jurisdiction on this Court.

I. *Law of the Case*

The "law of the case" doctrine is "part of a related set of preclusion principles that includes stare decisis, res judicata, and collateral estoppel." *Gonzalez v. Arizona*, 624 F.3d 1162, 1185 n.16 (9th Cir. 2010). These preclusion principles are all aimed at promoting the efficient operation of the courts. *Id.* They are distinguished, however, by the type or stage of litigation in which they separately apply. *Id.*

The law of the case doctrine generally precludes a court from "reconsidering an issue previously decided by the same court, or a higher court in the identical case." *Milgard Tempering, Inc. v. Selas Corp. of Am.*, 902 F.2d 703, 715 (9th Cir. 1990) (citing *Richardson v. United States*, 841 F.2d 993, 996 (9th Cir. 1988), *amended*, 860 F.2d 357 (9th Cir. 1988)). For the law of the case doctrine to apply, "the issue in question must have been 'decided explicitly or by necessary implication in [the] previous disposition.'" *Id.* (quoting *Liberty Mut. Ins. Co. v. EEOC*, 691 F.2d 438, 441 (9th Cir. 1982)). A court may exercise its discretion to depart from the law of the case in three instances: "(1) the first decision was clearly erroneous and would result in manifest injustice; (2) an intervening change in the law has occurred; or (3) the evidence on remand was substantially different." *Id.*

As the opinion of the Court correctly notes, the Court of Appeals for the Ninth Circuit dismissed the Bedrosians' appeal in this case for lack of jurisdiction because we had not entered a final judgment as to all claims. *See* op. Ct. p. 112. However, the opinion of the Court then erroneously concludes that this Court "must rule against the Bedrosians because we are bound by what the Court of Appeals for the Ninth Circuit has already decided in this case." *See id.* The opinion of the Court quotes the Court of Appeals' statement that "'the Tax Court never had jurisdiction over "such deficiency" in the first place.'" *See id.* (quoting *Bedrosian v. Commissioner*, 358 Fed. Appx. 868, 870 (9th Cir. 2009)).[2] The opinion of the Court overlooks the fact that the Court of Appeals' statements in this case constitute dicta. *See Md. Nat'l Bank v. Vessel Madam Chapel*, 46 F.3d 895, 902 (9th Cir. 1995) ("Because the * * * [Court of Appeals for the Fourth Circuit] action was dismissed for lack of jurisdiction, the statement upon which * * * [the claimant-appellee] relies is dicta and therefore not persuasive."); *United States v. Eccles*, 850 F.2d 1357, 1365 (9th Cir. 1988) ("Because we lack jurisdiction to hear the defendant's appeal, any statements that we could make here as to the appealability after trial of the defendant's claims would constitute dicta.").

The law in the Ninth Circuit, in which an appeal of this case would lie, *see* sec. 7482(b)(1)(A), is absolutely clear that dicta do not have preclusive effect for purposes of the law of the case doctrine, *see Milgard Tempering, Inc.*, 902 F.2d at 715 ("A significant corollary to the [law of the case] doctrine is that dicta have no preclusive effect."); *Ducey v. United States*, 830 F.2d 1071, 1072 (9th Cir. 1987) ("Dicta is not given preclusive effect under the law of the case doctrine in this circuit."); *Russell v. Commissioner*, 678 F.2d 782, 785 (9th Cir. 1982) ("Because the res judicata discussion in our prior * * * decision was dicta, it is not part of the law of the case."). Accordingly, the opinion of the Court is simply mis-

[2] The complete sentence from which the opinion of the Court extracts the quotation from the Court of Appeals' opinion reads as follows: "No assessment could possibly deprive the Tax Court of jurisdiction over that particular deficiency, because the Tax Court never had jurisdiction over 'such deficiency' in the first instance." *Bedrosian v. Commissioner*, 358 Fed. Appx. 868, 870 (9th Cir. 2009), *aff'g* T.C. Memo. 2007–376. This statement appears in the portion of the opinion dealing with the affected items notice issued in 2006 rather than in the separate section of the opinion dealing with the notice of deficiency issued in 2005. The exact meaning of the quoted statement is unclear, especially considering that in the previous paragraph of its opinion the Court of Appeals had expressly held that it lacked jurisdiction to consider an appeal with respect to the 2005 notice of deficiency because the appeal was interlocutory inasmuch as the Tax Court had dismissed the Bedrosian's challenge to the 2005 notice of deficiency only in part, "retaining jurisdiction" over certain issues reflected in the notice of deficiency. *Id.*

taken that the Court of Appeals' statements in dicta bind us in this case.

The opinion of the Court also contends that our prior holding in this case binds us.[3] We held in our prior opinion that we do not have jurisdiction over respondent's adjustments for 1999 in the April 19, 2005, notice of deficiency because the partnership proceeding was pending at the time that notice was issued. *See Bedrosian v. Commissioner*, T.C. Memo. 2007–375, slip op. at 7. The opinion of the Court correctly notes that "[f]ollowing either the section 6223(e) approach advocated by the Bedrosians or the section 6231(g)(2) approach would require that we reconsider our prior opinion", but then erroneously concludes that doing so would violate the law of the case doctrine. *See* op. Ct. p. 113.

To the contrary, "'[a]ll rulings of a trial court are subject to revision at any time before the entry of judgment.'" *City of Los Angeles, Harbor Div. v. Santa Monica Baykeeper*, 254 F.3d 882, 888 (9th Cir. 2001) (quoting *United States v. Houser*, 804 F.2d 565, 567 (9th Cir. 1986)); *see also* Fed. R. Civ. P. 54(b) ("[A]ny order or other decision, however designated, that adjudicates fewer than all the claims or the rights and liabilities of fewer than all the parties does not end the action as to any of the claims or parties and may be revised at any time before the entry of a judgment adjudicating all the claims and all the parties' rights and liabilities.").[4] It is undisputed that we did not enter a final judgment as to all claims in this case. *See Bedrosian v. Commissioner*, 358 Fed. Appx. at 870. Therefore, we have the power to reconsider, modify, or rescind our prior opinion (and the accompanying interlocutory order).

The holding in our prior opinion that we lacked jurisdiction over the items in the notice of deficiency for 1999 was based on an agreement of the parties, which we accepted, that these items were either partnership items or affected items. *See Bedrosian v. Commissioner*, T.C. Memo. 2007–375, slip op. at 7. We did not at the time consider the possible application of section 6231(g)(2), nor did we have the affidavits of

[3] Judge Goeke agrees with the opinion of the Court as to this point in his concurring opinion.

[4] Where, as here, there is no Tax Court Rule on point, we consult the Federal Rules of Civil Procedure for guidance. Rule 1(a); *Davis v. Commissioner*, T.C. Memo. 2006–272, slip op. at 5.

the IRS revenue agent and the Bedrosians' power of attorney (POA) with regard to the events that transpired during the course of the audit. The parties now dispute the characterization of the 1999 items, and it is most prudent for us to reconsider this issue on the merits. *See, e.g.*, *Rawls Trading, L.P. v. Commissioner*, 138 T.C. 271, 284 (2012) ("[W]e are under an affirmative duty to investigate the extent of our subject matter jurisdiction.").

Lastly, we consider the *Stone Canyon Partners* proceeding. The opinion of the Court correctly states that "[f]ollowing the section 6231(g)(2) approach would render the FPAA and the *Stone Canyon Partners* proceeding a nullity". *See* op. Ct. p. 113. But then the opinion of the Court suggests that both the law of the case doctrine and the collateral estoppel doctrine preclude us from reconsidering our ruling in that proceeding. *See id.* This is not so.

As previously stated, the law of the case doctrine precludes a court from "reconsidering an issue previously decided by the same court, or a higher court in the *identical* case." *Milgard Tempering, Inc.*, 902 F.2d at 715 (emphasis added). The *Stone Canyon Partners* proceeding is not identical to the case before us. The parties might be related. There might be issues in common. But, unquestionably, it is not the identical case.

The collateral estoppel doctrine likewise does not apply because it is an affirmative defense which was not raised by either party in this proceeding. *See* Rule 39; *Taylor v. Sturgell*, 553 U.S. 880, 907 (2008) ("Claim preclusion, like issue preclusion, is an affirmative defense."); *Kightlinger v. Commissioner*, T.C. Memo. 1998–357, slip op. at 24 ("[W]e observe that because res judicata and collateral estoppel are affirmative defenses and neither was pleaded by petitioner, they are deemed waived."). While this Court may raise collateral estoppel sua sponte, it is not obligated to do so. *Monahan v. Commissioner*, 109 T.C. 235, 250–251 (1997). "Sua sponte consideration of issue preclusion generally should be limited to circumstances where the parties are given an opportunity to address the applicability of the doctrine to a particular issue." *Id.* at 251. They have not been given that opportunity here. And, regardless, I seriously question whether the requirements of collateral estoppel would have even been met.[5]

Judge Goeke's concurring opinion relies on section 6226(h), which might, at first blush, appear to support its argument that the Bedrosians are precluded from contesting any of the adjustments in the FPAA as part of their deficiency case. Section 6226(h) generally provides that a court's dismissal of an action brought under the section is considered to be its decision that the FPAA is correct. However, no partnership action with respect to Stone Canyon was actually brought under section 6226. The TMP of Stone Canyon did not file a petition in response to the FPAA within 90 days under section 6226(a), nor did any other partner file a petition within 60 days after the close of the 90-day period under section 6226(b). The dismissal of a partnership action which was not properly brought under section 6226, as is the case here, has *no* preclusive effect. *See Cent. Valley AG Enters. v. United States*, 531 F.3d 750, 765–766 (9th Cir. 2008) ("TEFRA contains no provision stating that an FPAA has preclusive effect based solely on the failure to timely pursue TEFRA remedies and notwithstanding the lack of a Tax Court proceeding."); *see also A.I.M. Controls, L.L.C. v. Commissioner*, 672 F.3d 390, 392 n.2 (5th Cir. 2012) ("Because Royce Mitchell was not a tax matters partner of * * * [the partnership], he lacked authority to bring an action under * * * [section] 6226(a), and * * * [section] 6226(h)'s bar was not triggered by the district court's dismissal of his action.").

In short, there is no bar that prevents this Court from considering the merits of section 6231(g)(2). The reliance of the opinion of the Court on the law of the case doctrine is wholly

[5] In *Peck v. Commissioner*, 90 T.C. 162, 166–167 (1988), *aff'd*, 904 F.2d 525 (9th Cir. 1990), we set forth five requirements that must be met before application of collateral estoppel in the context of a factual dispute: (1) the issue in the second suit must be identical in all respects with the one decided in the first suit; (2) there must be a final judgment rendered by a court of competent jurisdiction; (3) collateral estoppel may be invoked against parties and their privies to the prior judgment; (4) the parties must actually have litigated the issues and the resolution of these issues must have been essential to the prior decision; and (5) the controlling facts and applicable legal rules must remain unchanged from those in the prior litigation. The opinion of the Court does not discuss these requirements, and it is far from clear whether the first, fourth, and fifth requirements have been met.

inapposite. One of the underlying rationales for preclusion doctrines, such as law of the case, is to prevent litigants from taking the proverbial second bite at the apple. But that is not what the Bedrosians ask of us. They have yet to take their first bite.

II. *The TEFRA Procedures*

I now arrive at section 6231(g)(2), which presents an issue largely of first impression in any court. I thus believe it is appropriate to take a step back and look at how that section fits into the statutory scheme of TEFRA as a whole.

A. *Background*

"TEFRA's design is premised on the conceptual dichotomy of partnership and nonpartnership items."[6] *Rawls Trading, L.P. v. Commissioner*, 138 T.C. at 286. The tax treatment of partnership items must be resolved under the TEFRA procedures at the partnership level. Sec. 6221. The tax treatment of nonpartnership items must be resolved under the normal deficiency procedures at the individual level.[7] *See* secs. 6212(a), 6230(a)(2); *Huff v. Commissioner*, 138 T.C. 258, 263 (2012). The House conference report, H.R. Conf. Rept. No. 97–760, at 611 (1982), 1982–2 C.B. 600, 668, makes these rules explicitly clear:

> Existing rules relating to administrative and judicial proceedings, statutes of limitations, settlements, etc., will continue to govern the deter-

[6] *Compare* sec. 6231(a)(3) (defining the term "partnership item", with respect to a partnership, to mean "any item required to be taken into account for the partnership's taxable year under any provision of subtitle A to the extent regulations prescribed by the Secretary provide that, for purposes of this subtitle, such item is more appropriately determined at the partnership level than at the partner level"), *with* sec. 6231(a)(4) (defining the term "nonpartnership item" to mean "an item which is (or is treated as) not a partnership item").

[7] There is a third category of items within TEFRA called affected items. An affected item, as its name implies, is a nonpartnership item which is affected by a partnership item. Sec. 6231(a)(5). There are two types of affected items: (1) items that require factual determinations to be made at the partner level (factually affected items), and (2) items that require merely a computational adjustment (computationally affected items). *See Petaluma FX Partners, LLC v. Commissioner*, 135 T.C. 581, 595 n.2 (2010). The normal deficiency procedures apply to factually affected items (other than penalties, additions to tax, and additional amounts that relate to adjustments to partnership items). Sec. 6230(a)(2)(A)(i).

mination of a partner's tax liability attributable to nonpartnership income, loss, deductions, and credits. Neither the Secretary nor the taxpayer will be permitted to raise nonpartnership items in the course of a partnership proceeding nor may partnership items, except to the extent they become nonpartnership items under the rules, be raised in proceedings relating to nonpartnership items of a partner.

As the opinion of the Court acknowledges, Congress intended the TEFRA procedures and the normal deficiency procedures to be "mutually exclusive". *See* op. Ct. p. 108; *see also* Internal Revenue Manual (IRM) pt. 4.31.2.1.1(1) (June 1, 2004) ("[T]he TEFRA partnership rules and the deficiency procedures are mutually exclusive."). Merriam Webster's Collegiate Dictionary 768 (10th ed. 1996) defines the term "mutually exclusive" as "being related such that each excludes or precludes the other". In other words, the IRS' choice to audit a partnership return using the TEFRA procedures precludes the IRS from conducting that same audit under the normal deficiency procedures. Likewise, the IRS' choice to audit a partnership return using the normal deficiency procedures precludes the IRS from conducting that same audit under the TEFRA procedures. The rules Congress prescribed require the IRS to choose one, and only one, of the procedures.

However, in this case, like many before it, the IRS has chosen to apply both procedures. This practice has resulted in duplicative audits, confusion among the taxpayers, an unnecessary burden on the court system, and in this case a rare IRS apology to the Court for a lack of consistency and candor.[8] *See* op. Ct. pp. 94–95. That makes this case the appropriate vehicle to start enforcing the rules.

B. *Section 6231(g)(2)*

So how does section 6231(g) fit into this picture? That section was Congress' attempt to address the difficulties faced by the IRS in determining which of the procedures to apply. *See* H.R. Rept. No. 105–148, at 587–588 (1997), 1997–4 C.B. (Vol. 1) 319, 909–910. The IRS' approach was (and still is) to

[8] We note that duplicative audits and litigation were some of the problems Congress sought to resolve in enacting TEFRA. *See Adams v. Johnson*, 355 F.3d 1179, 1186–1187 (9th Cir. 2004); *Maxwell v. Commissioner*, 87 T.C. 783, 787 (1986); H.R. Conf. Rept. No. 97–760, at 599–600 (1982), 1982–2 C.B. 600, 662–663.

disregard the rules and apply both procedures when the IRS is uncertain as to the correct procedures. *See* IRM pt. 4.31.2.1.8(1) (June 20, 2013) ("These key cases are controlled as both TEFRA and nonTEFRA. This is done when it is unclear whether a key case is TEFRA or nonTEFRA to protect the government's interest."). But Congress had a different approach in mind.

Congress' approach was to permit the IRS to rely on a partnership's return and to make that return determinative of the audit procedures to be followed. *See* H.R. Rept. No. 105–148, *supra* at 587–588, 1997–4 C.B. (Vol. 1) at 909–910 ("Partnership return to be determinative of audit procedures to be followed"); *see also* sec. 6231(g) ("Partnership Return To Be Determinative of Whether Subchapter Applies."). If the IRS selects the correct procedures, section 6231(g) does not come into play. If the IRS selects the wrong procedures, but is reasonable in doing so, section 6231(g) treats the wrong procedures as the correct ones. If the IRS acts unreasonably in its determination, it does so at its peril and "possibly jeopardize[s] any assessment". H.R. Rept. No. 105–148, *supra* at 587–588, 1997–4 C.B. (Vol. 1) at 909–910; *see also* IRM pt. 4.31.2.1.1(1) (June 1, 2004) ("If the Service applies the wrong procedures, e.g., erroneously proceeds at the partnership level rather than at the partner level, or vice versa, barred deficiencies and/or refunds can result.").

1. *Determination To Apply the Normal Deficiency Procedures*

The record in this case clearly establishes that the IRS selected the normal deficiency procedures to audit Stone Canyon's return. The very first notice the IRS sent to the Bedrosians in this case was a letter informing them that their Form 1040, U.S. Individual Income Tax Return, for 1999 had been selected for audit. A Form 1040 is an individual income tax return. The letter did not mention that the IRS had commenced, or was even considering, a TEFRA audit of Stone Canyon's return. The IRS enclosed in the letter a standard Form 872, Consent to Extend the Time to Assess Tax, which is used to extend the period of limitations with respect to nonpartnership items as part of an individual-level audit. *See* sec. 6501(c)(4). It does not extend the period of limitations with respect to partnership items or affected items (unless it has been specifically modified for that purpose—and it was not here). *See* sec. 6229(b)(3); *Ginsburg v. Commissioner*, 127 T.C. 75, 87 (2006).

The Bedrosians submitted to the IRS a Form 2848, Power of Attorney and Declaration of Representative, with respect to their individual income tax return for 1999, consistent with their understanding that the IRS had commenced an individual-level audit. At no point during the audit did the IRS request that a Form 2848 be executed for Stone Canyon, the LLC, or the S corporation.[9] Over the course of an audit lasting more than a year and a half, the IRS exchanged multiple communications with the Bedrosians and their POA, including information document requests, proposed settlement agreements (on Forms 870, Waiver of Restrictions on Assessment and Collection of Deficiency in Tax and Acceptance of Overassessment), and proposed audit changes. All of these actions were taken at the individual level.

On brief respondent admits that his "revenue agent erred in soliciting an extension of the limitations period on Forms 872 and in soliciting a settlement agreement on Form 870" but argues with respect to the other events that "the revenue agent focused on Petitioners' individual income tax liability as a matter of practicality in conducting an examination of a Son-of-Boss partnership subject to TEFRA, not because the revenue agent believed that the Partnership was not subject to the TEFRA provisions of the Code."

---

[9] Internal Revenue Manual (IRM) pt. 4.10.3.2.1.1(1) (Mar. 1, 2003) states:

> When a taxpayer obtains representation, the examiner will ensure that the authorization, Form 2848, Power of Attorney (POA), Form 8821, Tax Information Authorization (TIA), or a similar privately designed form, is properly executed. Service personnel are prohibited from disclosing tax information of a confidential nature to any unauthorized person. Upon receipt, the authorization must be date stamped and reviewed to ensure that it contains all required information. * * *

Had the IRS determined that the TEFRA procedures applied to Stone Canyon, the IRS should have at minimum secured a power of attorney from Mr. Bedrosian in his capacity as the sole managing member of the LLC (the TMP of Stone Canyon). *See id.* pt. 4.31.2.2.6(1) (June 20, 2013) ("A TMP may appoint a power of attorney (POA) to represent the partnership before the Service and to perform all acts for the partnership except for the execution of 'legally significant documents'.").

The opinion of the Court goes along with this argument and holds that all of the actions that take place before the issuance of an FPAA or a notice of deficiency are the "give-and-take of an ongoing examination." *See* op. Ct. p. 107. None of them matter. According to the opinion of the Court, the only action that matters for purposes of section 6231(g) is the final notice that concludes an audit. *See id.* at 106–107.

The opinion of the Court's backward-looking approach is contrary to both the statute and the legislative history. Neither the statute nor the legislative history provides any guidance as to the meaning of the phrase "on the basis of a partnership return". *See id.* The opinion of the Court does not attempt to come up with an appropriate definition. Instead, it simply reads this phrase out of the statute on the ground that "[l]ooking behind the notice is disfavored."[10] *See id.* at 108.

Under the opinion of the Court's approach, if the IRS issues an FPAA at the end of a partnership audit, then the IRS is said to have made a determination to apply the TEFRA procedures for purposes of section 6231(g), and vice versa, regardless of which procedures the IRS actually used throughout the audit. It matters not to the opinion of the Court whether the IRS even consulted the partnership's return. Such an approach is contrary to the basic principle of statutory construction that all words of a statute are to be given meaning. *See Market Co. v. Hoffman*, 101 U.S. 112, 115 (1879) ("It is a cardinal rule of statutory construction that significance and effect shall, if possible, be accorded to every word.").

This approach would also render meaningless any distinction between the TEFRA procedures and the normal deficiency procedures with respect to an audit. The legislative history to the statute is clear that a partnership's return is to be determinative of the *audit* procedures the IRS is to

---

[10] We note that there are exceptions to the rule that we generally do not look behind a notice of deficiency. An exception applies, for example, where there is "substantial evidence of unconstitutional conduct on respondent's part". *See Greenberg's Express, Inc. v. Commissioner*, 62 T.C. 324, 328 (1974). We believe that another exception is appropriate for purposes of sec. 6231(g) because the statute and the legislative history specifically speak to the audit procedures to be followed by the IRS. *See infra* p. 131.

apply. *See* H.R. Rept. No. 105–148, *supra* at 587–588, 1997–4 C.B. (Vol. 1) at 909–910. Similarly, the heading of the statute states that a "[p]artnership return [is] to be determinative of whether subchapter applies." Sec. 6231(g). The subchapter in question is subchapter C of chapter 63, otherwise known as the "unified partnership *audit* and litigation procedures of the Tax Equity and Fiscal Responsibility Act of 1982 (TEFRA)". *Rawls Trading, L.P. v. Commissioner*, 138 T.C. at 272 (emphasis added).

If, as the opinion of the Court contends, the IRS does not make its determination until it issues an FPAA or a notice of deficiency, then the determination, even if made on the basis of a partnership's return, would have no bearing on the audit procedures the IRS is to apply. An FPAA and a notice of deficiency are the final notices that conclude an audit. The opinion of the Court's reading of the statute would turn it into a provision that speaks solely to the proper litigation procedures going forward. This is simply not a logical construction of the statute. *See United States v. Koyomejian*, 946 F.2d 1450, 1458 (9th Cir. 1991) ("The role of the courts is to give legislative enactments a sensible and logical construction whenever it is possible to do so through the use of ordinary tools of reasoning and statutory construction, rather than to adopt a sterile and unreasonable interpretation that Congress itself would clearly find unacceptable.").

I believe that Congress intended the IRS to make its determination at the outset of an audit by examining a partnership's return and the attached Schedules K–1, Partner's Share of Income, Credits, Deductions, etc. This Court reached the same conclusion in *Harrell v. Commissioner*, 91 T.C. 242 (1988),[11] for purposes of two very similar TEFRA provisions. The issue in *Harrell* was how to apply the now-repealed same share rule of the small partnership exception. The same share rule was satisfied if "each partner's share of each partnership item * * * [was] the same as his share of every other item." Sec. 6231(a)(1)(B)(i)(II) (1982). We held in *Harrell v. Commissioner*, 91 T.C. at 246:

---

[11] *Z-Tron Computer Research & Dev. Program v. Commissioner*, 91 T.C. 258 (1988), is a companion case to *Harrell* and was filed on the same day.

> [F]or purposes of determining whether a partnership is a small partnership and whether the same share rule is satisfied, the test should be applied by determining whether the partnership reported more than one partnership item for the year and, if so, how those items were shared by each partner. *This determination should be made by respondent as of the date of commencement of the audit of the partnership (but not necessarily on that date) by examining the partnership return and the corresponding Schedules K–1, and any amendments thereto received prior to this date.* [Emphasis added.]

In reaching our holding in *Harrell*, we looked at the purpose of the small partnership exception in the context of TEFRA as a whole. We explained that the small partnership exception "serves the limited purpose of determining to whom to issue a statutory notice or whether to issue an FPAA". *Id.* at 247. Because of that, and for the sake of judicial economy, we would not for purposes of the same share rule "permit a partner or representative of a partnership or respondent to claim a result other than that identified in the return and Schedules K–1 as filed and amended prior to the date of commencement of the partnership audit." *Id.* We reasoned that "relying on the partnership returns and accompanying Schedules K–1" would minimize "the extent to which respondent must interpret the partnership agreement each year", *id.* at 248, and we concluded that said approach "best serves the purpose of simplicity that is behind the partnership audit and litigation provisions", *id.*

We also looked at section 6233, which prescribes in general that where an entity files a return as a partnership, it will be subject to the TEFRA procedures even though it is later determined that the putative partnership is not a partnership for tax purposes. We found that for purposes of section 6233 "Congress mandated that the information on the tax return would be determinative of the procedures to be followed, even if the underlying facts later prove the return to be incorrect." *Id.* We concluded that the approach in *Harrell* with respect to the same share rule was "totally consistent with the approach mandated by Congress in section 6233, i.e., *making the determination regarding the application of the TEFRA procedures on the basis of the partnership information return.*" *Id.* (emphasis added).

I believe that Congress intended the approach in *Harrell* to apply for purposes of section 6231(g). Section 6231(g) is similar to section 6231(a)(1)(B)(i)(II) (1982) (i.e., the same share rule of the small partnership exception) and section 6233, discussed above, in that all three provisions revolve around the IRS' selection of either the TEFRA procedures or the normal deficiency procedures by which to audit a partnership return. Moreover, for all three provisions, Congress sought to make the information on a partnership's return determinative of the audit procedures the IRS is to apply.

Unlike the opinion of the Court's approach, the *Harrell* approach gives effect to the phrase "on the basis of a partnership return". Moreover, the IRS' determination would actually govern the procedures to be used throughout the audit, as Congress had intended. And under the *Harrell* approach, there is no question that the IRS made a determination, on the basis of Stone Canyon's return, to apply the normal deficiency procedures. *See supra* pp. 128–129; *see also* op. Ct. p. 107 ("Undoubtedly, the IRS initially treated the examination underlying this case as though it was not a TEFRA examination.").

2. *Reasonableness*

The second half of the inquiry under section 6231(g)(2) is one of reasonableness. The statute applies only if the IRS' determination to follow the normal deficiency procedures was reasonable. The opinion of the Court holds that "the only reasonable conclusion is that TEFRA applies to Stone Canyon." *See* op. Ct. p. 111. The opinion of the Court acknowledges all of the inconsistencies on Stone Canyon's return, but chooses to disregard them, looking solely at the attached Schedules K–1. *Id.* The opinion of the Court also chooses to disregard the IRS' lack of candor in this case, calling it a "sideshow". *Id.* pp. 94–95. I do not dismiss such conduct so lightly, especially where, as here, it has a direct bearing on one of the issues in this case—the question of reasonableness.

On December 1, 2004, during the audit, the IRS' revenue agent participated in a conference call with IRS Office of Chief Counsel attorneys and the IRS Son-of-BOSS TEFRA coordinator. The revenue agent filed an affidavit in this case claiming that she wanted to discuss "how to proceed with this case in order to disallow the net operating loss carryforward deductions claimed on Petitioners' Form 1040 for the 2000 tax year, in view of * * * [her] determination that the limitations period for issuing a notice of final partnership administrative adjustment (FPAA) for the 1999 tax year had expired." The revenue agent explains in her affidavit that two months later, the TEFRA coordinator advised her that the IRS should issue an FPAA for 1999 in order to disallow the NOL carryforward deduction for 2000.

Actually, though, the IRS wanted to disallow a $17 million loss deduction on the Bedrosians' 1999 return, an amount that dwarfs the approximately $80,000 NOL carryforward deduction in comparison. The problem was that the IRS had been using the wrong audit procedures for more than a year and had allowed the correct period of limitations to lapse. [12]

On February 1, 2005, approximately a year and a half into the audit, the IRS' revenue agent called the Bedrosians' POA and told her that the IRS would soon issue an NBAP for 1999. The POA inquired as to why the IRS would issue an NBAP (a partnership-level notice) when the IRS was in the process of issuing audit reports with respect to the Bedrosians' individual income tax return for 1999. The revenue agent responded that "the NBAP was procedural and that the TEFRA examination would be 'opened and shut'." The POA in all likelihood had no idea what the revenue agent meant by that.

The very next day the revenue agent mailed the NBAP to the Bedrosians but not to their POA. The revenue agent instead mailed the POA proposed individual audit reports for 1999. Approximately two weeks later, the POA mailed the revenue agent a letter stating that the Bedrosians had forwarded the NBAP to her and inquiring whether the revenue agent needed, among other things, executed Forms 2848 for Stone Canyon, the LLC, and the S corporation. The revenue agent received the POA's letter but decided not to respond to it. [13] The following month, though, the revenue agent mailed the POA finalized audit reports making adjustments at the individual level.

In April 2005 the IRS issued an FPAA and a notice of deficiency separated by only 11 days. [14] The IRS disallowed the

[12] The general three-year periods of limitations under secs. 6229(a) and 6501(a) had both expired.

[13] The POA's letter was stamped "received" on February 22, 2005, by the IRS office in which the revenue agent worked.

[14] Both notices were actually drafted on the same day.

$17 million loss deduction for 1999 in the FPAA and in the notice of deficiency, the former at the partnership level and the latter at the individual level. The IRS knew or should have known that it was not proper to disallow this exact same loss deduction in both notices. *See* H.R. Conf. Rept. No. 97–760, *supra* at 611, 1982–2 C.B. at 668. In August 2005 the IRS assessed, and the Bedrosians paid, more than $4 million in tax and interest as a result of the $17 million loss deduction adjustment.

On October 19, 2006, at a hearing over which I presided, I asked respondent's counsel why the IRS had issued a notice of deficiency 11 days after it had issued an FPAA. Respondent's counsel offered three reasons. First, the $17 million loss was incurred at the level of the S corporation and not the partnership. Second, the characterization of the transaction fees was not clear. And the third reason offered by respondent's counsel was as follows:

> I think significantly, Your Honor, on the taxpayers' 1065, Form 1065, Schedule B, Question 4, 'Is this partnership subject to the consolidated audit procedures of Section 6221 through 6233?' Answer, 'No.' They put on their return that they weren't subject to the TEFRA procedures.

So it seemed, at least in part, that the IRS followed both procedures in the audit because it was not clear, on the basis of Stone Canyon's partnership return, which of the procedures was the correct one.

At a September 21, 2010, hearing before Chief Special Trial Judge Peter J. Panuthos, counsel for respondent made this point explicitly clear:

> The difficulty with the situation as the Service saw it was that the partnership return, on the partnership return when asked if this was a TEFRA partnership it had been marked no this was not a TEFRA partnership. Therefore, given the fact that also there was a TMP appointed, the Service did not quite have a complete handle on whether or not this was a TEFRA partnership, so they are caught between a rock and a hard place.

Then on September 20, 2012, in respondent's objection to Chief Special Trial Judge Panuthos' recommended findings of fact and conclusions of law, respondent's counsel once again affirmed:

> Respondent was unsure at the time the notice of deficiency was issued, whether the partnership was subject to the Code's TEFRA partnership

procedures and, if subject to the TEFRA procedures, whether certain items would be regarded by the Court as partnership items or affected items. Indeed, Mr. Bedrosian signed the partnership's Form 1065, on which a box was checked stating that the partnership was not subject to the TEFRA partnership procedures.

After the Court brought section 6231(g)(2) to the parties' attention, respondent changed his position. The uncertainties surrounding Stone Canyon's partnership return disappeared. On brief, respondent explained his new position as follows:

> [S]ince the information reported on the partnership return shows that both partners in the partnership were pass-thru partners, the small partnership exception does not apply to the partnership. Therefore, based on the partnership return, * * * [the IRS] could have reasonably determined only that the partnership was subject to the TEFRA partnership provisions.

Stone Canyon's representation that it was not subject to the TEFRA procedures no longer seemed to matter. In fact, respondent suggested on brief that the IRS might not have even considered it:

> The statement on the subject partnership return that the partnership taxable year is not subject to the TEFRA procedures cannot, in context, serve as evidence that * * * [the IRS] made a reasonable determination, on the basis of the partnership return, that the TEFRA procedures do not apply. While * * * [the IRS] could have considered such a statement in making * * * [its] determination, there is no authority for binding * * * [the IRS] to such a statement when the partnership return also provided a statement that there was at least one pass-thru partner.

Then, in respondent's response to petitioners' allegations of fraud (i.e., respondent's apology to the Court), respondent made the bold claim:

> Respondent has consistently taken the position that * * * [the] Stone Canyon Partnership is subject to the TEFRA provisions of the Code.

Needless to say, respondent's claim is simply not true.

In short, the IRS has been less than open and candid with both the Bedrosians and this Court. The opinion of the Court concludes that the IRS' conduct has no bearing on the outcome of this case. The opinion of the Court contends that "the Schedules K–1 that were included with and are part of the partnership return make it clear that the partnership must have been subject to TEFRA as a matter of law" and that "the only reasonable conclusion is that TEFRA applies to Stone Canyon." *See* op. Ct. p. 111. I respectfully disagree.

I do not believe the opinion of the Court's bright-line test is appropriate. The opinion of the Court seems to mistakenly equate the term "reasonable" with the term "correct". If every incorrect determination were also found to be unreasonable, then section 6231(g)(2) would serve no purpose. Section 6231(g)(2), by its terms, applies only if a determination is both incorrect and reasonable. I believe the question of reasonableness is most appropriately determined under *all* of the facts and circumstances. *See, e.g., Pac. Grains, Inc. v. Commissioner*, 399 F.2d 603, 606 (9th Cir. 1968) (stating that the reasonableness of compensation is a question of fact to be determined on the basis of all the facts and circumstances), *aff'g* T.C. Memo. 1967–7; *Patel v. Commissioner*, 138 T.C. 395, 417 (2012) (stating that reasonable cause and good faith are determined on a case-by-case basis, taking into account all pertinent facts and circumstances); *Price v. Commissioner*, 102 T.C. 660, 662 (1994) (stating that for purposes of an award of litigation costs, the determination of the reasonableness of the Commissioner's position is based on all the facts and circumstances), *aff'd without published opinion sub nom. TSA/Stanford Assocs., Inc. v. Commissioner*, 77 F.3d 490 (9th Cir. 1996); *Montgomery v. Commissioner*, 65 T.C. 511, 519 (1975) (stating that the existence of a reasonable prospect of recovery depends on the facts and circumstances); *Carithers-Wallace-Courtenay v. Commissioner*, 5 T.C. 942, 945 (1945) (stating that the reasonableness of an addition for a bad debt reserve depends upon the facts and circumstances); *EMI Corp. v. Commissioner*, T.C. Memo. 1985–386 (stating that whether a corporation's accumulation of earnings for a contingent liability is reasonable depends upon all the facts and circumstances).

When I look at all of the facts and circumstances of this case, there is no question in my mind that a determination to apply the normal deficiency procedures on the basis of Stone Canyon's return would be reasonable. The information on Stone Canyon's Form 1065, U.S. Partnership Return of Income, for 1999, including the attached Schedules K–1, was confusing and contradictory. As even the opinion of the Court points out, the return "contained conflicting and necessarily erroneous information." *See* op. Ct. p. 111.

Stone Canyon expressly reported that it was not subject to the TEFRA procedures, and yet it designated a TMP, which exists only in the world of TEFRA partnerships. Stone Canyon attached a Schedule K–1 to its return listing an LLC as one of its partners. However, Stone Canyon identified the LLC as an "INDIVIDUAL", which would not be a pass-through partner. *See* sec. 6231(a)(9). The opinion of the Court brushes aside these inconsistencies and places all of its reliance on a second Schedule K–1 in which Stone Canyon identified its other partner as an "S CORPORATION". How could one know, looking solely at the partnership return, whether this information was not also incorrect?

The information on Stone Canyon's return was plainly unreliable. I fail to see why Stone Canyon's representation that it was not subject to TEFRA is any less credible, and entitled to any less reliance, than the other information on the return. The statements respondent's counsel made to this Court in 2006, 2010, and 2012 clearly indicate that the IRS relied on Stone Canyon's representation. To impose upon the IRS an affirmative duty to seek out additional information from Stone Canyon or its partners for the sole purpose of discerning what information on the return was correct so that the IRS could apply the correct procedures in the audit would undercut the very purpose of section 6231(g). I believe that it would be reasonable for the IRS to apply either the normal deficiency procedures or the TEFRA procedures on the basis of the return.

My conclusion is bolstered by the Court of Appeals for the Seventh Circuit's opinion in *Cole v. Commissioner*, 637 F.3d 767 (7th Cir. 2011), *aff'g* T.C. Memo. 2010–31. In that case, the taxpayer husband incorrectly represented on a Form 1065 that an LLC (taxed as a partnership) owned by him, his wife, and his wife's family trust was not subject to the TEFRA procedures.[15] *Id.* at 770, 779. The taxpayers argued on appeal that the Tax Court erred in taking jurisdiction over the items originating from the LLC because the IRS failed to apply the TEFRA procedures to the LLC. *Id.* at 779.

[15] A trust, like an S corporation, is a passthrough partner. *See* sec. 6231(a)(9).

The Court of Appeals summarily dismissed the taxpayers' argument, finding that the taxpayers' attempt to raise TEFRA, when the taxpayer husband expressly stated that the LLC was not subject to TEFRA, was "misguided". *Id.*

3. *Whether Section 6231(g)(2) Confers Jurisdiction*

I would find that all three requirements of section 6231(g)(2) have been met in this case: (1) the IRS made a determination to follow the normal deficiency procedures on the basis of Stone Canyon's return; (2) it was reasonable for the IRS to do so; and (3) the determination turned out to be erroneous. Where, as here, the requirements of the statute are met, "the provisions of this subchapter shall not apply to such partnership (and its items) for such taxable year or to partners of such partnership". The statute should be construed to mean exactly what it says and the conclusion here should be: The TEFRA procedures do not apply to Stone Canyon and its partners for 1999. *See Conn. Nat'l Bank v. Germain*, 503 U.S. 249, 253–254 (1992) ("[C]ourts must presume that a legislature says in a statute what it means and means in a statute what it says there.").

Consequently, Stone Canyon would be treated as though it were subject solely to the normal deficiency procedures for 1999. Therefore, there would be no distinction between partnership items, nonpartnership items, and affected items of Stone Canyon. *See* sec. 6231(a)(3), (4) and (5). Nor would any items of Stone Canyon be properly determinable in a partnership-level proceeding. *See* sec. 6221. Instead, all items of Stone Canyon would be taken into account by the partners of Stone Canyon in accordance with their distributive shares, *see* secs. 701–704, and would be properly determinable on a partner-by-partner basis at the individual level, *see* sec. 6212. And that is exactly how the IRS audited and adjusted Stone Canyon's items in this case. I would hold that this Court has jurisdiction over all of the items in the notice of deficiency through the application of section 6231(g)(2).

III. *Conclusion*

The IRS' conduct in this case led both the Bedrosians and this Court down the wrong path. This Division of the Court issued the opinion in this case and the two related cases. At the time we knew little of what happened during the audit.

There had never been a trial in this case. Fortunately, neither the law of the case doctrine nor any other judicial doctrine of which I am aware prevents this Court from reaching the right result in the end. I do not know whether the Bedrosians are entitled to any of the loss deductions they claimed, but I wholeheartedly believe they are entitled to their day in court to make their case.

Judge Halpern writes in his concurring opinion that the Bedrosians missed their opportunity to have their day in court by failing to timely petition in response to the FPAA. *See* Halpern op. p. 116. Judge Halpern overlooks the fact that the IRS led the Bedrosians to believe that the April 19, 2005, notice of deficiency, in response to which they filed a timely petition, was the appropriate notice. It is the IRS, and not the taxpayer, that chooses audit procedures. In this case, the IRS chose the normal deficiency procedures and applied those procedures, and only those procedures, for approximately a year and a half. But at that late stage of the audit, the IRS changed course in an attempt to gain an unfair advantage over the Bedrosians. The IRS began a partnership-level audit, allegedly to disallow NOL carryforward deductions on the Bedrosians' Form 1040 for 2000, and told the Bedrosians' POA that said audit would be "opened and shut". All the while, the IRS continued to examine Stone Canyon at the individual level until the very last day of the audit. I would hold that section 6231(g)(2) applies to treat this case exactly as the IRS treated it from the outset—as an individual deficiency case.

Because the interests of substantial justice so require, I respectfully dissent.

THORNTON, COLVIN, and FOLEY, *JJ.*, agree with this dissent.

PARIMAL H. SHANKAR AND MALTI S. TRIVEDI, PETITIONERS *v.* COMMISSIONER OF INTERNAL REVENUE, RESPONDENT

Docket No. 24414–12. Filed August 26, 2014.

R disallowed Ps' deduction for contributions to their IRAs, which Ps claim are deductible because the limitations on deductibility either do not apply or are unconstitutional. R also included in Ps' gross income the value of an airline ticket that P–H received by redeeming "thank you" award points that P–H claims he never received. R also redetermined Ps' alternative minimum tax.

1. *Held*: Ps are not entitled to a deduction for IRA contributions because P–W is an "active participant" in an employer-sponsored retirement plan and Ps' combined modified adjusted gross income is above the phaseout ceiling.

2. *Held*, *further*, Ps must include in their gross income the value of the airline ticket received in redemption of "thank you" award points.

3. *Held*, *further*, AMT to be redetermined.

Parimal H. Shankar and Malti S. Trivedi, pro sese.
Lydia A. Branche and *Marco Franco*, for respondent.

HALPERN, *Judge*: Respondent determined a deficiency of $563 in petitioners' 2009 Federal income tax. The deficiency resulted principally from respondent's making the following adjustments to petitioners' reported 2009 tax. Respondent increased petitioners' gross income by $668 on account of that amount's being reported by Citibank, N.A. (Citibank), as the value of 50,000 "Thank You Points" (thank you points) petitioner husband (Mr. Shankar) redeemed in 2009 to purchase an airline ticket. Respondent disallowed petitioners' deduction of $11,000 reflecting their contributions of that sum under a qualified retirement arrangement (IRA). Respondent disallowed the deduction because petitioners' modified adjusted gross income (modified AGI) for 2009 exceeded the statutorily imposed ceiling for such contributions. Respondent reduced petitioners' alternative minimum tax (AMT) from $2,775 to zero. Respondent did not explain that last adjustment. By amendment to answer, respondent increased his claim of a deficiency to $6,883 on account of his recomputation of petitioners' 2009 AMT.

Unless otherwise indicated, all section references are to the Internal Revenue Code of 1986, as amended and in effect for 2009, and all Rule references are to the Tax Court Rules of Practice and Procedure. We round all dollar amounts to the nearest dollar.

FINDINGS OF FACT

Introduction

Petitioners, husband and wife, resided in New Jersey when they filed the petition.

Petitioners' Reported Income and Tax Return

For 2009, petitioners filed a joint Federal income tax return on Form 1040, U.S. Individual Income Tax Return.

During 2009, Mr. Shankar was a self-employed consultant who reported his self-employment income on Schedule C, Profit or Loss From Business, attached to the Form 1040.

During 2009, petitioner wife (Ms. Trivedi) was employed by University Group Medical Associates, PC (Associates). In addition to paying her a taxable salary, which she reported, Associates made contributions on her behalf to an annuity purchase plan described in section 403(b), which she was not required to report as an item of gross income. Ms. Trivedi also earned self-employment income, which she reported on a second Schedule C attached to the Form 1040.

Petitioners claimed a deduction of $11,000 for IRA contributions made in 2009.

They reported AGI of $243,729.

They also reported alternative minimum taxable income of $235,487 and AMT of $2,775.

Thank You Points

During 2009, Mr. Shankar banked at Citibank. Citibank reported to Mr. Shankar and to the Internal Revenue Service on a 2009 Form 1099–MISC, Miscellaneous Income, "Other income" of $668. Petitioners did not report the income shown on the 2009 Form 1099–MISC on the Form 1040. At trial, in order to show that the 2009 Form 1099–MISC properly and accurately reported the income shown thereon, respondent introduced into evidence as a business record the affidavit of Marilyn Kennedy, a duly authorized custodian of records for Citibank. Attached to the affidavit are documents and computer transcripts from Citibank showing that Mr. Shankar redeemed 50,000 thank you points on February 27, 2009, to purchase a restricted coach class airline ticket for travel in the lower 48 United States, Alaska, and Canada. Also attached to the affidavit is a letter from Ms. Kennedy, in which she, as the custodian of records for Citibank, represents that the fair market value of the airline ticket was $668. Respondent provided the affidavit and attachments to petitioners on September 9, 2013. Trial in this case was held on December 2, 2013.

Respondent's Adjustments

Respondent's adjustments are as described above.

OPINION

I. *IRA Contribution Deduction*

A. *Introduction*

Respondent disallowed petitioners' claimed IRA contribution deduction because he believes that the $11,000 petitioners contributed is in excess of the amount allowed for such deductions by section 219(g) ("Limitation on Deduction for Active Participants in Certain Pension Plans."), described *supra*. At trial, Mr. Shankar did not dispute the application of section 219(g); he argued only that it is unconstitutional. On brief, he suggests that the section 219(g) limitation on the deductibility of contributions to an IRA is inapplicable because Ms. Trivedi was not an "active participant" in a qualified retirement plan.

B. *Section 219*

In general, a taxpayer is entitled to deduct amounts that the taxpayer contributes to an IRA for the taxable year. *See* sec. 219(a). The deduction may not exceed the lesser of (1) the deductible amount, which was generally $5,000 for 2009, or (2) an amount equal to the compensation includible in the taxpayer's gross income for such taxable year. Sec. 219(b)(1), (5)(A). The $5,000 limitation is increased to $6,000 for a taxpayer who has attained the age of 50 before the close of the taxable year. *See* sec. 219(b)(5)(B).

The deductible amount allowed under section 219(a) may be further limited if the taxpayer or the taxpayer's spouse is "an active participant" during any part of the year. Sec. 219(g)(1), (5). For purposes of section 219(g), an active participant means, among others, an individual who actively participates in an annuity contract described in section 403(b). *See* sec. 219(g)(5)(A)(iv).

For a taxpayer who is an active participant and files a joint return, section 219(g)(2)(A)(ii) provides that the dollar amount of the allowable deduction under section 219(a) is phased out over a $20,000 range of AGI determined with certain modifications (i.e., modified AGI) beginning at the "applicable dollar amount." Section 219(g)(3)(A)(ii) provides, in part, that the individual's modified AGI is determined without regard to the IRA contribution deduction under section 219. For 2009 the applicable dollar amount at which the phaseout begins for a married taxpayer filing a joint return is the taxpayers' combined modified AGI of $89,000.[1] Notice 2008–102, 2008–45 I.R.B. 1106. Consequently, for 2009 the IRA contribution deduction is completely phased out for a married taxpayer who is an active participant and who files a joint return when the taxpayers' combined modified AGI exceeds $109,000.

For a married taxpayer filing a joint return who is not an active participant but who is the spouse of an active participant, section 219(g)(7) provides that the dollar amount of the allowable deduction under section 219(a) is phased out over a $10,000 range of combined modified AGI beginning at the applicable dollar amount for such taxpayers. For 2009, the applicable dollar amount for such a taxpayer is $166,000. Notice 2008–102, 2008–45 I.R.B. at 1107. That provision results in a total disallowance of the deduction whenever the spouses' combined modified AGI exceeds $176,000.

C. *Analysis and Conclusion*

Petitioners' 2009 modified AGI was $255,397 (AGI of $243,729 plus (1) an addback of an $11,000 IRA contribution deduction and (2) $668 of unreported income, *see infra*). Therefore, because (1) Ms. Trivedi was an active participant in a section 403(b) retirement plan provided to her by her employer as described under section 219(g)(5)(A)(iv), and (2)

[1] In applying the sec. 219(g) limitations, the Court will look to the combined modified AGI of married taxpayers filing jointly and not to an individual spouse's modified AGI to determine the reduction or elimination of the IRA contribution deduction. *See, e.g., Ho v. Commissioner*, T.C. Memo. 2005–133, 2005 WL 1314196, at *2; *Wade v. Commissioner*, T.C. Memo. 2001–114, 2001 WL 505210, at *2.

petitioners' 2009 combined modified AGI exceeds the section 219(g)(2) and (7) threshold and phaseout amounts, section 219(g) does apply to deny petitioners any 2009 deduction for contributions to an IRA. Petitioners' statutory arguments to the contrary are without basis.

Petitioners additionally argue that section 219 is unconstitutional because it discriminates against self-employed individuals who contribute to IRAs by imposing restrictions on IRA contribution deductions that do not apply to tax benefits afforded to participants in other types of retirement plans. Petitioners' argument is, essentially, that, because the statute treats individuals who file joint returns with active participants in a retirement plan differently from those who are not so described, the statute is discriminatory and, therefore, unconstitutional, presumably, in violation of the Equal Protection Clause. It is unclear whether petitioners believe that the statute is unconstitutional because it discriminates against Ms. Trivedi, Mr. Shankar, or both. If they are arguing that it discriminates against Ms. Trivedi who is herself an active participant in a qualified retirement plan, this Court considered that exact argument in *Guest v. Commissioner*, 72 T.C. 768, 775–778 (1979), and rejected it. There we held that, because the classification in section 219(b)(2) that differentiated between active participants in retirement plans and nonparticipants in retirement plans did not involve a fundamental right or a suspect category, it was constitutional if the classification had a reasonable basis. *Id.* at 776. Examining the legislative history in enacting deductions for IRA contributions, we determined that the reasonable basis was Congress' intent to make available "'a special deduction for amounts set aside for retirement by employees who are not covered under a qualified plan * * *, a government plan, or a tax exempt organization annuity plan (sec. 403(b)).'" *Id.* at 773 (quoting H.R. Rept. No. 93–807, at 126 (1974), 1974–3 C.B. (Supp.) 236, 361).

If petitioners are arguing that the statute discriminates against Mr. Shankar, who is not himself an active participant but who is married to an active participant, we also disagree. Although it is not precisely the same issue we addressed in *Guest*, the framework for the analysis remains the same. The limitation on the deductibility of IRA contributions by one who files a joint return with an active participant in a qualified retirement plan does not involve a fundamental right or suspect category and is, therefore, constitutional if the classification is reasonable and has a rational relationship to the purpose of the legislation. *Keeler v. Commissioner*, 70 T.C. 279, 285 (1978). In 1986, Congress reinstated restrictions on active participants contributing to IRAs that, in 1981, it had eliminated. *See* S. Rept. No. 99–313, at 542 (1986), 1986–3 C.B. (Vol. 3) 1, 542 (accompanying H.R. 3838, 99th Cong. (1985), enacted as the Tax Reform Act of 1986, Pub. L. No. 99–514, 100 Stat. 2085). The Committee on Finance explained the reinstatement of the restrictions as follows:

> [M]any employees of tax-exempt organizations are permitted to make significant elective deferrals under tax-sheltered annuity programs. The committee believes that the wide availability of the option to make elective deferrals under cash or deferred arrangements and tax-sheltered annuities reduces the prior concern that individuals in employer-maintained plans should be able to save additional amounts for retirement on a discretionary basis. [*Id.*]

We deem it reasonable to extend the foregoing rationale as a basis for limiting or denying an IRA contribution deduction to an individual where his or her spouse is an active participant. Whether the individual or the spouse (or each) is an active participant, the economic family unit has the ability to save in a tax-favored manner as much as Congress thinks proper through active participation in an employer-sponsored plan (or plans) and to the extent IRA contribution deductions are allowed. Although petitioners find themselves on the "wrong" side of the line Congress has drawn, they have not shown the slightest foundation for their constitutional attack on Congress' drawing of that line. Therefore, as in *Guest*, we reject petitioners' argument challenging the constitutionality of the deduction disallowance provision.

II. *Unreported Income*

Respondent increased petitioners' gross income by $668 on account of that amount's being reported as "Other income" on the 2009 Form 1099–MISC. Petitioners deny receipt of the income shown on the 2009 Form 1099–MISC. In general, the taxpayer bears the burden of proving facts to support his assignments of error to the Commissioner's determination of a deficiency. *See* Rule 142(a). Pursuant to section 6201(d), however, if, in any court proceeding, a taxpayer asserts a reasonable dispute with respect to the income reported on an information return and the taxpayer has fully cooperated with the Commissioner, then the Commissioner has the burden of producing reasonable and probative information in addition to the information return.

Because respondent has by way of Ms. Kennedy's affidavit and its attachments provided reasonable and probative information in addition to the information reported on the 2009 Form 1099–MISC that, during 2009, Mr. Shankar received from Citibank other income of $668, we need not consider whether he reasonably disputes that report or that he has fully cooperated with respondent. Respondent has carried any burden imposed on him by section 6201(d). Indeed, in carrying that burden, respondent has provided us with evidence in the form of Citibank records (i.e., computer transcripts) showing that, on February 27, 2009, Mr. Shankar redeemed 50,000 thank you points to purchase a restricted coach class airline ticket. Contradicting that evidence we have only Mr. Shankar's testimony that, in effect, he knows nothing about any thank you points and received no award. Petitioners had ample time between their receipt of the Citibank records on September 9, 2013, and the trial of this case on December 2, 2013, to investigate the information provided in the Citibank records and to show to us that it was in error. They did not do so. Ms. Trivedi did not appear at trial, so we do not have the benefit of her view of whether Mr. Shankar received the award. On balance, we give more weight to Citibank's records showing Mr. Shankar's receipt of an award than we do to his testimony to the contrary, and we find that he did in 2009 receive from Citibank in redemption of 50,000 thank you points a restricted coach class airline ticket. There are still the questions of whether receipt of the airline ticket constituted receipt of an item of gross income and, if so, its value.

Section 61(a) defines the term "gross income" to include "all income from whatever source derived". The term has been broadly interpreted. *See, e.g., Commissioner v. Glenshaw Glass Co.*, 348 U.S. 426, 431 (1955) (gross income includes "instances of undeniable accessions to wealth, clearly realized, and over which the taxpayers have complete dominion"). We are not here dealing with the taxability of frequent flyer miles attributable to business or official travel, with respect to which the Commissioner stated in Announcement 2002–18, 2002–1 C.B. 621, he would not assert that a taxpayer has gross income because he received or used frequent flyer miles attributable to business travel. Petitioners have provided us with no information concerning the reason Citibank awarded Mr. Shankar thank you points. Mr. Shankar did not object when, at the start of the trial in this case, respondent's counsel answered in the affirmative the Court's question as to whether, besides the IRA contribution, the other item in dispute, i.e., "Other income", involved the omission from the Form 1040 of interest. Respondent's counsel added that the omitted income was a noncash award for opening a bank account. We proceed on the assumption that we are dealing here with a premium for making a deposit into, or maintaining a balance in, a bank account. In other words, something given in exchange for the use (deposit) of Mr. Shankar's money; i.e., something in the nature of interest. In general, the receipt of interest constitutes the receipt of an item of gross income. *See* sec. 61(a)(4). Receipt of the airline ticket constituted receipt of an item of gross income, and petitioners have failed to show that it was worth any less than $668, which Citibank, which had purchased the ticket, said was its fair market value.[2] *But cf. Turner v. Commissioner*, T.C. Memo. 1954–38 (in which we determined that the "proper fair figure" to be included in the taxpayers' gross income on account of the taxpayer husband's winning steamship tickets on a radio quiz show was substantially less than the tickets' retail price because the tickets' value to the taxpayers was not equal to their retail cost). On account of Mr. Shankar's receipt of the airline ticket, petitioners omitted $668 of gross income from the Form 1040.

III. *Alternative Minimum Tax*

Petitioners reported on the Form 1040 an AMT of $2,775. Without explanation, respondent reversed that tax as part of his adjustments. By amendment to answer, respondent avers that petitioners' 2009 AMT is $6,320. By raising a new matter, respondent has the burden of proving that his AMT

[2] Neither party has addressed, nor do we consider, whether award of the thank you points, itself, may have been the taxable event.

adjustment is correct. *See* Rule 142(a)(1). Respondent explains that, in determining the deficiency in petitioners' 2009 Federal income tax, he made a computational error in computing petitioners' AMT. Since petitioners reported a 2009 AMT and they have furnished no evidence to controvert respondent's explanation of his computational error, we are satisfied that they are liable for the AMT for 2009. We will enter decision under Rule 155. Any dispute as to the correct calculation of the AMT can be raised in the Rule 155 computation.

IV. *Conclusion*

We sustain respondent's adjustments underlying his determination of a deficiency in tax.

Decision will be entered under Rule 155.

G. Douglas Barkett and Rita M. Barkett, Petitioners *v.* Commissioner of Internal Revenue, Respondent

Docket No. 28223–12. Filed August 28, 2014.

R issued a notice of deficiency concerning Ps' Federal income tax for taxable years 2006 to 2009. R sent the notice more than three years but less than six years after Ps filed their 2006 and 2007 returns. Ps argue under I.R.C. sec. 6501(a) that the notice is invalid as it relates to 2006 and 2007 because R sent it more than three years after they filed their returns for those years. R contends that the six-year limitations period under I.R.C. sec. 6501(e) applies because Ps' omitted gross income exceeded 25% of the gross income they stated in their returns. On their 2006 and 2007 returns Ps reported amounts realized from the sale of investments of more than $7 million and $4 million, respectively, and total gains from such sales of approximately $123,000 and $314,000, respectively. Ps argue that the amounts they realized, not their gains, should be included in "gross income they stated in their return" for purposes of I.R.C. sec. 6501(e). R contends that only their gains should be included. Our resolution of this dispute will determine the appropriate limitations period. We have held in other cases that gross income includes only a taxpayer's gains from the sale of investment property, not the taxpayer's entire amounts realized from such sales. Ps argue that those cases are inconsistent with the Supreme Court's recent decision in *United States v. Home*

Concrete & Supply, LLC, 566 U.S. ___, ___, 132 S. Ct. 1836, 1842 (2012). We must decide whether the *Home Concrete* decision affects our prior cases. *Held*: The *Home Concrete* decision does not affect our prior cases holding that "gross income" includes only gains from the sale of investments, not amounts realized from such sales. *Held*, *further*, the gross income Ps omitted from their 2006 and 2007 returns exceeds 25% of the gross income they stated in those returns, and therefore the six-year limitations period applies.

Ernest S. Ryder, *Richard V. Vermazen*, and *Lauren A. Rinsky*, for petitioners.

Mistala M. Cullen and *Monica D. Polo*, for respondent.

OPINION

GOEKE, *Judge*: This matter is before us on petitioners' motion for partial summary judgment under Rule 121(a).[1]

Respondent issued a notice of deficiency concerning petitioners' Federal income tax for the taxable years 2006 to 2009. Petitioners contend that the notice is invalid as it relates to 2006 and 2007 because respondent did not send it within the three-year limitations period provided by section 6501(a). Respondent argues that a six-year limitations period applies under section 6501(e) because petitioners omitted from their returns gross income exceeding 25% of the gross income they reported. We must determine the appropriate limitations period; we hold that a six-year limitations period applies.

Background

Petitioners resided in California when they filed their petition.

Petitioners filed their 2006 and 2007 Forms 1040, U.S. Individual Income Tax Return, on September 17, 2007, and October 2, 2008, respectively. Respondent sent petitioners a notice of deficiency on September 26, 2012, determining income tax deficiencies for taxable years 2006 to 2009.

In the notice of deficiency, respondent alleged that petitioners had omitted from their 2006 and 2007 returns gross

[1] Unless otherwise indicated, all section references are to the Internal Revenue Code in effect for the years at issue, and all Rule references are to the Tax Court Rules of Practice and Procedure.

income of $629,850 and $431,957, respectively.[2] On those returns petitioners reported gross income totaling $271,440 and $340,591, respectively, excluding their shares of the passthrough entity activity we describe below.

During the years at issue petitioners were 80.04% partners in Barkett Family Partners, a limited partnership. They were also 100% shareholders of Unicorn Investments, Inc., an S corporation. These entities reported extensive investment activity on their 2006 and 2007 returns. Combined, they reported capital gains from the sale of investments of approximately $123,000 for 2006 and $314,000 for 2007.[3] They reported amounts realized from the sale of investments of more than $7 million for 2006 and more than $4 million for 2007.[4] On their 2006 and 2007 returns petitioners reported their shares of the entities' gains and losses. For simplicity's sake, we will refer to the investment activities as if petitioners had engaged in them directly, i.e., not via the passthrough entities.

Discussion

I. *Summary Judgment*

Summary judgment is intended to expedite litigation and avoid unnecessary and expensive trials. *Fla. Peach Corp. v. Commissioner*, 90 T.C. 678, 681 (1988). The Court may grant summary judgment when there is no genuine dispute of material fact and a decision may be rendered as a matter of law. Rule 121(a) and (b); *Sundstrand Corp. v. Commissioner*, 98 T.C. 518, 520 (1992), *aff'd*, 17 F.3d 965 (7th Cir. 1994). The moving party bears the burden of proving that there is no genuine dispute of material fact, and the Court will draw any factual inferences in the light most favorable to the nonmoving party. *Dahlstrom v. Commissioner*, 85 T.C. 812, 821 (1985).

---

[2] These omissions are unrelated to the investment activities we discuss below. Respondent determined that petitioners omitted compensation they received for dental services they provided to Barkett Dental Corporation, a C corporation they wholly owned.

[3] Respondent concedes that these amounts represent gross income petitioners stated in their return.

[4] These amounts include proceeds petitioners reported from sales that generated losses.

II. *Limitations Periods*

Under the general rule set forth in section 6501(a), the Internal Revenue Service (IRS) must assess tax or send a notice of deficiency within three years after a return is filed. The limitations period extends to six years under section 6501(e)(1) "[i]f the taxpayer omits from gross income an amount properly includible therein and * * * such amount is in excess of 25 percent of the amount of gross income stated in the return".

Respondent issued the notice of deficiency here more than three years but less than six years after petitioners filed their 2006 and 2007 returns. Thus, the notice is timely with respect to those returns only if the six-year limitations period applies.

III. *Analysis*

To determine the appropriate limitations period, we must divide the amount of gross income petitioners omitted from their return by the amount of gross income they stated in their return. If the omitted amount is more than 25% of the included amount, the six-year limitations period applies. The parties agree that for the purpose of this calculation, the omitted amounts are $629,850 and $431,957 for taxable years 2006 and 2007, respectively. They disagree over the amounts of gross income petitioners stated in their returns. Petitioners argue that the gross income they stated in their returns should include the amounts realized they reported from the sale of investment assets; respondent argues that it should include only the gain they reported from those sales, i.e., amounts realized less bases of assets sold.

We have considered this issue before and have held that "capital gains, and not the gross proceeds,[5] are to be treated as the 'amount of gross income stated in the return' for purposes of sec. 6501(e)." *Insulglass Corp. v. Commissioner*, 84 T.C. 203, 204 (1985); *see also Schneider v. Commissioner*, T.C. Memo. 1985–139. We decided those cases on the basis of section 61(a), which defines gross income as "all income

[5] Gross proceeds in these cases referred to the amounts the taxpayers realized and reported on their returns.

from whatever source derived", including "[g]*ains* derived from dealings in property". (Emphasis added.)

In 2010 the Secretary promulgated section 301.6501(e)–1, Proced. & Admin. Regs., which provides instructions consistent with our jurisprudence. T.D. 9511, 2011–6 I.R.B. 455. The regulation also explains how to determine whether gross income has been omitted from a taxpayer's return. The Supreme Court addressed the validity of the regulation in *United States v. Home Concrete & Supply, LLC*, 566 U.S. ____, ____, 132 S. Ct. 1836, 1842 (2012), and determined that the portion concerning omitted gross income was invalid. Petitioners argue that the *Home Concrete* decision also invalidated the regulation's instructions concerning the calculation of gross income and consequently our cases on the matter. For the reasons we discuss below, we disagree.

To fully explain the import of the *Home Concrete* decision, we must first discuss the Supreme Court's decision in *Colony, Inc. v. Commissioner*, 357 U.S. 28 (1958). In *Colony* the taxpayer had overstated its basis in property it had sold and had consequently underreported its gain on the sale. The Commissioner argued that the underreported gain constituted "omitted gross income" for the purpose of determining whether the extended limitations period applied. The Court disagreed, citing the limitations statute's legislative history. The Court determined that in enacting the statute, Congress intended to give the Commissioner additional time to review a taxpayer's return when the taxpayer had reported no information about a given transaction. In such cases, the Court said, the Commissioner is particularly disadvantaged because the return does not alert him to suspicious activity requiring further investigation. When an understatement results from misreported information, rather than a complete omission, the IRS is at no such disadvantage, and the understatement should not contribute to triggering the limitations period extension.

As we noted above, in 2010 the Secretary promulgated section 301.6501(e)–1, Proced. & Admin. Regs., which explained when gross income should be considered omitted for the purpose of triggering the extended limitations period. The regulation provides that when taxpayers understate their income from a property sale because they overstated their basis in the property, the amount of the understatement shall be considered omitted income. Sec. 301.6501(e)–1(a)(1)(iii), Proced. & Admin. Regs. The regulation's guidance directly conflicts with *Colony*, which held that such an understatement is not omitted gross income.

The Court resolved the conflict between the regulation and the *Colony* holding in *Home Concrete*. There the taxpayer had overstated its basis in a partnership it had sold and had consequently underreported its gain on the sale. The Commissioner again argued, this time under the regulation, that the underreported gain constituted "omitted gross income". The Court held, after an administrative law discussion we will omit here, that the regulation was invalid because it conflicted with the *Colony* holding. The Court followed its *Colony* analysis and held that the underreported gain was not omitted gross income and that it did not belong in the numerator of the statute of limitations calculation. The *Home Concrete* holding addressed only when gross income is to be considered omitted. It did not address how to calculate gross income.[6]

Petitioners attempt to use the *Home Concrete* decision to support their position that "gross income" includes amounts realized from the sale of investment property without a corresponding basis adjustment. They state their argument as follows:

> Only when * * * [amounts realized[7]] are left out of the computation of gross income are they omitted for purposes of the six-year statute of limitations of section 6501(e)(1)(A). If * * * [amounts realized] are not left out of the computation of gross income, they are not omitted; when they are not omitted, they are included; when they are included, they are stated in the return; when they are stated in the return, they are included in the denominator of the 25% percent omitted calculation of section 6501(e)(1)(A).

We see nothing wrong with petitioners' logic, but it proves only that "gross income stated in the return" includes amounts realized stated in the return. That point is undis-

[6] In dictum, the Court did note that "the Code itself define[s] 'gross income' in this context as the difference between gross revenue (often the amount the taxpayer received upon selling the property) and basis (often the amount the taxpayer paid for the property)." *United States v. Home Concrete & Supply, LLC*, 566 U.S. ___, ___, 132 S. Ct. 1836, 1840 (2012).

[7] Petitioners use the term "gross receipts", but we believe petitioners mean "amounts realized" and will evaluate their argument accordingly.

puted; one component of gain is amount realized,[8] and respondent concedes that "gross income stated in the return" includes reported gains from the sale of investment property. The disputed issue, which petitioners' argument does not address, is whether "gross income stated in the return" includes only the excess of the amount realized over the bases of the assets sold. We have consistently held that it does, and the *Home Concrete* decision does not disturb our precedents on the matter.

Our Court's history with the issue the Supreme Court faced in *Home Concrete* and *Colony* demonstrates the difference between that issue and the one we face in this case. As we mentioned earlier, we have previously resolved the issue petitioners raise here. In *Insulglass* and *Schneider*, we determined that gross income includes gains from the sale of investment assets, not simply the amounts realized from such sales. Since we decided those cases, we have addressed the issue the Supreme Court decided in *Home Concrete* and *Colony* at least twice. *See Intermountain Ins. Serv. of Vail, LLC v. Commissioner*, 134 T.C. 211 (2010), *rev'd*, 650 F.3d 691 (D.C. Cir. 2011); *Bakersfield Energy Partners, LP v. Commissioner*, 128 T.C. 207 (2007), *aff'd*, 568 F.3d 767 (9th Cir. 2009). In *Bakersfield*, which we decided before the Secretary promulgated section 301.6501(e)–1, Proced. & Admin. Regs., we held consistently with *Colony*. In *Intermountain*, which we decided after the Secretary promulgated the regulation but before the Supreme Court decided *Home Concrete*, we determined that the regulation was invalid and again held consistently with *Colony*. We did not discuss *Insulglass* or *Schneider* in either of those cases, because they did not address the same issue. *Insulglass* and *Schneider* addressed how to calculate gross income (the issue we face here). *Bakersfield* and *Intermountain* addressed when gross income is omitted from the return (the issue the Supreme Court faced in *Home Concrete* and *Colony*).

Although the *Home Concrete* holding does not affect the issue in this case, we find support for our conclusion in dictum. In addressing one of the Commissioner's arguments,

[8] Sec. 1001 provides that "[t]he gain from the sale or disposition of property shall be the excess of the amount realized therefrom over the adjusted basis".

the Court explained how to calculate income under the general statutory definition of "gross income":

> the general statutory definition of "gross income" requires subtracting the cost from the sales price. Under such a definition of "gross income," the calculation would take (1) total revenue from sales, $40,000, minus (2) "the cost of such sales," say, $25,000. The $10,000 of revenue would thus amount to 67% of the "gross income" of $15,000. * * * [*Home Concrete & Supply, LLC*, 566 U.S. at ___, 132 S. Ct. at 1842.]

Our holding is consistent with this example.

An exception to the general statutory definition appears in section 6501(e)(1)(B)(i), which provides that "[i]n the case of a trade or business, the term 'gross income' means the total of the amounts received or accrued from the sale of goods or services * * * prior to diminution by the cost of such sales or services. The Court demonstrated the operation of this exception with the following example: "a merchant who fails to include $10,000 of revenue from sold goods has not met the 25% test if total revenue is more than $40,000, regardless of the cost paid by the merchant to acquire those goods." *Id.*

Petitioners essentially argue that we should calculate their gross income under this exception rather than under the general statutory definition of gross income. But they have not argued that the amounts realized at issue here resulted from sales of goods or services. They concede that they sold investment assets. Accordingly, the exception does not apply, and we calculate the gross income petitioners stated in their return under the general statutory definition of gross income.

IV. *Conclusion*

The *Home Concrete* decision invalidated a portion of a regulation that coincidentally included instructions for calculating gross income from the sale of investment assets. The decision treated favorably, however, the regulation's instructions for calculating gross income stated in the return, which are consistent with our caselaw. Accordingly, we see no reason to stray from our precedents; we hold that "gross income" includes gains from the sale of investment assets, not the entire amounts realized from such sales. Under this rule, petitioners' omitted gross income for 2006 and 2007 exceeds 25% of the gross income they stated in their returns for those years. Therefore, the six-year limitations period applies to those years and respondent's notice of deficiency is timely with respect to them.

In reaching our holdings herein, we have considered all arguments the parties made, and, to the extent not mentioned above, we conclude they are moot, irrelevant, or without merit.

To reflect the foregoing,

An appropriate order will be issued denying petitioners' motion for partial summary judgment.

STEVEN YARI, PETITIONER *v.* COMMISSIONER OF INTERNAL REVENUE, RESPONDENT

Docket No. 13925–12L. Filed September 15, 2014.

R assessed a penalty under I.R.C. sec. 6707A. R issued a notice of intent to levy to collect this penalty. P requested a collection due process hearing, challenging the collection action. While the hearing was pending Congress retroactively changed the manner in which I.R.C. sec. 6707A penalties are calculated. P requested that R recalculate the penalty using the amount of tax shown on subsequent amended returns. R decided the penalty should not be changed, and P appealed this decision. The IRS Appeals Office agreed that the penalty amount should not be changed, and R issued a notice of determination sustaining the collection action. P believes that the appropriate penalty calculation should use the actual tax due, not the tax shown on the return on which he was obliged but failed to disclose the reportable transaction. P seeks to change the penalty from the current amount assessed, $100,000, to the minimum under the statute, $5,000. *Held*: We have jurisdiction to consider the penalty. *Held, further*, the penalty is calculated by reference to the amount of tax shown on the return with respect to which the taxpayer had a disclosure obligation.

Steven R. Mather, for petitioner.
Michael W. Tan, for respondent.

OPINION

WHERRY, *Judge*: This case is before us on a petition for review of a Notice of Determination Concerning Collection

Action(s) Under Section 6320 and/or 6330 (notice of determination) sustaining a notice of intent to levy with respect to a penalty assessed for the 2004 tax year.[1] The case presents an issue of first impression as to whether section 6707A requires respondent to use the tax shown on the return giving rise to the disclosure obligation or whether respondent must use the tax as shown on subsequent, amended returns. We hold that respondent may calculate the amount of the penalty using the tax shown on the return giving rise to the violation of the disclosure obligation.

Background

This case was submitted fully stipulated pursuant to Rule 122. The parties' stipulation of settled issues and stipulation of facts, with accompanying exhibits, are incorporated herein by this reference. At the time he filed his petition, petitioner resided in California.

Petitioner formed Topaz Global Holdings, LLC (Topaz Global), on December 22, 2000. Under the regulations, Topaz Global was a disregarded entity for Federal income tax purposes. *See* sec. 301.7701–3, Proced. & Admin. Regs. On December 23, 2002, petitioner formed Faryar, Inc., a Nevada corporation, which elected to be treated as an S corporation for Federal income tax purposes. Faryar entered into agreements with Topaz Global and other companies to provide management services. We refer to Faryar's relationship with these companies as the management fee transaction.

In 2002 petitioner opened a Roth individual retirement account (Roth IRA) with an initial contribution of $3,000. The Roth IRA acquired all of the Faryar stock for $3,000, making the Roth IRA the sole shareholder of the S corporation.[2] For the 2002 through 2007 tax years Faryar reported a total net income of $1,221,778 in management fees and interest income less deductions. Because Faryar was an S

---

[1] All section references are to the Internal Revenue Code (Code) of 1986, as amended and in effect during the relevant period, and all Rule references are to the Tax Court Rules of Practice and Procedure, unless otherwise indicated.

[2] Such a structure does not work for Federal income tax purposes because a Roth IRA generally cannot be an eligible shareholder of an S corporation. *Taproot Admin. Servs., Inc. v. Commissioner*, 133 T.C. 202, 215 (2009), *aff'd*, 679 F.3d 1109 (9th Cir. 2012).

corporation, this income was not taxed at the corporate level, and because the shareholder was a nontaxable entity, the income was not taxed at the shareholder level. The practical effect of this transaction was twofold: it allowed petitioner to effectively exceed the Roth IRA contribution limits and decreased the amount of income petitioner otherwise would have reported from Topaz Global because Topaz Global deducted the amounts paid to Faryar as management fees.

The Internal Revenue Service (IRS) has identified transactions such as the one petitioner engaged in as abusive Roth IRA transactions. Notice 2004–8, 2004–1 C.B. 333. The IRS has also identified these transactions as listed transactions, potentially subjecting taxpayers who did not disclose participation in these transactions on their Federal income tax returns to penalties.

Petitioner and his wife signed and apparently filed a joint 2004 Federal income tax return on October 17, 2005. This return did not disclose petitioner's participation in the Roth IRA transaction. Respondent audited petitioner's returns for 2002 and 2003 and, following his marriage in 2004, petitioner and his wife's returns for 2004 through 2007 and issued notices of deficiency to petitioner for his 2002 and 2003 tax years and to petitioner and his wife for the 2004 through 2007 tax years. In these notices respondent determined that the management fee transactions were not valid business transactions and should result in an excise tax under section 4973. With respect to the 2004 tax year respondent determined that petitioner and his wife should have included in income $482,912 from the management fee transaction. According to respondent's calculations, this inclusion, along with corresponding computational adjustments, increased petitioner and his wife's tax liability by $135,215.

Petitioner, his wife, and respondent settled these deficiency cases and entered into a closing agreement in 2011. The closing agreement required petitioner to include in his income certain amounts for each of the tax years and provided that petitioner and his wife were not liable for the section 4973 excise tax. The Court entered stipulated decisions in the deficiency cases that reflected the parties' closing agreement.

During the course of the audit petitioner determined that he had made a substantial error on his 2004 tax return because he incorrectly transferred information from a Schedule K–1, Partner's Share of Income, Deductions, Credits, etc., to that return. Petitioner and his wife prepared an amended return (first amended return) including $51 of taxable interest, $482,912 of income as determined by respondent, deductions of $1,270,448 claimed on Schedule E, Supplemental Income and Loss, and $23,625 in itemized deductions. The first amended return resulted in a negative taxable income.

Petitioner and his wife filed a second amended return for the 2004 tax year during the pendency of the deficiency cases. This second amended return claimed a net operating loss carryback from the 2008 tax year of $2,856,026. On both amended returns petitioner and his wife reported the $482,912 from the management fee transaction as income. The stipulated decision entered by the Court for the 2004 tax year reflected the adjustments made in the first and second amended 2004 tax returns.

Respondent also assessed a section 6707A penalty of $100,000 for the 2004 tax year based on his belief that petitioner had failed to disclose his participation in a transaction identified in Notice 2004–8, *supra*, as a listed transaction. Respondent assessed this penalty on September 11, 2008.

Respondent sent petitioner a final notice of intent to levy on February 9, 2009. Petitioner timely requested a collection due process (CDP) hearing. During the pendency of the hearing, on September 27, 2010, Congress amended section 6707A to change the method of calculating the penalty. Small Business Jobs Act of 2010 (SBJA), Pub. L. No. 111–240, sec. 2041(a), 124 Stat. at 2560. This change was effective retroactively for penalties assessed after December 31, 2006, *id.* sec. 2041(b), and therefore the CDP hearing was suspended in October 2010 so respondent could reconsider the calculation of the penalty.[3] Respondent's revenue agent declined to change the penalty, and petitioner requested review by the IRS Appeals Office (Appeals), which also declined to modify

[3] The parties scarcely mention, much less substantively discuss, this midhearing "time-out" and apparent referral to the IRS examination function. We therefore will not further comment on these events.

the penalty. Petitioner did not request any collection alternatives during the CDP hearing, and counsel for petitioner requested that the settlement officer issue a notice of determination. Consequently, the settlement officer complied and issued the notice of determination sustaining the collection action.

Petitioner concedes that the Roth IRA transactions he engaged in were listed transactions under Notice 2004–8, *supra*, for the purposes of the section 6707A penalty. He admits that he is liable for a penalty but challenges the calculation of the penalty.

Discussion

I. *Jurisdiction*

The parties assume we have jurisdiction over the penalty issue in this case. But the Court has an independent obligation to determine whether it has jurisdiction over a case, and the parties cannot simply stipulate jurisdiction or waive jurisdictional defects. *Arbaugh v. Y & H Corp.*, 546 U.S. 500, 514 (2006); *Charlotte's Office Boutique, Inc. v. Commissioner*, 121 T.C. 89, 102 (2003), *aff'd*, 425 F.3d 1203 (9th Cir. 2005). Therefore, we begin our analysis with the jurisdictional question.

The Tax Court is a court of limited jurisdiction and may exercise jurisdiction only to the extent authorized by Congress. *Adkison v. Commissioner*, 592 F.3d 1050, 1052 (9th Cir. 2010), *aff'g on other grounds* 129 T.C. 97 (2007). But we "have jurisdiction to determine whether we have jurisdiction." *Smith v. Commissioner*, 133 T.C. 424, 426 (2009). In *Smith* we also held that we did not have jurisdiction to redetermine section 6707A penalties in a petition for redetermination of a deficiency. *Id.* at 428–430. Because the section 6707A penalty did not fit the statutory definition of a deficiency and because the Commissioner could assess and collect the penalty without issuing a statutory notice of deficiency, we lacked deficiency jurisdiction to redetermine the penalty. *Id.* at 429. We noted, however, that "we would presumably have jurisdiction to redetermine a liability challenge asserted by * * * [the taxpayers] in a collection due process hearing." *Id.* at 430 n.6. We now turn presumption into conviction and aver our jurisdiction.

We begin by noting that section 6707A allows a taxpayer to request the Commissioner to rescind all or part of the penalty that is imposed because of a violation with respect to a reportable transaction other than a listed transaction if rescission would promote compliance with the Code and effective tax administration. Sec. 6707A(d)(1). Congress explicitly denied taxpayers the ability to seek judicial review of the Commissioner's rescission decision. Sec. 6707A(d)(2). The provision prohibiting judicial review applies only to subsection (d) of section 6707A and does not otherwise preclude our jurisdiction to review this penalty under section 6330. *See* H.R. Rept. No. 108–548 (Part 1), at 262 n.233 (2004) (stating that this provision contained in the American Jobs Creation Act of 2004 (AJCA), Pub. L. No. 108–357, 118 Stat. 1418, "does not limit the ability of a taxpayer to challenge whether a penalty is appropriate (e.g., a taxpayer may litigate the issue of whether a transaction is a reportable transaction (and thus subject to the penalty if not disclosed) or not a reportable transaction (and thus not subject to the penalty))").

Section 6330(d)(1) as amended by the Pension Protection Act of 2006, Pub. L. No. 109–280, sec. 855(a), 120 Stat. at 1019, expanded the Court's review of collection actions to include collection actions where the underlying tax liability consists of penalties not reviewable in a deficiency action. *See Williams v. Commissioner*, 131 T.C. 54, 58 n.4 (2008); *Callahan v. Commissioner*, 130 T.C. 44, 48 (2008). In a CDP hearing a taxpayer may challenge "the existence or amount of the underlying tax liability for any tax period if the person did not receive any statutory notice of deficiency for such tax liability or did not otherwise have an opportunity to dispute such tax liability." Sec. 6330(c)(2)(B). In his hearing petitioner challenged the amount of the underlying tax liability that resulted from the section 6707A penalty. *See Callahan v. Commissioner*, 130 T.C. at 49 ("We have interpreted the phrase 'underlying tax liability' as including any amounts a taxpayer owes pursuant to the tax laws that are the subject of the Commissioner's collection activities."). Petitioner has not had an opportunity to dispute the amount of the penalty, and consequently, we have jurisdiction to redetermine the amount of the penalty.

II. *Standard of Review*

Ordinarily, our review of the determinations in a CDP hearing is for abuse of discretion. *Sego v. Commissioner*, 114 T.C. 604, 610 (2000); *Goza v. Commissioner*, 114 T.C. 176, 181–182 (2000). But when the underlying tax liability is properly at issue, we review the determination de novo. *Sego v. Commissioner*, 114 T.C. at 610; *Goza v. Commissioner*, 114 T.C. at 181–182. Petitioner challenges respondent's determination as to the amount of the penalty, and thus, we review that determination de novo.

III. *Section 6707A Penalty*

Section 6707A(a) imposes a penalty on "[a]ny person who fails to include on any return or statement any information with respect to a reportable transaction which is required under section 6011 to be included with such return or statement". The amount of the penalty before the SBJA depended on whether the transaction was a reportable transaction or a listed transaction. Sec. 6707A(b) (2006), *amended by* SBJA sec. 2041(a). For reportable transactions other than listed transactions, it was $10,000 for natural persons and $50,000 for others, and for listed transactions, it was $100,000 for natural persons and $200,000 for others. *Id.* The penalty applied regardless of whether the listed or reportable transaction is respected for Federal income tax purposes. Petitioner concedes he engaged in a listed transaction and that he failed to properly disclose his participation.

The penalty for failing to disclose a listed transaction on a return after enactment of the SBJA is "75 percent of the decrease in tax shown on the return as a result of such transaction (or which would have resulted from such transaction if such transaction were respected for Federal [income] tax purposes)." Sec. 6707A(b)(1). In the case of individuals, the statute prescribes minimum and maximum penalties for failing to disclose a listed transaction of $5,000 and $100,000, respectively. Sec. 6707A(b)(2) and (3). The parties disagree as to what return and what amount of tax we should use in calculating the tax. Petitioner urges us to use the amended returns to determine the decrease in tax, and respondent says we must look to the original return. These disparate positions stem from a fundamental disagreement as to what the phrase "decrease in tax shown on the return as a result of the transaction" means. To resolve this dispute, we must examine and interpret the statute.[4]

The starting point for interpreting a statute is its plain and ordinary meaning unless such an interpretation "would produce absurd or unreasonable results". *Union Carbide Corp. v. Commissioner*, 110 T.C. 375, 384 (1998). Undefined words take their "ordinary, contemporary, common meaning." *Hewlett-Packard Co. & Consol. Subs. v. Commissioner*, 139 T.C. 255, 264 (2012). We interpret statutes "'in their context and with a view to their place in the overall statutory scheme.'" *FDA v. Brown & Williamson Tobacco Corp.*, 529 U.S. 120, 133 (2000) (quoting *Davis v. Mich. Dep't of Treasury*, 489 U.S. 803, 809 (1989)). Where the statute is clear and unambiguous, we need not resort to other tools of statutory interpretation. *BedRoc Ltd., LLC v. United States*, 541 U.S. 176, 183 (2004). If the statute is silent or ambiguous, we may employ "'*traditional tools of statutory construction*'", *United States v. Home Concrete & Supply, LLC*, 566 U.S. ___, ___, 132 S. Ct. 1836, 1844 (2012) (quoting *Chevron, U.S.A., Inc. v. Natural Res. Def. Council, Inc.*, 467 U.S. 837, 843 n.9 (1984)), including legislative history, to ascertain congressional intent, *Burlington N. R.R. Co. v. Okla. Tax Comm'n*, 481 U.S. 454, 461 (1987); *Intermountain Ins. Serv. of Vail, LLC v. Commissioner*, 134 T.C. 211, 222–223 (2010), *rev'd*, 650 F.3d 691 (D.C. Cir. 2011), *vacated and remanded*, 566 U.S. ___, 132 S. Ct. 2120 (2012).

Petitioner urges us to interpret the statute as calculating the penalty using the tax savings produced by the listed transactions. He says we should ignore the tax reported on the return with respect to which he was required to report the listed transaction. Instead, petitioner asks us to focus on the returns prepared years after the reporting obligation arose. He urges us to look at the plain language of the statute, its place in the statutory scheme, and to the legislative history. Respondent, on the other hand, says that the

[4] The regulations are of no help here, as they merely parrot the statutory language. Sec. 301.6707A–1(a), Proced. & Admin. Regs. The IRS released these final regulations in 2011 with the explicit proviso that the regulations "do not give further guidance on how the amount of the penalty is computed" and stated that it intended to "provide guidance" at a "later time." T.D. 9550, 2011–47 I.R.B. 785, 786.

plain meaning of the statute does not support petitioner's position and urges us to compute the tax with reference only to the tax shown on the original tax return. In his view, we disregard the returns prepared during the audit, the mistakes on the prior return, and the correct tax owed by petitioner when calculating the penalty. To be clear about the stakes, if we adopt petitioner's reading of the statute, the penalty would be the statutory minimum, or $5,000; if we hold for respondent, the penalty will stand as $100,000.

We think the statute is clear and unambiguous: The penalty is calculated with reference to the "tax shown on the return". Sec. 6707A(b). When we look to the penalty provision as a whole, it is clear that Congress has penalized the failure to disclose participation in a listed or otherwise reportable transaction on the return or other information statement giving rise to the disclosure obligation. If the taxpayer fails to report the transaction on that return or information statement, then the penalty is based on the tax shown on that return or information statement, not some other, later filed return or some hypothetical tax. Congress did not say that the penalty should be calculated by reference to tax shown on *a* return; it did not say to calculate the penalty using the tax required to be shown; and it did not say to calculate the penalty using the decrease in tax resulting from participation in the transaction. Congress very clearly linked the penalty to the tax shown on a particular return—the return giving rise to the reporting obligation. Absent a "'clearly expressed legislative intent to the contrary'", we will regard the clear and unambiguous language of the statute as conclusive.[5] *Reves v. Ernst & Young*, 507

[5] We observe that the process of divining the legislative intent underlying a statute's language and structure, while subject to canons of construction and well-established methodologies, is hardly an exact science. *Compare, e.g., Halbig v. Burwell*, 758 F.3d 390, 406–412 (D.C. Cir. 2014) (having found sec. 36B unambiguous, concluding that weight of legislative history, including overall congressional policy goals, did not override statute's plain meaning, which was that tax credits were unavailable to participants in health insurance exchanges established by the Federal Government), *rehearing en banc granted, vacated by* ___ F.3d ___, 2014 WL 4627181 (D.C. Cir. Sept. 4, 2014), *with King v. Burwell*, 759 F.3d 358, 371–372 (4th Cir. 2014) (having found sec. 36B ambiguous, concluding that legislative history did not support either plausible interpretation, and defer-

Continued

U.S. 170, 177 (1993) (quoting *United States v. Turkette*, 452 U.S. 576, 580 (1981)). The plain meaning of the statute does not support petitioner's position.

Petitioner also contends that the legislative history supports his position, but he fails to point to any actual legislative history. In any event, the documentary evidence referencing the penalty provision does not support petitioner's position. Congress initially enacted section 6707A with a flat penalty of $100,000 for individuals with respect to listed transactions. AJCA sec. 811(a), 118 Stat. at 1575. There was no variable minimum and no variable maximum and no 75% of tax savings calculation. Congress added the current calculation as part of the SBJA, likely because of concern that an inflexible penalty would create harsh results. *See* H.R. Rept. No. 111–447, at 15 (2010).

Unfortunately, no direct legislative history exists to explain the change. What we do have is the rationale behind an almost identical amendment included in a bill that never became law.[6] H.R. 4849, 111th Cong., sec. 111 (2010). The House passed H.R. 4849 partly out of concern for the potential inequities an inflexible penalty may create. H.R. Rept. No. 111–447, *supra* at 15. Congress had heard from the National Taxpayer Advocate that the potential magnitude of the penalties had an overly harsh impact on individuals and small businesses. *Id.* at 15–16. The tax advisers may not have told these taxpayers of the reporting obligation, and the penalties, for an individual conducting business through an S corporation, could reach $300,000 per year for a listed transaction that yielded little or no tax benefit. *See* National Taxpayer Advocate, 2008 Annual Report to Congress (Vol. One) 342–343, 419–421 (2008); *see also* sec. 6707A(b)(2) (2004) (imposing a $200,000 penalty on nonindividual taxpayers for failing to disclose a listed transaction).

Transactions that span multiple tax years magnify the effect as the reporting obligation exists for each return.

ring to agency's determination that statute permitted tax credits for participants in Federal health insurance exchanges, as consistent with overall congressional policy goals).

[6] The only difference between the enacted and proposed amendments was the inclusion in the proposed amendment to sec. 6707A(b)(2) of the additional words "for any taxable year" between the words "transaction" and "shall not exceed".

National Taxpayer Advocate, 2008 Annual Report to Congress (Vol. One), *supra*, at 420. The House Ways and Means Committee explained that the new penalty calculation would "provide a mechanism for establishing a penalty amount that will be proportionate to the misconduct to be penalized, without discouraging compliance with the requirement to disclose reportable transactions." H.R. Rept. No. 111–447, *supra* at 16.

Petitioner believes other legislative history inextricably links the penalty calculation to the tax savings. He points to the Joint Committee on Taxation's general explanation, also known as the Blue Book, to bolster his position. *See* Staff of J. Comm. on Taxation, General Explanation of Tax Legislation Enacted in the 111th Congress 476–480 (J. Comm. Print 2011). The Joint Committee explained that Congress desired to spare small businesses and individuals "unconscionable hardship * * * as a result of the magnitude of the penalty" where the penalty "exceed[ed] the tax savings claimed on these returns". *Id.* at 478. Contrary to petitioner's position, the Blue Books are not legislative history, though they can sometimes be relevant if persuasive. *United States v. Woods*, 571 U.S. ____, ____, 134 S. Ct. 557, 568 (2013). In any event, we remain unconvinced that the combined import of the Blue Book and the earlier bill override our prior conclusions as to the statute's plain meaning.

It is clear that in the earlier bill Congress intended to blunt the effect of section 6707A for taxpayers who failed to disclose a transaction but nonetheless did not benefit much from that transaction. But it is equally clear that Congress was concerned with the "tax reported on the participant's income tax return as a result of participation in the transaction", not the tax required to be shown. H.R. Rept. No. 111–447, *supra* at 16. It is also clear that what Congress intended to penalize is the failure to disclose participation, not the tax savings produced by the transaction. *Id.* at 15.[7] That Congress linked the penalty to the tax savings does not change the fact that the culpable act here is the failure to

[7] *See also* Staff of J. Comm. on Taxation, General Explanation of Tax Legislation Enacted in the 108th Congress 361 (J. Comm. Print 2005) (discussing the American Jobs Creation Act of 2004, Pub. L. No. 108–357, sec. 811, 118 Stat. at 1575, including "[r]easons for [c]hange").

disclose. Furthermore, the 2010 change linked the penalty not to the tax savings calculated with the benefit of hindsight but rather to the tax savings as claimed on the tax return. In this vein, even the Blue Book fails to persuade as the Joint Committee explained the change as aimed at "achiev[ing] proportionality between the penalty and the tax savings that were the object of the transaction," and not to the actual tax saved. Staff of J. Comm. on Taxation, General Explanation of Tax Legislation Enacted in the 111th Congress, *supra* at 479.

We note also section 6651(a)(2), which imposes an addition to tax for failure "to pay the amount shown as tax on any return specified [by parts of the Code]". At first glance, this addition to tax would ignore the correct tax liability, and a taxpayer who reported a tax greater than the actual tax due would suffer. But section 6651(c)(2) ameliorates this potentially harsh result by providing: "If the amount required to be shown as tax on a return is less than the amount shown as tax on such return, subsections (a)(2) and (b)(2) shall be applied by substituting such lower amount."

Congress obviously knows how to link a penalty or an addition to tax to the tax required to be shown on the return and has done so. Consequently, the fact that it did not do so in section 6707A tends to bolster our holding that the penalty applies to the amount shown on petitioner's first filed return.[8] *See Marx v. Gen. Revenue Corp.*, 568 U.S. ____, ____, 133 S. Ct. 1166, 1177 (2013) (declining to read into 15 U.S.C. sec. 1692k(a)(3) a limitation on the ability of courts to award costs under rule 54 of the Federal Rules of Civil Procedure in part because other "[s]tatutes confirm that Congress knows how to limit a court's discretion * * * when it

[8] We note that, here, petitioner amended his first filed return after the date prescribed for filing a return for the 2004 tax year. We do not express an opinion as to the result had he filed his first amended return before that date. *See Goldstone v. Commissioner*, 65 T.C. 113, 116 (1975) (where taxpayers sought to avoid a credit's recapture in a later year by amending the return on which the credit was claimed, holding that the Commissioner was entitled to reject the amended return and recapture the credit in the later year but observing that courts had upheld the validity of amended returns in other circumstances, such as where the amended returns were filed before the filing deadline for the subject tax year).

so desires").[9] Congress did not do so in section 6707A, instead opting to impose the penalty as a percentage "of the decrease in tax shown on the return as a result of such transaction (or which would have resulted from such transaction if such transaction were respected for Federal tax purposes)." Sec. 6707A(b)(1). Without a subsection analogous to section 6651(c)(2), we calculate the penalty by reference to the tax shown on the return and do not consider the amount required to be shown.

Section 6707A imposes a strict liability penalty. *See* H.R. Rept. No. 111–447, *supra* at 13. While it may be harsh in situations where a taxpayer mistakenly overstates his tax, such is the result of the plain meaning of the statutory language.[10] Legislative history does not indicate a clear congressional intent to the contrary, and we therefore find that the settlement officer did not err in the calculation of the penalty.

The Court has considered all of petitioner's contentions, argument, requests, and statements. To the extent not discussed herein, we conclude that they are moot, irrelevant, or without merit. To reflect the foregoing,

Decision will be entered for respondent.

---

[9] We note also that a net operating loss carryback from a subsequent tax year does not reduce the tax required to be shown on the return for purposes of calculating the sec. 6651(a)(2) addition to tax. *See Vines v. Commissioner*, T.C. Memo. 2009–267, slip op. at 15, *aff'd*, 418 Fed. Appx. 900 (11th Cir. 2011).

[10] A court's "obligation to avoid adopting statutory constructions with absurd results is well-established" and can, in rare cases, override the literal meaning of unambiguous statutory language. *Halbig v. Burwell*, 758 F.3d at 402 (citing *Public Citizen v. DOJ*, 491 U.S. 440, 454–455 (1990)). *See generally* John F. Manning, "The Absurdity Doctrine", 116 Harv. L. Rev. 2387 (2003). The statutory construction we adopt here does not, in petitioner's case, yield "'an outcome so contrary to perceived social values that Congress could not have intended it.'" *See Halbig v. Burwell*, 758 F.3d at 402 (quoting *United States v. Cook*, 594 F.3d 883, 891 (D.C. Cir. 2010)). Different facts—such as, for example, a mere scrivener's error in a decimal place, resulting in tax shown on the return of 10 or even 100 times the facially correct amount—might entail a different analysis.

GREENOAK HOLDINGS LIMITED, SOUTHBROOK PROPERTIES LIMITED AND WESTLYN PROPERTIES LIMITED, PETITIONERS *v.* COMMISSIONER OF INTERNAL REVENUE, RESPONDENT

Docket No. 12075–13L. Filed September 16, 2014.

R issued a final notice of intent to levy to estate (E) to collect unpaid estate tax. E requested a hearing before an IRS Appeals officer (AO) pursuant to I.R.C. sec. 6330. Following the hearing, AO issued a notice of determination to E sustaining the proposed levy as to E's nonprobate assets. Among the nonprobate assets reported on the estate tax return was an offshore trust that owned certain entities (Ps). Ps petitioned the Tax Court for review of the notice of determination issued to E. No petition was filed on behalf of E. R moved to dismiss for lack of jurisdiction. *Held*: The "person" entitled to the rights and protections set forth in I.R.C. sec. 6330 is the taxpayer liable for unpaid Federal tax. *Held*, *further*, under I.R.C. sec. 6330(d), this Court lacks jurisdiction over a petition filed by a party who is neither the taxpayer nor an authorized representative of the taxpayer.

Michael Ben-Jacob, for petitioners.
Frederick C. Mutter, for respondent.

RUWE, *Judge*: Respondent issued a notice of determination to the personal representative of the Estate of James B. Irwin on May 1, 2013. Greenoak Holdings Limited, Southbrook Properties Limited, and Westlyn Properties Limited (petitioners) filed a petition for judicial review with the Tax Court on May 30, 2013. The issues for decision are: (1) whether petitioners' alleged ownership interest in property that might be subject to levy by respondent entitles them to the rights afforded to "persons" under section 6330 [1] and (2) whether this Court has jurisdiction under section 6330(d) of an appeal filed by entities other than the taxpayer liable for the unpaid Federal tax.

FINDINGS OF FACT

At the time the petition was filed, petitioners' principal place of business was in Nassau, Bahamas.

[1] All section references are to the Internal Revenue Code in effect at all relevant times, and all Rule references are to the Tax Court Rules of Practice and Procedure, unless otherwise indicated.

James B. Irwin (decedent) died on September 21, 2009. On November 19, 2009, Howard L. Crown was appointed personal representative of decedent's estate (estate). Respondent received from the estate a Form 706, United States Estate (and Generation-Skipping Transfer) Tax Return (estate tax return), in December 2010, which was signed by Mr. Crown as executor and reported the estate's probate and nonprobate assets. Among the nonprobate assets listed on the estate tax return was the Karamia Settlement, an offshore trust governed by the laws of Jersey in the Channel Islands, to which decedent allegedly made property transfers before death. The Karamia Settlement is the owner of petitioners.[2]

The estate failed to timely pay the estate tax reported on the estate tax return because, according to Mr. Crown, it did "not have funds available * * * which [is] attributable to the inclusion of the Karamia Settlement in the decedent's gross estate." Respondent assessed the tax reported on the estate tax return on January 31, 2011, along with an addition to tax for failure to timely pay tax shown on the estate tax return and accrued interest.

On November 28, 2012, respondent issued to Mr. Crown a Final Notice of Intent to Levy and Notice of Your Right to a Hearing. Although the record before the Court does not indicate the exact amount reported on the estate tax return, the July 2, 2012, notice of intent to levy states that the estate owes a balance of $7,526,038.88. Mr. Crown timely submitted a request for a collection due process (CDP) hearing on December 27, 2012. The CDP hearing between Mr. Crown, his representative Mr. Pearson, and respondent was conducted via telephone conference on April 18, 2013. During the CDP hearing the estate argued that the penalties for failure to timely pay the estate tax due should be abated in the light of the estate not having sufficient liquid assets.

On May 1, 2013, respondent sent to the estate, in care of Mr. Crown, a notice of determination. The notice of determination (1) sustained the proposed levy against the estate's nonprobate assets (i.e., those assets not in the custody of the

[2] The record before the Court does not specify what assets are included in the Karamia Settlement other than petitioners. Mr. Crown, however, contends that the Karamia Settlement consists of various "worldwide properties and entities."

Probate Court), (2) did not sustain the proposed levy as to the estate's probate assets (i.e., those assets in the custody of the Probate Court), and (3) denied the estate's request for penalty abatement. According to the notice of determination, the proposed levy was sustained as to only the nonprobate assets because "the Internal Revenue Service (Service) cannot administratively collect if the property is in the custody of the court." While not identifying the nonprobate assets subject to levy, the notice of determination instructed that "Collection has to properly determine which assets are probate and which are not probate."

Mr. Crown did not file a petition for review of the May 1, 2013, notice of determination on behalf of the estate. However, after receiving a copy of the notice of determination from Mr. Crown, petitioners, on their own behalf, filed a petition with the Tax Court on May 30, 2013.

Upon receiving petitioners' petition, we issued an order to show cause on June 19, 2013, directing the parties and the estate to show cause in writing why the estate should not be substituted as petitioner. On July 11, 2013, respondent filed a motion to dismiss for lack of jurisdiction (motion to dismiss), arguing that this Court does not have jurisdiction over the instant matter because the proper party to petition the Court for review of the notice of determination (the estate) did not timely petition and no determination was made with respect to petitioners that would confer jurisdiction upon the Court. Mr. Crown, on behalf of the estate, filed a response that essentially agreed with respondent and asked that the case be dismissed.

On January 16, 2014, Mr. Crown filed a notice of substitution of personal representative, indicating that he had resigned as personal representative of the estate and that Jill McCrory had been appointed as the successor personal representative. On May 6, 2014, Ms. McCrory filed supplemental responses to our order to show cause and respondent's motion to dismiss, arguing that: (1) petitioners have standing to pursue the instant litigation on their own behalf; (2) the case should not be dismissed for lack of jurisdiction; or alternatively, that (3) the estate should be substituted as party petitioner and petitioners should be allowed to intervene.

OPINION

The issue before us is whether petitioners are the proper parties to petition this Court for review of the May 1, 2013, notice of determination which was sent to the estate in care of Mr. Crown. Petitioners assert that they have an ownership interest in the nonprobate property that might be subject to levy and argue that they "did not receive proper notice of the proposed levy action and were not afforded a fair opportunity to contest the proposed levy action and underlying tax liability". Petitioners further argue that "[r]espondent's failure to provide proper notice under IRC Section 6330 * * * deprived [p]etitioner[s] of * * * [their] due process right to contest the amount of tax due in a hearing before an impartial Appeals Officer under IRC Section 6330(c), and to seek judicial review of any determination thereof under IRC Section 6330(d)." Petitioners nonetheless conclude that the "substance" of the May 1, 2013, notice of determination supports the proposition that this Court has jurisdiction over the instant appeal.

Respondent argues that Mr. Crown, as the personal representative of the estate, was the appropriate party to receive prelevy notice and to exercise any CDP hearing rights. Moreover, respondent argues that the taxpayer (i.e., the estate in care of Mr. Crown) was the proper party to appeal the May 1, 2013, notice of determination. Respondent concludes that "[p]etitioners have not demonstrated that a [n]otice of [d]etermination sufficient to confer jurisdiction on this Court with respect to the estate tax liability of the [e]state was issued to them by * * * [respondent] as required by I.R.C. §§ 6330(c) and/or 6330(d)." We will begin by discussing the relevant law pertaining to collection actions and then will explain why we lack jurisdiction over petitioners' appeal.

When "any person liable to pay any tax neglects or refuses to pay the same within 10 days after notice and demand", the Commissioner is authorized to collect the unpaid tax "by levy upon all property and rights to property * * * belonging to such person". Sec. 6331(a). Section 6330(a)(1) provides that "[n]o levy may be made on any property or right to property of any person unless the Secretary has notified such person in writing of their right to a hearing under this section before such levy is made." If timely requested by "the person", a CDP hearing is held by an Appeals officer within the Commissioner's office who has had no prior involvement with respect to the unpaid tax. Sec. 6330(b); *see Offiler v. Commissioner*, 114 T.C. 492, 496 (2000). At the hearing "[t]he person" may raise any relevant issue, including appropriate spousal defenses, challenges to the appropriateness of the collection action, and collection alternatives. Sec. 6330(c)(2)(A). The person is also entitled to raise issues regarding the underlying tax liability "if the person did not receive any statutory notice of deficiency for such tax liability". Sec. 6330(c)(2)(B). Following the CDP hearing the Appeals officer will determine whether proceeding with the proposed levy is appropriate and issue a notice of determination. Sec. 6330(c)(3); *Offiler v. Commissioner*, 114 T.C. at 498.

If dissatisfied with the determination of Appeals, "[t]he person" may seek judicial review in the Tax Court. Sec. 6330(d). During such review the suspension of levy continues. Sec. 6330(e); *Blaga v. Commissioner*, T.C. Memo. 2010–170, 2010 Tax Ct. Memo LEXIS 206, at *12. We have jurisdiction to review the determination made by Appeals, and said determination is the focus of this Court under section 6330(d). *See Offiler v. Commissioner*, 114 T.C. at 498. We generally review the Appeals officer's determination for abuse of discretion. *See Sego v. Commissioner*, 114 T.C. 604, 610 (2000); *Goza v. Commissioner*, 114 T.C. 176, 181–182 (2000). Under the abuse of discretion standard, we decide whether the determination of the Appeals officer was arbitrary, capricious, or without a sound basis in fact or law. *Murphy v. Commissioner*, 125 T.C. 301, 320 (2005), *aff'd*, 469 F.3d 27 (1st Cir. 2006). However, we review a determination regarding the underlying tax liability de novo where "the person did not receive any statutory notice of deficiency for such tax liability or did not otherwise have an opportunity to dispute such tax liability." Sec. 6330(c)(2)(B); *see Montgomery v. Commissioner*, 122 T.C. 1, 8 (2004); *Sego v. Commissioner*, 114 T.C. at 610; *Goza v. Commissioner*, 114 T.C. at 181–182. The only person entitled to receive a notice of deficiency is the taxpayer. *See* secs. 6212 and 6213.

Thus far, all of the reported cases under section 6330(d) where we have recognized jurisdiction have been based on petitions filed by taxpayers or their authorized personal representatives. *See, e.g.*, *Lunsford v. Commissioner*, 117 T.C. 159 (2001); *Offiler v. Commissioner*, 114 T.C. at 492; *Thompson v. Commissioner*, T.C. Memo. 2013–260; *Estate of Deese v. Commissioner*, T.C. Memo. 2007–362, 2007 Tax Ct. Memo LEXIS 378. However, petitioners argue that they are the proper parties to appeal the May 1, 2013, notice of determination that was sent to the estate—and that this Court has jurisdiction over the instant appeal—because section 6330(d) "does not limit the Court's jurisdiction with respect solely to a designated party." Specifically, petitioners argue that the term "person" in section 6330 includes any person who might claim a right in property that is intended to be levied upon even if that person is not the taxpayer or the taxpayer's authorized representative. Petitioners cite no previous Court opinions that support their argument, and their argument presents us with an issue of first impression.

Petitioners go on to argue that their property does not constitute property of the estate that is subject to levy by respondent. Nevertheless, they argue that respondent intends to levy upon their property because the Karamia Settlement was shown on the estate tax return as property of the estate. (Neither the notice of determination nor the notice of intent to levy identified the specific property on which respondent intends to levy). Since petitioners allege that they, not the estate, are the owners of the property, they conclude that section 6330 applies to them and that they are a "person" who was entitled to receive notice, a CDP hearing, and to appeal the May 1, 2013, notice of determination sent to the estate. We disagree.

The meaning of the word "person" throughout section 6330 is critical to the resolution of this case. Section 6330 provides, in pertinent part:

SEC. 6330. NOTICE AND OPPORTUNITY FOR HEARING BEFORE LEVY.

(a) REQUIREMENT OF NOTICE BEFORE LEVY.

(1) IN GENERAL.——No levy may be made on any property or right to property of any *person* unless the Secretary has notified such *person* in writing of their right to a hearing under this section before such levy is made. Such notice shall be required only once for the taxable period to which the unpaid tax specified in paragraph (3)(A) relates.

* * * * * * *

(b) RIGHT TO FAIR HEARING.—

* * * * * * *

(2) ONE HEARING PER PERIOD.—A *person* shall be entitled to only one hearing under this section with respect to the taxable period to which the unpaid tax specified in subsection (a)(3)(A) relates.

* * * * * * *

(c) MATTERS CONSIDERED AT HEARING.—In the case of any hearing conducted under this section—

* * * * * * *

(2) ISSUES AT HEARING.—

(A) IN GENERAL.—The *person* may raise at the hearing any relevant issue relating to the unpaid tax or the proposed levy, including—

(i) appropriate spousal defenses;

(ii) challenges to the appropriateness of collection actions; and

(iii) offers of collection alternatives, which may include the posting of a bond, the substitution of other assets, an installment agreement, or an offer-in-compromise.

(B) UNDERLYING LIABILITY.—The *person* may also raise at the hearing challenges to the existence or amount of the underlying tax liability for any tax period if the *person* did not receive any statutory notice of deficiency for such tax liability or did not otherwise have an opportunity to dispute such tax liability.

* * * * * * *

(d) PROCEEDING AFTER HEARING.—

(1) JUDICIAL REVIEW OF DETERMINATION.—The *person* may, within 30 days of a determination under this section, appeal such determination to the Tax Court (and the Tax Court shall have jurisdiction with respect to such matter).

(2) JURISDICTION RETAINED AT IRS OFFICE OF APPEALS.—The Internal Revenue Service Office of Appeals shall retain jurisdiction with respect to any determination made under this section, including subsequent hearings requested by the *person* who requested the original hearing on issues regarding—

(A) collection actions taken or proposed with respect to such determination; and

(B) after the *person* has exhausted all administrative remedies, a change in circumstances with respect to such person which affects such determination.

[Emphasis added.]

Petitioners interpret "person" broadly so as to include any third party claiming an ownership right in property that might be subject to levy to collect the unpaid taxes of another person. Thus, they claim all of the rights conferred in section 6330, including the right to appeal a notice of determination to this Court, even if the notice of determination was issued only to the person who owed tax. In analyzing the text of a statute, this Court is guided by the basic principle that a statute should be read as a harmonious whole, with its separate parts being interpreted within their broader statutory context in a manner that furthers the statutory purpose. *See K Mart Corp. v. Cartier, Inc.*, 486 U.S. 281, 291 (1988); *Guardian Indus. Corp. v. Commissioner*, 143 T.C. 1, 21 (2014). A comprehensive reading of section 6330 in its context demonstrates that "[t]he person" contemplated within the statutory framework is the person who owes the unpaid tax and that the only property that is subject to levy is the property of the person who owes the tax.

When section 6330 was enacted in 1998, it provided taxpayers with new procedural protections in the case of a levy which was already authorized by section 6331.[3] The levy authority provided in section 6331 is restricted to property of "the person" liable to pay the tax. Section 6331(a) provides:

> SEC. 6331(a). AUTHORITY OF SECRETARY.—If *any person liable to pay any tax* neglects or refuses to pay the same within 10 days after notice and demand, it shall be lawful for the Secretary to collect such tax (and such further sum as shall be sufficient to cover the expenses of the levy) by levy upon all *property and rights to property* (except such property as is exempt under section 6334) *belonging to such person* or on which there is a lien provided in this chapter for the payment of such tax. * * * [Emphasis added.]

The only property that is properly subject to levy under section 6331 is property and rights to property belonging to the person who owes the tax. Section 6330(d) allows a "person" whose property is going to be levied upon pursuant to section 6331 to appeal a notice of determination to the Tax Court and provides the Tax Court with jurisdiction over the appeal. Petitioners would have us believe that any person other than the delinquent taxpayer who alleges an ownership interest in property that might be subject to levy, is able to petition the Court for review of a notice of determination issued to a delinquent taxpayer. However, when read in its entirety and in context, section 6330 is unambiguously a taxpayer-oriented statute that provides *the taxpayer* with rights, defenses, and the ability to appeal a notice of determination.

[3] Sec. 6331, which authorized levy on a taxpayer's property, already contained certain notice and procedural provisions.

Section 6330(a)(3)(A) provides that the person will be delivered a prelevy notice which includes "the amount of unpaid tax". Section 6330(b)(2) instructs that the person who received the prelevy notice is "entitled to only one hearing under this section with respect to the taxable period to which the unpaid tax * * * relates." Section 6330(c)(2)(A) allows the person to raise at the hearing any relevant issue relating to the unpaid tax or proposed levy, including "appropriate spousal defenses" and "collection alternatives". Furthermore, section 6330(c)(2)(B) allows the person in certain cases to raise at the hearing any "challenges to the existence or amount of the underlying tax liability" if the person did not receive a notice of deficiency. These provisions involve due process protections and defenses pertaining to the taxpayer, not any third party who claims an ownership interest in property that might be subject to a proposed levy. Accordingly, we find that none of petitioners is a "person" as contemplated by section 6330, and therefore they cannot appeal a notice of determination issued to the estate in care of Mr. Crown.

The legislative history of section 6330 buttresses our conclusion that only the taxpayer or an authorized representative is to be provided with prelevy notice, CDP hearing rights, and the ability to petition for judicial review. Section 6330 was enacted as part of the Internal Revenue Service Restructuring and Reform Act of 1998, Pub. L. No. 105–206, sec. 3401(b), 112 Stat. at 747, in order to establish "formal procedures designed to insure due process where the IRS seeks to collect taxes by levy". H.R. Conf. Rept. No. 105–599, at 263 (1998), 1998–3 C.B. 747, 1017. The portion of the House conference report titled "Conference Agreement" that accompanied the enactment of section 6330 makes clear that it is the taxpayer, not a third party with alleged ownership interests, who is afforded prelevy notice and due process protections:

> The IRS would be required to provide the *taxpayer* with a "Notice of Intent to Levy," formally stating its intention to collect a tax liability by levy against the *taxpayer's* property or rights to property. * * *
>
> [T]he *taxpayer* may demand a hearing before an appeals officer who has had no prior involvement with the *taxpayer's* case, other than in connection with a hearing after the filing of a notice of tax lien. * * * In general, any issue that is relevant to the appropriateness of the proposed

> collection against the *taxpayer* can be raised at the pre-levy hearing. * * *
>
> [*Id.* at 265, 1998–3 C.B. at 1019; emphasis added.]

The House conference report indicates that the provision was initiated in the Senate. The portion of the report titled "Senate Amendment" states that it is the taxpayer who has the right to appeal a notice of determination in the Tax Court:

> The *taxpayer* may contest the determination of the appellate officer in Tax Court by filing a petition within 30 days of the date of the determination. The IRS may not take any collection action pursuant to the determination during such 30-day period or while the *taxpayer's* contest is pending in Tax Court. [*Id.* at 264, 1998–3 C.B. at 1018; emphasis added.]

Moreover, the regulations prescribed under section 6330 support our conclusion that petitioners are not appropriate parties to appeal a notice of determination issued to the estate. Petitioners cite section 301.6330–1(a)(3), Q&A–A1, Proced. & Admin. Regs., in support of the proposition that any "person whose property or right to property is intended to be levied upon" is required to receive a notice of intent to levy. From this language, petitioners glean that, because they allege an ownership interest in property that might be levied upon, this Court maintains jurisdiction over their appeal. Again, we disagree.

Section 301.6330–1(a)(3), Q&A–A1, Proced. & Admin. Regs., explains "[w]ho is the person to be notified under section 6330" of the Commissioner's intent to levy. The regulation plainly provides that the person to be notified is "the person liable to pay the tax due after notice and demand who refuses or neglects to pay (referred to here as the taxpayer). A prelevy or postlevy CDP Notice therefore will be given only to *the taxpayer*." *Id.* (emphasis added). Furthermore, the regulation explains that a party in petitioners' position is not entitled to receive notice:

> Q–B5. Will the IRS give pre-levy or post-levy CDP Notices to known nominees of, persons holding property of, or persons holding property subject to a lien with respect to the taxpayer?
>
> A–B5. No. Such person is not the person described in section 6331(a) and is, therefore, not entitled to a CDP hearing or an equivalent hearing * * *. Such person, however, may seek reconsideration by the IRS office collecting the tax, assistance from the National Taxpayer Advocate, or an administrative hearing before Appeals under its Collection Appeals

> Program. However, any such administrative hearing would not be a CDP hearing under section 6330 and any determination or decision resulting from the hearing would not be subject to judicial review.
> [Sec. 301.6330–1(b)(2), Q&A–B5, Proced. & Admin. Regs.]

The regulations provide that a notice of intent to levy is required to be sent only to the taxpayer. In the matter sub judice, it is undisputed that the taxpayer liable for the payment of Federal tax is the estate and the personal representative of the estate, not petitioners. *See* sec. 2002. The regulations further provide that "persons holding property of" the taxpayer are not entitled to prelevy or postlevy notice; however, they may seek other avenues of redress which are not subject to judicial review in the Tax Court.[4] Sec. 301.6330–1(b)(2), Q&A–B5, Proced. & Admin. Regs.

Upon replacing Mr. Crown as personal representative of the estate on January 16, 2014, Ms. McCrory filed supplemental responses to our order to show cause and respondent's motion to dismiss. In her responses Ms. McCrory took a position contrary to Mr. Crown. Specifically, Ms. McCrory argued that: (1) petitioners have standing to pursue the instant litigation; (2) the case should not be dismissed for lack of jurisdiction; or alternatively, that (3) the estate should be substituted as party petitioner and petitioners should be allowed to intervene "in order to adequately protect their interests" in property subject to levy.

Concerning our jurisdiction over petitioners' appeal, Ms. McCrory looks to the legislative history underlying section 6330 to support the proposition that "'affected third parties' are entitled to collection due process rights under I.R.C. § 6330." Specifically, Ms. McCrory quotes the following language from the portion of the House conference report titled "Senate Amendment":

> The taxpayer (or affected third party) is allowed to raise any relevant issue at the hearing. Issues eligible to be raised include (but are not limited to):
> (1) challenges to the underlying liability as to existence or amount;
> (2) appropriate spousal defenses;
> (3) challenges to the appropriateness of collection actions; and

---

[4] While the regulations under sec. 6330 are consistent with our position, we do not base our decision on the regulations. *See SECC Corp. v. Commissioner*, 142 T.C. 225, 234 n.5 (2014) ("We owe no deference to what an administrative agency says about our jurisdictional bounds.").

(4) collection alternatives, which could include the posting of a bond, substitution of other assets, an installment agreement or an offer-in-compromise.

[H.R. Conf. Rept. No. 105–599, *supra* at 264, 1998–3 C.B. at 1018.]

See S. Rept. No. 105–174, at 68 (1998), 1998–3 C.B. 537, 604. From this language Ms. McCrory concludes that it was "the express will of Congress" to provide affected third parties—such as petitioners—with the same due process rights under section 6330 as taxpayers liable for unpaid Federal tax. We find Ms. McCrory's argument unconvincing.

To begin with, the quoted portion of the legislative history concerns the original Senate Amendment and only mentions "affected third parties" with respect to attending and raising specified issues at the CDP hearing. While the Senate Amendment portion of the legislative history suggests that an affected third party might be permitted to participate in a CDP hearing, there is no suggestion that persons who are not taxpayers have notice or appeal rights. The subsequent conference report plainly states that notice and appeal rights are conferred only to the taxpayer, and the subsequent conference agreement omits the parenthetical regarding affected third parties that Ms. McCrory relies upon. Secondly, if we were to accept Ms. McCrory's argument that affected third parties are entitled to prelevy notice, it would prove administratively inconsistent with the express intent of the legislature concerning notice. The House conference report states that "[t]he Notice of Intent to Levy would not be required to itemize the property the Secretary seeks to levy on." H.R. Conf. Rept. No. 105–599, *supra* at 265, 1998–3 C.B. at 1019. Because the Commissioner is not required to itemize the property of the taxpayer subject to levy—as is the case in the matter sub judice—it would be impossible to provide alleged owners of the yet-to-be-determined property with prelevy notice. We conclude that the legislative history does not support the argument that "affected third parties" are entitled to notice or appeal rights.

Furthermore, Ms. McCrory's attempt to substitute the estate as a party is contrary to Mr. Crown's original position. Mr. Crown did not file a timely petition, and did not intend to petition, for review of the May 1, 2013, notice of determination. On May 6, 2014—nearly one year after the deadline to appeal from the May 1, 2013, notice of determination—Ms. McCrory filed a supplemental response attempting to support petitioners' right to petition and to reverse the original position of the estate. However, it is clear that the estate and its original personal representative did not intend to file a petition on the estate's behalf during the time for filing a petition, and any belated attempt to do so cannot be the basis for our jurisdiction. *See* Rule 41(a) ("No amendment shall be allowed after expiration of the time for filing the petition, however, which would involve conferring jurisdiction on the Court over a matter which otherwise would not come within its jurisdiction under the petition as then on file.").[5]

Section 6330 was enacted to give new procedural rights to taxpayers who owned property that the Commissioner intended to levy upon. Persons other than taxpayers who claimed ownership rights in property subject to levy already had procedural rights to contest a levy on the ground that they were the true owners. Section 7426(a)(1) provides:

> (1) WRONGFUL LEVY.—If a levy has been made on property or property has been sold pursuant to a levy, any person (other than the person against whom is assessed the tax out of which such levy arose) who claims an interest in or lien on such property and that such property was wrongfully levied upon may bring a civil action against the United States in a district court of the United States. Such action may be brought without regard to whether such property has been surrendered to or sold by the Secretary.

If the Internal Revenue Service levies upon a third party's property to collect taxes owed by another, the third party may bring a wrongful levy action against the United States pursuant to section 7426(a)(1). Section 7426(a)(1) provides the exclusive remedy for third-party wrongful levy claims. *See EC Term of Years Trust v. United States*, 550 U.S. 429, 435 (2007); *Elias v. Commissioner*, 100 T.C. 510, 519 n.10 (1993); *Cutler v. Commissioner*, T.C. Memo. 2013–119, at *32. Section 7426(a) gives the District Courts jurisdiction to hear wrongful levy actions. This Court has no jurisdiction

---

[5] We have allowed ratification and amendment of an imperfect petition where it was clear that the original filing was made on behalf of the taxpayer by a person duly authorized to do so. *See Fletcher Plastics, Inc. v. Commissioner*, 64 T.C. 35, 37 (1975); *Brooks v. Commissioner*, 63 T.C. 709, 714 (1975). The matter sub judice does not fall within these parameters because a duly authorized representative of the estate did not file, nor intend to file, a timely petition for review of the May 1, 2013, notice of determination.

over section 7426 claims. *See Cutler v. Commissioner*, T.C. Memo. 2013–119, at *32.

We hold that a person, other than the taxpayer, who alleges an ownership interest in property which the Commissioner seeks to levy upon is not entitled to receive a notice of intent to levy and is not able to seek judicial review in this Court pursuant to a notice of determination issued to a delinquent taxpayer. Accordingly, we lack jurisdiction under section 6330(d) to hear petitioners' appeal.

In reaching our decision, we have considered all arguments made by the parties, and to the extent not mentioned or addressed, they are irrelevant or without merit.

To reflect the foregoing,

An order of dismissal for lack of jurisdiction will be entered.

DYNAMO HOLDINGS LIMITED PARTNERSHIP, DYNAMO, GP, INC., TAX MATTERS PARTNER, PETITIONER *v.* COMMISSIONER OF INTERNAL REVENUE, RESPONDENT

BEEKMAN VISTA, INC., PETITIONER *v.* COMMISSIONER OF INTERNAL REVENUE, RESPONDENT

Docket Nos. 2685–11, 8393–12. Filed September 17, 2014.

R requests that Ps produce electronically stored information contained on two backup storage tapes or, alternatively, the tapes themselves (or copies thereof). Ps acknowledge that the tapes contain tax-related information but assert that the tapes also contain privileged information that Ps have a right or duty to protect. Ps assert that they must review the responsive information on the tapes before giving the information to R to ensure that privileged or confidential information is not disclosed. Ps request that the Court let them use "predictive coding", a technique prevalent in the technology industry but not yet formally sanctioned by this Court, to help identify the information that is responsive to R's request. *Held*: Ps may use predictive coding in responding to R's request.

Martin R. Press, *Edward A. Marod*, *Lu-Ann Mancini Dominguez*, and *Alan Stuart Lederman*, for petitioners.

David B. Flassing and *Lisa Goldberg*, for respondent.

OPINION

BUCH, *Judge*: These consolidated cases are before the Court on respondent's motion to compel production of documents.[1] The cases concern various transfers from Beekman Vista, Inc. (Beekman), to a related entity, Dynamo Holdings Limited Partnership (Dynamo). Respondent determined that the transfers are disguised gifts to Dynamo's owners. Petitioners assert that the transfers are loans.

Respondent requests that petitioners produce the electronically stored information (ESI) contained on two specified backup storage tapes or, alternatively, that they produce the tapes themselves (or copies thereof). Petitioners assert that it will take many months and cost at least $450,000 to fulfill respondent's request because they would need to review each document on the tapes to identify what is responsive and then withhold privileged or confidential information. Petitioners request that the Court deny respondent's motion as a "fishing expedition" in search of new issues that could be raised in these or other cases. Alternatively, petitioners request that the Court let them use predictive coding, a technique prevalent in the technology industry but not yet formally sanctioned by this Court, to efficiently and economically identify the nonprivileged information responsive to respondent's discovery request.

Respondent counters that he wants the backup tapes to review the ESI's metadata and verify the dates on which certain documents were created. Respondent states that he also wants the backup tapes to ascertain all transfers relevant to this proceeding. Respondent opposes petitioners' request to use predictive coding because, he states, predictive coding is an "unproven technology". Respondent adds that petitioners need not devote their claimed time or expense to this matter because they can simply give him access to all data on the two tapes and preserve the right (through a "clawback agreement") to later claim that some or all of the data is privileged information not subject to discovery.[2]

---

[1] Respondent also moved to compel interrogatories. We will separately address that motion in an order.

[2] We understand respondent's use of the term "clawback agreement" to mean that the disclosure of any privileged information on the tapes would not be a waiver of any privilege that would otherwise apply to

The Court held an evidentiary hearing on respondent's motion. We will grant respondent's motion to the limited extent stated herein. Specifically, we hold that petitioners must respond to respondent's discovery request but that they may use predictive coding in doing so.

Background

I. *Relevant Entities*

A. *Beekman*

Beekman is a corporation wholly owned by a Canadian entity which is controlled by Delia Moog. Beekman's mailing address was in Florida when its petition was filed.

B. *Dynamo*

Dynamo is a limited partnership owned by a corporation and two trusts that were established for Ms. Moog's daughter and nephew. Dynamo's tax matters partner is Dynamo GP, Inc. Dynamo, through its tax matters partner, alleges that its principal place of business was in Delaware when its petition was filed. Respondent alleges that Dynamo's principal place of business was in Florida at that time.

II. *Backup Tapes*

Dynamo backs up onto tapes its entire exchange server (inclusive of emails, operating system, and configuration information). Dynamo performs this backup work every four weeks and at the end of every month. Dynamo generally retains its backup tapes for one year.

Respondent seeks two of the backup tapes, specifically, the "Month End August 2010 ORANGE" and the "Month End Jan 08 ORANGE". These tapes contain data backed up from (1) an exchange server and (2) a domain controller and file server (KSH–DC). The exchange server database has approximately 200 mailboxes ranging in size from 500 megabytes to 1 gigabyte each. The KSH–DC has a common group and a user group. The common group has shares where assigned users may store data to be shared with other assigned users. The common group has approximately 50 common top-level file shares and an undetermined number of

---

that information.

subfolders, and ownership of these files may not be limited to the authors of the documents. The user group is in a section of the network assigned to a specific individual and has approximately 200 user share folders.

III. *Petitioners' Request To Use Predictive Coding*

Petitioners acknowledge that the two requested backup tapes contain tax-related information but assert that the tapes also contain "personal identification information, health insurance information, HIPAA protected information and other confidential information that Petitioners have a duty to protect."[3] Petitioners assert that if they must respond to respondent's discovery request, they must review the documents on the backup tapes to ensure that no privileged or confidential information is disclosed before giving any information to respondent. Petitioners ask the Court to let them use predictive coding to efficiently and economically help identify the nonprivileged information that is responsive to respondent's discovery request. More specifically, petitioners want to implement the following procedure to respond to the request:

> 1. Restore some or all of the data from the tapes.
>
> 2. Qualify the restored data; i.e., remove NIST files, system files, etc. [4]
>
> 3. Index and load the qualified restored data into a review environment.
>
> 4. Apply criteria to the loaded data to remove duplicate messages and other nonrelevant information.
>
> 5. Through the implementation of predictive coding, review the remaining data using search criteria that the parties agree upon to ascertain, on the one hand, information that is relevant to the matter, and on the other hand, potentially relevant information that should be withheld as privileged or confidential information.

---

[3] The Health Insurance Portability and Accountability Act of 1996 (HIPAA), Pub. L. No. 104–191, secs. 261–264, 110 Stat. at 2021–2033, contains privacy rules and gave rise to privacy regulations relating to individually identifiable health information.

[4] The National Institute of Standards and Technology (NIST), which is an agency of the U.S. Department of Commerce, maintains a database of hash values of files that typically are part of an operating system or a piece of software. A hash value, which is essentially a fingerprint of a file, is a numeric computation of a file's content which is used to identify the file. Two files with the same hash values are exact copies of each other.

6. Produce the relevant nonprivileged information and a privilege log that sets forth the claimed privileged documents and sufficient information supporting that claim.

Discussion

I. *Discovery in General*

A party in this Court generally may obtain discovery of documents and ESI to the extent that the information contained therein is not privileged and is relevant to the subject matter of the case. *See* Rule 70(a)(1), (b);[5] *see also* Rule 72(a).[6] In this context, documents and ESI include "writings, drawings, graphs, charts, photographs, sound recordings, images, and other data compilations stored in any medium from which information can be obtained, either directly or translated, if necessary, by the responding party into a reasonably usable form".[7] Rule 72(a)(1). And a party is gen-

---

[5] Rule references are to the Tax Court Rules of Practice and Procedure.

[6] Rule 72(a) provides:

RULE 72. PRODUCTION OF DOCUMENTS, ELECTRONICALLY STORED INFORMATION, AND THINGS

(a) Scope: Any party may, without leave of Court, serve on any other party a request to:

(1) Produce and permit the party making the request, or someone acting on such party's behalf, to inspect and copy, test, or sample any designated documents or electronically stored information (including writings, drawings, graphs, charts, photographs, sound recordings, images, and other data compilations stored in any medium from which information can be obtained, either directly or translated, if necessary, by the responding party into a reasonably usable form), or to inspect and copy, test, or sample any tangible thing, to the extent that any of the foregoing items are in the possession, custody, or control of the party on whom the request is served * * *

[7] Literature on electronic data storage has characterized electronically stored data as falling within five categories. *See Zubulake v. UBS Warburg LLC*, 217 F.R.D. 309, 318 (S.D.N.Y. 2003). These categories are active, online data (e.g., hard drives); near-line data (e.g., optical disks); offline storage/archives (i.e., removable optical disk or magnetic tape media); backup tapes (i.e., a device that reads data from and writes it onto a tape); and fragmented, erased, or damaged data (fragmented data consists of files that are broken up and placed randomly throughout the disk). *See id.* at 318–319. The first three categories are generally considered accessible, while the remaining categories are generally considered inaccessible. *See*

Continued

erally required to produce documents or electronically stored information in the form in which they are maintained. Rule 72(b)(3). A party, however, is not required to provide discovery of ESI from sources that the party establishes are not reasonably accessible because of undue burden or cost unless the Court concludes that the requesting party has shown good cause for the discovery.[8] *See* Rule 70(c)(2). These Rules are all similar to corresponding provisions found in the Federal Rules of Civil Procedure. *See* Fed. R. Civ. P. 34(a)(1)(A), (b)(2)(E), 26(b)(2)(B).

II. *Respondent's Request*

Respondent requests access to petitioners' ESI. Petitioners resist this request, primarily because of cost and of concern that privileged or confidential information will be improperly disclosed. Respondent essentially responds that he can alleviate both concerns if petitioners give him all of the requested information, with the condition that he will allow them to later claim that some or all of that information should not be disclosed further because it is privileged. Petitioners remain mindful of their need to protect their privileged or confidential information, as well as the projected cost of protecting that information, and ask the Court to allow them to use predictive coding in responding to respondent's request.

In this respect, we note that this request is somewhat unusual. Our Rules are clear that "the Court expects the parties to attempt to attain the objectives of discovery through informal consultation or communication" before resorting to formal discovery procedures. Rule 70(a)(1). And although it is a proper role of the Court to supervise the discovery process and intervene when it is abused by the parties, the Court is not normally in the business of dictating to parties the process that they should use when responding to discovery. If our focus were on paper discovery, we would not (for example) be dictating to a party the manner in which it should review documents for responsiveness or privilege, such as whether that review should be done by a paralegal,

---

id. at 319–320.

[8] Petitioners do not claim that, if they use predictive coding, the requested ESI is not reasonably accessible because of undue burden or cost.

a junior attorney, or a senior attorney. Yet that is, in essence, what the parties are asking the Court to consider—whether document review should be done by humans or with the assistance of computers. Respondent fears an incomplete response to his discovery request. If respondent believes that the ultimate discovery response is incomplete and can support that belief, he can file another motion to compel at that time. Nonetheless, because we have not previously addressed the issue of computer-assisted review tools, we will address it here.

III. *Expert Witnesses*

Each party called a witness to testify at the evidentiary hearing as an expert. Petitioners' witness was James R. Scarazzo. Respondent's witness was Michael L. Wudke. The Court recognized the witnesses as experts on the subject matter at hand.

We may accept or reject the findings and conclusions of the experts, according to our own judgment. *See Chapman Glen, Ltd. v. Commissioner*, 140 T.C. 294, 329 (2013). We also may be selective in deciding what parts (if any) of their opinions to accept. *See id.*

IV. *Analysis*

The Court applies the standard of relevancy liberally when it comes to matters of discovery, *see, e.g., Zaentz v. Commissioner*, 73 T.C. 469, 471 (1979), and a party challenging the requested production of a document (including ESI) has the burden of establishing that the document is not discoverable, *see Rutter v. Commissioner*, 81 T.C. 937, 948 (1983); *Branerton Corp. v. Commissioner*, 64 T.C. 191, 192–193 (1975).

We believe that respondent's request for the ESI is within the bounds of our Rules, and petitioners do not appear to contest this point. At the same time, however, we are faced with the competing interests of the parties. On one hand, we do not consider it appropriate to order petitioners to give all of their ESI to respondent, subject to a right to later claim that some or all of the information that he has reviewed is privileged or confidential information and thus outside the bounds of discovery. Although the use of a clawback agreement may be an option to which the parties might consent, petitioners reasonably resist entering into any such agreement as part of a plan under which they would voluntarily allow respondent to see all of the privileged or confidential information on the requested tapes. On the other hand, given the time and expense involved with petitioners' review of all the ESI to identify any privileged or confidential information, we likewise do not consider it appropriate to order petitioners to go to that extreme either.

We find a potential happy medium in petitioners' proposed use of predictive coding. Predictive coding is an expedited and efficient form of computer-assisted review that allows parties in litigation to avoid the time and costs associated with the traditional, manual review of large volumes of documents. Through the coding of a relatively small sample of documents, computers can predict the relevance of documents to a discovery request and then identify which documents are and are not responsive. The parties (typically through their counsel or experts) select a sample of documents from the universe of those documents to be searched by using search criteria that may, for example, consist of keywords, dates, custodians, and document types, and the selected documents become the primary data used to cause the predictive coding software to recognize patterns of relevance in the universe of documents under review. The software distinguishes what is relevant, and each iteration produces a smaller relevant subset and a larger set of irrelevant documents that can be used to verify the integrity of the results. Through the use of predictive coding, a party responding to discovery is left with a smaller set of documents to review for privileged information, resulting in savings both in time and in expense. The party responding to the discovery request also is able to give the other party a log detailing the records that were withheld and the reasons they were withheld.

Magistrate Judge Andrew Peck published a leading, oft-cited article on predictive coding which is helpful to our understanding of that method. *See* Andrew Peck, "Search, Forward: Will Manual Document Review and Keyboard Searches be Replaced by Computer-Assisted Coding?", L. Tech. News (Oct. 2011). The article generally discusses the mechanics of predictive coding and the shortcomings of manual review and of keyword searches. The article explains that predictive coding is a form of "computed-assisted coding", which in turn means "tools * * * that use sophisticated algorithms to enable the computer to determine relevance, based on interaction with (i.e., training by) a human reviewer." *Id.* at 29. The article explains that

> [u]nlike manual review, where the review is done by the most junior staff, computer-assisted coding involves a senior partner (or team) who review and code a "seed set" of documents. The computer identifies properties of those documents that it uses to code other documents. As the senior reviewer continues to code more sample documents, the computer predicts the reviewer's coding. (Or, the computer codes some documents and asks the senior reviewer for feedback.)
>
> When the system's predictions and the reviewer's coding sufficiently coincide, the system has learned enough to make confident predictions for the remaining documents. Typically, the senior lawyer (or team) needs to review only a few thousand documents to train the computer.
>
> Some systems produce a simple yes/no as to relevance, while others give a relevance score (say, on a 0 to 100 basis) that counsel can use to prioritize review. For example, a score above 50 may produce 97% of the relevant documents, but constitutes only 20% of the entire document set.
>
> Counsel may decide, after sampling and quality control tests, that documents with a score of below 15 are so highly likely to be irrelevant that no further human review is necessary. Counsel can also decide the cost-benefit of manual review of the documents with scores of 15–50.
>
> [*Id.*]

The substance of the article was eventually adopted in an opinion that states: "This judicial opinion now recognizes that computer-assisted review is an acceptable way to search for relevant ESI in appropriate cases." *Moore v. Publicis Groupe*, 287 F.R.D. 182, 183 (S.D.N.Y. 2012), *adopted sub nom. Moore v. Publicis Groupe SA*, No. 11 Civ. 1279 (ALC)(AJP), 2012 WL 1446534 (S.D.N.Y. Apr. 26, 2012).

Respondent asserts that predictive coding should not be used in these cases because it is an "unproven technology". We disagree. Although predictive coding is a relatively new technique, and a technique that has yet to be sanctioned (let alone mentioned) by this Court in a published Opinion, the understanding of e-discovery[9] and electronic media has advanced significantly in the last few years, thus making predictive coding more acceptable in the technology industry

[9] We use the term "e-discovery" to refer to "electronic discovery", which in turn means the obtaining of ESI in the discovery phase of litigation.

than it may have previously been. In fact, we understand that the technology industry now considers predictive coding to be widely accepted for limiting e-discovery to relevant documents and effecting discovery of ESI without an undue burden.[10] *See Progressive Cas. Ins. Co. v. Delaney*, No. 2:11–cv–00678–LRH–PAL, 2014 WL 3563467, at *8 (D. Nev. July 18, 2014) (stating with citations of articles that predictive coding has proved to be an accurate way to comply with a discovery request for ESI and that studies show it is more accurate than human review or keyword searches); *F.D.I.C. v. Bowden*, No. CV413–245, 2014 WL 2548137, at *13 (S.D. Ga. June 6, 2014) (directing that the parties consider the use of predictive coding). *See generally* Nicholas Barry, "Man Versus Machine Review: The Showdown between Hordes of Discovery Lawyers and a Computer-Utilizing Predictive-Coding Technology", 15 Vand. J. Ent. & Tech. L. 343 (2013); Lisa C. Wood, "Predictive Coding Has Arrived", 28 ABA Antitrust J. 93 (2013). The use of predictive coding also is not unprecedented in Federal litigation. *See, e.g.*, *Hinterberger v. Catholic Health Sys., Inc.*, No. 08–CV–3805(F), 2013 WL 2250603 (W.D.N.Y. May 21, 2013); *In re Actos*, No. 6:11–md–2299, 2012 WL 7861249 (W.D. La. July 27, 2012); *Moore*, 287 F.R.D. 182. Where, as here, petitioners reasonably request to use predictive coding to conserve time and expense, and represent to the Court that they will retain electronic discovery experts to meet with respondent's counsel or his experts to conduct a search acceptable to respondent, we see no reason petitioners should not be allowed to use predictive coding to respond to respondent's discovery request. *Cf. Progressive Cas. Ins. Co.*, 2014 WL 3563467, at *10–*12 (declining to allow the use of predictive coding where the record lacked the necessary transparency and cooperation among counsel in the review and production of ESI responsive to the discovery request).

Mr. Scarazzo's expert testimony supports our opinion.[11] He testified that discovery of ESI essentially involves a two-step

[10] Predictive coding is so commonplace in the home and at work in that most (if not all) individuals with an email program use predictive coding to filter out spam email. *See Moore v. Publicis Groupe*, 287 F.R.D. 182, 184 n.2 (S.D.N.Y. 2012), *adopted sub nom. Moore v. Publicis Groupe SA*, No. 11 Civ. 1279 (ALC)(AJP), 2012 WL 1446534 (S.D.N.Y. Apr. 26, 2012).

[11] Mr. Wudke did not persuasively say anything to erode or otherwise

process. First, the universe of data is narrowed to data that is potentially responsive to a discovery request. Second, the potentially responsive data is narrowed down to what is in fact responsive. He also testified that he was familiar with both predictive coding and keyword searching, two of the techniques commonly employed in the first step of the two-step discovery process, and he compared those techniques by stating:

> [K]ey word searching is, as the name implies, is a list of terms or terminologies that are used that are run against documents in a method of determining or identifying those documents to be reviewed. What predictive coding does is it takes the type of documents, the layout, maybe the whispets of the documents, the format of the documents, and it uses a computer model to predict which documents out of the whole set might contain relevant information to be reviewed.
>
> So one of the things that it does is, by using technology, it eliminates or minimizes some of the human error that might be associated with it. Sometimes there's inefficiencies with key word searching in that it may include or exclude documents, whereas training the model to go back and predict this, we can look at it and use statistics and other sampling information to pull back the information and feel more confident that the information that's being reviewed is the universe of potentially responsive data.

He concluded that the trend was in favor of predictive coding because it eliminates human error and expedites review.

In addition, Mr. Scarazzo opined credibly and without contradiction that petitioners' approach to responding to respondent's discovery request is the most reasonable way for petitioners to comply with that request. Petitioners asked Mr. Scarazzo to analyze and to compare the parties' dueling approaches in the setting of the data to be restored from Dynamo's backup tapes and to opine on which of the approaches is the most reasonable way for petitioners to comply with respondent's request. Mr. Scarazzo assumed as to petitioners' approach that the restored data would be searched using specific criteria, that the resulting information would be reviewed for privilege, and that petitioners would produce the nonprivileged information to respondent. He assumed as to respondent's approach that the restored data would be searched for privileged information without using specific search criteria, that the resulting privileged

undercut Mr. Scarazzo's testimony.

information would be removed, and that petitioners would then produce the remaining data to respondent. As to both approaches, he examined certain details of Dynamo's backup tapes, interviewed the person most knowledgeable on Dynamo's backup process and the contents of its backup tapes (Dynamo's director of information technology), and performed certain cost calculations.

Mr. Scarazzo concluded that petitioners' approach would reduce the universe of information on the tapes using criteria set by the parties to minimize review time and expense and ultimately result in a focused set of information germane to the matter. He estimated that 200,000 to 400,000 documents would be subject to review under petitioners' approach at a cost of $80,000 to $85,000, while 3.5 million to 7 million documents would be subject to review under respondent's approach at a cost of $500,000 to $550,000.

Our Rules, including our discovery Rules, are to "be construed to secure the just, speedy, and inexpensive determination of every case." Rule 1(d). Petitioners may use predictive coding in responding to respondent's discovery request. If, after reviewing the results, respondent believes that the response to the discovery request is incomplete, he may file a motion to compel at that time. *See* Rule 104(b), (d).

Accordingly,

An appropriate order will be issued.

JAMES C. COOPER AND LORELEI M. COOPER, PETITIONERS *v.* COMMISSIONER OF INTERNAL REVENUE, RESPONDENT

Docket No. 17284–12. Filed September 23, 2014.

In 1997 P–H, an inventor, transferred several patents to T, a corporation. Ps own 24% of the outstanding stock of T. P–W's sister and Ps' friend own the remaining stock. P–H controlled T through its officers, directors, and shareholders. Ps reported royalty income that P–H received from T in exchange for the transfer of the patents as capital gain under I.R.C. sec. 1235(a) for 2006, 2007, and 2008. In 2006 P–H paid the engineering expenses of a related corporation. Ps deducted these expenses as professional fees on a Schedule C, Profit or Loss From Business, attached to their 2006 Federal income tax return. Between 2005 and 2008 Ps advanced $2,046,901 to X, a corporation, under the terms of a working capital promissory note. P–H owned 24% of the outstanding stock of X during the years at issue. X contracted with an Indian company to develop a new product, and it used Ps' loans in part to fund the development of the new product. In 2008 the Indian company abandoned its development of the new product. Ps claimed that X was insolvent and claimed a bad debt deduction under I.R.C. sec. 166 of $2,046,570 for 2008. R determined that (1) the royalty payments P–H received from T did not qualify for capital gain treatment; (2) the engineering expenses were the ordinary and necessary expenses of a related corporation and Ps were not entitled to deduct those expenses; (3) Ps were not entitled to a bad debt deduction for 2008; and (4) Ps were liable for an accuracy-related penalty under I.R.C. sec. 6662(a) for each of the years at issue. *Held*: P–H did not transfer all substantial rights in the subject patents to T within the meaning of I.R.C. sec. 1235(a) because P–H controlled T during the years at issue. *See Charlson v. United States*, 525 F.2d 1046, 1053 (Ct. Cl. 1975). Ps are therefore not entitled to capital gain treatment under I.R.C. sec. 1235(a) for the royalties P–H received from T in exchange for the subject patents. *Held*, *further*, Ps are entitled to deduct the engineering expenses for 2006. Under *Lohrke v. Commissioner*, 48 T.C. 679, 688 (1967), P–H's primary motive in paying the expenses was to protect or promote his business as an inventor, and the expenditures constituted ordinary and necessary expenses in the furtherance or promotion of P–H's business. *Held*, *further*, Ps are not entitled to a bad debt deduction under I.R.C. sec. 166 because Ps have failed to prove that the promissory note became worthless in 2008. *Held*, *further*, Ps are liable for an accuracy-related penalty under I.R.C. sec. 6662(a) for each of the years at issue.

Lawrence T. Ullmann, for petitioners.
Nhi T. Luu and *Christian A. Speck*, for respondent.

MARVEL, *Judge*: Respondent determined deficiencies in petitioners' Federal income tax of $580,961, $384,705, and $496,236 for 2006, 2007, and 2008, respectively, and accuracy-related penalties under section 6662(a)[1] of $116,192, $76,941, and $99,247 for 2006, 2007, and 2008, respectively. After concessions,[2] the issues for decision are:

[1] Unless otherwise indicated, all section references are to the Internal Revenue Code (Code) in effect for the years at issue, and all Rule references are to the Tax Court Rules of Practice and Procedure. Some monetary amounts have been rounded to the nearest dollar.

[2] The parties stipulated or conceded that petitioners are entitled to de-

Continued

(1) whether royalties petitioner James Cooper received during 2006, 2007, and 2008 qualified for capital gain treatment pursuant to section 1235; (2) whether petitioners may deduct professional fees paid during 2006 that were attributable to expenses charged by Holmes Development for work performed with respect to U.S. Patent # 5,157,489 (489 patent);[3] (3) whether petitioners' advance of $2,046,570[4] to Pixel Instruments Corp. (Pixel) is deductible as a nonbusiness bad debt for 2008 pursuant to section 166; and (4) whether petitioners are liable for section 6662(a) accuracy-related penalties for the years at issue.

FINDINGS OF FACT

Some of the facts have been stipulated and are so found. The stipulations of facts are incorporated herein by this reference. Petitioners resided in Nevada when they petitioned this Court.

I. *Patent Royalties*

Mr. Cooper is an engineer and inventor. He has an undergraduate degree in electrical engineering from Oklahoma State University and is the named inventor on more than 75 patents in the United States.[5] His patents are primarily for products and components used in the transmission of audio and video signals. Petitioner Lorelei Cooper has an undergraduate degree in communications from Kent State University. She is not the named inventor on any patents.

In 1988 Mr. Cooper consulted Daniel Leckrone, an attorney specializing in patent law and patent licensing, regarding Mr. Cooper's portfolio of intellectual property. These con-

---

duct on Schedule C, Profit or Loss From Business: (1) travel expenses of $30,072, $18,432, and $21,444 for 2006, 2007, and 2008, respectively; and (2) professional fees of $82,585, $241,153, and $109,007 for 2006, 2007, and 2008, respectively.

[3] The 489 patent was titled "Apparatus and Method for Reducing Quantizing Distortion".

[4] The parties stipulated that on December 31, 2008, the outstanding balance on the promissory note was $2,046,901. However, petitioners claimed a nonbusiness bad debt deduction for the outstanding balance on the promissory note of $2,046,570 for 2008.

[5] Mr. Cooper is also a patent agent entitled to represent third parties before the U.S. Patent and Trademark Office.

sultations led to an agreement (commercialization agreement)[6] among Mr. Leckrone, Mr. Cooper, and Pixel wherein Mr. Cooper and Pixel assigned their portfolio of audio and video patents to VidPro,[7] a licensing company formed by Mr. Leckrone.

A number of disputes arose between Mr. Cooper and Mr. Leckrone under the commercialization agreement. In 1997 Mr. Cooper sent Mr. Leckrone notice that he was terminating the commercialization agreement. Mr. Cooper contended that under the terms of the commercialization agreement the patent rights held by VidPro automatically reverted to him as a result of the termination notice. Mr. Leckrone disagreed. Ultimately, this dispute led to litigation between Mr. Cooper and Mr. Leckrone, VidPro, and an attorney on VidPro's board of directors (Cooper-Leckrone litigation).[8]

Subsequently, petitioners, believing that all rights in VidPro's audio and video patents reverted to Mr. Cooper, incorporated Technology Licensing Corp., a California corporation (TLC),[9] with Lois Walters and Janet Coulter. Ms. Walters is petitioner Lorelei Cooper's sister, and Ms. Coulter is a longtime friend of Ms. Cooper and Ms. Walters. Ms. Coulter and Ms. Walters resided in Ohio from 1997 through

---

[6] The commercialization of a patent generally includes finding companies to manufacture products using the patent as well as finding and suing patent infringers for damages.

[7] At the time the commercialization agreement was signed, VidPro was known as VideoTech.

[8] The Cooper-Leckrone litigation ended in 2004 when a final arbitration award was entered determining, among other things, that the commercialization agreement was properly terminated as of January 21, 1997, and all rights, title, and interest that VidPro claimed in the patents were returned to Mr. Cooper or his assignee.

[9] Petitioners moved their principal residence from California to Nevada in November 2003. Petitioners, Ms. Walters, and Ms. Coulter then formed a second Technology Licensing Corp. with the Nevada secretary of state (TLC Nevada). Petitioners as cotrustees of the Cooper Trust U.D.T. December 11, 1991 (Cooper Trust), contributed $240 to TLC Nevada in exchange for 240 shares in TLC Nevada, and Ms. Walters and Ms. Coulter each contributed $380 to TLC Nevada in exchange for 380 shares in TLC Nevada (38%). Ms. Walters, Ms. Cooper, and Ms. Coulter were the president and chief financial officer, vice president, and secretary of TLC, respectively. On February 24, 2004, TLC merged into TLC-Nevada with TLC-Nevada as the surviving corporation. We refer to TLC Nevada as TLC unless otherwise indicated.

2013, and both worked full time with companies other than TLC during the years at issue.[10] Neither Ms. Coulter nor Ms. Walters had any experience in patent licensing or patent commercialization before their involvement with TLC.

Petitioners incorporated TLC to engage in patent licensing and patent commercialization. They wanted TLC to have the "aura" of a fully operating licensing corporation but also wanted people Mr. Cooper could trust—such as their close friend Ms. Coulter and their relative Ms. Walters—to be the shareholders, officers, and directors of TLC.[11]

Petitioners engaged Attorney R. Gordon Baker, Jr., to provide advice on forming TLC. Among other things, Mr. Baker advised petitioners on the requirements of section 1235 and qualifying the royalty payments Mr. Cooper would receive from TLC as capital gain under that section. Mr. Baker advised petitioners that (1) they could not control TLC directly or indirectly and (2) their stock ownership in TLC had to be less than 25% of the total outstanding stock.

Consistent with Mr. Baker's advice, the outstanding stock of TLC at formation was as follows: petitioners as cotrustees of the Cooper Trust owned 240 shares (24%); (2) Lois Walters owned 380 shares (38%); and (3) Janet Coulter owned 380 shares (38%). Ms. Walters and Ms. Coulter each made an initial contribution of $3,800 to TLC in exchange for their shares while petitioners as cotrustees of the Cooper Trust contributed $2,400 for the trust's shares. Ms. Walters, Ms. Cooper, and Ms. Coulter were the president and chief financial officer, vice president, and secretary of TLC, respectively.[12] Mr. Cooper was the general manager of TLC.

---

[10] Ms. Walters has a B.A. degree in finance from Cleveland State University. During the years at issue she was an employee of the National Multiple Sclerosis Society in Independence, Ohio. Ms. Coulter has a B.S. degree in animal science from Ohio State University and an M.S. in agricultural economics from the University of Wyoming. She owns her own construction company, Multi-Maintenance, Inc., in Ohio and was an employee of Multi-Maintenance during the years at issue.

[11] TLC did not have an office or other formal business location.

[12] Beginning in 2004 or 2005 and continuing through the years at issue, Ms. Coulter performed most of Ms. Walters' duties at TLC. At that time, Ms. Walters was working more than 50 hours per week for the National Multiple Sclerosis Society and spending substantial time caring for her ill father.

On March 15, 1997, Mr. Cooper and Pixel entered into agreements (collectively, TLC agreements) with TLC purportedly transferring all of Mr. Cooper's and Pixel's rights in the patents (subject patents) giving rise to the royalties at issue in this case to TLC. Under each TLC agreement, the licensor (i.e., Mr. Cooper or Pixel) receives 40% of all gross proceeds received by TLC for any sublicense and 40% of all damages received in litigation or settlement of litigation. The licensor then receives 90% of all remaining net proceeds as defined in the TLC agreements.

By 1999 TLC had begun experiencing financial difficulty. It could not effectively license its patents because the patents were the subject of the Cooper-Leckrone litigation and potential licensees were wary of TLC's authority to license the patents. Furthermore, TLC needed legal representation to pursue patent infringement cases.

In an effort to solve TLC's financial difficulties, Mr. Cooper contacted Anthony Brown, who was in the business of helping inventors protect and enforce their patents. Mr. Brown owned IP Innovation, LLC (IP Innovation). Subsequently, TLC, Mr. Cooper, and Pixel entered into an agreement (IP Innovation assignment agreement) with IP Innovation assigning an undivided interest in Patent # 5,424,780 (780 patent) to IP Innovation.[13] Then, IP Innovation, Mr. Cooper, Pixel, and TLC engaged the patent law firm of Niro, Scavone, Haller & Niro (Niro firm) to represent their interests with respect to the 780 patent. Mr. Cooper agreed to provide technical assistance to the Niro firm as necessary to assist the firm in interpreting the patents, technology, and devices that would be the subject of the licensing and infringement matters the firm was pursuing. Mr. Cooper was not compensated for providing technical assistance to the Niro firm.

On February 28, 2003, TLC and its shareholders adopted a stock restriction agreement providing in relevant part that

[13] On August 12, 2002, TLC, Pixel, Mr. Cooper, and IP Innovation executed an agreement (exclusive license agreement) expanding IP Innovation's license beyond the 780 patent by providing an exclusive, perpetual, and irrevocable license to several additional patents. TLC, Pixel, Mr. Cooper, and IP Innovation amended the exclusive license agreement on October 31, 2002, and on November 12, 2004, the exclusive license agreement was terminated.

TLC's shares could not be sold, assigned, or transferred except according to the terms of the stock restriction agreement. Under the agreement petitioners were permitted to transfer shares of TLC stock to their issue or any trust for the benefit of their issue. No other TLC shareholder (i.e., Ms. Coulter or Ms. Walters) was permitted to transfer shares of TLC stock to her issue or any party other than a shareholder. Mr. Baker drafted the stock restriction agreement in his role as petitioners' estate planning attorney. Despite owning a majority of TLC's outstanding stock and being on the board of directors, neither Ms. Coulter nor Ms. Walters negotiated the terms of the stock restriction agreement.[14]

In 2004 Anthony Brown formed New Medium, LLC (New Medium), and AV Technologies, LLC (AV Technologies), to pursue patent commercialization. TLC, Pixel, and Mr. Cooper subsequently entered into licensing agreements for certain patents with both New Medium and AV Technologies (collectively, New Medium and AV Technologies agreements). In or about 2004 Acacia Technologies Group (Acacia) purchased IP Innovation and IP Innovation became a subsidiary of Acacia. On March 23, 2005, the parties to the New Medium and AV Technologies agreements and the IP Innovation assignment agreement clarified by agreement (letter agreement) that all material decisions (i.e., licensing, litigation, and prosecution) with respect to the New Medium and AV Technologies agreements and the IP Innovation assignment agreement were to be made according to a majority vote of Mr. Cooper, Acacia,[15] and Anthony Brown. Under the letter agreement TLC did not have a vote with respect to the material decisions under either the IP Innovation assignment agree-

[14] Neither Ms. Coulter nor Ms. Walters consulted an attorney before signing the stock restriction agreement, and neither could recall the circumstances of her signing the agreement. They did not receive any consideration for giving up their right to transfer their shares in TLC. Mr. Baker testified that the restrictions on Ms. Walters' and Ms. Coulter's ability to transfer shares in TLC were inadvertent and done in error. We find Mr. Baker's testimony unconvincing in the light of our finding that Mr. Cooper indirectly controlled TLC. *See infra* p. 213. Mr. Cooper had ample motivation to ensure that the stock of TLC was not transferred to parties he could not control.

[15] Under the letter agreement Acacia was defined as IP Innovation, New Medium, and AV Technologies.

ment or the New Medium and AV Technologies agreements.[16]

Among the patents transferred by Mr. Cooper to TLC under the terms of the TLC agreements were three patents known as the "Lowe patents". The Lowe patents included the 489 patent. On January 18, 2006, TLC transferred the Lowe patents back to Mr. Cooper. He did not pay any money or transfer any other consideration to TLC for the return of the Lowe patents. The agreement transferring the Lowe patents from TLC to Mr. Cooper simply states that the parties completed the transfer because TLC had not licensed the Lowe patents and TLC and Mr. Cooper desired to return the Lowe patents to Mr. Cooper.

On January 23, 2006, Mr. Cooper transferred the Lowe patents to Watonga Technology, Inc. (Watonga). The shareholders of Watonga were as follows: the Cooper Trust (1%); petitioners' son (11.5%); petitioners' daughter (11.5%); Ms. Coulter and Ms. Walters (76% combined). Ms. Coulter was the president of Watonga.[17] Under the agreement transferring the Lowe patents to Watonga, Mr. Cooper received 55% of all net revenue (as defined in the agreement), and

[16] The letter agreement provides that "all material decisions with respect to the * * * [IP Innovation assignment agreement and the New Medium and AV Technologies agreements] will be made by a majority of Cooper, the Acacia Companies, and Anthony Brown, including without limitation, all licensing, litigation, and prosecution decisions." Petitioners contend that the above-referenced provision in the letter agreement mistakenly uses the term Cooper instead of "Cooper Parties". "Cooper Parties" was defined in the letter agreement to include TLC, while "Cooper" was defined as J. Carl Cooper (petitioner James C. Cooper).

Generally, where the terms of a contract are unambiguous, we presume that the contracting parties intended what they stated and will interpret the contract as written. *See, e.g., Peco Foods, Inc. v. Commissioner*, T.C. Memo. 2012–18, *aff'd*, 522 Fed. Appx. 840 (11th Cir. 2013); *see also Canfora v. Coast Hotels & Casinos, Inc.*, 121 P.3d 599, 603 (Nev. 2005) (holding that when a contract is clear on its face it will be enforced as written). As a result, we presume the parties intended what they stated in the letter agreement and infer that Mr. Cooper (and not TLC) was entitled to vote on material decisions regarding the IP Innovation assignment agreement and the New Medium and AV Technologies agreements.

[17] Although she was Watonga's president, Ms. Coulter testified that she did not know whether Watonga licensed any patents during 2006.

Watonga retained 20% of all net revenue.[18] Watonga received $120,000 in gross receipts from the license of the 489 patent in 2007.[19]

The amount of the royalties paid each year to Mr. Cooper was determined under the TLC agreements by accountants hired by TLC. Neither Ms. Walters nor Ms. Coulter, who were the majority shareholders as well as officers and directors, reviewed and verified the amount of royalties paid to Mr. Cooper each year.[20] Similarly, neither Ms. Walters nor Ms. Coulter negotiated the terms of TLC's agreements to license the subject patents to other companies. Instead, Ms. Walters and Ms. Coulter relied on TLC's attorneys and the technical expertise of Mr. Cooper with regard to TLC's licensing activities. During the years at issue, Ms. Walters and Ms. Coulter's duties as directors and officers consisted largely of signing checks and transferring funds as directed by TLC's accountants and signing agreements as directed by TLC's attorneys. The only compensation Ms. Walters and Ms. Coulter received from TLC was director's fees paid during some years and long-term care insurance policies purchased by TLC in 2003. TLC had no employees and paid no compensation to any party.

We infer from the record and find that substantially all of TLC's decisions regarding licensing, patent infringement, and patent transfers were made either by Mr. Cooper or at his

---

[18] The remaining 25% of net revenue was payable to Virgil Lowe or his nominee. Mr. Lowe was the original owner of the Lowe patents. He sold the Lowe patents to Mr. Cooper in 1995 for $40,000 and 25% of all net revenue received from any third party in connection with the license of the patents.

[19] Watonga purportedly paid TLC $72,000 in 2007 with respect to the 489 patent. It is unclear from the record whether such a payment was made and, if so, pursuant to what agreement the payment was made. Mr. Cooper testified at trial that he could not recall the details of the payment and was not sure whether Watonga had a licensing agreement with TLC. He further testified that the document notating the payment could be in error or that the payment could be the result of a prior agreement that was not in the record. In the light of Mr. Cooper's testimony and our review of the record, we do not find credible the contention that Watonga paid TLC anything of value with respect to the 489 patent in 2007.

[20] Ms. Coulter testified that her review of the royalties paid annually to Mr. Cooper consisted solely of reviewing the statement provided by the accountants regarding the amount of royalties to be paid and agreeing with it.

direction. We further find that Mr. Cooper controlled TLC in all material respects. Ms. Coulter and Ms. Walters acted in their capacities as directors and officers of TLC at the direction of Mr. Cooper. They did not make independent decisions in accordance with their fiduciary duties to TLC or act in their best interests as shareholders.

II. *Professional Fees*

During late 2005 and 2006 Mr. Cooper engaged Mike Holmes of Holmes Development to complete reverse engineering and related services with respect to the 489 patent (reverse engineering services). The reverse engineering services included disassembling televisions and DVD recorders to determine how the products were designed and manufactured and whether any of the products were infringing on Mr. Cooper's patents.

The invoices for the reverse engineering services were addressed to Mr. Cooper individually and not to TLC or Watonga.[21] Yet TLC and Watonga were the principal owners of the 489 patent during the period when Mr. Holmes completed the reverse engineering services. Mr. Cooper owned the 489 patent for only a few days in 2006. He paid Holmes Development $108,519 in 2006 for the reverse engineering services.

III. *Pixel Instruments/Bad Debt*

Petitioners incorporated Pixel in 1983 for the purpose of designing and manufacturing audio and video signal processing products. Specifically, Pixel designed products to measure and correct errors in the synchronization of sound and video images. Mr. Cooper was the president of Pixel at all relevant times. Ms. Cooper held various positions with Pixel from 1983 to 2004, including the position of vice president.

In September 1995 Pixel executed a working capital promissory note (promissory note) wherein it promised to pay to the Cooper Trust all sums advanced to Pixel by the Cooper

---

[21] Mr. Cooper transferred the 489 patent to TLC in 1997. TLC returned the 489 patent to Mr. Cooper on January 18, 2006, and Mr. Cooper transferred the 489 patent to Watonga on January 23, 2006. *See supra* pp. 201–202.

Trust up to \$1.5 million. On May 14, 2004, Pixel and the Cooper Trust amended the promissory note to increase the maximum loan amount to \$2.5 million.

Until some point in 2006 petitioners wholly owned Pixel. In 2006 petitioners transferred 76% of their shares in Pixel to Mirko Vojnovic and Christopher Smith. Mr. Smith was a longtime consultant to Pixel. He and Mr. Vojnovic owned 22% and 54% of Pixel's shares, respectively, during the years at issue.[22] They paid nothing or a de minimis amount for their shares. However, in conjunction with the Cooper Trust's transfer of shares to Mr. Smith and Mr. Vojnovic, Pixel transferred certain intellectual properties—including its rights to royalties from the patents Pixel previously licensed to TLC—to Mr. Cooper.

When televisions changed from standard definition to high definition in the mid-to-late 2000s, many of Pixel's products became obsolete. In an effort to better compete in the marketplace, Pixel began developing a product known as Liptracker to correct lip synchronization errors in high definition televisions. Between 2005 and 2008 petitioners as co-trustees of the Cooper Trust advanced funds to Pixel under the terms of the promissory note. These funds were used in part to fund the Liptracker program.

Pixel contracted with an Indian company to complete the software development necessary for Liptracker. Pixel's goal was to have a working and salable Liptracker product for presentation at the National Association of Broadcasters convention in April 2008. Unfortunately, the Indian company could not fulfill its promise to develop the Liptracker software, and Pixel was unable to proceed with the development on its own. Pixel met with representatives from the Indian company in July 2008 who confirmed the company was abandoning its development of the Liptracker software.

In 2008 Pixel faced financial difficulty. It had no new products in development—aside from the stalled Liptracker product—and few older products that were still marketable. Its gross receipts were in excess of \$525,000 in both 2005 and 2006 but decreased significantly in 2007 and 2008.

---

[22] Mr. Vojnovic sold all of his Pixel shares to Mr. Smith in April 2011 for \$1.

However, Pixel continued business operations through at least 2012. It was the assignee of many patents in 2008 and thereafter and had an active licensing agreement with TLC.[23] Pixel's gross receipts were $92,603, $148,968, $26,912, $22,500, and $22,500[24] for 2008, 2009, 2010, 2011, and 2012, respectively. Pixel had total yearend assets each year from 2008 through 2012 in excess of $172,000, including more than $319,000 in both 2011 and 2012.

Mr. Cooper continued to advance funds to Pixel under the terms of the promissory note throughout 2008. On December 31, 2008, the outstanding balance on the promissory note was $2,046,901. Mr. Cooper concluded at that time that Pixel could not pay the outstanding balance on the Pixel note, and petitioners treated the balance as a nonbusiness bad debt on petitioners' 2008 Federal income tax return. Petitioners did not initiate any type of litigation[25] to recover the amounts they lent Pixel under the terms of the promissory note and it is unclear from the record what demands, if any, they made for payment of the outstanding balance.

IV. *Petitioners' Tax Reporting and Notice of Deficiency*

Petitioners jointly filed Forms 1040, U.S. Individual Income Tax Return, for each of the years at issue. They reported the royalty payments Mr. Cooper received from TLC as capital gain on Schedules D, Capital Gains and Losses, attached to their Forms 1040. The amounts of royalty payments petitioners reported for 2006, 2007, and 2008 were $3,248,886, $1,933,010, and $1,597,450, respectively. Petitioners also reported income and expenses from Mr. Cooper's patent licensing business on Schedules C attached to their

[23] Pixel was the assignee or assignor on a number of filings with the U.S. Patent and Trademark Office from 2010 through 2012. Mr. Cooper testified that these assignments were confirming assignments that had occurred many years before and did not transfer anything new of value to Pixel. According to Mr. Cooper, these confirmatory assignments were necessary to show proper chain of title.

[24] The gross receipts of $22,500 in 2011 and 2012 consisted of a single annual trademark royalty that will continue for the foreseeable future.

[25] Mr. Cooper testified that he consulted Attorney Mitch Mitchell, who had previously represented Mr. Cooper in the Cooper-Leckrone litigation, regarding pursuing litigation against Pixel for the balance due on the promissory note. Mr. Cooper claimed that he subsequently determined that litigation against Pixel would be futile.

Form 1040 for each of the years at issue. Among the deductions claimed for 2006 was $108,519 for professional fees paid to Holmes Development during 2006. Finally, for 2008, petitioners claimed a bad debt deduction of $2,046,570 on a Schedule D attached to their Form 1040. This deduction was for the purportedly uncollectible loan to Pixel under the terms of the promissory note.

On April 4, 2012, respondent issued the notice of deficiency to petitioners. Respondent determined that (1) the royalties Mr. Cooper received from TLC did not qualify for capital gain treatment under section 1235 because Mr. Cooper controlled TLC; (2) petitioners could not deduct certain expenses for the years at issue; and (3) petitioners were not entitled to a bad debt deduction under section 166 for the promissory note because petitioners had not shown that the promissory note became worthless in 2008.

OPINION

I. *Burden of Proof*

Ordinarily, the Commissioner's determinations in a notice of deficiency are presumed correct, and the taxpayer bears the burden of proving that the determinations are erroneous. Rule 142(a); *Welch v. Helvering*, 290 U.S. 111, 115 (1933). The burden of proof shifts to the Commissioner, however, if the taxpayer produces credible evidence to support the deduction or position, the taxpayer complied with any substantiation requirements, and the taxpayer cooperated with the Secretary[26] with regard to all reasonable requests for information. Sec. 7491(a); *see also Higbee v. Commissioner*, 116 T.C. 438, 440–441 (2001).

Petitioners do not assert nor have they proven that they are entitled to a shift in the burden of proof under section 7491(a)(1). Accordingly, petitioners bear the burden of proof with respect to respondent's deficiency determinations.

[26] The term "Secretary" means the Secretary of the Treasury or his delegate. Sec. 7701(a)(11)(B).

II. *Section 1235 Gain*

A. *Whether a Holder's Control Over an Unrelated Corporate Transferee Defeats Capital Gain Treatment Under Section 1235*

Section 1235(a) provides that a transfer (other than by gift, inheritance, or devise) of all substantial rights to a patent by any holder[27] shall be treated as the sale or exchange of a capital asset held for more than 1 year, regardless of whether the payments in consideration of such transfer are contingent on the productivity, use, or disposition of the property transferred. Thus, in order for the transfer of a patent to qualify as a sale or exchange, the owner must transfer "all substantial rights"[28] to the property. *See* sec. 1235(a); *see also Juda v. Commissioner*, 90 T.C. 1263, 1281 (1988), *aff'd*, 877 F.2d 1075 (1st Cir. 1989). For purposes of section 1235, the term "all substantial rights"[29] means "all rights * * * which are of value at the time the rights * * * are transferred." Sec. 1.1235–2(b)(1), Income Tax Regs.[30] The retention of the right to terminate the transfer at will is the retention of a substantial right under section 1235.[31] Sec.

[27] The term "holder" includes any individual whose efforts created such property. Sec. 1235(b)(1).

[28] Generally, an assignment is a transfer of all substantial rights to a patent, *see Juda v. Commissioner*, 877 F.2d 1075, 1078 (1st Cir. 1989), *aff'g* 90 T.C. 1263 (1988), while a license is a transfer of less than all substantial rights in a patent, *see Kueneman v. Commissioner*, 68 T.C. 609, 613 (1977), *aff'd*, 628 F.2d 1196 (9th Cir. 1980).

[29] We have previously stated that transactions between shareholders and their closely held corporations should be closely scrutinized in determining whether there has been a transfer of all substantial rights in a patent. *See McDermott v. Commissioner*, 41 T.C. 50, 59 (1963).

[30] Sec. 1.1235–1(b), Income Tax Regs., provides that if a transfer is not one described in sec. 1.1235–1(a), Income Tax Regs. (transfer of all substantial rights to a patent by a holder to a person other than a related person), then sec. 1235 does not apply to determine whether such transfer is the sale or exchange of a capital asset. In other words, a transfer by a person other than a holder or a transfer by a holder to a related person is not governed by sec. 1235. Sec. 1.1235–1(b), Income Tax Regs. Instead, the tax consequences of such transactions are determined under other provisions of the Code. *Id.* Petitioners do not contend that Mr. Cooper is entitled to capital gain treatment under any provisions of the Code (e.g., sec. 1221 or sec. 1231) other than sec. 1235.

[31] In determining whether a transfer of all substantial rights to a patent

Continued

1.1235–2(b)(4), Income Tax Regs. Finally, under section 1235(d), transfers between related persons, as defined in section 267(b), are not eligible for capital gain treatment, and for purposes of section 1235, a corporation and an individual owning 25% or more of the stock of such corporation directly or indirectly are related persons. Sec. 267(b)(2), (c).

Respondent does not dispute that (1) the transfer of the patents to TLC under the TLC agreements was other than by gift, inheritance, or devise; (2) Mr. Cooper qualified as a holder of the subject patents; and (3) petitioners owned less than 25% of TLC for purposes of section 1235(d). However, respondent contends that Mr. Cooper effectively retained a right to terminate the transfers under the TLC agreements, *see* sec. 1.1235–2(b)(4), Income Tax Regs., because he indirectly controlled TLC through its directors, officers, and shareholders. Therefore, respondent contends that Mr. Cooper did not transfer all substantial rights in the subject patents and is not entitled to capital gain treatment. Petitioners contend that Mr. Cooper did not control TLC and that the directors, officers, and shareholders of TLC acted independently of Mr. Cooper in their corporate decision-making.

Neither the Code nor applicable regulations specifically address whether section 1235 applies to transfers to a corporation that is not related to the holder but is indirectly controlled by the holder. Whether a holder's control over a corporate transferee that is unrelated (within the meaning of section 1235(d)) defeats capital gain treatment appears to be an issue of first impression for this Court. However, the Court of Claims[32] in *Charlson v. United States*, 525 F.2d

has occurred, the language of the transfer agreement is not controlling. Sec. 1.1235–2(b)(1), Income Tax Regs. Instead, the entire agreement and the form of the transaction must be examined to see if all substantial rights were transferred. *See Juda v. Commissioner*, 877 F.2d at 1078.

[32] The Federal Courts Improvement Act of 1982, Pub. L. No. 97–164, 96 Stat. 25, merged the United States Court of Claims into the newly created Court of Appeals for the Federal Circuit and, in effect, reconstituted the trial division of the Court of Claims into a newly created United States Claims Court, a so-called Article I court. Subsequently, the United States Claims Court was renamed the United States Court of Federal Claims. Federal Courts Administration Act of 1992, Pub. L. No. 102–572, sec. 902(a)(1), 106 Stat. at 4516.

1046, 1053 (Ct. Cl. 1975),[33] considered this issue and concluded that such control could prohibit the transfer of substantially all rights in a patent and therefore preclude capital gain treatment under section 1235.

The Court of Claims in *Charlson* examined the legislative history of section 1235 and stated that "it is * * * clear that retention of control by a holder over an unrelated corporation can defeat capital gains treatment, if the retention prevents the transfer of 'all substantial rights.'" *Id.* The court supported its conclusion by reasoning that the holder's control over the unrelated corporation "places him in essentially the same position as if all substantial rights had not been transferred." *Id.* The court found further support for its reasoning in the legislative history of section 1235, noting that a court should closely examine all of the facts and circumstances of transactions under section 1235 and not rely solely on the terms of the transfer agreement to determine whether the owner transferred substantially all rights in the patent to the transferee. *See id.* (citing S. Rept. No. 83–1622, at 439–440 (1954), 1954 U.S.C.C.A.N. 4621, 5083).

We agree that retention of control places the holder in essentially the same position as if the patent had not been transferred, thereby precluding the application of section 1235. *See id.* We further agree that Congress intended for a "transferor's acts to speak louder than his words in establishing whether a sale of a patent has occurred". *Id.* Accordingly, we hold that retention of control by a holder over an unrelated corporation can defeat capital gain treatment under section 1235 because the retention prevents the transfer of "all substantial rights" in the patent.

B. *Whether Mr. Cooper Retained Control Over TLC and Therefore Did Not Transfer All Substantial Rights in the Subject Patents to TLC*

Petitioners rely on the facts regarding control in *Lee v. United States*, 302 F. Supp. 945 (E.D. Wis. 1969), and *Charlson* to support their contention that the directors, offi-

[33] In *Charlson v. United States*, 525 F.2d 1046 (Ct. Cl. 1975), the Court of Claims found that on the facts of that case the taxpayer did not control the transferee corporation and thus the taxpayer was not precluded from claiming capital gain treatment under sec. 1235. *See infra* pp. 210–211.

cers, and shareholders of TLC acted independently of Mr. Cooper in their corporate decisionmaking and that they are entitled to capital gain treatment under section 1235. We disagree because the facts regarding control in *Lee* and *Charlson* are distinguishable from the facts regarding control in this case. Here, the facts support our finding that Mr. Cooper indirectly controlled TLC. We explain below.

In *Lee*, the taxpayer transferred patents to Lee Custom Engineering, Inc. (Lee Engineering), a closely held corporation. The three shareholders of Lee Engineering were unrelated but were all friends. The taxpayer owned 24% of the outstanding stock of Lee Engineering. The Government argued that the taxpayer had not transferred all substantial rights in his patents because he controlled Lee Engineering—the exclusive licensee of the patents. Therefore, the Government argued that the taxpayer did not effectively transfer his patents under section 1235.[34] The District Court rejected the Government's contentions, stating among other things, that there was "no evidence presented which suggested * * * [the taxpayer] was * * * able to force the other stockholders or directors to do his bidding." *Lee*, 302 F. Supp. at 950.

In *Charlson*, the taxpayer transferred an exclusive license to Germane Corp. (Germane) to use, manufacture, and sell items incorporating his patents in exchange for 80% of the royalties that Germane received from licensing the patents to others. Germane was formed for the specific purpose of purchasing and licensing the taxpayer's patents, and the shareholders and directors of Germane were all trusted business associates, friends, and employees of the taxpayer.

The taxpayer treated the royalties he received from Germane as capital gain under section 1235. The Government argued that the taxpayer had not transferred all substantial

[34] The court in *Lee* interpreted the Government's argument to be that no transfer had occurred under sec. 1235 because the purported transfer was between parties within the same economic group. *Lee v. United States*, 302 F. Supp. 945, 950 (E.D. Wis. 1969). The court rejected the Government's argument because it reasoned that under sec. 1235(d) Congress considered transfers within the same economic group to be "transfers to a corporation in which 25% or more of the outstanding stock was owned by the transferor. Congress did not at any point in the legislative history of this section indicate an intent to prohibit as a matter of course transfers to a closed corporation." *Id.*

rights in the patents to Germane because he controlled Germane. In effect, the Government argued that the taxpayer had a tacit understanding with Germane that he would have final veto over any license agreement that Germane made with respect to his patents.

The court found that although the relationships among the taxpayer, Germane, and the shareholders made more probable the existence of prohibited retained control, the evidence did not establish that the taxpayer was able to exercise such control over Germane. *Charlson* 525 F.2d at 1055. Instead, the court found that Germane exercised its rights in the patents according to its own discretion even though it frequently sought, received, and followed the taxpayer's advice. *Id.* at 1056.

The court noted, among other things, that the shareholders in Germane all had skills valuable to a small patent licensing company. *Id.* at 1049. These skills included legal, engineering, design, and business expertise. *Id.* Further, the court found that although the taxpayer was present in many of Germane's licensing negotiations, this was mutually beneficial to both parties since it would potentially lead to higher royalties. Moreover, there was no evidence that the taxpayer—and not Germane—decided the terms of the licensing agreements. Finally, although the taxpayer participated as a joint plaintiff with Germane in patent infringement actions, there was no evidence that the taxpayer controlled or directed the details of the litigation. *Id.* at 1055. In short, the court rejected the Government's position that the taxpayer controlled the operation of Germane. As a result, the court held that the taxpayer had transferred all substantial rights in his patents to Germane—entitling him to capital gain treatment under section 1235. *Id.* at 1057.

By contrast, TLC did not exercise its rights in the subject patents according to its own discretion. Both *Lee* and *Charlson* are distinguishable because the taxpayers in those cases did not control the transferee corporations. Here, Mr. Cooper—troubled by his deteriorated business relationship with Mr. Leckrone—formed TLC with individuals he could trust and ultimately control. Ms. Coulter and Ms. Walters—the shareholders and directors of TLC (along with Ms. Cooper)—did not have the patent, engineering, or other such skills to make them particularly valuable to a small patent licensing company. Instead, they were individuals whom Mr. Cooper could trust to follow his direction on patent licensing issues. Indeed, Ms. Coulter testified that the technical negotiations regarding licensing and patent infringement were over her head and she deferred to Mr. Cooper on such issues. She further testified that she signed licensing and infringement agreements when directed to do so by TLC's attorneys and signed checks and transferred funds when directed to do so by TLC's accountants.

As officers and directors of TLC, Ms. Coulter and Ms. Walters took numerous actions that are inconsistent with acting independently and in the best interest of the corporation. Among other things, Ms. Coulter and Ms. Walters approved TLC's transfer of potentially valuable patents to Mr. Cooper for no consideration. At least in one instance, Mr. Cooper almost immediately licensed one of these patents to another related corporation for which that corporation received a royalty of $120,000 in 2007. As shareholders Ms. Coulter and Ms. Walters signed a stock restriction agreement placing restrictions on their ability to transfer shares of stock in TLC to anyone other than petitioners, without receiving any consideration in exchange. The stock restriction agreement did not place similar restrictions on petitioners.

Indeed, it is unclear what material decisions, if any, the officers and directors of TLC made independent of Mr. Cooper.[35] Mr. Cooper—and not the officers or directors of TLC—provided technical assistance to the Niro firm in interpreting the subject patents and relevant technology and in formulating patent enforcement strategies. Mr. Cooper conducted all technical matters for TLC—which in substance was all or a large part of TLC's activities. Furthermore, in his role as general manager of TLC and under the terms of the letter agreement, Mr. Cooper made all material decisions for TLC with respect to the IP Innovation assignment agreement and the New Medium and AV Technologies agreements.

---

[35] Ms. Coulter testified that she often followed the advice of TLC's attorneys, but she did not know who at TLC was directing TLC's attorneys. We infer from the record and find that TLC's attorneys drafted licensing agreements and patent infringement agreements largely at the direction of Mr. Cooper.

We do not find credible any testimony by petitioners that TLC was an independent corporation that Mr. Cooper did not control. We conclude that petitioners have failed to meet their burden of establishing that they transferred all substantial rights in the subject patents to TLC pursuant to section 1235(a). *See* Rule 142(a). Accordingly, we sustain respondent's determination that petitioners' royalty income for 2006, 2007, and 2008 did not qualify for capital gain treatment under section 1235(a).

III. *Professional Fees*

Generally, a taxpayer is entitled to deduct ordinary and necessary expenses paid or incurred in carrying on a trade or business. *See* sec. 162(a); *Am. Stores Co. v. Commissioner*, 114 T.C. 458, 468 (2000).[36] An expense is ordinary if it is customary or usual within the particular trade, business, or industry or if it relates to a transaction "of common or frequent occurrence in the type of business involved." *Deputy v. du Pont*, 308 U.S. 488, 495 (1940). An expense is necessary if it is appropriate and helpful for the development of the business. *See Commissioner v. Heininger*, 320 U.S. 467, 471 (1943). To be deductible, ordinary and necessary expenses must be "directly connected with or pertaining to the taxpayer's trade or business". Sec. 1.162–1(a), Income Tax Regs. Deductions are a matter of legislative grace, and a taxpayer must prove that he is entitled to the deductions he claims. *INDOPCO, Inc. v. Commissioner*, 503 U.S. 79, 84 (1992).

Generally, a taxpayer who pays another taxpayer's business expenses may not treat those payments as ordinary and necessary expenses incurred in the payor's trade or business. *See Deputy v. du Pont*, 308 U.S. at 494–495; *Columbian Rope Co. v. Commissioner*, 42 T.C. 800, 815 (1964). An exception exists for cases in which the taxpayer paid another taxpayer's ordinary and necessary business expenses in order to "protect or promote" the taxpayer's own business. *See, e.g., Scruggs-Vandervoort-Barney, Inc. v. Commissioner*, 7 T.C.

[36] Additionally, sec. 212 generally allows a taxpayer to deduct the ordinary and necessary expenses paid or incurred during the taxable year for the production or collection of income. Such expenses must be reasonable in amount and bear a proximate relationship to the production or collection of taxable income. Sec. 1.212–1(d), Income Tax Regs.

779, 787 (1946). In *Lohrke v. Commissioner*, 48 T.C. 679, 688 (1967), we articulated a two-part test for determining whether a taxpayer's payments are eligible for this exception: (1) the taxpayer's primary motive for paying the expenses was to protect or promote the taxpayer's business and (2) the expenditures constituted ordinary and necessary expenses in the furtherance or promotion of the taxpayer's business.

Under the *Lohrke* test, we must first "ascertain the purpose or motive which cause[d] the taxpayer to pay the obligations of the other person." *Id.* To meet this prong, Mr. Cooper's purpose in paying the Holmes Development expenses must have been for the benefit of his business as an inventor. We "must then judge whether it is an ordinary and necessary expense of the * * * [taxpayer's] trade or business; that is, is it an appropriate expenditure for the furtherance or promotion of that trade or business? If so, the expense is deductible by the individual paying it." *Id.*

Petitioners claimed a deduction of $108,519 in 2006 for professional fees paid to Mr. Holmes for reverse engineering services. Respondent disallowed this deduction in its entirety. Respondent contends that these expenses are properly chargeable to Watonga or TLC and are not Mr. Cooper's ordinary and necessary business expenses. Petitioners contend that these expenses are the ordinary and necessary expenses of Mr. Cooper's business as an inventor. Alternatively, petitioners contend that even if we find that the expenses are properly chargeable to Watonga or TLC, petitioners are still entitled to deduct the expenses.

Mr. Holmes' reverse engineering services included the disassembling of televisions and DVD recorders to determine how the products were designed and manufactured and whether any of the products infringed on Mr. Cooper's patents. The invoices for the reverse engineering expenses indicated that the services were completed with respect to the 489 patent. However, Mr. Cooper testified that most of these expenses were unrelated to the 489 patent. For example, according to Mr. Cooper, the reverse engineering services included the reverse engineering of plasma televisions that use random dithering and not coherent dithering—the subject of the 489 patent. Regardless, petitioners stipulated that the reverse engineering expenses were for services performed with respect to the 489 patent.[37] Petitioners are bound by their stipulation. *See, e.g.*, *Dorchester Indus., Inc. v. Commissioner*, 108 T.C. 320, 330 (1997), *aff'd without published opinion*, 208 F.3d 205 (3d Cir. 2000); *see also* Rule 91(e). Because TLC and Watonga, as applicable, owned the 489 patent during the period in which Mr. Holmes completed his services, *see supra* pp. 201–202, we conclude that the reverse engineering expenses were the ordinary and necessary business expenses of TLC and Watonga. Nevertheless, because petitioners paid the reverse engineering expenses for TLC and Watonga, they still may be entitled to deduct the expenses under *Lohrke v. Commissioner*, 48 T.C. at 688.

Respondent does not dispute that Mr. Cooper was in the trade or business of patent commercialization and being an inventor during the years at issue. Mr. Cooper testified that he had a long-term working relationship with Mr. Holmes. The Holmes Development invoices, while referencing that the services were completed with respect to the 489 patent, also list Mr. Cooper as the obligor and account holder. Thus, it appears Holmes Development understood its client relationship to be with Mr. Cooper individually and not with Watonga or TLC.[38] We find credible Mr. Cooper's testimony that Holmes Development's business relationship was with him personally, that Holmes Development trusted Mr. Cooper to pay for the services completed, and that nonpayment of the Holmes Development expenses would have adversely affected Mr. Cooper's business reputation. *See, e.g.*,

---

[37] The parties filed a stipulation of settled issues on June 10, 2013, stating that "[t]he legal and professional services expenses not allowed by respondent for taxable year 2006 in the amount of $108,518.60 are attributable to expenses charged by Holmes Development for works performed by Holmes Development during the period from December 15, 2005 through November 30, 2006 with respect to U.S. Patent # 5,157,489."

[38] The Holmes Development invoices further support our conclusion that Mr. Cooper controlled TLC and his portfolio of patents. *See supra* p. 212. Although Mr. Cooper purportedly transferred all substantial rights in the 489 patent to TLC and Watonga, Holmes Development understood its relationship to be with Mr. Cooper individually. We do not believe that Holmes Development would have considered its business relationship to be with Mr. Cooper if TLC and Watonga, as applicable, owned all substantial rights in the 489 patent and TLC and Watonga functioned as independent corporations.

Jenkins v. Commissioner, T.C. Memo. 1983–667. Furthermore, Holmes Development's work on the 489 patent owned by Watonga had the potential to directly benefit Mr. Cooper's trade or business as an inventor because Mr. Cooper stood to receive 55% of Watonga's net revenue. Accordingly, we conclude that Mr. Cooper's payment of the reverse engineering expenses was for the benefit of his trade or business as an inventor and his ongoing relationship with Holmes Development. Therefore, petitioners have satisfied the first part of *Lohrke*'s two-part test. *See Lohrke v. Commissioner*, 48 T.C. at 688.

Mr. Cooper further testified that the services performed by Holmes Development were necessary in his trade or business to keep him apprised of current developments and current engineering practices for audio and video technology. He further testified that the services performed by Holmes Development helped him ascertain whether certain products infringed on any patents that he had developed and commercialized. We conclude that the reverse engineering expenses were proximately related to Mr. Cooper's business as an inventor and their payment by him was ordinary and necessary. *See id.* at 689. Accordingly, we conclude that petitioners have satisfied the second part of the *Lohrke* test, *see id.*, and they are entitled to deduct the reverse engineering expenses.

IV. *Bad Debt*

Section 166 authorizes a taxpayer to deduct any debt that becomes worthless within the taxable year. Section 166 distinguishes between business and nonbusiness bad debts. Nonbusiness bad debts are treated as losses resulting from the sale or exchange of a short-term capital asset.[39] Secs. 166(d)(1), 1211(b), 1212(b). A nonbusiness debt is a debt other than "(A) a debt created or acquired (as the case may be) in connection with a trade or business of the taxpayer; or (B) a debt the loss from the worthlessness of which is incurred in the taxpayer's trade or business." Sec. 166(d)(2). "To qualify for a deduction for a worthless debt a taxpayer

[39] A business bad debt is deductible as an ordinary loss to the extent of the taxpayer's adjusted basis in the debt. Sec. 166(b). Petitioners do not contend that the loan to Pixel is deductible as a business bad debt.

must show that he and his alleged debtor intended to create a debtor-creditor relationship, that a genuine debt in fact existed, and that the debt became worthless within the tax year." *Andrew v. Commissioner*, 54 T.C. 239, 244–245 (1970); *see also* sec. 1.166–1(c), Income Tax Regs. "The year a debt becomes worthless is fixed by identifiable events that form the basis of reasonable grounds for abandoning any hope of recovery." *Aston v. Commissioner*, 109 T.C. 400, 415 (1997).

The question of whether a debt became worthless during a taxable year is determined on the basis of all the facts and circumstances. *See, e.g., Halliburton Co. v. Commissioner*, 93 T.C. 758, 774 (1989), *aff'd*, 946 F.2d 395 (5th Cir. 1991). "Specifically, * * * [a taxpayer] must prove that the debt had value at the beginning of the taxable year and that it became worthless during that year." *Milenbach v. Commissioner*, 106 T.C. 184, 204 (1996), *aff'd in part, rev'd in part on other grounds*, 318 F.3d 924 (9th Cir. 2003). The taxpayer "must show sufficient objective facts from which worthlessness could be concluded; mere belief of worthlessness is not sufficient." *Fincher v. Commissioner*, 105 T.C. 126, 138 (1995). Furthermore, legal action is not required to show worthlessness if surrounding circumstances indicate that a debt is worthless and uncollectible and that any legal action in all likelihood would be futile because the debtor would not be able to satisfy a favorable judgment. Sec. 1.166–2(b), Income Tax Regs.

A debt is not worthless for purposes of a section 166 deduction merely because it might be difficult, or uncomfortable, to collect. *See Reading & Bates Corp. v. United States*, 40 Fed. Cl. 737, 757 (1998). A creditor's determination that there is no hope of recovery of a debt due and owing must be made in the exercise of sound business judgment and must be based upon information that is as complete as is reasonably obtainable regarding the debtor's financial condition or ability to satisfy the debt. *See Andrew v. Commissioner*, 54 T.C. at 248.

An analysis regarding the deductibility of a bad debt must examine whether the debt was truly worthless, and if so, when it became worthless. The conclusions depend on the particular facts and circumstances of the case, and there is no bright-line test or formula for determining worthlessness within a given taxable year. *Lucas v. Am. Code Co.*, 280 U.S.

445, 449 (1930). To be worthless, a debt must not only be lacking current value and be uncollectible at the time the taxpayer takes the deduction, but it must also be lacking potential value due to the likelihood that it will remain uncollectible in the future. *Dustin v. Commissioner*, 53 T.C. 491, 501 (1969), *aff'd*, 467 F.2d 47 (9th Cir. 1972); *see also Fox v. Commissioner*, 50 T.C. 813, 822 (1968) ("Mere belief that a debt is bad is insufficient to support a deduction for worthlessness"). The fact that a business is on the decline, that it has failed to turn a profit, or that its debt obligation may be difficult to collect does not necessarily justify treating the debt obligation as worthless. *Intergraph Corp. & Subs. v. Commissioner*, 106 T.C. 312, 323 (1996), *aff'd without published opinion*, 121 F.3d 723 (11th Cir. 1997). This is especially true where the debtor continues to be a going concern with the potential to earn a future profit. *See Rendall v. Commissioner*, 535 F.3d 1221, 1228 (10th Cir. 2008) (citing *Roth Steel Tube Co. v. Commissioner*, 620 F.2d 1176, 1182 (6th Cir. 1980), *aff'g* 68 T.C. 213 (1977)), *aff'g* T.C. Memo. 2006–174; *ABC Beverage Corp. v. Commissioner*, T.C. Memo. 2006–195.

Petitioners contend that the promissory note became worthless in 2008 following the Indian company's abandonment of the Liptracker program. This action, according to petitioners, gave rise to the conclusion that there was no hope of recovering the outstanding amounts under the promissory note. We disagree.

Pixel had total yearend assets each year from 2008 through 2012 in excess of $172,000, including more than $319,000 in assets in 2011 and 2012. It appears to us that Pixel remained a going concern well past 2008. The outcome of Pixel's arrangement with the Indian company and the failure of the Liptracker program do not support petitioners' claim that there was no longer any prospect of recovery of their loans to Pixel. More importantly, the proper inquiry in this case is not whether petitioners acted reasonably in their recovery efforts, but whether sufficient objective facts show that the debt became worthless during the year in question. Here, the facts do not support such a determination.

Pixel experienced a decline in its business in 2008, but its gross receipts increased in 2009. Petitioners as cotrustees of the Cooper Trust continued to advance funds to Pixel under the terms of the promissory note throughout 2008. Indeed, petitioners advanced $148,255 to Pixel under the terms of the promissory note between July and December 2008. We do not find it credible that petitioners would have advanced nearly $150,000 to Pixel after July 2008 if they believed the promissory note had been rendered worthless in July 2008 by the difficulties with the Liptracker program.[40] The evidence shows that Pixel had substantial assets at the end of the 2008 tax year and that its gross receipts increased in 2009. Moreover, at the very least, Pixel was entitled to an indefinitely continuing annual royalty of $22,500 and owned rights in several other patents.

Mr. Cooper claimed that he consulted with Mr. Mitchell and they determined that filing a lawsuit against Pixel would be futile. Mr. Cooper then concluded that the promissory note was worthless. But petitioners failed to introduce evidence proving what information Mr. Mitchell analyzed to determine that litigation against Pixel would be futile and failed to introduce evidence proving the basis on which Mr. Mitchell made his purported conclusion. Petitioners have failed to satisfy their burden of proving that no prospect of recovery existed in 2008 and failed to prove that the promissory note became worthless in 2008.[41] *See* Rule 142(a). Accordingly, we sustain respondent's disallowance of petitioners' bad debt deduction for 2008.

V. *Accuracy-Related Penalties*

A. *Introduction*

Section 6662 authorizes the imposition of a 20% penalty on the portion of an underpayment of tax that is attributable to, among other things, (1) negligence or disregard of rules or regulations or (2) any substantial understatement of income tax. Sec. 6662(a) and (b)(1) and (2). Only one accuracy-

---

[40] Generally, advances made to an insolvent debtor are not debts for tax purposes but are characterized as capital contributions or gifts. *See Dixie Dairies Corp. v. Commissioner*, 74 T.C. 476, 497 (1980); *Davis v. Commissioner*, 69 T.C. 814, 835–836 (1978). Furthermore, advances made by an investor to a closely held or controlled corporation may properly be characterized not as a bona fide loan but as a capital contribution. *See Fin Hay Realty Co. v. United States*, 398 F.2d 694, 697 (3d Cir. 1968).

[41] Pixel's liabilities to petitioners under the terms of the promissory note constituted substantially all of Pixel's liabilities in 2008.

related penalty may be imposed with respect to any given portion of an underpayment, even if that portion is attributable to more than one of the reasons identified in section 6662(b). Sec. 1.6662–2(c), Income Tax Regs.

The Commissioner bears the initial burden of production with respect to the taxpayer's liability for the section 6662 penalty. Sec. 7491(c). The Commissioner must introduce sufficient evidence "indicating that it is appropriate to impose the relevant penalty." *Higbee v. Commissioner*, 116 T.C. at 446. Once the Commissioner meets his burden of production, the taxpayer must come forward with persuasive evidence that the Commissioner's determination is incorrect or that the taxpayer had reasonable cause or substantial authority for the position. *Id.* at 446–447.

B. *Petitioners' Liability for the Section 6662 Penalties*

1. *Substantial Understatement of Income Tax*

A substantial understatement of income tax exists if the amount of the understatement exceeds the greater of 10% of the tax required to be shown on the return or $5,000. Sec. 6662(d)(1)(A). The term "understatement" means the excess of the amount of tax required to be shown on the return for the taxable year over the amount of tax imposed that is shown on the return, reduced by any rebate. Sec. 6662(d)(2)(A). The amount of the understatement is reduced by that portion of the understatement that is attributable to (1) the tax treatment of any item if there is or was substantial authority for such treatment or (2) any item if the relevant facts affecting the item's tax treatment are adequately disclosed in the return or in a statement attached to the return and there is a reasonable basis for the taxpayer's treatment of the item. Sec. 6662(d)(2)(B).

Respondent has introduced sufficient evidence to demonstrate that petitioners have substantially understated their income tax liability for each of the years at issue. Petitioners have not alleged nor have they proven that they had substantial authority for all or any portion of the understatements or that they adequately disclosed their tax positions on their returns. Accordingly, if the Rule 155 computations confirm a substantial understatement, petitioners are liable for the section 6662(a) underpayment penalty for a substantial understatement of income tax.

2. *Negligence or Disregard of Rules or Regulations*

The term "negligence" includes any failure to make a reasonable attempt to comply with the provisions of the internal revenue laws, and the term "disregard" includes any careless, reckless, or intentional disregard. Sec. 6662(c); sec. 1.6662–3(b)(1) and (2), Income Tax Regs. Negligence is strongly indicated where a taxpayer fails to make a reasonable attempt to ascertain the correctness of a deduction, credit, or exclusion on a return that would seem to a reasonable and prudent person to be "too good to be true" under the circumstances. Sec. 1.6662–3(b)(1)(ii), Income Tax Regs. Disregard of rules or regulations "is 'careless' if the taxpayer does not exercise reasonable diligence to determine the correctness of a return position" and "is 'reckless' if the taxpayer makes little or no effort to determine whether a rule or regulation exists, under circumstances which demonstrate a substantial deviation from the standard of conduct that a reasonable person would observe." Sec. 1.6662–3(b)(2), Income Tax Regs.; *see also Neely v. Commissioner*, 85 T.C. 934, 947 (1985).

Respondent has met his burden to show that petitioners acted negligently or with careless disregard of rules and regulations with respect to the royalty payments Mr. Cooper received from TLC and with respect to the bad debt deduction for the promissory note. We have found that Mr. Cooper did not transfer all substantial rights to TLC within the meaning of section 1235 because Mr. Cooper indirectly controlled TLC. Further, we have found that the promissory note did not become worthless in 2008 and therefore petitioners were not entitled to claim a bad debt deduction for the promissory note on their 2008 return. Petitioners reported the royalty payments from TLC as capital gain without considering how Mr. Cooper's involvement with TLC affected their qualification for capital gain treatment under section 1235. Similarly, petitioners reported the promissory note as a bad debt on their 2008 return without reasonably attempting to collect the debt and without identifying specific events that made recovery of the debt futile in the future. We conclude that petitioners did not make a reasonable attempt to ascertain the correctness of their bad debt deduction for 2008 or their right to treat the royalty payments received from TLC as capital gain.

C. *Petitioners' Reasonable Cause / Good Faith Defense*

Taxpayers may avoid liability for the section 6662 penalty if they demonstrate that they had reasonable cause for the underpayment and that they acted in good faith with respect to the underpayment. Sec. 6664(c)(1). Reasonable cause and good faith are determined on a case-by-case basis, taking into account all pertinent facts and circumstances. Sec. 1.6664–4(b)(1), Income Tax Regs. The most important factor is the extent of the taxpayer's efforts to assess his or her proper tax liability. *Id.* Reliance on professional advice may constitute reasonable cause and good faith, but "it must be established that the reliance was reasonable." *Freytag v. Commissioner*, 89 T.C. 849, 888 (1987), *aff'd on another issue*, 904 F.2d 1011 (5th Cir. 1990), *aff'd*, 501 U.S. 868 (1991). We have previously held that the taxpayer must satisfy a three-prong test to be found to have reasonably relied on professional advice to negate a section 6662(a) accuracy-related penalty: (1) the adviser was a competent professional who had sufficient experience to justify the reliance; (2) the taxpayer provided necessary and accurate information to the adviser; and (3) the taxpayer actually relied in good faith on the adviser's judgment. *Neonatology Assocs., P.A. v. Commissioner*, 115 T.C. 43, 99 (2000), *aff'd*, 299 F.3d 221 (3d Cir. 2002).

Petitioners contend that they acted with reasonable cause and good faith based on their reliance on professional advice and therefore no section 6662(a) accuracy-related penalty is applicable. With regard to the royalty payments Mr. Cooper received from TLC, petitioners contend they sought the advice of Mr. Baker, a tax attorney and competent professional. With regard to their bad debt deduction, petitioners contend they sought and relied on the advice of Mr. Baker and Mr. Mitchell. Petitioners contend that they provided Mr. Baker and Mr. Mitchell with all necessary and accurate information, and that they reasonably relied in good faith on Mr. Baker and Mr. Mitchell's advice. *See Freytag v. Commissioner*, 89 T.C. at 888.

Mr. Baker testified with respect to the royalty payments and petitioners' compliance with section 1235 that he advised petitioners that Mr. Cooper could not indirectly control TLC. Moreover, Mr. Baker did not provide advice to petitioners before they filed their Forms 1040 for the years at issue, nor did he provide advice to petitioners regarding whether Mr. Cooper controlled TLC following TLC's incorporation. Petitioners did not follow Mr. Baker's advice to ensure that Mr. Cooper did not indirectly control TLC. Consequently, petitioners cannot claim reliance on the professional advice of Mr. Baker to negate the section 6662(a) penalty with respect to their erroneous capital gain treatment of the royalty payments Mr. Cooper received during the years at issue.

With regard to the bad debt deduction, petitioners have failed to introduce evidence regarding what information they provided to Mr. Baker and Mr. Mitchell to enable them to determine whether the promissory note was worthless within the meaning of section 166 in 2008. Petitioners did not call Mr. Mitchell to testify or otherwise introduce any evidence regarding Mr. Mitchell's advice. Similarly, Mr. Baker did not testify regarding any advice he may have given to petitioners that would indicate that it was his opinion that the promissory note became worthless in 2008. In short, petitioners have failed to prove that they received or relied on the professional advice of Mr. Baker and Mr. Mitchell with respect to their erroneous section 166 bad debt deduction in 2008.

Because respondent has met his initial burden of production under section 7491(c) with respect to the section 6662(a) penalty for each of the years at issue and petitioners have failed to prove either that they are not liable for the penalties or that they had reasonable cause and acted in good faith, we conclude that respondent properly determined that petitioners are liable for the penalties. Accordingly, if the Rule 155 computations show that the understatement of tax exceeds the greater of 10% of the tax required to be shown on the return or $5,000, *see* sec. 6662(d)(1)(A), then petitioners are liable for the section 6662(a) penalty for an underpayment of tax attributable to a substantial understatement of income tax for each of the years at issue. Alternatively, petitioners are liable for the section 6662(a) penalty for negligence or disregard of rules and regulations with respect to the royalty payments and the section 166 bad debt deduction.

We have considered the remaining arguments made by the parties and, to the extent not discussed above, conclude those arguments are irrelevant, moot, or without merit.

To reflect the parties' concessions and the foregoing,

Decision will be entered under Rule 155.

DENNIS E. BOHNER, PETITIONER *v.* COMMISSIONER OF INTERNAL REVENUE, RESPONDENT

Docket No. 24166–12. Filed September 23, 2014.

While P worked for the Federal Government, he participated in the Civil Service Retirement System (CSRS). After P retired, he received a letter explaining that he could elect to increase his CSRS retirement annuity by remitting a fixed sum. P remitted the funds to CSRS. Because P did not have sufficient funds in his bank account, he borrowed a portion of the fixed sum. P paid off the loan and replenished his bank account by making withdrawals from his traditional individual retirement account (IRA). P did not report any of the amounts he withdrew from his IRA as taxable income. P contends that he engaged in a tax-free rollover. R contends that rollover contributions cannot be made to CSRS. *Held*: Because CSRS did not accept his remittance as a rollover, P must include his withdrawals in his taxable income for the year at issue.

Kathryn L. Everlove-Stone, for petitioner.

Joel D. McMahan, for respondent.

KERRIGAN, *Judge*: Respondent determined a deficiency of $4,590 with respect to petitioner's Federal income tax for tax year 2010.

Unless otherwise indicated, all section references are to the Internal Revenue Code in effect for the year in issue, and all Rule references are to the Tax Court Rules of Practice and Procedure.

The sole issue for consideration is whether a tax-free rollover occurred when petitioner withdrew funds from his traditional individual retirement account (IRA) to cover a deposit of the same amount to the Civil Service Retirement System (CSRS).

FINDINGS OF FACT

Some facts have been stipulated and are so found. Petitioner resided in Florida when he filed the petition.

Petitioner was an employee of the Social Security Administration in 2009 and retired before April 13, 2010. He was eligible to participate in Federal Government retirement plans offered through the Office of Personnel Management (OPM), and he participated in CSRS during his years of Government service.

After petitioner retired, OPM mailed him a letter on April 13, 2010, explaining that he could elect to increase his CSRS retirement annuity by remitting $17,832 with respect to creditable Government service for a period during which no retirement contributions had been withheld from his salary. The letter required that petitioner remit the funds within 15 days of the date of the letter. The letter was silent as to whether the remittance could be made through a tax-free rollover contribution.

Petitioner elected to remit to CSRS the $17,832 to increase his retirement annuity. Because petitioner did not have sufficient funds to make the entire payment directly from his bank account, he borrowed a portion of the $17,832 from a friend. On April 27, 2010, petitioner mailed a check to OPM for $17,832.

During 2010 petitioner maintained a traditional IRA with Fidelity Investments (Fidelity). Petitioner made two separate requests to withdraw funds from his Fidelity IRA, one in April 2010 and another in May 2010. Petitioner's monthly Fidelity investment report for April 2010 shows that he requested a $5,000 distribution, of which $4,500 was sent to him on April 15, 2010, and $500 was withheld to satisfy Federal income tax liability in connection with the distribution. Petitioner's Fidelity investment report for May 2010 shows that he requested a $12,832 distribution, which was sent entirely to him on May 3, 2010; no Federal tax was withheld. Petitioner used the funds he received from Fidelity to reimburse his friend and to replenish his bank account.

Fidelity issued petitioner a Form 1099–R, Distributions From Pensions, Annuities, Retirement or Profit-Sharing Plans, IRAs, Insurance Contracts, etc., in which it reported $17,832 in distributions and listed the entire $17,832 as taxable income. On his Form 1040A, U.S. Individual Income Tax Return, for tax year 2010 petitioner reported receipt of the $17,832 in distributions from his Fidelity IRA on line 11a, IRA Distributions. He did not report any of the $17,832 as taxable income as a result of those distributions on line 11b, Taxable Amount.

On July 2, 2012, respondent issued petitioner a notice of deficiency which determined a deficiency of $4,590 and treated the $17,832 withdrawal from the IRA as taxable income.

OPINION

Generally, the Commissioner's determinations in a notice of deficiency are presumed correct, and the taxpayer bears the burden of proving those determinations are erroneous. Rule 142(a)(1); *Welch v. Helvering*, 290 U.S. 111, 115 (1933). The parties do not dispute any material facts; therefore, the burden of proof is not at issue.

I. *CSRS*

CSRS is a statutorily created retirement plan designed to provide retirement benefits in the form of annuities and lump-sum benefits to Federal civil service employees. *See generally* 5 U.S.C. secs. 8331–8351 (2006). The statutory provisions governing CSRS do not include a provision allowing pretax employee contributions. *Id.* An eligible employee contributes portions of his or her salary to CSRS, and the employing agency withholds the contributions from the employee's salary. *Id.* sec. 8334(a)(1)(A); *Malbon v. United States*, 43 F.3d 466, 467 (9th Cir. 1994); *see also Logsdon v. Commissioner*, T.C. Memo. 1997–8, slip op. at 3–4. Matching contributions are made from funds appropriated for the employing agency. 5 U.S.C. sec. 8334(a)(1)(B)(i).

To assure that income will be taxed only once, the Internal Revenue Code deems an annuity, such as one for a CSRS participant, to have two components: one taxable, one not. *See* sec. 72; *Montgomery v. United States*, 18 F.3d 500 (7th Cir. 1994). The employing agency withholds a mandatory contribution from the employee's salary, and that withheld amount is after-tax income because it is taxable for the year in which it is withheld. *Malbon*, 43 F.3d at 467. On distribution that portion is nontaxable because it was already subject to tax. *See Montgomery*, 18 F.3d at 500. The amount contributed by the employing agency and any interest earned on the employee's investment are not taxed to the employee until distributed. Secs. 72, 402(a). This portion of the distribution is the taxable component. *Montgomery*, 18 F.3d at 500.

Petitioner contends that all distributions from CSRS are taxable and that unless the distributions from his IRA are excluded from income, he will be subject to double taxation. Petitioner will not be subject to double taxation, however, because under section 72 he will be able to exclude from his gross income CSRS distributions attributable to his previously taxed contributions to the plan. *See* sec. 72(c)(1)(A). Section 72(c)(1)(A) and (B) defines "investment in the contract" as of the annuity starting date as "the aggregate amount of premiums or other consideration paid for the contract, minus * * * the aggregate amount received under the contract before such date, to the extent that such amount was excludable from gross income under this subtitle or prior income tax laws."

CSRS provisions include that "[e]ach employee or Member credited with civilian service after July 31, 1920, for which retirement deductions or deposits have not been made, may deposit with interest an amount equal to * * * [certain statutorily defined] percentages of his basic pay received for that service". 5 U.S.C. sec. 8334(c). This provision allows civil service employees to elect to make a deposit for creditable Government service and thus increase their CSRS retirement annuity. *See Dela Cruz v. OPM*, 553 Fed. Appx. 977 (Fed. Cir. 2014).

II. *Rollover Contributions Under Section 408(d)(3)*

In general, any amount paid or distributed out of an individual retirement plan is included in the gross income of the payee or distributee as provided in section 72. Sec. 408(d)(1); *Arnold v. Commissioner*, 111 T.C. 250, 253 (1998). This general rule does not apply to a rollover contribution. *See* sec. 408(d)(3)(A). A rollover contribution is any amount paid or distributed out of an IRA or individual retirement annuity to the individual for whose benefit the account or annuity is maintained if the entire amount received is paid into an eligible retirement plan no later than 60 days after receipt. Sec. 408(d)(3)(A)(ii); *see also Schoof v. Commissioner*, 110 T.C. 1, 7 (1998). An "eligible retirement plan" is defined as any (1) qualified trust; (2) annuity plan described in section 403(a); (3) eligible deferred compensation plan described in section 457(b) which is maintained by an eligible employer described in section 457(e)(1)(A); or (4) annuity contract described in section 403(b). Secs. 408(d)(3)(A), 402(c)(8)(B). A "qualified trust" is any employees' trust described in section 401(a) which is exempt from tax under section 501(a). Sec. 402(c)(8)(A). Respondent does not dispute that CSRS is a qualified trust. [1]

Respondent contends, however, that petitioner's deposit to CSRS does not constitute a rollover contribution under section 408(d)(3) because CSRS does not, and is not required to, accept rollovers. [2]

Even though there is no specific provision in the Internal Revenue Code concerning whether a qualified trust must accept a rollover that is an indirect transfer from an IRA in order to constitute an eligible retirement plan for purposes of section 408(d)(3), this issue is contemplated in similar cir-

---

[1] The Commissioner has taken the position in published guidance that CSRS is a qualified trust under sec. 401(a). *See* Rev. Rul. 74–138, 1974–1 C.B. 29, 30 ("[CSRS] is a qualified trust under section 401(a) of the Code and is exempt from Federal income tax under section 501(a)."); Rev. Rul. 68–486, 1968–2 C.B. 184; Rev. Rul. 58–472, 1958–2 C.B. 30; IRS Publ'n 721, Tax Guide to U.S. Civil Service Retirement Benefits 13 (rev. Feb. 22, 2011) ("CSRS, FERS, and TSP are considered qualified retirement plans" for the purpose of determining whether a CSRS distribution can be used in a tax-free rollover to another plan or trust). CSRS is a plan that meets the requirements of sec. 401(a). *Guilzon v. Commissioner*, 97 T.C. 237, 241 (1991), *aff'd*, 985 F.2d 819 (5th Cir. 1993); *Gomez v. Commissioner*, T.C. Memo. 1996–212, slip op. at 5; *Roundy v. Commissioner*, T.C. Memo. 1995–298, *aff'd*, 122 F.3d 835 (9th Cir. 1997); *Shimota v. United States*, 21 Cl. Ct. 510, 519 (1990), *aff'd*, 943 F.2d 1312 (Fed. Cir. 1991).

[2] Respondent also contends that petitioner's deposit to CSRS is not a rollover because the funds paid to CSRS were not a distribution from an IRA. We have held that the phrase "if the entire amount is contributed into an eligible retirement plan" is not to be read so narrowly as to require the taxpayer to roll over the exact same money that he or she received in the distribution from the IRA. *Zaklama v. Commissioner*, T.C. Memo. 2012–346, at *68. Respondent did not raise the issue of the second IRA distribution's taking place after petitioner's deposit to CSRS, and we deem respondent to have waived that issue. In any event, our disposition of this case does not require addressing the timing of the second distribution.

cumstances. Section 401(a)(31)(E) and the legislative history associated with the rollover provision of section 402 address this issue in the context of transfers from other qualified trusts. For the purpose of a direct transfer of eligible rollover distributions, a qualified trust plan must permit distributees to elect to have a distribution paid directly to an eligible retirement plan, which for this purpose must be a defined contribution plan that permits the acceptance of rollover distributions. The Senate report explaining this provision includes the following statement: "As under present law, a transfer cannot be made to another qualified plan unless the terms of the transferee plan permit the acceptance of such transfer." 138 Cong. Rec. S8180 (1992).

The instant case does not involve a defined contribution plan; rather, it involves a defined benefit plan. However, for the reasons explained below, we conclude and hold that because CSRS did not accept petitioner's remittance as a rollover, he must include his withdrawals in his taxable income for 2010.

The letter that OPM sent to petitioner after he retired explained how he could make a deposit to make up for years for which no retirement contributions were withheld from his pay. The letter requested that a check be sent to OPM for these contributions; it is silent on whether the deposit can be made as a rollover. Title 5 U.S.C. sec. 8334(c) does not specifically permit civil service employees to remit the deposit by means of a tax-free rollover contribution from an IRA or another eligible retirement plan. The regulations promulgated under 5 U.S.C. sec. 8334(a)(2) likewise do not require CSRS to accept tax-free rollovers as a form of deposit. 5 C.F.R. sec. 831.303 (2001).

Amounts deposited under 5 U.S.C. sec. 8334(c) allow civil service employees to make up for years in which there were no contributions from their salaries. *See* 5 C.F.R. sec. 831.303. Deposited amounts take the place of after-tax contributions that were not originally made. *See* 5 U.S.C. sec. 8334(a), (c). Only the portion of a distribution from an IRA that is otherwise includible in gross income may be rolled over from the IRA to an eligible retirement plan other than an IRA. Sec. 408(d)(3)(A)(ii); *see* Janine H. Bosley & Martha L. Hutzelman, Qualified Plans—Taxation of Distributions, 370–3d Tax Mgmt. (BNA), at A–158. After-tax contributions that were made to an IRA cannot be rolled over. *See* sec. 408(d)(3)(A)(ii); *see also* Bosley & Hutzelman, *supra*, at A–158. A rollover contribution does not result in taxation until distribution. *See* secs. 72, 408(d)(3)(A).

The instant case involves an indirect transfer. Because it was not a direct transfer, CSRS was likely not aware that petitioner was attempting to make a tax-free rollover contribution, and there is nothing in the record to suggest that petitioner informed CSRS of his attempt to make a rollover. Unless it explicitly accepted rollovers, a qualified plan such as CSRS would not be aware of the proper tax treatment of the payment upon distribution.

Even if CSRS accepted rollovers, section 408(d)(3)(A)(ii) would permit it to accept as a rollover only the portion of the IRA distribution includible in gross income. Petitioner attempted to effect a rollover in order to make the payment to CSRS with pretax dollars. Petitioner did not distinguish for CSRS the extent to which the payment was made with pre- or post-tax dollars. Petitioner's deposit was to make up for wage contributions which were not withheld in prior years; those contributions would have been taxable. CSRS does not provide for the acceptance of rollovers. Because the payment was not accepted as a pretax contribution, it is taxable. *See Montgomery*, 18 F.3d at 500. Therefore, section 408(d)(3) does not apply and the $17,832 petitioner withdrew from his Fidelity IRA must be included in gross income under section 408(d)(1).

Any contention we have not addressed is irrelevant, moot, or meritless.

To reflect the foregoing,

Decision will be entered for respondent.

Reviewed by the Court.

THORNTON, COLVIN, GALE, GOEKE, PARIS, LAUBER, and NEGA, *JJ.*, agree with this opinion of the Court.

VASQUEZ, *J.*, concurring: I concur with the opinion of the Court's holding that petitioner's payment to the Civil Service Retirement System (CSRS) was not a rollover. I write separately to emphasize that this case can be resolved solely on the basis of the Office of Personnel Management's (OPM) authority to choose whether to accept rollovers. I also take this opportunity to address Judge Buch's dissent.

I agree with the facts as laid out by the opinion of the Court. OPM gave petitioner an opportunity to make a payment to CSRS in order to increase his annuity, as provided by 5 C.F.R. sec. 831.303(b) (2001). *See* op. Ct. p. 225. Within a two-month period, petitioner borrowed money from a friend, made a withdrawal from his Fidelity Investments individual retirement account (IRA), made the payment, made a second withdrawal from the same IRA, and repaid his friend. *See id.* The only question before us is whether one or both of the withdrawals from the IRA were rollover contributions to CSRS under section 408(d)(3).

As the opinion of the Court recognizes, CSRS is a qualified trust. *See id.* p. 228 and note 1. OPM administers CSRS. 5 U.S.C. sec. 8347(a) (2006); *see also* 5 C.F.R. sec. 838.101(a)(1) (2001) ("[T]he Civil Service Retirement System * * * [is] administered by the Office of Personnel Management[.]"). OPM's policy is to not accept rollovers to CSRS. *See* op. Ct. p. 230. Petitioner has failed to provide any authority requiring OPM to accept rollovers, and OPM did not treat petitioner's payment as a rollover. These are the only facts necessary to decide the issue before us.

"A trustee * * * has broad powers that are only 'limited by statute or the terms of the trust'". *Dabney v. Commissioner*, T.C. Memo. 2014–108, at *10 (quoting 3 Restatement, Trusts 3d, sec. 85 (2007)). In *Dabney*, the taxpayer attempted to invest in real property through an IRA he held with Charles Schwab & Co., Inc. (Charles Schwab). *Id.* at *3. The Internal Revenue Code does not prohibit IRAs from holding real estate. *Id.* at *10. However, Charles Schwab did not permit IRAs to purchase or hold real property. *Id.* at *3. We held that, because it was the trustee or custodian of the IRA, Charles Schwab's policies controlled and the taxpayer would not have been able to use his Charles Schwab IRA to hold the real property regardless of how he had structured the transaction. *Id.* at *11–*12.

The same analysis holds true here. As the administrator of CSRS, OPM may choose whether to accept rollover contributions to CSRS. No statute or regulation restricts OPM's authority to do so. OPM chose not to accept rollovers. Therefore, petitioner's payment to CSRS was not a rollover contribution.

In his dissent, Judge Buch raises the issue of the plain language of section 408(d)(3). The Supreme Court has stated:

> There is, of course, no more persuasive evidence of the purpose of a statute than the words by which the legislature undertook to give expression to its wishes. Often these words are sufficient in and of themselves to determine the purpose of the legislation. * * * Frequently, however, even when the plain meaning did not produce absurd results but merely an unreasonable one "plainly at variance with the policy of the legislation as a whole" this Court has followed that purpose, rather than the literal words. * * * [*United States v. Am. Trucking Ass'ns, Inc.*, 310 U.S. 534, 543, 544 (1940); fn. refs. omitted.; quoting *Ozawa v. United States*, 260 U.S. 178, 194 (1922).]

Under Judge Buch's reading of the statute, neither CSRS nor any other qualified plan or trust has the discretion to choose whether to accept rollover contributions. I do not believe that such an approach is reasonable or in keeping with Congress' intent. *See* H.R. Rept. No. 107–51 (Part 1), at 81 (2001) ("Qualified plans are not required to accept rollovers."). The term "qualified plan" refers to "a plan which satisfies the requirements of section 401(a)." Sec. 1.401–0(b)(1), Income Tax Regs. As the opinion of the Court states: "CSRS is a plan that meets the requirements of sec. 401(a)." *See* op. Ct. p. 228 note 1. Qualified plans have the discretion to decide whether to accept rollover contributions, and OPM exercised that discretion. No further analysis is required.

LAUBER, *J.*, agrees with this concurring opinion.

HALPERN, *J.*, dissenting: I join Judge Buch's dissent and write separately to explain why the second distribution fails. It fails under the statutory definition of a rollover. Mr. Bohner made his payment into CSRS on April 27, 2010, before he received the second distribution on May 3, 2010. Section 408(d)(3)(A) requires that the amount received as a distribution be paid into the eligible retirement plan no later than 60 days *after* distribution. A distribution cannot be rolled over before it is received. Judge Buch may not have included that reason because some joining his side opinion may have objected that that ground was not raised by respondent. That is not necessarily a valid objection.

A deficiency determination may be sustained upon any legal ground that supports it, even though the grounds relied upon by the Commissioner may have been different or unsound. *Blansett v. United States*, 283 F.2d 474, 478 (8th Cir. 1960); *Metrocorp, Inc. v. Commissioner*, 116 T.C. 211, 232 (2001); *Smith v. Commissioner*, 56 T.C. 263, 291 n.17 (1971); *Wilkes-Barre Carriage Co. v. Commissioner*, 39 T.C. 839, 845–846 (1963), *aff'd*, 332 F.2d 421 (2d Cir. 1964); *Williams v. Commissioner*, T.C. Memo. 1997–326. As we said in *Barnette v. Commissioner*, T.C. Memo. 1992–595, *aff'd without published opinion sub nom. Allied Mgmt. Corp. v. Commissioner*, 41 F.3d 667 (11th Cir. 1994):

> It is the Court's right and obligation to decide the case upon what it considers to be the correct application of the law, based upon the record presented, whether the parties have properly pleaded the controlling issues or not. * * * [I]f the Court feels that a full and fair opportunity to present the facts has been given, and the Court feels that no further briefing on the law is necessary, the Court can go forward and decide the case on the record presented.

We have sufficient facts to permit us to determine that the second distribution fails under the statutory definition of a rollover because it could not be rolled over before it was received, and I believe that we are obligated to so conclude.

HOLMES and BUCH, *JJ.*, agree with this dissent.

BUCH, *J.*, dissenting: The opinion of the Court turns on the question of whether CSRS accepts rollovers, yet in that opinion a majority of the Court candidly states that "there is no specific provision in the Internal Revenue Code concerning whether a qualified trust must accept a rollover that is an indirect transfer from an IRA in order to constitute an eligible retirement plan for purposes of section 408(d)(3)". *See* op. Ct. p. 228. They then go on to create such a rule.

This may or may not be a good or wise rule, but that should be irrelevant. It is not our role to act as rulemaker. Indeed, on the same day the Court Conference considered this Opinion, the Court of Appeals for the D.C. Circuit made this very point: "The Tax Court is in the business of interpreting and applying the internal revenue laws, *see Freytag*, 501 U.S. at 891, not in the business of making those laws."

Kuretski v. Commissioner, 755 F.3d 929, 943 (D.C. Cir. 2014), *aff'g* T.C. Memo. 2012–262. After noting what the statute says (and does not say), we are to apply what is written. The Court of Appeals for the Eleventh Circuit (where an appeal of this case could be taken) reminded us of that earlier this year: "The 'preeminent canon of statutory interpretation' requires the court to 'presume that the legislature says in a statute what it means and means in a statute what it says there.'" *Packard v. Commissioner*, 746 F.3d 1219, 1222 (11th Cir. 2014) (quoting *Bed Rock, Ltd., LLC v. United States*, 541 U.S. 176, 183 (2004)), *rev'g* 139 T.C. 390 (2012).

Indeed, over the years circuit after circuit has had occasion to remind us of this point. *See Textron, Inc. v. Commissioner*, 336 F.3d 26, 32 (1st Cir. 2003) ("Statutory language 'is the most persuasive evidence of the statutory purpose' and should not have been avoided by the Tax Court in this case." (quoting *Woodral v. Commissioner*, 112 T.C. 19, 22 (1999))), *rev'g* 115 T.C. 104 (2000); *Estate of Swan v. Commissioner*, 247 F.2d 144 (2d Cir. 1957) (reversing the Tax Court for failing to apply the plain meaning of the statute), *aff'g in part, rev'g in part* 24 T.C. 829 (1955); *Zackim v. Commissioner*, 887 F.2d 455 (3d Cir. 1989) (reversing the Tax Court for looking beyond the statute to a Senate report when the language of the statute is clear), *rev'g* 91 T.C. 1001 (1988); *Hillman v. IRS*, 263 F.3d 338, 342–343 (4th Cir. 2001) (holding that the plain meaning rule applies unless the literal application of the statute "produces an outcome that is demonstrably at odds with clearly expressed congressional intent to the contrary" or when literal application of the statute "produces an absurd result"), *rev'g* 114 T.C. 103 (2000); *Estate of Monroe v. Commissioner*, 124 F.3d 699 (5th Cir. 1997) (holding that the Tax Court incorrectly applied the law when it interpreted a statute in a way that conflicts with the statutory language), *rev'g* 104 T.C. 352 (1995); *Limited, Inc. v. Commissioner*, 286 F.3d 324, 336 (6th Cir. 2002) ("[I]t is not the Tax Court's role to inject its own policy determinations into the plain language of statutes."), *rev'g* 113 T.C. 169 (1999); *De Soto Sec. Co. v. Commissioner*, 235 F.2d 409, 411 (7th Cir. 1956) ("The courts can only interpret congressional acts. They cannot legislate."), *rev'g* 25 T.C. 175 (1955); *Estate of Farnam v. Commissioner*, 583 F.3d 581 (8th Cir. 2009) (holding that when the language of the statute is plain and unambiguous, there is no need to look to policy considerations), *aff'g* 130 T.C. 34 (2008); *Easson v. Commissioner*, 294 F.2d 653, 657 (9th Cir. 1961) (reversing the Tax Court for "failing to adhere to the unambiguous language contained in the statutes in question"), *rev'g* 33 T.C. 963 (1960); *Hawkins v. Commissioner*, 86 F.3d 982, 989 (10th Cir. 1996) (holding that the Tax Court's interpretation of the statute was "unduly narrow" and ran counter to the plain meaning of the statute), *rev'g* 102 T.C. 61 (1994); *Matthews v. Commissioner*, 907 F.2d 1173, 1179 (D.C. Cir. 1990) (holding that the language of the statute is "too plain to be mistaken"), *aff'g* 92 T.C. 351 (1989).

And the Supreme Court has reminded us. *Badaracco v. Commissioner*, 464 U.S. 386, 398 (1984) (affirming the Court of Appeals for the Third Circuit's reversal of the Tax Court and stating that "[c]ourts are not authorized to rewrite a statute because they might deem its effects susceptible of improvement"), *aff'g* 693 F.2d 298 (3d Cir. 1982).

We have acknowledged this point, as well. *See Belk v. Commissioner*, 140 T.C. 1, 10 (2013) ("When the plain language of the statute is clear and unambiguous, that is where the inquiry should end."). We often make this point in apologetic tones when denying a taxpayer a tax benefit not clearly contemplated by the Internal Revenue Code. *See, e.g.*, *Eichelburg v. Commissioner*, T.C. Memo. 2013–269 at *7–*8 ("We acknowledge that the result we reach may seem harsh. * * * However, this Court may not rely on general equitable principles to expand the statutorily prescribed time for filing a petition." (Citations omitted.)); *Cutler v. Commissioner*, T.C. Memo. 2013–119, at *34 ("While we sympathize with her children, we must apply the law as written; it is up to Congress to address questions of fairness and to make improvements to the law."); *Moody v. Commissioner*, T.C. Memo. 2012–268, at *8 ("We are sympathetic to petitioner's plight; however, we are bound by the statute as written and the accompanying regulations when consistent therewith."); *Ball v. Commissioner*, T.C. Memo. 1995–520, slip op. at 13 ("While the result to petitioner may seem harsh, we cannot ignore the plain language of the statute and, in effect, rewrite the statute to achieve what might be an equitable result.").

So with that, I would look to the law as written and apply it to the material facts, which are fairly straightforward. Mr. Bohner worked for the Social Security Administration and participated in the CSRS during his years of service. After Mr. Bohner retired, he received a letter from OPM explaining that he could increase his CSRS retirement annuity by remitting $17,832 to make up for years when he did not have retirement contributions withheld. The letter required the amount to be paid within 15 days. The letter was silent as to whether that payment could be made through an indirect rollover. [1]

During 2010 Mr. Bohner maintained an IRA with Fidelity Investments. Mr. Bohner made two requests for distributions from his IRA. Here, the chronology becomes important. Fidelity made a first distribution of $5,000 on April 15, 2010, withholding $500 of Federal income tax. Mr. Bohner then borrowed money from a friend and mailed a check for the full $17,832 to OPM for payment into CSRS on April 27, 2010. Fidelity then made a second distribution of $12,832 on May 3, 2010. Mr. Bohner used these funds to reimburse his friend and replenish his bank account.

The question for us to decide under the arguments properly preserved by the parties is whether Mr. Bohner made valid rollovers. [2]

The relevant statute is section 408(d). To begin, an IRA distribution is taxable as provided under section 72. Sec. 408(d)(1). However, that distribution is not taxable if it is a rollover. Sec. 408(d)(3)(A). That section sets forth the requirements of a rollover as follows:

> Paragraph (1) [providing that distributions are taxable] does not apply to any amount paid or distributed out of an individual retirement account or individual retirement annuity to the individual for whose benefit the account or annuity is maintained if—
>
> * * * * * * *
>
> (ii) the entire amount received (including money and any other property) is paid into an eligible retirement plan for the benefit of such individual not later than the 60th day after the date on which the pay-

---

[1] Such a statement would not affect the outcome the opinion of the Court reaches, and whether any such statement would affect the outcome under the analysis in this dissent is not an issue before us.

[2] *See* op. Ct. p. 228 and note 2.

ment or distribution is received, except that the maximum amount which may be paid into such plan may not exceed the portion of the amount received which is includible in gross income (determined without regard to this paragraph).

CSRS is an "eligible retirement plan". Through a series of cross-references, a qualified trust is an eligible retirement plan. *See* secs. 408(d)(3) (flush language), 402(c)(8)(B). In Rev. Rul. 58–472, 1958–2 C.B. 30, the IRS held that CSRS, which was first created by the Civil Service Retirement Act of 1920, Pub. L. No. 66–215, 41 Stat. 614, is a qualified trust under section 401(a). Although revenue rulings are not binding on the Court, they may serve to bind the Commissioner where a longstanding revenue ruling that has not been modified or revoked is relevant to the case before us. *Rauenhorst v. Commissioner*, 119 T.C. 157, 173 (2002). The IRS has not revoked this revenue ruling, and respondent did not challenge CSRS' status as a qualified trust here. Accordingly, CSRS is a qualified trust and therefore an eligible retirement plan.

So we must see whether either of the two distributions qualifies as a rollover. The opinion of the Court denies rollover treatment for both distributions in one fell swoop.

Like the facts, the law is fairly straightforward. The requirements for a distribution to be treated as a rollover are found in section 408(d)(3)(A)(ii). A distribution from an IRA will not be included in gross income if the entire amount received from the IRA is paid into an eligible retirement plan no later than 60 days after the date the payment is received. Mr. Bohner received the first distribution on April 15, 2010. Twelve days later, Mr. Bohner wrote a check exceeding the amount of the distribution to OPM for payment into CSRS. Accordingly, he fulfilled all of the requirements for a rollover contribution under section 408(d)(3)(A)(ii), and the first distribution should not be included in his gross income.

The opinion of the Court makes it abundantly clear that there is no rule that overrides the rollover treatment allowed under section 408. The opinion cites section 401(a)(31), which relates to the qualification of a plan, not the tax treatment of a rollover.[3] The opinion cites section 402, which relates to

[3] Both the opinion of the Court and respondent cite a regulation for the

Continued

rollovers from exempt trusts, not rollovers from IRAs. In fact, the opinion does not cite any specific provision in section 402 but rather cites the legislative history of 1992 amendments to section 402.

In looking to analogous provisions to assist in interpreting section 408, the opinion of the Court has done the exact opposite of what canons of statutory construction instruct. Canons of statutory construction encourage courts to look to analogous provisions when resolving ambiguity in the provision under consideration. *Atl. Cleaners & Dyers, Inc. v. United States*, 286 U.S. 427, 433 (1932) ("Undoubtedly, there is a natural presumption that identical words used in different parts of the same act are intended to have the same meaning."). Where one provision contains a specific rule and another is silent, canons of statutory construction tell us that the omission is intentional. *Rand v. Commissioner*, 141 T.C. 376, 390–391 (2013). And we should interpret the provision consistent with the omission; we do not add a rule to the statute that Congress did not itself include.

The strongest statutory authority the opinion of the Court can muster is the statement "[t]he statutory provisions governing CSRS do not include a provision allowing pretax employee contributions." *See* op. Ct. p. 226. But the statutory framework of CSRS also does not include a provision prohibiting pretax employee contributions. A review of that statutory framework reveals that it is silent on the subject of its Federal income tax treatment. 5 U.S.C. secs. 8331–8351 (2006). The only tax-related provisions within CSRS's governing statutes relate to State taxes and withholding. *Id.* sec. 8345(k).

The provisions governing the tax treatment of CSRS distributions and rollovers into the CSRS are (unsurprisingly) found in title 26, the Internal Revenue Code. Section 408(d)(3) governs rollovers from an IRA. That provision tells us that a rollover distribution is to be treated as income on the contract when contributed to the new plan. Sec. 408(d)(3)(H)(ii)(II). If treated properly, that amount would be

---

proposition that eligible retirement plans are not required to accept rollovers. Sec. 1.401(a)(31)–1, Q&A–13, Income Tax Regs. The regulation is irrelevant because it not only addresses the qualification requirements for a plan (an issue not before us); it also relates to accepting direct rollovers, which are not at issue here.

taxable when paid out by CSRS. Sec. 72(b) (because it is not treated as an investment in the contract, it is not part of the amount that is excluded from income).

The opinion of the Court seems intent on solving a problem that does not exist. The statutory scheme places no weight on whether CSRS has a practice of accepting rollover contributions. Indeed, the statute places no weight on a plan's preferences regarding accepting rollovers when determining the taxability of a rollover distribution. The Internal Revenue Code, however, would tax that rollover when it comes out of CSRS. If CSRS does not properly account for that (a fact that is not in the record), then that is a problem for those who administer CSRS to resolve, not the Court.

The concurring opinion cites *Dabney v. Commissioner*, T.C. Memo. 2014–108, for the proposition that the trustee or custodian of a plan can restrict the types of investments the plan will allow, even when the statute would otherwise permit the investment. *See* concurring op. p. 231. *Dabney* is inapposite because the question presented to the Court was whether the distribution at issue was either an investment by Mr. Dabney's IRA or a transfer between IRA trustees. Mr. Dabney did not intend or attempt to make a rollover contribution under section 408(d)(3) from one retirement account to another; rather, Mr. Dabney attempted to change the investments within his IRA in violation of the trustee's internal policies. Mr. Dabney claimed that he acquired an investment in real property as agent for the IRA trustee; however, he could not act as agent for the trustee where the trustee had a policy against investing in real property. Our approval of the IRA trustee's right to restrict the investment of IRA funds is not authority for the proposition that an otherwise qualified recipient of an IRA rollover contribution may, through its internal policies, cause the contribution not to qualify as such. Thus the analysis in *Dabney* has no bearing on the case before us.

On the basis of the foregoing, the first distribution fulfills the necessary requirements for a rollover contribution. As for the second of the two Fidelity distributions, that distribution may fail to qualify as a rollover for reasons not addressed here.

Because Mr. Bohner complied with all the necessary steps to make a rollover contribution as to the first distribution, I dissent.

HALPERN, FOLEY, HOLMES, GUSTAFSON, and MORRISON, *JJ.*, agree with this dissent.

GERD TOPSNIK, PETITIONER *v.* COMMISSIONER OF INTERNAL REVENUE, RESPONDENT

Docket No. 22577–11. Filed September 23, 2014.

In 2004, P, a German citizen, made an installment sale of his stock in a U.S. corporation, and he received payments in 2004–09 (years in issue) pursuant to a promissory note executed in connection with the sale. The 2004 payments consisted of a large downpayment and four smaller, equal monthly payments, which continued throughout 2005–09. He filed U.S. individual income tax returns for 2004 and 2005 on which he erroneously reported identical portions of the gain. He did not file U.S. returns for 2006–09. R challenged P's installment sale reporting for 2004 and 2005 and filed substitutes for returns for 2006–09 on which he included in P's income appropriate portions of P's installment sale gain. R alleges that P is liable for income tax deficiencies for 2004 and 2006–09, almost entirely attributable to the gain on his installment sale of stock, additions to tax under I.R.C. sec. 6651(a)(1) and (2) for 2004 and 2006–09, and an addition to tax under I.R.C. sec. 6654 for 2005, all of which were included in a jeopardy assessment pursuant to which R levied on the installment payments due P in partial satisfaction of P's liabilities. P alleges that, during the years in issue, he was a German resident and a U.S. nonresident alien, having "informally" abandoned his status as a lawful permanent resident (LPR) (i.e., a resident alien taxable on his worldwide income) in 2003 and, therefore, was not subject to U.S. taxation pursuant to arts. 4 and 13 of the U.S.-Germany Income Tax Treaty (treaty). R counters that (1) because P did not formally abandon his LPR status (obtained in 1977) until 2010, he remained an LPR during the years in issue and (2) because he was not taxable by Germany as a German resident during those years, he was not a German resident under art. 4 of the treaty. Therefore, he was not exempted from U.S. taxation by the treaty. P also alleges that, because R moved to dismiss P's 2011 Federal District Court suit to review R's jeopardy assessments and levies encompassing the years in issue, in part, for improper venue on the ground that P was a resident of Germany, R is now judicially estopped from arguing that P was not a German resident during the years in issue.

1. *Held*: Because he did not formally abandon his LPR status pursuant to sec. 301.7701(b)–1(b)(1) and (3), Proced. & Admin. Regs., until 2010, P remained an LPR during the years in issue, taxable by the United States on his worldwide income, including the gain on his 2004 installment sale of stock.

2. *Held, further*, LPR status for Federal income tax purposes turns on Federal income tax law and is only indirectly determined by immigration law.

3. *Held, further*, because P was not subject to German taxation as a German resident during the years in issue, he was not a German resident pursuant to art. 4 of the treaty and, therefore, is not exempted by the treaty from U.S. taxation during those years.

4. *Held, further*, as a U.S. but not a German resident, P is taxable by the United States, pursuant to art. 13, para. 5 of the treaty, on his gain recognized during the years in issue from his 2004 installment sale of stock in a U.S. corporation.

5. *Held, further*, because the prior Federal District Court litigation concerned only P's status as a German resident for a year after the years in issue, R is not estopped from asserting that P was not a German resident under the treaty during the years in issue.

6. *Held, further*, R's additions to tax sustained except for the I.R.C. sec. 6651(a)(2) addition to tax for 2004, which must be recalculated.

Charles Herbert Magnuson, for petitioner.
Najah J. Shariff and *Catherine G. Chang*, for respondent.

HALPERN, *Judge*: By notice of deficiency (notice) respondent determined deficiencies and related additions to tax for petitioner's 2004–09 tax years as follows:

		Additions to tax	
Year	*Deficiency*	*Sec. 6651(a)(1)*	*Sec. 6654*
2004	$135,316	$28,893	---
2005	---	---	$224
2006	75,167	16,913	---
2007	62,766	14,122	---
2008	61,068	13,740	---
2009	60,858	5,477	---

The notice also seeks to impose additions to tax for 2004 and 2006–09 under section 6651(a)(2)[1] (failure to timely pay tax shown on return) but alleges that the "[a]mount cannot be determined at this time."

The issues for decision are (1) whether petitioner was subject to U.S. taxation as a resident alien during the years in issue and (2) if so, whether petitioner is liable for additions to tax under sections 6651(a)(1) (failure to timely file tax return), 6651(a)(2) (failure to pay tax shown on return), and 6654 (failure to pay estimated tax).[2] Petitioner alleges that he was a German resident during the years in issue and, therefore, was exempt from U.S. taxation pursuant to articles 4 and 13 of the Convention for the Avoidance of Double Taxation and the Prevention of Fiscal Evasion With Respect to Taxes on Income and Capital and to Certain Other Taxes, U.S.-Ger., Aug. 29, 1989, 1708 U.N.T.S. 3 (entered into force Aug. 21, 1991), *available at* https://treaties.un.org/doc/Publication/UNTS/Volume%201708/volume–1708–1–29534–English.pdf (U.S.-Germany Treaty or treaty).[3] Petitioner, thus, seeks our determination that there are no deficiencies in, or additions to, tax for the years in issue and that he is entitled to a refund of all payments made by him (for 2004 and 2005) and all amounts collected by respondent pursuant to a jeopardy assessment and levy on the installment pay-

---

[1] Unless otherwise indicated, all section references are to the Internal Revenue Code in effect for the years in issue, and all Rule references are to the Tax Court Rules of Practice and Procedure. We round all dollar amounts to the nearest dollar.

[2] In his pretrial memorandum, petitioner alleges that he "is to be granted an allowance of entitlements such as for IRC § 7430 cost and fees and any other further relief a court may deem appropriate under the circumstances", and he seeks "reasonable fees and costs" in both his petition and amended petition. Petitioner's claim for litigation and administrative costs is not timely. *See* Rule 231. In any event, on brief, petitioner has not pursued those claims for relief. Therefore, we consider them to have been abandoned. *See Mendes v. Commissioner*, 121 T.C. 308, 312–313 (2003) ("If an argument is not pursued on brief, we may conclude that it has been abandoned.").

[3] In response to respondent's argument that petitioner spent more time in the Philippines and Thailand than he did in Germany during the years in issue, petitioner suggests that, if respondent is correct, petitioner was a resident of one or the other and, therefore, exempt from U.S. taxation under U.S. bilateral treaties with those two countries. *See* discussion *infra* note 19.

ments arising out of petitioner's 2004 installment sale of stock.

FINDINGS OF FACT[4]

The parties have stipulated certain facts and the authenticity of certain documents. The facts stipulated are so found, and the documents stipulated are accepted as authentic.

At the time petitioner filed the petition, he resided in Germany.

Principal Transaction Resulting in Proposed Deficiencies

In 1986, petitioner and another individual organized Gourmet Foods, Inc. (GFI), a California corporation in the business of producing, preparing, purchasing, and selling gourmet foods, with its principal place of business in Rancho Dominguez, California. In 2001, petitioner sued a number of individuals and entities involved with GFI's business for, in effect, maneuvering to prohibit him from cashing in on his investment in the business. The parties to that litigation ultimately settled their dispute. Pursuant to the settlement, on July 30, 2004, petitioner sold his interest in GFI, to GFI, for $5,427,000.[5] The purchase price was paid in installments, a 2004 "down payment" of $1.6 million "less any advances previously made", and monthly payments (pursuant to a promissory note) of $42,500 commencing in October 2004.[6] That arrangement resulted in payments to petitioner of $1.77 million in 2004 ($1.6 million plus four payments of $42,500) and $510,000 (12 × $42,500) in each of the subsequent years in

---

[4] In his answering brief, petitioner does not object to any of respondent's proposed findings of fact. We will, therefore, assume that they are correct except to the extent that they are clearly inconsistent with either evidence in the record or petitioner's proposed findings of fact. *See, e.g.*, *Jonson v. Commissioner*, 118 T.C. 106, 108 n.4 (2002), *aff'd*, 353 F.3d 1181 (10th Cir. 2003); *Bland v. Commissioner*, T.C. Memo. 2012–84, 2012 WL 967651, at *1 n.3.

[5] Presumably, the "sale" was, in substance, GFI's redemption of petitioner's GFI stock.

[6] The settlement agreement states that petitioner received advances before 2004 totaling $766,418, which, pursuant to the terms of the settlement agreement, should have been deducted from the $1.6 million down payment in 2004. The parties have stipulated, however, and the stipulated exhibits confirm, that GFI did, in fact, make a $1.6 million down payment to petitioner in 2004.

issue (2005–09). All of the monthly installment payments were reduced by California withholding taxes. GFI mailed the checks and the yearend Forms 1099–MISC, Miscellaneous Income, to petitioner at his daughter's British Columbia, Canada, address.

Petitioner's Return Filings for the Years in Issue

Petitioner filed an untimely 2004 Form 1040, U.S. Individual Income Tax Return, on June 4, 2007. On his 2004 return, petitioner reported $723,600 as the gross sale proceeds from the sale of a capital asset acquired on June 30, 1986, and sold on June 30, 2004, a $99,789 basis for the asset, and net long-term capital gain of $623,811. Petitioner also reported net losses of $73,569 from Gourmet Foods, Thailand, and "Gerd Topsnik Reitershausen" and from "operating a hotel". Petitioner reported his daughter's British Columbia, Canada, address as his home address.

Petitioner untimely filed his 2005 Form 1040 on December 10, 2007. As he did for 2004, petitioner reported net long-term capital gain of $623,811 from the sale of a capital asset acquired on June 30, 1986, and sold on June 30, 2004. Also consistent with his 2004 return, petitioner reported net losses of $61,671 from the same business operations in Thailand and Reitershausen. Petitioner also reported $983 of taxable interest. On that return, too, he reported his daughter's British Columbia address as his home address.

Petitioner did not file Forms 1040 for 2006–09. Consequently, respondent made substitutes for returns (SFRs) for petitioner for those years pursuant to section 6020(b). On each of the SFRs for 2006–09, respondent listed capital gain income of $439,671, provided offsets for the applicable standard deduction and personal exemption, and, for 2006, included $35,700 for "state tax refunds, credits or offsets." Also, for each year, respondent imposed additions to tax under section 6651(a)(1) and (2).

In November 2009, petitioner filed a Form 1040X, Amended U.S. Individual Income Tax Return, for 2005 seeking a refund of his tax payments for that year and, in May 2010, he filed Forms 1040NR, U.S. Nonresident Alien Income Tax Return, for 2006–09 showing zero tax due for each of those years.

Respondent's Adjustments [7]

Respondent challenges the accuracy of petitioner's 2004 and 2005 installment sale reporting of his gain on the installment sale of his GFI stock. [8]

Respondent first computed the gross profit percentage (GPP) under section 453(c) by dividing petitioner's $4,678,582 total gain on the sale (derived by subtracting petitioner's $748,418 basis for his GFI stock, as determined by respondent, from the total sale price of $5,427,000) by the sale price of $5,427,000, which results in a GPP of 0.8621. Applying the GPP to the total payments petitioner received in 2004 results in installment sale gain of $1,525,917 (0.8621 × $1.77 million) for 2004 and installment sale gain of $439,671 (0.8621 × $510,000 [9]) for 2005–09. Those computations resulted in an increase in petitioner's capital gain

---

[7] In addition to his capital gain adjustments and imposition of additions to tax under secs. 6651(a)(1) and (2) and 6654, respondent (1) adjusted petitioner's reported itemized deductions for 2004 and 2005, (2) made adjustments to his reported alternative minimum tax (AMT) for 2004 and 2005 and imposed AMT for 2006–09, (3) included taxable interest in his income for 2006, (4) for 2006 and 2007, disallowed expenses subject to the 2% adjusted gross income limitation, and (5) made adjustments with respect to unreported State tax refunds and a deduction for tax preparation fees for 2006. Petitioner disputes all of the adjustments, but solely on the basis that he was exempt from U.S. taxation under the U.S.-Germany Treaty. He does not dispute respondent's computation of the adjustments that give rise to the tax deficiencies. Because the entire discussion by both parties focuses on whether petitioner is required to pay U.S. income tax on the capital gain arising from his installment sale of GFI stock, and because that is by far respondent's largest adjustment and is responsible for the AMT adjustments and the deduction disallowances, we shall limit our discussion of respondent's adjustments to his computation of that gain for each of the years at issue, which, as noted, petitioner appears to accept as accurate. For the same reasons, we shall limit our discussion of petitioner's taxability by the United States to his taxability on that gain.

[8] With exceptions not relevant herein, an installment sale constitutes a "disposition of property where at least 1 payment is to be received after the close of the taxable year in which the disposition occurs." Sec. 453(b)(1). The gain from such a sale must be reported under the installment method, i.e., by recognizing as gain for each taxable year in which payments are received "that proportion of the payments received in that year which the gross profit * * * [on the sale or other disposition] bears to the total contract price." *See* sec. 453(a), (c).

[9] This $510,000 is the amount petitioner received annually (12 monthly payments of $42,500) from 2005–09.

income for 2004 of $902,106 ($1,525,917 less the $623,811 gain petitioner reported) and a decrease in petitioner's capital gain income reported for 2005 of $184,140 ($623,811 reported less the $439,671 gain derived by application of the GPP to the $510,000 paid to petitioner during the year).

Because petitioner did not initially file returns or pay tax for 2006–09, respondent's adjustment for each of those years, with respect to petitioner's sale of his GFI stock, was to attribute to petitioner the gain of $439,671 he realized with respect to the $510,000 he received during the year.

Jeopardy Assessment, Levies, and Subsequent Litigation

On March 16, 2011, respondent issued a jeopardy assessment of petitioner's liabilities for taxes, penalties, and interest for the years in issue and, thereafter, levied on the GFI installment payments in partial satisfaction of those liabilities.

On August 23, 2011, petitioner filed a complaint and, thereafter, an amended complaint against the United States in the U.S. District Court for the Central District of California requesting a review of respondent's jeopardy assessments and levies, including the foregoing jeopardy assessment and levies, refunds for 2004 and 2005, and damages for unauthorized collection actions. The defendant United States moved to dismiss the case on several grounds, including improper venue. After noting that petitioner "does not reside in any judicial district since he currently resides in Germany", the District Court held that, under the venue provisions of 28 U.S.C. sec. 1402(a)(1), petitioner "may not file his claim in a district court" and that his "only recourse is to prosecute his claim in the United States Claims Court, which has concurrent jurisdiction over tax refund actions." *Topsnik v. United States*, No. 2:11–cv–06958–JHN–MRW, 2012 WL 10637570, at *1 (C.D. Cal. Jan. 17, 2012), *aff'd*, 554 Fed. Appx. 630 (9th Cir. 2014) (*Topsnik I*). On that basis, the District Court granted defendant's motion to dismiss. *Id.* [10]

[10] Following the District Court's dismissal of petitioner's suit due to improper venue and while petitioner's appeal of that ruling was pending before the Court of Appeals for the Ninth Circuit, petitioner brought suit for refund in the Court of Federal Claims. The defendant United States moved

Petitioner's Ties to the United States

On January 25, 1977, petitioner applied for and, on February 3, 1977, was issued a Form I–551, "Resident Alien" card (green card), thereby becoming a "lawful permanent resident" (LPR) of the United States and, hence, a resident alien taxable on his worldwide taxable income.[11] Also, in 1977, petitioner moved from Calgary, Canada, to Honolulu, Hawaii.

On November 21, 2002, petitioner flew from Frankfurt, Germany, to San Francisco International Airport where he presented himself as a returning LPR. At that time he signed and submitted to the Department of Justice Immigration and Naturalization Service (INS) an affidavit stating, in part, that (1) the purpose of his trip to the United States was to return home to Honolulu where he had been residing since 1977, (2) he was a partner in GFI, and (3) he traveled every six weeks on business in connection with a company that he owned in Thailand and properties in Germany and Thailand. At that time he also listed "U.S.A." as his country of residence on a customs declaration.

On March 3, 2003, petitioner renewed his LPR status by filing a Form I–90, Application to Replace [Expiring] Permanent Residence Card, on which he listed his status in the United States as "Permanent Resident—(Not a Commuter)" and his U.S. mailing address as 2938 Pacific Heights Road in Honolulu. His application for renewed LPR status through March 1, 2014, was approved by the INS on March 1, 2004. Petitioner retained his LPR status until November 20, 2010, when he abandoned it by filing a U.S. Citizenship and Immigration Services (USCIS) Form I–407, Abandonment of Lawful Permanent Resident Status, on which he stated that his "intended or actual permanent residence abroad" would

to continue a temporary stay of the case pending the outcome of petitioner's appeal of the District Court ruling. The Court of Federal Claims denied the motion on the ground that there was no venue issue before it, and that, whatever disposition the Court of Appeals were to make of petitioner's appeal, it would retain subject matter jurisdiction over petitioner's refund claim and, therefore, could proceed to address the merits of that claim. *See Topsnik v. United States*, 114 Fed. Cl. 1 (2013) (*Topsnik II*).

[11] *See* sec. 7701(b)(1)(A)(i) (codifying the resident alien status of a lawful permanent resident for taxable years beginning after 1984); sec. 1.1–1(a)(1), (b), Income Tax Regs.

be in the Philippines, and he surrendered his green card to the USCIS.

Petitioner sold his Hawaiian residence in 2003, but the new owner continued to let him list it as a home address when registering at hotels, and he continued to receive mail there, which the new owner forwarded to him.

Petitioner's Ties to Germany

Petitioner was born in Germany and has a German driver's license and a German passport. Beginning in 1964, petitioner had access to a room in his brother's house in Freiburg, Germany, where he stays and has in the past stayed on frequent occasions. In 2002, petitioner purchased a small inn in Oerlenbach, district of Rottershausen, Germany. One of the rooms at the inn was always available to him, and he stayed in that room, during the years in issue, whenever he was there. The inn was some 400 kilometers from Freiburg. Also, during all or a part of that period petitioner owned an old farmhouse and farm; some industrial or commercial properties in the former East Germany, which remain undeveloped and are still held by petitioner for potential gain; and a small "cafhouse" in Markelsheim, Germany. According to petitioner's own logbook entries for five of the six years in issue, he was physically present in Germany for a total of 98 days in 2005, 92 days in 2006, 44 days in 2007, 40 days in 2008, and 14 days in 2009.

In response to a request by the U.S. competent authority to his German counterpart under article 26 of the U.S.-Germany Treaty (article 26: "Exchange of Information and Administrative Assistance"), the latter, pursuant to a letter dated May 4, 2011, furnished the following information regarding petitioner's contacts with Germany during the years in issue, which he, in turn, had obtained from German tax authority records:

(1) Petitioner was not registered in the community of Oerlenbach, the situs of the aforementioned inn. Therefore, he failed to establish residency in that community.[12]

[12] A member of the U.S. competent authority office in Frankfurt, Germany, testified, without objection by petitioner's counsel, that one registers in a particular city or town in order to establish that that is the community in which he intends to become a German resident.

(2) It is not clear whether petitioner had or has a domicile or habitual residence in Germany.

(3) Beginning with the 2002 assessment period, petitioner has been registered with the German tax authority as a taxpayer with limited liability, i.e., as a nonresident individual generally chargeable only on German source income, including income from German assets, a status equivalent to the status, for U.S. tax purposes, of a nonresident alien.

(4) For 2002–04, value added tax returns were submitted with respect to rental income that petitioner collected from customers of the Oerlenbach inn.

(5) In cash basis accounting statements for 2002–04, Oerlenbach inn rental revenues of €4,541.02 were declared for 2002, €1,034.48 for 2003, and €1,879.92 for 2004. No cash basis accounting statements were filed for 2005 and subsequent years.

(6) Petitioner did not file the required tax returns for a limited liability taxpayer despite the German tax authority's repeated requests that he do so. Therefore, the German tax authority estimated the German income tax tax bases for the 2002–08 assessment periods and submitted SFRs on his behalf.

(7) Because the German tax authority did not consider petitioner to be a German resident, it would not have considered the gain on petitioner's installment sale of his GFI stock to be income taxable in Germany, and, in fact, the German tax authority had no record of his filing income tax returns in Germany for 2004 and subsequent years.

Petitioner's Ties to Thailand

During the years in issue, petitioner operated a winery business in Thailand called Gourmet Foods Thailand Co. Ltd. During that period, he maintained a bank account in Thailand, spent significant time there visiting with his son, who lived there, and ran his winery business.

Petitioner's Ties to the Philippines

During the years in issue, petitioner spent considerable time in the Philippines. In January 2007, petitioner rented premises in the Philippines as a residence for himself and his family, and, on November 20, 2010, when he surrendered his green card, he listed those premises as his permanent residence. The lease is to run for 10 years, from February 1, 2007, until January 31, 2016.

Situs of Petitioner's Physical Presence

During the years in issue, petitioner traveled extensively among, and had substantial physical presence in, the Philippines, Thailand, the United States, Canada, Germany, and a number of other countries in Asia and Africa.

OPINION

I. *Burden of Proof*

As discussed *infra*, the factual issue before us is whether, during the years in issue, petitioner was a resident of either or both the United States and Germany, as that term is defined under the U.S.-Germany Treaty.

In general, a taxpayer bears the burden of proof. Rule 142(a)(1). However, section 7491(a) shifts the burden of proof to the Commissioner in certain situations if the taxpayer raises the issue, introduces credible evidence with respect to any factual issue relevant to ascertaining the proper tax liability, and demonstrates compliance with the applicable requirements of section 7491(a)(2).

Because we base our decision regarding petitioner's status as a German resident during the years in issue upon a preponderance of the evidence, it is not necessary that we assign the burden of proof. *See, e.g., Estate of Black v. Commissioner*, 133 T.C. 340, 359 (2009); *Estate of Bongard v. Commissioner*, 124 T.C. 95, 111 (2005).

II. *Whether Petitioner Is Subject to U.S. Taxation of His Installment Sale Gain*

A. *Applicable Law*

1. *Introduction*

As noted *supra*, petitioner's sole claim is that he was a resident of Germany and a nonresident alien vis-a-vis the United States during the years in issue and, therefore, was exempt, under the U.S.-Germany Treaty, from U.S. taxation of his installment sale gain realized during those years.

2. *Applicable Provisions of the Internal Revenue Code and Regulations*

Pursuant to sections 61(a)(3) and 1001(a) and (c), a taxpayer is taxable on gain (amount realized in excess of basis) from the sale or exchange of property in the year of the sale or exchange. The taxpayer may defer recognition of the gain in the case of an installment sale of a capital asset. Such sales are reported under the installment method whereby the gain recognized during the taxable year is that portion of the payment(s) received during the year that is determined by applying thereto the ratio of the gross profit on the sale to the total contract price. *See* sec. 453(c).

As noted *supra*, a U.S. resident alien is taxable by the United States on his worldwide taxable income. Sec. 1.1–1(a)(1) and (b), Income Tax Regs. Section 7701(b)(1)(A)(i) defines a resident alien, "with respect to any calendar year", in pertinent part, as "[a]n alien individual" who is "[l]awfully admitted for permanent residence * * * [and] is * * * [an LPR] of the United States at any time during such calendar year." Section 301.7701(b)–1(b)(1), Proced. & Admin. Regs., defines an LPR as follows:

> Lawful permanent resident.—(1) Green card test.—An alien is a resident alien with respect to a calendar year if the individual is a lawful permanent resident at any time during the calendar year. A lawful permanent resident is an individual who has been lawfully granted the privilege of residing permanently in the United States as an immigrant in accordance with the immigration laws. Resident status is deemed to continue unless it is rescinded or administratively or judicially determined to have been abandoned.

Section 7701(b)(6) also concerns the duration of an individual's status as an LPR and provides as follows:

> (6) Lawful permanent resident.—For purposes of this subsection, an individual is a lawful permanent resident of the United States at any time if—
>
> (A) such individual has the status of having been lawfully accorded the privilege of residing permanently in the United States as an immigrant in accordance with the immigration laws, and
>
> (B) such status has not been revoked (and has not been administratively or judicially determined to have been abandoned).
>
> An individual shall cease to be treated as a lawful permanent resident of the United States if such individual commences to be treated as a resident of a foreign country under the provisions of a tax treaty between the United States and the foreign country, does not waive the

benefits of such treaty applicable to residents of the foreign country, and notifies the Secretary of the commencement of such treatment.

The definitions of resident alien and LPR set forth in section 7701(b)(1)(A)(i) and (6) were enacted as part of the Deficit Reduction Act of 1984, Pub. L. No. 98–369, sec. 138, 98 Stat. at 672. The House Ways and Means Committee report accompanying the House bill (adopted in conference with modifications not pertinent herein), in describing the definition of an LPR set forth in those provisions, states as follows:

> The bill defines lawful permanent resident to mean an individual who has the status of having been lawfully accorded the privilege of residing permanently in the United States as an immigrant in accordance with the immigration laws, if such status has not been revoked or administratively or judicially determined to have been abandoned. Therefore, an alien who comes to the United States so infrequently that, on scrutiny, he or she is no longer legally entitled to permanent resident status, but who has not officially lost or abandoned that status, will be a resident for tax purposes. [H.R. Rept. No. 98–432 (Part 2), at 226 (1983), 1984 U.S.C.C.A.N. 697, 1166.]

Section 301.7701(b)–1(b)(3), Proced. & Admin. Regs., sets forth the requirements for an administrative or judicial determination of an alien's abandonment of U.S. resident status as follows:

> (3) Administrative or judicial determination of abandonment of resident status.—An administrative or judicial determination of abandonment of resident status may be initiated by the alien individual, the Immigration and Naturalization Service (INS), or a consular officer. If the alien initiates this determination, resident status is considered to be abandoned when the individual's application for abandonment (INS Form I–407) or a letter stating the alien's intent to abandon his or her resident status, with the Alien Registration Receipt Card (INS Form I–151 or Form I–551) enclosed, is filed with the INS or a consular officer. If INS replaces any of the form numbers referred to in this paragraph or § 301.7701(b)–2(f), refer to the comparable INS replacement form number. For purposes of this paragraph, an alien individual shall be considered to have filed a letter stating the intent to abandon resident status with the INS or a consular office if such letter is sent by certified mail, return receipt requested (or a foreign country's equivalent thereof). A copy of the letter, along with proof that the letter was mailed and received, should be retained by the alien individual. If the INS or a consular officer initiates this determination, resident status will be considered to be abandoned upon the issuance of a final administrative order of abandonment. If an individual is granted an appeal to a federal court of competent jurisdiction, a final judicial order is required.

3. *Applicable Provisions of the U.S.-Germany Treaty*

The U.S.-Germany Treaty, as applicable to the years in issue, consists of three documents: (1) the original treaty, which was signed in 1989 but which entered into force in 1991, (2) the 1989 protocol executed in 1989 on the same day the treaty was signed and which entered into force contemporaneously with the treaty, and (3) the 2006 protocol, which entered into force on December 28, 2007, and is effective for taxes other than withholding taxes (e.g., for income taxes) as of January 1, 2008. Therefore, the treaty (sometimes, original treaty) as amended by the 2006 protocol (sometimes, post-2006 treaty) is applicable for petitioner's 2008 and 2009 taxable years.

Article 4 of the treaty defines the term "resident" for purposes thereof. Before its amendment by the 2006 protocol, article 4, paragraph 1, provided as follows:

> For the purposes of this Convention, the term "resident of a Contracting State" means any person who, under the laws of that State, is liable to tax therein by reason of his domicile, residence, place of management, place of incorporation, or any other criterion of a similar nature, provided, however, that
>
> (a) this term does not include any person who is liable to tax in that State in respect only of income from sources in that State or capital situated therein; and
>
> (b) in the case of income derived or paid by a partnership, estate, or trust, this term applies only to the extent that the income derived by such partnership, estate, or trust is subject to tax in that State as the income of a resident, either in its hands or in the hands of its partners or beneficiaries.

The 2006 protocol modified article 4, paragraph 1, to read as follows:

> For the purposes of this Convention, the term "resident of a Contracting State" means any person who, under the laws of that State, is liable to tax therein by reason of his domicile, residence, place of management, place of incorporation, or any other criterion of a similar nature, and also includes that State and any political subdivision or local authority thereof. The term, however, does not include any person who is liable to tax in that State in respect only of income from sources in that State or of profits attributable to a permanent establishment in that State or capital situated therein. [Protocol Amending the Convention for the Avoidance of Double Taxation and the Prevention of Fiscal Evasion With Respect to Taxes on Income and Capital and to Certain Other Taxes Signed on 29th August 1989, U.S.-Ger., Jun. 1, 2006, 2504 U.N.T.S.

90, *available at* https://treaties.un.org/doc/Publication/UNTS/Volume%202504/v2504.pdf.]

Article 4, paragraph 1, of the original treaty, through subparagraph (a) (as applicable to individuals) is identical, in substance, to article 4, paragraph 1 of the post-2006 treaty. Both define a "resident of a Contracting State" to include an individual "liable to tax therein by reason of his * * * [domicile or residence]", and both exclude from the definition "any person who is liable to tax in that State in respect only of income from sources in that State * * * or capital situated therein."[13]

Article 13, paragraph 1 (the same in both the original and post-2006 treaties), provides:

> Gains derived by a resident of a Contracting State from the alienation of immovable property * * * [i.e., real property] situated in the other Contracting State may be taxed in that other State.

Article 13, paragraph 2 (also unchanged by the 2006 protocol), provides in pertinent part:

> For the purposes of this Article, the term "immovable" property situated in the other Contracting State shall include
>
> * * * * * * *
>
> (b) shares * * * in a company that is * * * a resident of that other Contracting State, the assets of which company consist or consisted wholly or principally of immovable property situated in such other Contracting State * * *

Article 13, paragraph 5, of both the original and post-2006 treaties provides, for relevant purposes, that gains from the alienation of intangible property (other than the shares referred to in article 13, paragraph 2(b)) "shall be taxable only in the Contracting State of which the alienator is a resident."

---

[13] Article 4, paragraph 2, of the treaty sets forth tiebreaker rules where "by reason of the provisions of paragraph 1 an individual is a resident of both Contracting States". Because, for the reasons stated *infra*, we find petitioner to be a U.S., but not a German, resident for the years in issue, paragraph 2 is not germane to this case. Moreover, even if we were to find that petitioner was a dual resident taxpayer during the years in issue, he failed to follow the required procedures for claiming German residency under the tiebreaker rules of article 4, paragraph 2. *See* sec. 6114; sec. 301.7701(b)–7(b) and (c), Proced. & Admin. Regs.

B. *Analysis*

1. *Petitioner's Status as a U.S. Resident*

Petitioner does not appear to dispute that he became a U.S. LPR (resident alien) in 1977, when he applied for and was issued a green card. Nor does he dispute that he periodically renewed his LPR-resident alien status and did not formally renounce or abandon that status until November 10, 2010, when he filed a Form I–407 and surrendered his green card to the USCIS consistent with the requirements of section 301.7701(b)–1(b)(3), Proced. & Admin. Regs. Petitioner argues, however, that he informally abandoned his U.S. resident status when he sold his Hawaiian residence in 2003 and allegedly moved back to Germany. In support of his argument that one may informally abandon resident alien status, petitioner cites *United States v. Yakou*, 428 F.3d 241 (D.C. Cir. 2005).

In *Yakou*, the Court of Appeals for the D.C. Circuit affirmed a District Court decision dismissing an indictment charging the defendant with engaging in brokering activities in violation of the Arms Export Control Act and its implementing regulations, the International Traffic in Arms Regulations (ITAR). Among the errors alleged by the Government to have been committed by the District Court was its ruling that the defendant's LPR status changed without formal administrative action by immigration officials so that the defendant was not a "U.S. person", as defined by the ITAR, subject to prosecution for brokering activities. *Id.* at 243. The defendant in that case, while under investigation by Federal agents, left his home in California in 1993, lived in London until 1998, and then returned to his native Baghdad where he lived and worked thereafter, making occasional trips to the United States of short duration to visit his family. He never formally renounced his LPR status by filing Form I–407 with the immigration authorities, and the Board of Immigration Appeals (BIA) had not adjudged that his LPR status had changed. *Id.* at 244. After noting that the controlling statutes and the ITAR "are all silent regarding the manner and the point at which LPR status changes", the court looked to decisions of the BIA for guidance on the issue. *Id.* at 247–248. It found that "[n]umerous BIA decisions express in dicta the BIA's view that LPR status can change outside the formal adjudicatory process associated with removal." *Id.* at 248. The court distinguished *United States v. Grimley*, 137 U.S. 147, 151–152 (1890), in which the Supreme Court rejected the argument that an individual who had falsified his qualifications for enlistment in the U.S. military could avoid a court-martial for desertion because he was never a soldier subject to court-martial. The Court of Appeals noted that "LPR status [in *Yakou*] turns on immigration law, and the United States fails to show that LPR status operates in a way comparable to the military relationship at issue in *Grimley*." *Yakou*, 428 F.3d at 249.

Correspondingly, LPR status for Federal income tax purposes turns on Federal income tax law and is only indirectly determined by immigration law. Unlike the controlling statutes and the ITAR considered in *Yakou*, the Internal Revenue Code and the regulations are not "silent regarding the manner and the point at which LPR status changes", and they do circumscribe the means by which an LPR may abandon that status for Federal income tax purposes. *See* sec. 7701(b)(6)(B) (LPR continues until "revoked" or "administratively or judicially determined to have been abandoned"); sec. 301.7701(b)–1(b)(1), Proced. & Admin. Regs. ("Resident status is deemed to continue unless it is rescinded or administratively or judicially determined to have been abandoned."); sec. 301.7701(b)–1(b)(3) ("If the alien initiates this determination, resident status is considered to be abandoned when the individual's application for abandonment (INS Form I–407) or a letter stating the alien's intent to abandon his or her resident status * * * is filed with the INS or a consular officer."). The immigration law itself (including the ITAR), which governed the result in *Yakou*, contains no such requirements for abandoning residency status. Therefore, *Yakou* is not on point and does not furnish a basis for petitioner's contention that he abandoned his LPR status before filing a Form I–407 with the immigration authorities on November 20, 2010. For the same reason, the fact that the immigration authorities may deport, or deny reentry to, an LPR under certain circumstances, *see Alaka v. Elwood*, 225 F. Supp. 2d 547, 553 (E.D. Pa. 2002), cited by petitioner, is of no relevance herein.

Nor are the requirements set forth in section 7701(b)(6)(B) and section 301.7701(b)–1(b)(1) and (3), Proced. & Admin.

Regs., for abandoning LPR status vitiated by petitioner's 2003 sale of his Hawaiian residence or by his arguably infrequent visits to the United States thereafter. As is made clear by the House Ways and Means Committee report accompanying the enactment of section 7701(b)(1)(A)(i) and (6), "an alien who comes to the United States so infrequently that, on scrutiny, he or she is no longer legally entitled to permanent resident status, but who has not officially lost or abandoned that status, will be a resident for tax purposes." H.R. Rept. No. 98–432 (Part 2), *supra* at 226, 1984 U.S.C.C.A.N. at 1166.[14]

Petitioner also alleges that, because respondent argued before the District Court in *Topsnik I* that petitioner is a German resident, and because the court dismissed the case for improper venue on that basis, respondent is estopped, under the doctrine of judicial estoppel, from asserting a contrary position in this case.

Judicial estoppel is an equitable doctrine that prevents a party in a judicial proceeding from asserting a position contrary to one that that party has successfully persuaded a court to accept in a prior judicial proceeding. *See New Hampshire v. Maine*, 532 U.S. 742, 749–750 (2001); *see also Huddleston v. Commissioner*, 100 T.C. 17, 26 (1993).

In *Topsnik I*, the Government's motion for dismissal was based, in part, on its claim that Mr. Topsnik was a German resident in 2011, the year in which he filed his complaint. In its opinion, the District Court stated: "It is undisputed that Plaintiff [petitioner herein] is a resident of Germany", and, on that basis, granted the Government's motion to dismiss

---

[14] The House Ways and Means Committee explained its rationale for requiring official loss or abandonment of U.S. residency status as follows:

> The committee believes that aliens who have entered the United States as permanent residents and who have not officially lost or surrendered the right to permanent U.S. residence should be taxable as U.S. residents. These persons have rights that are similar to those afforded [U.S.] citizens (including the right to enter the United States at will); equity demands that they contribute to the cost of running the government as much as citizens. [H.R. Rept. No. 98–432 (Part 2), at 223 (1983), 1984 U.S.C.C.A.N. 697, 1163.]

Clearly, petitioner, as one who retained (and exercised) the right to enter the United States at will throughout the years in issue, is among the class of individuals targeted by the 1984 legislation.

the complaint for improper venue. In a subsequent proceeding before the District Court for the District of Columbia, *Topsnik v. United States*, 12 F. Supp. 3d 1 (D.D.C. 2013) (*Topsnik III*), the court determined that "the most that the Central District of California held was that the plaintiff was a resident of Germany in 2011 when he filed his complaint in that court or alternatively when the court issued its ruling on January 17, 2012." *Id.* at 7. We agree with that determination.[15] In *Topsnik I*, Mr. Topsnik's status as a German resident during the years in issue herein (2004–09) was not addressed by the parties and was not in issue. Therefore, respondent is not judicially estopped from arguing that petitioner was not a German resident during those years.[16] For the same reason, respondent is not barred by the doctrines of res judicata and collateral estoppel from asserting petitioner's U.S. residency during the years in issue, both of which doctrines petitioner briefly invokes for support.

We find that petitioner was an LPR of the United States (i.e., a resident alien subject to U.S. taxation of his worldwide income) during the years in issue and, therefore a "resident" of the United States as defined by article 4, paragraph 1, of the U.S.-Germany Treaty.

2. *Petitioner's Status as a German Resident*

Having found that petitioner was an LPR of the United States during the years in issue, we must sustain respond-

---

[15] We do not reject petitioner's argument on the basis of collateral estoppel because the court, in *Topsnik v. United States*, 12 F. Supp. 3d 1 (D.D.C. 2013) (*Topsnik III*), made clear that its determination that the court in *Topsnik v. United States*, No. 2:11–cv–06958–JHN–MRW, 2012 WL 10637570 (C.D. Cal. Jan. 17, 2012), *aff'd*, 554 Fed. Appx. 630 (9th Cir. 2014) (*Topsnik I*), found only that petitioner "currently resides in Germany" was not essential to its decision. *See Topsnik III*, 12 F. Supp. 3d at 7. Thus, the court's decision in *Topsnik III* lacks one of the required factors for applying collateral estoppel. *See Peck v. Commissioner*, 90 T.C. 162, 166–167 (1988), *aff'd*, 904 F.2d 525 (9th Cir. 1990).

[16] Petitioner also attempts to support his judicial estoppel argument by referring to exhibits attached to respondent's motion to dismiss in *Topsnik I*. Those exhibits, for the most part, supply background information, and one (a series of IRS transcripts relating to petitioner) is, at best, ambiguous regarding the IRS' position with respect to petitioner's residency during the years in issue. In any event, those exhibits cannot be said to alter or expand respondent's actual argument, adopted by the court in *Topsnik I*, that petitioner was a German resident in 2011.

ent's adjustments for those years unless we find that petitioner is exempt from U.S. tax under the U.S.-Germany Treaty. That will be the result if we find that petitioner was also a German resident under article 4, paragraph 1 of the treaty and, pursuant to the tiebreaker rules of article 4, paragraph 2 of the treaty, he is to be considered a German resident.

Aside from his estoppel arguments, which we have rejected, petitioner's claim of German residency rests on his contacts with Germany during the years in issue. Those contacts include a room at his inn in Oerlenbach, a room at his brother's house in Freiburg, his ownership and operation of the Oerlenbach inn, his ownership of a farmhouse, farm, property used for "industrial and various purposes", and a small "cafhouse". Petitioner also alleges that he "views Germany as his center of vital interest, and where he has his country of closer connection and did so for * * * [the years in issue,] [a]ll of which is underscored by petitioner's obligatory and necessary personal German driver's license."

As noted *supra*, with respect to individuals, both the original U.S.-Germany Treaty and the post-2006 treaty limit the definition of a "'resident of a Contracting State'" to individuals "liable to tax therein by reason of * * * [domicile or residence]", and both exclude from the definition "any person who is liable to tax in that State in respect only of income from sources in that State * * * or capital situated therein." Thus, the treaty test for residence in a contracting State is the individual's liability to pay tax to the State as a resident, which, in the case of Germany, means that the individual must be taxable on his or her worldwide income. *See* Staff of J. Comm. on Taxation, Explanation of Proposed Protocol to the Income Tax Treaty Between the United States and Germany, at 9 (J. Comm. Print 2007) ("Individuals resident in Germany are subject to tax on their worldwide income."); Tax Treaties (CCH) para. 3229, p. 77,181. That that is the test for residency under the U.S.-Germany Treaty is confirmed by the commentary with respect to article 4 of the Organization for Economic Cooperation and Development (OECD) Model Double Tax Convention on Income and Capital (1977) (OECD Model Treaty), article 4, paragraph 1 of which is, in all pertinent respects, identical to article 4, paragraph 1, of the original and post-2006

U.S.-Germany treaties.[17] The commentary to article 4 paragraph 1 states, in pertinent part: "As far as individuals are concerned, the definition aims at covering the various forms of personal attachment to a State which, in the domestic taxation laws, form the basis of a comprehensive taxation (full liability to tax)." OECD Committee on Fiscal Affairs, Model Tax Convention on Income and on Capital, at C(4–9) (1997).[18]

Thus, petitioner's recitation of his contacts with Germany during the years in issue is not relevant to his status as a German resident during those years except insofar as they served to subject him to German taxation of his worldwide income. Petitioner does not allege that he is subject to German taxation on his worldwide income, and the evidence in the record is uniformly to the contrary.

As noted *supra*, the information obtained by the German competent authority from the German tax authority reveals that (1) beginning in 2002, petitioner was registered with the German tax authority as a taxpayer with limited liability, taxable only on German source income, (2) petitioner failed to file even the tax returns required of a limited liability taxpayer despite the tax authority's repeated requests that he do so, (3) the German tax authority had no record of his filing income tax returns in Germany for 2004 and subsequent years, and (4) because there was no evidence to indicate that petitioner has or had a domicile or habitual residence in Germany, the German tax authority would not have considered him to be a German resident and, therefore, would not have considered the gain on his installment sale of GFI stock to be income taxable in Germany. There is no

---

[17] Where the parties to a bilateral tax treaty were both OECD members when the model treaty and commentary were drafted (which is the case herein) and the bilateral treaty language is substantially the same as the model treaty language (also the case herein), we have used the model treaty commentary to interpret provisions of the bilateral tax treaty. *See Podd v. Commissioner*, T.C. Memo. 1998–418, 1998 WL 800961, at *4 (and the cases cited thereat).

[18] Subsequent updates of the OECD Model Treaty left unchanged, in all pertinent respects, the article 4, paragraph 1, definition of resident contained in the 1977 OECD Model Treaty as it pertains to individuals. Therefore, the above-quoted commentary with respect to that definition applies to all of the OECD Model Treaties published since 1977. *See, e.g.*, Tax Treaties (CCH) paras. 200.04, 200A.04.

evidence in the record to refute the information obtained by the German competent authority. Therefore, we find that petitioner was not a “resident” of Germany as defined by article 4, paragraph 1, of the U.S.-Germany Treaty.

C. *Conclusion*

Both parties appear to assume that the right of the United States to tax petitioner’s gain on his 2004 sale of GFI stock is governed by article 13, paragraph 5, of the treaty, which grants the country of residence the right to tax gains from the sale of intangible personal property. That assumption implies the parties’ agreement that GFI’s assets did not consist “wholly or principally of immovable property [i.e., real property] situated in [the United States]”, in which event petitioner’s gain from his sale of his GFI stock would be taxable in the United States under article 13, paragraphs 1 and 2(b) of the U.S.-Germany Treaty, regardless of petitioner’s residence. There is no evidence in the record indicating the extent to which GFI’s assets consisted of “immovable property”. In the absence of such evidence and because respondent has not argued for the application of article 13, paragraph 2(b), we decide petitioner’s taxability on the basis of his residence during the years in issue. We find that petitioner was a U.S. and not a German resident during that period. Therefore, pursuant to article 13, paragraph 5 of the U.S.-Germany Treaty, petitioner is taxable by the United States on his gain recognized during the years in issue from the 2004 installment sale of his GFI stock. [19]

---

[19] In his opening brief, respondent supports his argument that petitioner may not be considered a German resident during the years in issue, in part, by noting that petitioner spent little actual time in Germany and a great deal of time in other countries, in particular, in Thailand, where he operated a winery business and visited with his son, and the Philippines, where, in 2007, he rented a house under a 10-year lease for the ostensible purpose of providing a home for himself and his family. In petitioner’s amended opening brief, filed more than a month after respondent’s opening brief, petitioner characterizes respondent’s references to his travels and activities during the years in issue as an argument that petitioner was a resident of either Thailand or the Philippines during those years, and he concludes that, therefore, he is entitled to the benefits provided by the income tax treaties between the United States and one or the other of those countries. Respondent argues in his reply brief that he has not had an op-

Continued

III. *Additions to Tax*

A. *Introduction*

Respondent determined that petitioner is liable for additions to tax pursuant to sections 6651(a)(1) and (2) and 6654. Respondent has the burden of production with respect to those additions to tax. *See* sec. 7491(c). To meet that burden, respondent must produce evidence showing that the additions to tax are appropriate. *See id.*; *Higbee v. Commissioner*, 116 T.C. 438, 446 (2001). Once respondent satisfies that burden, petitioner has the burden of proof with respect to exculpatory factors such as reasonable cause. *See Higbee v. Commissioner*, 116 T.C. at 446–447.

---

portunity to consider petitioner's argument or whether petitioner's contacts with either Thailand or the Philippines were sufficient to make him a resident of either for any or all of the years in issue. Therefore, he requests that we "not further consider this new issue as it will greatly prejudice respondent." Without addressing respondent's argument regarding timeliness and prejudice, we note that petitioner has failed to prove that his ties to either Thailand or the Philippines were sufficient to make him a "resident" of either country as that term is defined by the United States' tax treaties with those two countries. *See, e.g.*, Convention With Respect to Taxes on Income, U.S.-Phil., art. 3, para. 1(a)(ii), (2) (definition of "resident"), art. 14, para. 2 (treatment of gains), Oct. 1, 1976, 34 U.S.T. 1277, *available at* http://www.irs.gov/pub/irs-trty/philip.pdf; Convention for the Avoidance of Double Taxation and the Prevention of Fiscal Evasion With Respect to Taxes on Income, U.S.-Thai., art. 4, para.1, Nov. 26, 1996, S. Treaty Doc. No. 105–2 (1997), *available at* http://www.gpo.gov/fdsys/pkg/CDOC–105tdoc2/pdf/CDOC–105tdoc2.pdf. For example, although petitioner has shown that he rented premises in the Philippines in 2007, ostensibly to be used as a residence for himself and his family, he has not shown the number of days in 2007–09 that he actually treated those premises as his residence; and, aside from frequent business trips, during which he stayed in a hotel, he has not shown significant ties to the Philippines before 2007. Nor has petitioner analyzed either treaty to show that residence therein, even if established, would necessarily negate the United States' right to tax petitioner's gain on the sale of his GFI stock. See, e.g., the U.S.-Thai. treaty, art. 13, para. 1, which provides, with exceptions not relevant herein, that "each Contracting State may tax gains from the alienation of property in accordance with the provisions of its domestic law." Therefore, we reject petitioner's suggestion that respondent is barred from taxing that gain pursuant to the United States' tax treaties with either Thailand or the Philippines.

B. *Respondent's Section 6651(a)(1) and (2) and 6654 Determinations*

1. *Analysis*

Section 6651(a)(1) provides for an addition to tax in the event a taxpayer fails to file a timely return (determined with regard to any extension of time for filing), unless it is shown that such failure is due to reasonable cause and not due to willful neglect. The amount of the addition is equal to 5% of the amount required to be shown as tax on the delinquent return for each month or fraction thereof during which the return remains delinquent, up to a maximum addition of 25% for returns more than four months delinquent.

Section 6651(a)(2) provides for an addition to tax for failure to timely pay the amount of tax shown on a return, unless the taxpayer establishes that the failure was due to reasonable cause and not willful neglect. The addition is calculated as 0.5% of the amount shown as tax on the return but not paid, with an additional 0.5% for each month or fraction thereof during which the failure to pay continues, up to a maximum of 25%. *Id.* The amount of the addition to tax under section 6651(a)(2) reduces the addition to tax under section 6651(a)(1) for any month for which both additions to tax apply. *See* sec. 6651(c)(1). Pursuant to section 6651(g)(2), SFRs prepared by the Commissioner under section 6020(b) are treated as taxpayer returns for purposes of determining the addition to tax under section 6651(a)(2).

Section 6654(a) and (b) provides for an addition to tax in the event of an underpayment of a required installment of individual estimated tax. Each required installment of estimated tax is equal to 25% of the "required annual payment", which in turn is equal to the lesser of (1) "90 percent of the tax shown on the return for the taxable year (or, if no return is filed, 90 percent of the tax for such year)", or (2) if the individual filed a return for the immediately preceding year, 100% of the tax shown on that return. Sec. 6654(d)(1)(A) and (B). Except in very limited circumstances not applicable herein, *see* sec. 6654(e)(3)(B), section 6654 provides no exception for reasonable cause or lack of willful neglect.

It is undisputed that petitioner's (1) late filing of his 2004 and 2005 returns and failure to file returns for 2006–09, (2) untimely payment of the amount of tax shown on his 2004 return, (3) nonpayment of his tax liabilities as reflected on the SFRs filed for 2006–09, and (4) failure (made clear on the face of his 2005 return) to pay any estimated tax for 2005 demonstrate that respondent has satisfied his burden of production, under section 7491(c), with respect to his imposition of additions to tax under sections 6651(a)(1) and (2) and 6654.

With respect to the additions to tax, petitioner's only argument against respondent's imposition thereof is that he "acted due to reasonable cause and not due to willful neglect." Specifically, he states: "[A]ny amount of additional tax arising from a miscalculation of installment capital gain amounts brought about by the tax return preparer is not to be attributable to petitioner", and further "that nonresident alien filings are a product of instructions from counsel for petitioner, and asserted penalties in this regard are not attributed to petitioner." Petitioner's arguments are unpersuasive. The additions to tax do not relate to the miscalculations of petitioner's capital gain for 2004 and 2005. Nor do they relate to any "nonresident alien filings" (presumably, the zero tax liability Forms 1040NR that petitioner late-filed for 2006–09) by petitioner. If petitioner is attempting to escape the section 6651(a)(1) late-filing penalty by arguing that any and all of his late filings (and nonfilings) were the product of instructions from counsel, and, therefore, not attributable to him, that argument must be rejected as well under the authority of *United States v. Boyle*, 469 U.S. 241, 252 (1985) ("The failure to make a timely filing of a tax return is not excused by the taxpayer's reliance on an agent, and such reliance is not 'reasonable cause' for a late filing under § 6651(a)(1).").

We note, however, that respondent appears to be overreaching in his imposition of the section 6651(a)(2) addition to tax for 2004. The Form 5278, Statement—Income Tax Changes, attached to the notice computes a $49,358 addition to tax for 2004 under section 6651(a)(2), which is 25% of the $197,433 total amount due for that year. Moreover, in respondent's discussion of petitioner's liability for that addition to tax, respondent states that "petitioner failed to pay the tax due for the 2004, and 2006 through 2009 taxable years by the due dates of the returns." While it is proper to base the section 6651(a)(2) addition to tax on the amounts due for 2006–09, which are the amounts shown on the SFRs for those years, it is not proper to base it on the amount due for 2004 because petitioner filed a return for that year and "the amount shown as tax" on that return (the late payment of which is the basis for the addition to tax under section 6651(a)(2)) is $62,117, which petitioner paid in two installments: $10,990 on June 4, 2007, with his late-filed 2004 return, and $51,127 on July 5, 2007. Therefore, we direct that, in connection with the Rule 155 computation, respondent compute the section 6651(a)(2) addition to tax for 2004 on the basis of (1) petitioner's late payment of the $62,117 shown on his 2004 return, and (2) the number of months between the due date of that return and the dates of payment.

2. *Conclusion*

We sustain respondent's imposition of additions to tax, with the foregoing caveat regarding his imposition of an addition to tax under section 6651(a)(2) for 2004.

Decision will be entered under Rule 155.

LAW OFFICE OF JOHN H. EGGERTSEN P.C., PETITIONER *v.* COMMISSIONER OF INTERNAL REVENUE, RESPONDENT*

Docket No. 15479–11. Filed October 1, 2014.

R filed a motion for reconsideration of findings or opinion in *Law Office of John H. Eggertsen P.C. v. Commissioner*, 142 T.C. 110 (2014) (*Eggertsen I*), and a motion to vacate decision (collectively, R's motions). In *Eggertsen I*, we addressed whether I.R.C. sec. 4979A(a) imposes a Federal excise tax (excise tax) on P for its taxable year 2005. We held that it does. We also addressed in *Eggertsen I* whether the period of limitations for assessing that tax has expired (statute of limitations issue). It was R's position with respect to the statute of limitations issue in *Eggertsen I* that I.R.C. sec. 4979A(e)(2)(D), not I.R.C. sec. 6501, controls resolution of that issue. In *Eggertsen I*, we accepted that position. We held that the period of limitations under I.R.C. sec. 4979A(e)(2)(D) for assessing the excise tax that I.R.C. sec. 4979A(a) imposes on

---

* This Supplemental Opinion supplements *Law Office of John H. Eggertsen P.C. v. Commissioner*, 142 T.C. 110 (2014).

petitioner has expired. It is R's position in R's motions that I.R.C. sec. 6501, not I.R.C. sec. 4979A(e)(2)(D), controls resolution of the statute of limitations issue. According to R, because P did not file Form 5330, Return of Excise Taxes Related to Employee Benefit Plans, or any other document that qualifies as a return for I.R.C. sec. 4979A(a) excise tax purposes within the meaning of I.R.C. sec. 6501(a), I.R.C. sec. 6501(c)(3) permits R to assess at any time the excise tax that I.R.C. sec. 4979A(a) imposes on P. *Held*: Upon reconsideration of the statute of limitations issue in *Eggertsen I*, I.R.C. sec. 6501, not I.R.C. sec. 4979A(e)(2)(D), controls resolution of that issue because P did not file Form 5330 or any other document that qualifies as a return for I.R.C. sec. 4979A(a) excise tax purposes within the meaning of I.R.C. sec. 6501(a). I.R.C. sec. 4979A(e)(2)(D) serves only to extend under the circumstances set forth therein the period of limitations prescribed by I.R.C. sec. 6501. *Held, further*, the excise tax that I.R.C. sec. 4979A(a) imposes on P for its taxable year 2005 may be assessed at any time under I.R.C. sec. 6501(c)(3).

Stephen Wasinger, for petitioner.

David S. Weiner, *John W. Stevens*, and *Shawn P. Nowlan*, for respondent.

SUPPLEMENTAL OPINION

CHIECHI, *Judge*: This case is before us on respondent's motion for reconsideration of findings or opinion (respondent's motion for reconsideration) and respondent's motion to vacate decision (respondent's motion to vacate).[1] We shall grant respondent's motions.

Background

We incorporate herein by reference the facts set forth in *Law Office of John H. Eggertsen P.C. v. Commissioner*, 142 T.C. 110 (2014) (*Eggertsen I*).[2] We repeat here only those facts relevant to this Supplemental Opinion.

---

[1] Respondent filed a memorandum (respondent's memorandum) in support of respondent's motion for reconsideration. (We shall refer collectively to respondent's motion for reconsideration, respondent's motion to vacate, and respondent's memorandum as respondent's motions). Petitioner filed a response to each of respondent's motion for reconsideration and respondent's motion to vacate, and respondent filed a reply to each of those responses.

[2] The parties stipulated all of the facts in *Law Office of John H. Eggertsen P.C., v. Commissioner*, 142 T.C. 110 (2014), and submitted the case under Rule 122, Tax Court Rules of Practice and Procedure.

At all relevant times, 100% of the stock of petitioner was allocated to John H. Eggertsen under an employee stock ownership plan that petitioner, an S corporation, maintained (ESOP in question).

Around April 26, 2006, petitioner filed Form 1120S, U.S. Income Tax Return for an S Corporation, for its taxable year 2005 (2005 Form 1120S). Petitioner attached to that form Schedule K–1, Shareholder's Share of Income, Deductions, Credits, etc.

In petitioner's 2005 Form 1120S, petitioner showed, inter alia, that during 2005 the ESOP in question owned 100% of the stock of petitioner.

On a date not established by the record during 2006, the ESOP in question filed Form 5500, Annual Return/Report of Employee Benefit Plan (employee benefit plan 2005 annual return), for its taxable year 2005. The ESOP in question attached to that form Schedule E, ESOP Annual Information. The ESOP in question also attached to the employee benefit plan 2005 annual return Schedule I, Financial Information—Small Plan, and Schedule SSA, Annual Registration Statement Identifying Separated Participants With Deferred Vested Benefits.

In the employee benefit plan 2005 annual return, the ESOP in question showed that (1) its effective date was January 1, 1999; (2) it was maintained by petitioner during 2005; (3) it had three participants during 2005, two of whom were not identified and were described as "Active participants" and one of whom was identified as Kerry C. Duggan and described as "Other retired or separated participants entitled to future benefits"; (4) it held assets at the end of 2005 valued at $401,500; and (5) its assets consisted exclusively of "Employer securities".

On a date not established by the record, the ESOP in question filed an amended Form 5500 (amended employee benefit plan 2005 annual return) for its taxable year 2005. The ESOP in question attached to that form Schedule I.

In the amended employee benefit plan 2005 annual return, the ESOP in question showed information that was identical in most respects to the information that it had showed in the employee benefit plan 2005 annual return, except that (1) the ESOP in question did not identify in the amended employee benefit plan 2005 annual return the individual described in that return as "Other retired or separated participants entitled to benefits" and (2) the ESOP in question showed in the amended employee benefit plan 2005 annual return that it held assets at the end of 2005 valued at $868,833, which included "Employer securities" valued at that yearend at $401,500.

Petitioner did not file Form 5330, Return of Excise Taxes Related to Employee Benefit Plans, for its taxable year 2005. Respondent filed a substitute for Form 5330 for petitioner for that taxable year.

In *Eggertsen I*, we addressed whether section 4979A(a)[3] imposes a Federal excise tax (excise tax) on petitioner for its taxable year 2005. We held that it does. We also addressed in *Eggertsen I* whether the period of limitations for assessing that tax has expired (statute of limitations issue). In *Eggertsen I*, it was respondent's position that section 4979A(e)(2)(D), not section 6501, controls resolution of the statute of limitations issue. On brief, respondent argued in *Eggertsen I*:

> I.R.C. § 6501(a) is not the governing period of limitations under the facts of this case. By its terms * * * I.R.C. § 4979A(e) (2) (D) is the applicable statute of limitations in this case.[4]
>
> The specific triggering requirement to begin the running of the statute under the circumstances of this case is the later of the date of the allocation or ownership at issue or the date when the taxpayer provides notification to the respondent of the ownership or allocation at issue. I.R.C. § 4979A(e) (2) (D).
>
> By contrast, the event that triggers the running of I.R.C. § 6501 is the filing of an original return. I.R.C. § 6501(a); *See also*, *Beard v. Commissioner*, 82 T.C. 766, 780 (1984). This specific triggering device (i.e. the filing of a return) was not incorporated into I.R.C. § 4979A.
>
> [4]To the extent I.R.C. §§ 4979A and 6501 might create differing results here, this Court should be guided by the rules of resolving statutory conflicts. First, the Court should look for means to harmonize apparently conflicting statutes. *Beal v. Commissioner*, 13 B.T.A. 677, 683 (1928). If they may not be harmonized, only when two statutes irreconcilably conflict and the conflict cannot be resolved by interpretation, then the more specific statute controls over the more general one. *Estate of Morgens v. Commissioner*, 133 T.C. 402, 423 (2009) (citing 2B Singer & Singer, Statutes and Statutory Construction, sec. 51:2, at 216218 (7th ed. 2008)). In addition, where two irreconcilably conflicting statutes are involved, the more recent of the two prevails. *Id.*

[3] All section references are to the Internal Revenue Code (Code) in effect for the year at issue.

In this case, if the Court applies these statutory conflict rules, both rules point to the primacy of I.R.C. § 4979A(e) (2) (D) over I.R.C. § 6501. First, § 4979A is the more specific statute, and second, it was more recently amended.

In *Eggertsen I*, we accepted respondent's position that section 4979A(e)(2)(D), not section 6501, controls resolution of the statute of limitations issue. We held that the period of limitations under section 4979A(e)(2)(D) for assessing the excise tax that section 4979A(a) imposes on petitioner has expired.

Discussion

The granting of a motion for reconsideration rests within our discretion. *See Westbrook v. Commissioner*, 68 F.3d 868, 879 (5th Cir. 1995), *aff'g per curiam* T.C. Memo. 1993–634; *Estate of Quirk v. Commissioner*, 928 F.2d 751, 759 (6th Cir. 1991), *aff'g in part, remanding in part* T.C. Memo. 1988–286; *Klarkowski v. Commissioner*, 385 F.2d 398, 401 (7th Cir. 1967), *aff'g* T.C. Memo. 1965–328. A motion for reconsideration will be denied unless substantial error or unusual circumstances are shown. *See Westbrook v. Commissioner*, 68 F.3d at 879; *Estate of Quirk v. Commissioner*, 928 F.2d at 759; *Alexander v. Commissioner*, 95 T.C. 467, 469 (1990), *aff'd without published opinion sub nom. Stell v. Commissioner*, 999 F.2d 544 (9th Cir. 1993); *Vaughn v. Commissioner*, 87 T.C. 164, 167 (1986).

In *Eggertsen I*, it was respondent's position that section 4979A(e)(2)(D), not section 6501, controls resolution of the statute of limitations issue. In support of that position, respondent advanced the following arguments on brief in *Eggertsen I*:

I.R.C. § 6501(a) is not the governing period of limitations under the facts of this case. By its terms * * * I.R.C. § 4979A(e) (2) (D) is the applicable statute of limitations in this case.[4]

The specific triggering requirement to begin the running of the statute under the circumstances of this case is the later of the date of the allocation or ownership at issue or the date when the taxpayer provides notification to the respondent of the ownership or allocation at issue. I.R.C. § 4979A(e) (2) (D).

By contrast, the event that triggers the running of I.R.C. § 6501 is the filing of an original return. I.R.C. § 6501(a); *See also, Beard v. Commissioner*, 82 T.C. 766, 780 (1984). This specific triggering device (i.e. the filing of a return) was not incorporated into I.R.C. § 4979A.

[4]To the extent I.R.C. §§ 4979A and 6501 might create differing results here, this Court should be guided by the rules of resolving statutory conflicts. First, the Court should look for means to harmonize apparently conflicting statutes. *Beal v. Commissioner*, 13 B.T.A. 677, 683 (1928). If they may not be harmonized, only when two statutes irreconcilably conflict and the conflict cannot be resolved by interpretation, then the more specific statute controls over the more general one. *Estate of Morgens v. Commissioner*, 133 T.C. 402, 423 (2009) (citing 2B Singer & Singer, Statutes and Statutory Construction, sec. 51:2, at 216218 (7th ed. 2008)). In addition, where two irreconcilably conflicting statutes are involved, the more recent of the two prevails. *Id.*

In this case, if the Court applies these statutory conflict rules, both rules point to the primacy of I.R.C. § 4979A(e) (2) (D) over I.R.C. § 6501. First, § 4979A is the more specific statute, and second, it was more recently amended.

In *Eggertsen I*, we accepted respondent's position that section 4979A(e)(2)(D), not section 6501, controls resolution of the statute of limitations issue. We held that the period of limitations under section 4979A(e)(2)(D) for assessing the excise tax that section 4979A(a) imposes on petitioner has expired.

In respondent's motions, it is the position of respondent that section 6501, not section 4979A(e)(2)(D), controls resolution of the statute of limitations issue. In support of that position, respondent advances the following arguments in respondent's motions:

[T]he limitations period under I.R.C. § 4979A(e)(2)(D) supplements but does not replace the general limitations period under I.R.C. § 6501 or the specific limitations period under I.R.C. § 6501(c)(3). In this case, because the interaction between I.R.C. § 6501 and I.R.C. § 4979A was not discussed, the Opinion contains a substantial error of law when it implies that I.R.C. § 4979A replaces I.R.C. § 6501. Instead, because the limitations period under I.R.C. § 6501 is not superseded and has not expired, the period during which Respondent can assess the excise tax under I.R.C. § 4979A remains open.

Upon reconsideration of our holding in *Eggertsen I* that the period of limitations under section 4979A(e)(2)(D) for assessing the excise tax that section 4979A(a) imposes on P for its taxable year 2005 has expired, we conclude that we committed substantial error.[4] That is because in so holding

[4]The circumstances involved here are materially distinguishable from the circumstances involved in certain other cases where we denied motions for reconsideration because theories or issues were raised in those motions that could have been, but were not, raised before we issued our original

we concluded implicitly, as respondent had argued expressly, that section 4979A(e)(2)(D), a specific statute applicable to the excise tax imposed by section 4979A(a), took precedence over section 6501, a general statute applicable to all taxes imposed by the Code. We conclude upon reconsideration that section 4979A(e)(2)(D) serves only to extend under the circumstances set forth therein the period of limitations prescribed by section 6501. *Cf. BLAK Invs. v. Commissioner*, 133 T.C. 431, 435–436 (2009); *Rhone-Poulenc Surfactants & Specialties, L.P. v. Commissioner*, 114 T.C. 533, 542–543 (2000).

We consider now whether the period of limitations under section 6501 has expired for assessing the excise tax under section 4979A(a) for petitioner's taxable year 2005 that was triggered by an event described in section 4979A(a)(3). Petitioner is liable for that excise tax. *See* sec. 4979A(c)(2). Form 5330 is the form that the Commissioner of Internal Revenue has prescribed as the form in which, inter alia, the excise tax under section 4979A is required to be reported. We found in *Eggertsen I* that petitioner did not file Form 5330 for its taxable year 2005. Unless petitioner filed another document that qualifies as a return for section 4979A(a) excise tax purposes within the meaning of section 6501(a), the excise tax that section 4979A(a) imposes on petitioner for its taxable year 2005 may be assessed at any time under section 6501(c)(3).

We shall examine the record that the parties fully stipulated in *Eggertsen I*, *see supra* note 2, in order to determine whether petitioner filed for its taxable year 2005 a document that qualifies as a return for section 4979A(a) excise tax purposes within the meaning of section 6501(a). In order for a document filed by a taxpayer to qualify as a return within the meaning of section 6501(a), it must (1) contain sufficient information to calculate the taxpayer's tax liability, (2) pur-

---

opinion. *See, e.g.*, *CWT Farms, Inc. v. Commissioner*, 79 T.C. 1054, 1057 (1982) ("We will generally not grant reconsideration to resolve issues which could have been raised during the prior proceedings[.]"), *supplementing* 79 T.C. 86 (1982), *aff'd*, 755 F.2d 790 (11th Cir. 1985); *Lowry v. Commissioner*, T.C. Memo. 2004–10, slip op. at 4 ("On motions for reconsideration we do not, except under extraordinary circumstances, address any new issue which a party could have addressed but failed to address prior to the Court's deciding the case."), *supplementing* T.C. Memo. 2003–225, *aff'd*, 171 Fed. Appx. 6 (9th Cir. 2006).

port to be a return, (3) constitute an honest and reasonable attempt by the taxpayer to satisfy the requirements of the Federal tax law, and (4) be executed under penalties of perjury.[5] *See Beard v. Commissioner*, 82 T.C. 766, 777 (1984), *aff'd per curiam*, 793 F.2d 139 (6th Cir. 1986).

The record contains the 2005 Form 1120S that petitioner filed around April 26, 2006, the employee benefit plan 2005 annual return that the ESOP in question filed on a date not established by the record during 2006, and the amended employee benefit plan 2005 annual return that the ESOP in question filed on a date not established by the record.

We turn first to petitioner's 2005 Form 1120S. In that form, petitioner showed, inter alia, that during 2005 the ESOP in question owned 100% of the stock of petitioner. In order for the 2005 Form 1120S to qualify as a return for section 4979A(a) excise tax purposes within the meaning of section 6501(a), it must, inter alia, contain sufficient information to calculate petitioner's excise tax liability for its taxable year 2005 under section 4979A(a). *See Beard v. Commissioner*, 82 T.C. at 777. The information necessary to calculate petitioner's excise tax liability under section 4979A(a) for its taxable year 2005 includes information regarding the total value of all deemed-owned shares of all disqualified persons with respect to the ESOP in question. *See* sec. 4979A(a), (e)(2)(C). Petitioner's 2005 Form 1120S did not contain that information.[6]

On the record in *Eggertsen I*, we find that petitioner's 2005 Form 1120S does not qualify as a return for section 4979A(a) excise tax purposes within the meaning of section 6501(a).

We turn next to the employee benefit plan 2005 annual return that the ESOP in question filed on a date not established by the record during 2006 and the amended employee

[5] As pertinent here, sec. 6501(b)(4) provides that for purposes of sec. 6501 the filing of a return for a specified period in which an entry has been made with respect to a tax imposed under, inter alia, sec. 4979A, including a return in which an entry has been made showing no liability for such tax for such period, shall constitute the filing of a return of all amounts of such tax which, if properly paid, would be required to be reported in such return for such period.

[6] Petitioner made no entry in petitioner's 2005 Form 1120S with respect to an excise tax imposed by sec. 4979A, not even an entry that showed no liability for that tax for taxable year 2005. *See supra* note 5.

benefit plan 2005 annual return that that ESOP filed on a date not established by the record. In the employee benefit plan 2005 annual return, the ESOP in question showed that (1) its effective date was January 1, 1999; (2) it was maintained by petitioner during 2005; (3) it had three participants during 2005, two of whom were not identified and were described as "Active participants" and one of whom was identified as Kerry C. Duggan and described as "Other retired or separated participants entitled to future benefits"; (4) it held assets at the end of 2005 valued at $401,500; and (5) its assets consisted exclusively of "Employer securities".

In the amended employee benefit plan 2005 annual return, the ESOP in question showed information that was identical in most respects to the information that it had showed in the employee benefit plan 2005 annual return, except that (1) the ESOP in question did not identify in the amended employee benefit plan 2005 annual return the individual described in that return as "Other retired or separated participants entitled to benefits" and (2) the ESOP in question showed in the amended employee benefit plan 2005 annual return that it held assets at the end of 2005 valued at $868,833, which included "Employer securities" valued at that yearend at $401,500.

As discussed above, petitioner is liable for its taxable year 2005 for the excise tax under section 4979A(a) that we found in *Eggertsen I* was triggered by an event described in section 4979A(a)(3). *See* sec. 4979A(c)(2). The ESOP in question, not petitioner, filed the employee benefit plan 2005 annual return and the amended employee benefit plan 2005 annual return. Assuming arguendo that petitioner had filed those returns, they did not contain the information regarding the total value of all deemed-owned shares of all disqualified persons with respect to the ESOP in question that was necessary to calculate petitioner's excise tax liability under section 4979A(a) for its taxable year 2005.[7] *See* sec. 4979A(a), (e)(2)(C).

---

[7] The ESOP in question made no entry in the employee benefit plan 2005 annual return that it filed with respect to an excise tax imposed by sec. 4979A, not even an entry that showed no liability for that tax for taxable year 2005. *See supra* note 5.

On the record in *Eggertsen I*, we find that neither the employee benefit plan 2005 annual return nor the amended employee benefit plan 2005 annual return that the ESOP in question filed qualifies as a return for section 4979A(a) purposes within the meaning of section 6501(a).

On the record in *Eggertsen I*, we find that petitioner did not file with respondent any document that qualifies as a return for purposes of section 4979A(a) within the meaning of section 6501(a). On that record, we hold that the excise tax under section 4979A(a) for petitioner's taxable year 2005 may be assessed at any time under section 6501(c)(3).

We have considered all of the contentions and arguments of the parties that are not discussed herein, and we find them to be without merit, irrelevant, and/or moot.

To reflect the foregoing,

An order granting respondent's motions and vacating the decision for petitioner entered on February 12, 2014, and decision for respondent will be entered.

THOMAS M. COMPARINI AND VICKI COMPARINI, PETITIONERS *v.* COMMISSIONER OF INTERNAL REVENUE, RESPONDENT

Docket No. 6674–13W. Filed October 2, 2014.

Ps filed with R's Whistleblower Office (W) a claim for a whistleblower award under I.R.C. sec. 7623(b). In 2012 W mailed four essentially identical letters to Ps stating that Ps are not eligible for an award and inviting Ps to contact W with any questions. Ps later submitted additional information to W in support of Ps' claim. In 2013 W sent a letter (2013 letter) to Ps stating that W "determined your claim still does not meet our criteria for an award", "[o]ur determination remains the same", and "we are closing this claim." Ps petitioned this Court under I.R.C. sec. 7623(b)(4) within 30 days after receiving the 2013 letter. R moved to dismiss this case for lack of jurisdiction. *Held*: The 2013 letter constitutes a determination for purposes of I.R.C. sec. 7623(b)(4). R's motion to dismiss for lack of jurisdiction will be denied.

Thomas M. and Vicki Comparini, pro sese.

Rachel G. Borden, for respondent.

OPINION

COLVIN, *Judge*: This case is before the Court on respondent's motion to dismiss for lack of jurisdiction. For reasons discussed below we will deny respondent's motion.

Petitioners commenced this whistleblower proceeding pursuant to section 7623(b)(4).[1] Respondent then moved to dismiss for lack of jurisdiction, and petitioners filed an objection to respondent's motion. Neither party requested a hearing, and we conclude that none is necessary to decide respondent's motion.

For purposes of deciding respondent's motion, we consider the following undisputed information contained in the pleadings and documents relating to respondent's motion to dismiss.

Background

Petitioners resided in Illinois when they filed the petition.

On February 6, 2012, petitioners filed with the Internal Revenue Service (IRS) a Form 211, Application for Award for Original Information. The form was forwarded to the IRS Whistleblower Office in Ogden, Utah.

The Whistleblower Office processed petitioners' application as four separate claims designated with numbers ending in 48, 49, 50, and 51. The Whistleblower Officer treated two of the claims (48 and 49) as if they had been made only by petitioner husband and the two other claims (50 and 51) as if they had been made only by petitioner wife. The record does not indicate why the Whistleblower Office treated petitioners' application as four separate claims.[2] The Whistleblower Office denied petitioners' claims in four separate letters. The two letters sent to petitioner husband dated October 30, 2012, stated:

> We have considered your application for an award dated 01/11/12. Under Internal Revenue Code Section 7623, an award may be paid only if the

[1] Unless otherwise indicated, section references are to the Internal Revenue Code in effect at all relevant times, and Rule references are to the Tax Court Rules of Practice and Procedure. We round monetary amounts to the nearest dollar.

[2] Neither party contends, nor do we believe, that the fact that the Whistleblower Office used four letters in 2012 instead of one to deny petitioners' application has any bearing on the issues in dispute in this case.

> information provided results in the collection of additional tax, penalties, interest or other proceeds. In this case, the information you provided did not result in the collection of any proceeds. Therefore, you are not eligible for an award.
>
> Although the information you submitted did not qualify for an award, thank you for your interest in the administration of the internal revenue laws.
>
> If you have any further questions in regards to this letter, please feel free to contact the Informant Claims Examination Team at * * *.
>
> Sincerely,
> /s
> Cindy Wilde
> Supervisor—Whistleblower Office, Ogden

The Whistleblower Office denied petitioner wife's claims in two substantially identical letters dated November 15, 2012. Petitioners received the four letters (2012 letters) in November 2012. None of these letters refers to a determination or states that a determination had been made.

Around January 18, 2013, petitioners sent a letter to the Whistleblower Office in which they stated that they were submitting additional information and making additional claims for the years covered by the 2012 letters. The Whistleblower Office replied by letter dated February 12, 2013 (February 2013 letter). The February 2013 letter referred only to claim No. 48 and stated:

> We considered the additional information you provided and determined your claim still does not meet our criteria for an award. Our determination remains the same despite the information contained in your latest letter.
>
> Please keep in mind the confidentiality of the informants' claims process and understand that we cannot disclose the facts surrounding an examination, i.e. taxes collected and audit examination.
>
> Although we are closing this claim, we appreciate your interest in the compliance with the tax laws and in the Informants' Claims for Award Program.
>
> Sincerely,
> /s
> Cindy Wilde
> Supervisor—Whistleblower Office, Ogden

Petitioners filed a petition with this Court on March 19, 2013, under section 7623(b)(4). Petitioners mailed the petition to the Court in an envelope postmarked March 14, 2013.

Discussion

The issue for decision is whether we have jurisdiction as a result of petitioners' filing a petition within 30 days after respondent mailed the 2013 letter.

I. *Introduction*

The Tax Court may exercise jurisdiction only to the extent expressly provided by Congress. *See* sec. 7442; *Breman v. Commissioner*, 66 T.C. 61, 66 (1976); *see, e.g.*, Rules 13, 340(b). Section 7623(b)(4) provides that this Court has jurisdiction with respect to matters addressed in any determination made in response to a whistleblower claim under section 7623(b). More specifically, section 7623(b)(4) provides that "[a]ny determination regarding an award under paragraph (1), (2), or (3)[3] may, within 30 days of such determination, be appealed to the Tax Court (and the Tax Court shall have jurisdiction with respect to such matter)." Thus, this Court has jurisdiction under section 7623(b)(4) when (1) the IRS makes any determination regarding an award under section 7623(b)(1), (2), or (3); and (2) a petition invoking our jurisdiction over that matter is timely filed. *See Kasper v. Commissioner*, 137 T.C. 37, 41 (2011).

To decide whether we have jurisdiction, first we consider whether the 2013 letter constitutes a determination under section 7623(b)(4). Second, if it constitutes a determination, we decide what effect, if any, the 2012 letters had on petitioners' opportunity to invoke our jurisdiction under section 7623(b)(4) upon receipt of the 2013 letter.

II. *Whether the 2013 Letter Is a Determination Under Section 7623(b)(4)*

We first decide whether the 2013 letter is a determination for purposes of section 7623(b)(4). Petitioners filed the peti-

[3] Para. (1) generally requires that the IRS award an individual anywhere from 15% to 30% of the proceeds the IRS collects as a result of pursuing an administrative or judicial action based on information furnished by an individual. Para. (2) generally provides that if proceeding with the action was primarily based on certain information other than that furnished by the individual, the award should be no more than 10% of the collected proceeds. Para. (3) provides that the IRS may reduce or deny an award otherwise payable under para. (1) or (2) if the individual planned or initiated the conduct he or she reported.

tion within 30 days after the Whistleblower Office sent the 2013 letter.[4] That letter stated in pertinent part that "[w]e considered the additional information you provided and determined your claim still does not meet our criteria for an award", "our determination remains the same", and "we are closing this claim."[5]

The 2013 letter was the only letter the Whistleblower Office sent to petitioners stating that a determination had been made on their claim. By referring to the determination and stating that the claim was being closed, the letter made clear that the administrative process had concluded. *See Cooper v. Commissioner*, 135 T.C. 70, 72–76 (2010) (holding that a letter rejecting whistleblower claims was a determination for purposes of section 7623(b)(4) where the letter included the clause "'an award determination * * * [could not] be made'"); *see also SECC Corp. v. Commissioner*, 142 T.C. 225, 229 (2014) (holding that a letter not identified as a determination but stating that "[t]he employment tax liability as determined by Appeals will be assessed and you will receive a Notice and Demand for payment of the tax, penalty, and interest owed" was a determination for purposes of section 7436(a)).

A letter rejecting a whistleblower claim can be a determination under section 7623(b)(4) even if it is not formatted as a determination. *See Whistleblower 11332–13W v. Commissioner*, 142 T.C. 396, 398, 404 (2014); *Cooper v. Commissioner*, 135 T.C. 70. We have reached a similar holding in other contexts. *See SECC Corp. v. Commissioner*, 142 T.C. at 231; *Corbalis v. Commissioner*, 142 T.C. 46, 57–58 (2014) (holding that letters stating they were not final determinations with respect to interest abatement were final determinations for purposes of section 6404(h)); *Craig v.*

---

[4] Respondent does not challenge the timeliness of the petition as to the 2013 letter.

[5] Our holding is based on the text of the 2013 letter. Petitioners contend that they provided 300 additional documents supporting and expanding their claims. In holding that we have jurisdiction we have not considered the substance or significance of additional information petitioners submitted after they received the 2012 letters. We discuss *infra* pp. 283–284 an alternative ground for jurisdiction favored by Judge Halpern and Judge Lauber in their joint concurring opinion and based on petitioners' disputed claims about the significance of these additional documents.

Commissioner, 119 T.C. 252, 259 (2002) (holding that a form decision letter issued after a CDP hearing erroneously labeled as an "equivalent hearing" was a determination conferring jurisdiction under section 6330(d)(1)); *Lunsford v. Commissioner*, 117 T.C. 159, 164 (2001) (holding that a written notice to proceed with a collection action constituted a determination under section 6330).

The 2013 letter contained a statement on the merits of petitioners' whistleblower claim, referred for the first time in a letter to claimants to a "determination" made on that claim, and did not indicate that further administrative procedures were available to petitioners. [6] We conclude that it constitutes a determination for purposes of section 7623(b)(4). [7]

III. *The Effect, If Any, of the 2012 Letters on Our Jurisdiction Over the 2013 Letter*

We next consider respondent's contention that we lack jurisdiction over the petition filed in response to the 2013 letter because it was filed untimely as to the 2012 letters.

A. *Respondent's Argument*

Respondent's contention that the petition was untimely is based on opinions of this Court in *Friedland v. Commissioner*, T.C. Memo. 2011–90 (*Friedland I*), and *Friedland v. Commissioner*, T.C. Memo. 2011–217 (*Friedland II*) (collectively, *Friedland* cases). In the *Friedland* cases, the Whistleblower Office sent to the claimant a letter in response to which the claimant did not file a petition, and the Whistleblower Office later sent another letter in response to which the claimant filed a petition. We held that we lacked jurisdiction in both of those cases. We discuss *infra* part III.B. the texts of the 2012 letters in this case and the letters sent in the *Friedland* cases. We conclude *infra* part III.C. that,

---

[6] In contrast, for example, 30-day letters sent by the Examination Division typically state a proposed result and invite the taxpayer to seek review by the IRS Office of Appeals.

[7] It is well established that no particular words are required for our jurisdiction under sec. 7623(b)(4). *Cooper v. Commissioner*, 135 T.C. 70, 75 (2010). In describing the text of the 2013 letter in the accompanying text, we do not mean to imply that any of the particular words in the 2013 letter must be present in letters sent by the Whistleblower Office in other cases in order for this Court to have jurisdiction.

unlike the letters in the *Friedland* cases, the 2012 letters do not affect petitioners' opportunity to invoke our jurisdiction over the 2013 letter.

B. *Respondent's Letters Sent to Whistleblower Claimants in This Case, the Cooper Case, and the Friedland Cases Cause Confusion About the Claimants' Opportunity To Seek Review in This Court.*

In considering the effect, if any, the 2012 letters had on our jurisdiction over the petition filed in response to the 2013 letter, we will review the text of letters sent by the Whistleblower Office to claimants in the instant case, the *Friedland* cases, and, to provide perspective, the letter sent in *Cooper.*

The 2012 letters stated that petitioners are not eligible for an award and invited them to contact the Whistleblower Office. As stated *supra* p. 276, the 2012 letters stated that "you are not eligible for an award" and that "[i]f you have any further questions in regards to this letter, please feel free to contact the Informant Claims Examination Team" at a phone number stated in the letter.[8]

The letter rejecting the whistleblower claim in *Cooper v. Commissioner*, 135 T.C. at 72, stated that "'an award determination * * * [could not] be made under section 7623(b)' because petitioner 'did not identify * * * federal tax issue[s] upon which the IRS will take action.'" (Fn. ref. omitted.) The letter also indicated that an award was not warranted for either claim because the taxpayer's information did not "result in the detection of the underpayment of taxes." *Id.* We held that the letter contained a determination for purposes of section 7623(b)(4) and that we have jurisdiction over the petition timely filed on the basis of that letter. *Id.* at 75–76.

In *Friedland I* the whistleblower received four letters from the Whistleblower Office relating to his claim. The first letter, dated November 13, 2009, denied the claim and made no reference to further administrative procedures available to the whistleblower. In addition, the Whistleblower Office sent a letter to the claimant in *Friedland I* stating that "he would

[8] We do not have before us a petition filed in response to the 2012 letters, and so we have no occasion to express our views as to whether we would have had jurisdiction if petitioners had filed a petition in 2012.

have to appeal the determination through the court system, not the Whistleblower Office." *Friedland I*, slip op. at 6. The claimant in *Friedland I* was also the claimant in *Friedland II*.

In *Friedland II* the claimant received three letters from the Whistleblower Office relating to his claim. The first of those letters, dated March 3, 2011, denied the claim and made no reference to administrative procedures available to the whistleblower.

Whatever the significance of the differences among these letters, we do not expect whistleblower award claimants to parse letters they receive from the Whistleblower Office to identify slight variations in those letters for clues as to whether the 30-day period to file a petition has commenced. As discussed below, section 7623(b)(4) does not impose this burden.

C. *Respondent's Argument Gives Insufficient Regard to the Text of Section 7623(b)(4).*

As noted *supra* p. 277, section 7623(b)(4) provides that this Court has jurisdiction with respect to matters addressed in "any" determination issued in response to a whistleblower claim under section 7623(b). The Tax Court did not expressly consider the significance of the grant of jurisdiction in section 7623(b)(4) over "any" timely petitioned determination in *Cooper*,[9] in the *Friedland* cases, or in any other prior opinion. We do so here.

The word "any" does not modify "determination" in any other statute describing our jurisdiction. In comparison, section 6015(e) provides our jurisdiction to determine whether a taxpayer who filed jointly is entitled to relief from joint liability after the Commissioner sends to the taxpayer a "final" determination.

By providing the Tax Court with jurisdiction over "any" timely petitioned determination, section 7623(b)(4) in some respects parallels section 6212. Section 6212 authorizes the Commissioner to send more than one notice of deficiency for a taxable period unless the taxpayer has timely filed a Tax

[9] In *Cooper* we found that the determination over which we exercised jurisdiction was "final". We did not have before us a determination which was not "final", and so in *Cooper* we made no holding regarding whether we would have jurisdiction over a determination which is not final.

Court petition in response to a prior notice of deficiency for that taxable period.[10] This aspect of section 6212 shows that in another area of our jurisdiction—deficiency cases—a petitioner may file a petition in response to more than one letter from the Commissioner.

Petitioners received letters from the Whistleblower Office in 2012 in response to which they did not file a petition and a letter in 2013 in response to which they did file a petition. Because section 7623(b)(4) provides this Court with jurisdiction over "any" determination, we hold that we have jurisdiction over the petition filed in response to the 2013 letter.[11] If it were otherwise, the Commissioner could largely frustrate judicial review by issuing ambiguous denials that did not seem to be, but were, determinations. Section 7623(b)(4) provides an opportunity for petitioners to file a petition in

---

[10] Sec. 6212 provides in pertinent part as follows:

SEC. 6212. NOTICE OF DEFICIENCY.

(a) IN GENERAL.—If the Secretary determines that there is a deficiency in respect of any tax imposed by subtitle A or B or chapter 41, 42, 43, or 44, he is authorized to send notice of such deficiency to the taxpayer by certified mail or registered mail. * * *

* * * * * * *

(c) FURTHER DEFICIENCY LETTERS RESTRICTED.—(1) GENERAL RULE.—If the Secretary has mailed to the taxpayer a notice of deficiency as provided in subsection (a), and the taxpayer files a petition with the Tax Court within the time prescribed in section 6213 (a), the Secretary shall have no right to determine any additional deficiency of income tax for the same taxable year, * * *

See also Gmelin v. Commissioner, T.C. Memo. 1988–338, *aff'd without published opinion*, 891 F.2d 280 (3d Cir. 1989).

[11] Dictionary definitions are entirely consistent with everyday understanding of "any". The American Heritage Dictionary 81 (5th ed. 2011) defines "any" as follows: "adj. 1. One, some, every, or all without specification * * * 2. Exceeding normal limits, as in size or duration". Similarly, in defining "any", Webster's Third New International Dictionary 97 (2002) states: "adj. 1. : one indifferently out of more than two: one or some indiscriminately of whatever kind: a: one or another * * * b: one, no matter what one * * * c: one or some of whatever kind or sort * * * 2. one, some or all indiscriminately of whatever quantity * * * 3. a: great, unmeasured, or unlimited in amount, quantity, number, time, or extent". Of course, when construing the word "any" (as when construing any statutory term), we avoid literalistic interpretations that would contradict congressional intent or produce absurd results. *Cf. Util. Air Regulatory Grp. v. EPA*, 573 U.S. ____, ____, 134 S. Ct. 2427, 2439–2445 (2014).

response to the 2013 letter even though they did not file a petition in response to the 2012 letters.

The Court has gained a broader perspective on issues arising in the developing whistleblower area in the time since we decided the *Friedland* cases. In particular, we have considered here distinctive language in section 7623(b)(4)—i.e., "[*a*]*ny* determination" (emphasis added)—that was not discussed by the Court in the *Friedland* cases. Taking into account this broader perspective and the language of the statute, the Court will not follow the holdings in the *Friedland* cases to the extent they state or imply that it is not possible for the Whistleblower Office to issue, as to a given claim, more than one "determination" on which our jurisdiction might be based.

IV. *The Joint Concurring Opinion*

The joint concurring opinion by Judge Halpern and Judge Lauber agrees with the Court that we have jurisdiction here but prefers an alternative basis for our jurisdiction. We base our jurisdiction on the text of the 2013 letter, while the joint concurring opinion would base our jurisdiction on petitioners' representations about materials they sent to the Whistleblower Office after receiving the 2012 letters.

The "main concern with the opinion of the Court" expressed in the joint concurring opinion is "the way it handles the *Friedland* cases", which the joint concurring opinion would distinguish on their facts. *See* joint concurring op. pp. 288, 291–292. Contrary to the suggestion of the joint concurring opinion and as demonstrated by the difference of opinion evidenced between this report and the joint concurring opinion, reasonable minds may differ as to the breadth and contours of the holdings in the *Friedland* cases. Indeed, the joint concurring opinion finds it necessary to resort to the record in *Friedland I* to draw conclusions about its holding that are not apparent or inevitable from the text of the opinion itself. *See* joint concurring op. p. 288. We believe that the need to delve into the record of *Friedland I* to posit a theory of the scope of its holding illustrates as well as anything can that both *Friedland* cases are susceptible to the types of interpretations which we expressly disapprove today without the need to decide hypothetical issues not before us in this case.

In addition, while it is possible, as the joint concurring opinion does, to parse the *Friedland* cases and find factual nuances that might be thought to distinguish them in one way or another from this case, ultimately the factual distinctions are so tenuous that seeking to define our jurisdiction by reference to them risks contributing to confusion for claimants as to the proper time for filing a petition, as described *infra* pp. 287–288 of the joint concurring opinion, while also increasing the burdens on the Court.

The joint concurring opinion states that in *Friedland II* the claimant provided no new information to the Whistleblower Office after receiving the first letter and in *Friedland I* the claimant furnished additional information consisting not of factual documentation but of alleged legal authority that the Court found to be gratuitous, joint concurring op. pp. 290–291; but here, in contrast, petitioners "apparently" provided 300 additional documents supporting and expanding their claims. *See id.* p. 291. Thus, the essential difference between the analysis of the opinion of the Court and that of the joint concurring opinion is that the opinion of the Court bases our Court's jurisdiction on the text of the 2013 letter, and the joint concurring opinion would find jurisdiction because petitioners represent that they made new claims and submitted additional materials to the Whistleblower Office after receiving the 2012 letters.

However, the dispute between petitioners and the Whistleblower Office about the significance of those additional materials could not be more stark. Petitioners state that on January 18, 2013, they provided 300 documents supporting and expanding their claims (in addition to 500 documents they say they provided in their original submission to the Whistleblower Office).[12] In contrast, on the basis of the flat rejection of petitioners' claim made by the 2013 letter, it appears that the Whistleblower Office completely disagreed with petitioners' expansive representations about additional materials.

---

[12] Because the claimed 800 documents are not in the record, we cannot confirm petitioners' description of the submissions.

The joint concurring opinion thus accepts as a basis for our jurisdiction petitioners' unverified assertion that the additional materials are new or noteworthy. We believe this could invite abuse by unconscientious claimants in future cases.[13] Equally problematic, it would be burdensome and awkward for the Court to verify claimants' assertions about the newness or significance of additional materials by comparing them to the materials originally submitted to the Whistleblower Office—all to decide not the merits of the case but merely the threshold question of jurisdiction.

The joint concurring opinion envisions the following process for delving into potentially massive amounts of materials merely to resolve jurisdiction: "If there is any uncertainty about * * * [whether petitioners made additional claims supported by additional documentation], the Court has ample tools at its disposal, from stipulations to evidentiary hearings, to eliminate that uncertainty." *See* joint concurring op. p. 291. The joint concurring opinion would "resolve any doubt against respondent as the movant and in petitioners' favor and we treat their followup letters as making a different or supplemental claim." *See id.* This approach is further explained as follows: "If there are factual uncertainties that must be resolved before ruling on a motion to dismiss, the proper procedure is to resolve them or to assume facts as not favoring the movant (respondent)." *See id.* note 2.

Thus, using the approach urged by the joint concurring opinion, claimants' assertions about the newness or significance of their claims would be assumed correct unless the Court undertakes a hearing (using for purposes of discussion petitioners' assertions about the record here) to see whether the 300 additional documents raise new or noteworthy claims compared to the 500 documents previously submitted. We find it unnecessary to address those knotty factual matters in deciding our jurisdiction and instead base our jurisdiction on the text of the 2013 letter.

The joint concurring opinion misstates the Court's holding as follows: "The Court[ ] hold[s] that a claimant may file a petition, at his option, in response to any of a series of [iden-

[13] This discussion relates to possible future cases and not to the conduct of petitioners.

tical] letters referring to the denial of his claim". *See id.* p. 295. On the contrary, the Court provides no views on a hypothetical case involving "any of a series of [identical] letters" and simply decides that the 2013 letter constitutes a determination and that its status as a determination is not negated, as respondent contends in reliance on the *Friedland* cases, by the fact that the Whistleblower Office sent the 2012 letters.

The joint concurring opinion criticizes the statute because it fails "to specify an unambiguous 'ticket to the Tax Court'". Joint concurring op. pp. 287–288. The joint concurring opinion also disagrees with the reliance by the opinion of the Court on the statute's grant of our jurisdiction over "any" determination. *See id.* p. 294. The joint concurring opinion would provide jurisdiction here only if the 2013 letter acted on a new, different, or supplemental claim. *See id.* p. 291. In contrast, we simply apply the plain language of the statute in the most straightforward fashion, giving effect as best we can to every word that Congress enacted, including the word "any".

V. *Conclusion*

In deciding whether we have jurisdiction, we are mindful that "[w]here a statute is capable of various interpretations, we are inclined to adopt a construction which will permit the Court to retain jurisdiction without doing violence to the statutory language. *See Lewy v. Commissioner*, 68 T.C. at 781, 783–786 [1977]". *Smith v. Commissioner*, 140 T.C. 48, 51 (2013). Congress intended to provide a whistleblower claimant with the opportunity to invoke our jurisdiction after the Commissioner acts on the claim. To date many of those letters we have seen do not give claimants clear notice that the statutory 30-day period to file a petition has begun to run. We believe that adoption of the Commissioner's contentions in this case would create an unnecessary trap for individuals seeking to invoke our jurisdiction under section 7623(b). We conclude that the 2013 letter constitutes a determination for purposes of section 7623(b)(4).

To reflect the foregoing,[14]

An appropriate order denying respondent's motion to dismiss will be issued.

Reviewed by the Court.

THORNTON, FOLEY, VASQUEZ, GALE, GUSTAFSON, PARIS, MORRISON, and NEGA, *JJ.*, agree with this opinion of the Court.

HALPERN and LAUBER, *JJ.*, concurring: We agree that the February 2013 letter from the Internal Revenue Service (IRS) Whistleblower Office (Office) embodies a "determination regarding an award" within the meaning of section 7623(b)(4) and that, because petitioners filed a petition within 30 days of that letter, the Court has jurisdiction over this controversy. We therefore concur in the result reached by the opinion of the Court. We write separately because we have concerns about certain portions of the analysis in the opinion and about how it treats our precedents in *Friedland v. Commissioner*, T.C. Memo. 2011–90, 101 T.C.M. (CCH) 1422 (*Friedland I*), and *Friedland v. Commissioner*, T.C. Memo. 2011–217, 102 T.C.M. (CCH) 247 (*Friedland II*) (collectively, *Friedland* cases).

Section 7623(b)(4) provides that "[a]ny determination regarding an award * * * may, within 30 days of such determination, be appealed to the Tax Court (and the Tax Court shall have jurisdiction with respect to such matter)." Unlike most statutory provisions granting us jurisdiction, section 7623(b)(4) does not prescribe any particular form of notice to the taxpayer or would-be petitioner. Indeed, the statute does not literally require written notice of any kind; it simply requires the making of a "determination."

The statute's failure to specify an unambiguous "ticket to the Tax Court" has created serious interpretative and practical problems, both for whistleblowers and for the Court. These problems have been compounded by the Office's

---

[14] While the February 2013 letter referred only to what the Whistleblower Office treated as one of four claims, the record does not show in what respect it may have been a denial of part, instead of all, of petitioners' claim, and so we treat it as a denial of petitioners' entire claim.

habit—commendable in many respects—of communicating frequently with claimants during the claims investigation process. These communications have employed verbiage that is sometimes inconsistent about the status of the claim under review. In some cases, this has caused claimants to file premature petitions in our Court, fearing that the 30-day jurisdictional deadline would be triggered by an ambiguous communication that might later be deemed a "determination." In other situations, such as in the *Friedland* cases and the instant case, claimants have engaged in further discussions with the IRS after receiving the initial letter. They may then find themselves confronted with the assertion that they should have petitioned the Court immediately in response to the first letter and that their claims are now time barred.

Our main concern with the opinion of the Court is the way it handles the *Friedland* cases, whose facts resemble those here. If the Court is going to hold that it has jurisdiction on the basis of the February 2013 letter notwithstanding the prior mailing of the 2012 letters, it must either distinguish the *Friedland* cases or disapprove them. The Court declines to do the former. And while not explicitly overruling those precedents, it does do the latter, stating: "[T]he Court will not follow the holdings in the *Friedland* cases to the extent they state or imply that it is not possible for the Whistleblower Office to issue, as to a given claim, more than one 'determination' on which our jurisdiction might be based." *See* op. Ct. p. 283.

We disagree with this action for two reasons. First, the *Friedland* cases are distinguishable on their facts and, accordingly, in order to find jurisdiction here, there is no need to overrule or disapprove them. Second, it is error to disapprove these cases because the Court has not shown that they were wrongly decided.

In *Friedland I*, 101 T.C.M. (CCH) at 1422, the Office issued the claimant a letter stating that the claim had been evaluated and rejected. The claimant made further inquiries, by letter and telephone, and he supplied "additional information" regarding his claim. The record in *Friedland I* indicates that this additional information consisted, not of new factual material, but of a letter attaching legal authorities. The Court described this information as "gratuitous[ ]." *Ibid.*

The Office in *Friedland I* issued subsequent letters to the claimant "confirming that * * * [his] additional information had been received and considered but stating that the 'determination remains the same despite the information contained'" in the followup letters. 101 T.C.M. at 1422–1423. The Court held that the first letter constituted a "determination" denying the whistleblower's claim and that "[t]he subsequent three letters merely reaffirmed the initial determination in the first letter." *Id.* at 1423. Because the claimant did not file his petition within 30 days after the first letter was issued, the Court held that it lacked jurisdiction under section 7623(b)(4).

Friedland II involved the same claimant but a different claim. In *Friedland II*, 102 T.C.M. (CCH) 247, the Office issued a letter on March 3, 2011, in which it "denied * * * [the whistleblower's] claim." The claimant made one or more phone calls disputing the denial of his claim and sent a letter asking the Office to reconsider its decision. The Office sent him two subsequent letters, dated March 23 and April 11, 2011, that reaffirmed the March 3 determination. There is no indication that the claimant submitted additional information of any kind after receiving the March 3 letter. He filed his Tax Court petition on April 13, 2011, 41 days after issuance of the March 3 letter. The Court held that the March 3 letter constituted "the determination" under section 7623(b)(4) and that it lacked jurisdiction because the claimant did not petition within 30 days of that determination. *Id.* at 248.

In the instant case, the Office processed petitioners' application "as four separate claims designated with numbers ending in 48, 49, 50, and 51." *See* op. Ct. p. 275. The Office denied these claims in substantially identical letters dated October 30 and November 15, 2012. These letters informed petitioners that "the information you provided did not result in the collection of any proceeds" and stated that "you are not eligible for an award." *See id.* pp. 275–276. Because the IRS is authorized to make a nondiscretionary award only if it collects proceeds "based on information brought to the Secretary's attention by * * * [the claimant]," sec. 7623(b)(1), these letters unambiguously informed petitioners that their claim was denied. The letters clearly embodied "a final administrative decision regarding petitioner[s'] whistleblower claims," *Cooper v. Commissioner*, 135 T.C. 70, 76 (2010), and thus constituted a "determination regarding an award" that would have enabled petitioners to seek review in this Court under section 7623(b)(4). [1]

In January 2013 "petitioners sent a letter to the Whistleblower Office in which they stated that they were submitting additional information and making additional claims for the years covered by the 2012 letters." *See* op. Ct. p. 276. This information, according to petitioners, included 300 additional documents "supporting and expanding their claims." *See id.* note 5.

In response to this supplemental submission, the Office sent petitioners a letter dated February 12, 2013, which "referred only to claim number 48." It stated that "your claim still does not meet our criteria for an award" and that "[o]ur determination remains the same despite the information contained in your latest letter." *See* op. Ct. p. 276. The petition was filed on March 12, 2013, within 30 days of the mailing of the February 12, 2013, letter, but more than three months after the mailing of the October and November 2012 letters.

Here, as in the *Friedland* cases, the Office sent petitioners an initial letter embodying a "determination" that would have provided this Court with jurisdiction, then sent a subsequent letter addressing their claims. In the *Friedland* cases, we held that the claimant was required to petition the Court in response to the first letter and that his attempted petition in response to the subsequent letter(s) was jurisdictionally out of time. Thus, unless the *Friedland* cases are distinguished or disapproved, or unless they are regarded as nonbinding because they were issued as Memorandum Opinions, their holdings dictate that we lack jurisdiction in the instant case because the petition was not filed within 30 days of the first letter.

We believe that the *Friedland* cases are factually distinguishable. In *Friedland II*, the claimant did nothing after

---

[1] The opinion of the Court declines to express a view on the question whether "we would have had jurisdiction if petitioners had filed a petition in 2012." *See* op. Ct. note 8. The Court could answer this question in the negative, however, only by disavowing our reasoning and result in *Cooper*, 135 T.C. at 76. And unless that question is answered in the affirmative, there would be an obvious basis for distinguishing the *Friedland* cases and no apparent reason for this case to be reviewed by the Court Conference.

receiving the first letter except complain about it; he provided no new information but simply sought reconsideration of the Office's prior adverse determination. In *Friedland I*, 101 T.C.M. at 1422, the claimant furnished additional information consisting, not of factual documentation, but of alleged legal authority that the Court found to be "gratuitous[ ]." Here, petitioners stated that they were providing 300 additional documents and also said they were "making additional claims for the years covered by the 2012 letters." *See* op. Ct. p. 276 and note 5.

Because petitioners in their followup letters stated that they were making additional claims supported by additional documentation, it seems perfectly reasonable to regard them as having made a new, additional, or supplemental claim for an award and to treat the February 2013 letter as a "determination" denying this new, additional, or supplemental claim. If there is any uncertainty about this, the Court has ample tools at its disposal, from stipulations to evidentiary hearings, to eliminate that uncertainty. Since the Court declines to deploy these tools, we resolve any doubt against respondent as the movant and in petitioners' favor and we treat their followup letters as making a different or supplemental claim. Since the petition was filed within 30 days of the Office's determination denying that different or supplemental claim, we can assume jurisdiction over this controversy consistently with our holdings in the *Friedland* cases.[2]

The opinion of the Court declines to address these factual differences between the *Friedland* cases and the instant case, stating: "In holding that we have jurisdiction we have not considered the substance or significance of additional information petitioners submitted after they received the 2012 letters." *See* op. Ct. note 5. We agree that in assessing its jurisdiction the Court should focus carefully on "the text of the 2013 letter." *Ibid.* But the Court necessarily must also

[2] Contrary to the Court's assertion, we are not "accept[ing] as a basis for our jurisdiction petitioners' unverified assertion that the additional materials are new or noteworthy." *See* op. Ct. p. 285. The Court seems to forget that it is ruling on a motion to dismiss. If there are factual uncertainties that must be resolved before ruling on a motion to dismiss, the proper procedure is to resolve them or to assume facts as not favoring the movant (respondent).

consider *to what* that letter was responding. Was the Office simply reiterating a determination that it had previously made, as in the *Friedland* cases? Or was it responding to something new and different?[3]

The IRS determination that affords this Court jurisdiction is a determination regarding a "claim for an award." *See* sec. 7623(b)(3). Petitioners stated in their January 2013 letter that they were "making additional claims for the years covered by the 2012 letters" and were submitting additional documentation to support those claims. *See* op. Ct. p. 276. If in fact petitioners were making additional claims to which the January 2013 letter was responding, that is a fact that cannot properly be ignored. Whether petitioners made different or additional claims is critical in assessing whether this case differs in a legally significant way from the *Friedland* cases.[4]

The opinion of the Court declines to examine the substance of petitioners' supplemental claims or to distinguish the *Friedland* cases on their facts. But where it actually leaves the *Friedland* holdings is not entirely clear. The Court says that it "will not follow the holdings in the *Friedland* cases to the extent they state or imply that it is not possible for the Whistleblower Office to issue, as to a given claim, more than

---

[3] Courts must consider the substance of a claimant's communications with the IRS when addressing the scope of its jurisdiction in other contexts. For example, when evaluating a jurisdictional challenge in a tax refund suit under the "variance doctrine," a court must determine whether the claims asserted in the taxpayer's refund suit vary from the claims asserted in the administrative refund claim. *See, e.g.*, *El Paso CGP Co., L.L.C. v. United States*, 748 F.3d 225, 228–229 (5th Cir. 2014); *IA 80 Grp., Inc. v. United States*, 347 F.3d 1067, 1073–1074 (8th Cir. 2003); *Charter Co. v. United States*, 971 F.2d 1576, 1579 (11th Cir. 1992); *Ottawa Silica Co. v. United States*, 699 F.2d 1124, 1138 (Fed. Cir. 1983).

[4] The opinion of the Court suggests that it will be a daunting mission to ascertain, when ruling on a motion to dismiss, whether the Office is simply reiterating a prior determination or rejecting a new or supplemental claim. *See* op. Ct. p. 285. We disagree with that assessment. In *Friedland II*, it was obvious that the claimant, who submitted no new information, was simply quarreling with the prior determination. And in *Friedland I*, 101 T.C.M. at 1422, the Court had no difficulty discerning that the claimant's supplemental information was "gratuitous[ ]." The track record so far does not suggest that this exercise will be burdensome. In any event, the Court is obligated to resolve factual disputes that bear upon the propriety of granting a motion to dismiss.

one 'determination' on which our jurisdiction might be based." *See* op. Ct. p. 283. But this apparent disapproval of the *Friedland* cases makes little sense, because neither opinion states or implies any such thing.

The Court in *Friedland II* said that it was confronted with "a substantially identical situation" as in *Friedland I*, namely, a situation where the Office's subsequent letters "'merely reaffirmed the initial determination in the first letter.'" *Friedland II*, 102 T.C.M. (CCH) at 248 (quoting *Friedland I*, 101 T.C.M. (CCH) at 1423). The *Friedland* cases do not hold that it is *impossible* for the Office to make more than one determination on the same claim. Rather, they hold that this did not happen on the facts presented because the second letter was not a distinct "determination" but in effect a mere cross-reference to a prior "determination."

The key questions, we think, are whether "the claim" and "the determination" remain the same. The *Friedland* cases considered the claims not to have changed and treated the subsequent letters as simply reiterating the denial of those claims. But if the claim does change—e.g., if the claimant submits substantial additional documentation, expands his existing claim, or makes new claims—it is entirely possible for the Office to make a second determination (positive or negative) that will afford us jurisdiction. Indeed, that is exactly what we think happened here: the Office *did make* a second determination regarding petitioners' universe of claims and, because those claims had changed, we have jurisdiction to review the second determination consistently with the *Friedland* cases. [5]

If a rule of law is to be generalized from the *Friedland* cases, it is that, if a claimant fails timely to file a petition in response to a determination letter and receives a subsequent letter reiterating the same determination on the same claim, the subsequent letter does not start another 30-day period for petitioning the Tax Court. The opinion of the Court declines to address that critical question, namely, whether a second, substantially identical, denial letter can

[5] Again, if there is any uncertainty about the substantiality of petitioners' supplemental claims or the Office's denial of them, the proper procedure is to resolve that factual dispute by an evidentiary hearing or otherwise.

start another petition period. The Court rationalizes its refusal to address this problem on the ground that it presents "a hypothetical case." *See* op. Ct. p. 286. But this is exactly the fact pattern that the Court believed it faced in both *Friedland* cases. We do not understand how the Court can conclude that the *Friedland* cases must be disapproved while declining to address as "hypothetical" the fact pattern that they display.

In ruling that a claimant may file a petition in response to any of a series of similar letters involving a negative determination on the same claim, the Court focuses on the phrase "[a]ny determination regarding an award" in section 7623(b)(4). It infers from Congress' use of the word "any" that a claimant may be able to file a petition "in response to more than one letter from the Commissioner." *See* op. Ct. pp. 281–283. The Court analogizes this situation to one where the IRS sends multiple notices of deficiency for a particular year, enabling the taxpayer to file separate petitions in response to the various notices. *See id.* pp. 281–282.

This analogy does not hold water. When the Commissioner sends multiple notices of deficiency for a given year, the second notice invariably involves different determinations—e.g., different items of income, different deductions, or different dollar amounts—from those in the first notice. That is not so in the *Friedland* paradigm. In those cases, the IRS made a determination in the first letter—that the claim for an award was rejected—and issued a second letter that refused to disturb that very same determination. [6]

In any event, Congress' use of the word "any" will not bear the weight that the opinion of the Court places upon it. A common meaning of "any" is simply "a" or "one." *See* op. Ct. note 11. In the *Friedland* cases, the Office made "a determination" in the first letter. The Office then sent the claimant a second letter that said in effect: "We are not changing our determination." That second letter did not constitute a

---

[6] The Court's analogy is also strained because there is a statutory regime in place to deal with the problem of multiple notices of deficiency. Section 6212(c)(1) prohibits the sending of a second notice of deficiency once the taxpayer has timely petitioned the Court in response to an initial notice of deficiency for the same year, except in cases of fraud, jeopardy and termination assessments, and correction of mathematical errors.

distinct "determination"; it simply repeated the determination that had already been made.

The Court's holding that a claimant may file a petition, at his option, in response to any of a series of letters referring to the denial of his claim is difficult to reconcile with the 30-day jurisdictional filing period that Congress placed in section 7623(b)(4). The Office has not hesitated to send multiple letters to claimants in an effort to demonstrate its good faith in acknowledging their queries and submissions. A claimant who has received a determination letter denying his claim and who has neglected to file a Tax Court petition within 30 days may have little difficulty stimulating the issuance by that Office of one or more additional letters reaffirming the previous letter(s). If each subsequent letter falls within the statutory phrase "any determination," claimants can end-run the 30-day jurisdictional filing period with comparative impunity. The Court provides no reason to believe that Congress intended so unlikely a result. [7]

In sum, there is no dispute that the Office can make more than one "determination" with respect to a claimant's claim or universe of claims. If the claim is different, then the determination will be different, and this Court can properly assume jurisdiction over the subsequent determination. That is what we think the Court should do here. But if the claim is not different and the determination is the same, and if the petition is filed more than 30 days after the original determination, the Court should hold that it lacks jurisdiction, as the Court in the *Friedland* cases correctly did. [8]

---

[7] In light of the Court's holding, the Office might change its letter-writing habits. Once it has sent the claimant a "determination" that denies his claim—that is, a letter that "constitutes a final administrative decision regarding [his] claim," *Cooper*, 135 T.C. at 76—any response to a request for reconsideration might simply say: "We issued our determination denying your claim on [date.]" One would hope that the Court would not regard this as a distinct "determination" that begins another 30-day jurisdictional filing period. Otherwise, the Office might be better off just ignoring all subsequent communications from claimants about their rejected claims.

[8] On the basis of the text of the February 2013 letter and petitioners' timely petition thereto, the opinion of the Court holds that the February 2013 letter constitutes a "determination" that we may review. During that review, surely respondent will ask us to undertake what the Court suggests is a "knotty factual [inquiry]," *see* op. Ct. p. 285, as to whether, by

Continued

GOEKE, HOLMES, KERRIGAN, and BUCH, *JJ.*, agree with this concurring opinion.

GOEKE and KERRIGAN, *JJ.*, concurring: We continue to believe that *SECC v. Commissioner*, 142 T.C. 225 (2014), was incorrectly decided, and we find the citations of that Opinion in the opinion of the Court in this case to be misleading and unnecessary. However, the present matter does not involve a liability subject to assessment, which in itself distinguishes it from *SECC*.

Our dissent in *SECC* rested on Congress' instruction to treat determinations of worker classification like notices of deficiency. *See id.* at 242 (Goeke and Kerrigan, JJ., dissenting) (citing section 7436(d)(1)). On the basis of that instruction, we relied on our notice of deficiency jurisprudence to determine that the letter at issue was not a notice of determination of worker classification.

Congress has not instructed us to treat whistleblower award determinations like notices of deficiency. We noted this in our *SECC* dissent in criticizing the Court's reliance on whistleblower cases to bolster its Opinion. *Id.* at 246. Similarly, we think the opinion of the Court's references to *SECC* here are misplaced.

As the opinion of the Court notes, we have often found that generic letters concerning whistleblower awards trigger our

---

the February 2013 letter, the Office simply reiterated a prior determination (respondent's view) or rejected a new or supplemental claim (petitioners' view). Let us assume that the Court finds the former (i.e., that the Office merely reiterated a prior determination). What would the Court then do? Would we put that finding aside and consider the merits of respondent's twice-made determination? If so, we would be sanctioning a clear end run around the 30-day jurisdictional filing provision that Congress has placed in the statute. If we would not put the finding aside, but instead dismiss the case for what at bottom would be petitioners' failure to have petitioned timely in response to the first determination, would we not (however we labeled it) be dismissing for lack of jurisdiction, as we did in the *Friedland* cases? In any event, the knotty factual inquiry likely cannot be avoided, and we see no reason to postpone making it.

jurisdiction under section 7623(b)(4). On the basis of our whistleblower jurisprudence only, we concur in the result here.

MICA RINGO, PETITIONER *v.* COMMISSIONER OF INTERNAL REVENUE, RESPONDENT

Docket No. 29562–12W. Filed October 6, 2014.

P filed with R's Whistleblower Office (W) an application for a whistleblower award under I.R.C. sec. 7623. On Nov. 7, 2012, W mailed to P a letter stating that P was ineligible for such an award because P did not provide R with information that resulted in the collection of any tax from the target. P timely filed a petition with this Court. I.R.C. sec. 7623(b)(4) provides that "[a]ny determination regarding an award under paragraph (1), (2), or (3) [of I.R.C. sec. 7623(b)] may, within 30 days of such determination, be appealed to the Tax Court (and the Tax Court shall have jurisdiction with respect to such matter)." On June 11, 2013, W notified P that W was still considering P's application and that W had mailed the Nov. 7, 2012, letter to P in error. R then moved to dismiss this case for lack of jurisdiction. *Held*: The Nov. 7, 2012, letter was a determination and this Court has jurisdiction with respect to the matter. *Held, further*, the fact that R continued to consider P's application after sending the Nov. 7, 2012, letter does not terminate this Court's jurisdiction.

Thomas C. Pliske and *Shine Lin*, for petitioner.
Jonathan D. Tepper, for respondent.

OPINION

COLVIN, *Judge*: The Internal Revenue Service (IRS) Whistleblower Office mailed to petitioner a letter on November 7, 2012, stating that he was ineligible for a whistleblower award under section 7623. Petitioner commenced this whistleblower proceeding by timely filing a petition pursuant to section 7623(b)(4).[1] Respondent moves to dismiss the case for lack of jurisdiction. As discussed below, we will deny respondent's motion.

---

[1] Section references are to the Internal Revenue Code in effect at all relevant times. Rule references are to the Tax Court Rules of Practice and Procedure.

Neither party requested a hearing, and we conclude that none is necessary to decide respondent's motion to dismiss. The following undisputed information appears in the pleadings or respondent's motion to dismiss.

Petitioner resided in Texas when the petition was filed.

Background

On February 17, 2011, petitioner filed with the Whistleblower Office a Form 211, Application for Award for Original Information. Petitioner filed an amended Form 211 with that office on October 6, 2011.

On November 7, 2012, the Whistleblower Office mailed to petitioner a letter (November 7, 2012, letter) stating that he was ineligible for a whistleblower award under section 7623 because he had not provided the IRS with information that resulted in the collection of any proceeds. That letter stated:

> Dear Mica Ringo:
>
> We have considered your application for an award dated February 11, 2011. Under Internal Revenue Code Section 7623, an award may be paid only if the information provided results in the collection of additional tax, penalties, interest or other proceeds. In this case, the information you provided did not result in the collection of any proceeds. Therefore, you are not eligible for an award.
>
> Although the information you submitted did not qualify for an award, thank you for your interest in the administration of the internal revenue laws.
>
> If you have any further questions in regards to this letter, please feel free to contact the Informant Claims Examination Team at * * *.
>
> Sincerely,
> /s
> Cindy Wilde
> Supervisor—Whistleblower Office, Ogden

Petitioner petitioned the Court on December 7, 2012, to invoke our jurisdiction under section 7623(b)(4). On June 11, 2013, the Whistleblower Office sent a letter (June 11, 2013, letter) to petitioner stating that the November 7, 2012, letter had been sent in error and that the Whistleblower Office was still considering his application for an award. That letter said:

Dear Mr Ringo:

The L–1010 letter dated November 7 2012 [i.e., the November 7, 2012, letter] was sent to you in error. We are still considering your application for award F–211. We are sorry for this inconvenience.

Sincerely,
/s
Cindy Wilde
Supervisor—Whistleblower Office, Ogden

Discussion

The Tax Court may exercise jurisdiction only to the extent expressly provided by Congress. *See* sec. 7442; *Breman v. Commissioner*, 66 T.C. 61, 66 (1976); *see also* Rule 13. Respondent contends that the Court lacks jurisdiction in this case, and petitioner does not object to respondent's assertion. However, our jurisdiction is not expanded or contracted by the positions of the parties. Thus, it is not dispositive that both parties claim that we lack jurisdiction. *SECC Corp. v. Commissioner*, 142 T.C. 225, 230 (2014); *Charlotte's Office Boutique, Inc. v. Commissioner*, 121 T.C. 89, 102 (2003), *aff'd*, 425 F.3d 1203 (9th Cir. 2005). We will independently decide whether we have jurisdiction.

In the June 11, 2013, letter, the Whistleblower Office said it was still considering information petitioner had provided. Thus, respondent contends that the November 7, 2012, letter was not a "definitive determination" as to petitioner's application and that we lack jurisdiction in this case.

We disagree. Whether the Court has jurisdiction in a case depends on facts as of the time that our jurisdiction is invoked. *See Charlotte's Office Boutique, Inc. v. Commissioner*, 425 F.3d at 1208; *NT, Inc. v. Commissioner*, 126 T.C. 191, 194 n.2 (2006); *see also Smith v. Sperling*, 354 U.S. 91, 93 n.1 (1957) ("'It is quite clear that the jurisdiction of the Court depends upon the state of things at the time of the action brought, and that after vesting, it cannot be ousted by subsequent events.'" (quoting *Mollan v. Torrance*, 22 U.S. (9 Wheat.) 537, 539 (1824) (Marshall, C.J.))). Once the Court acquires jurisdiction over a matter, our jurisdiction generally continues unimpaired until we enter our decision or our jurisdiction is otherwise terminated by the Court. *See NT, Inc. v. Commissioner*, 126 T.C. at 194 n.2; *Wagner v. Commissioner*, 118 T.C. 330 (2002); *Naftel v. Commissioner*,

85 T.C. 527, 529–530 (1985); *see also Grupo Dataflux v. Atlas Global Grp. L.P.*, 541 U.S. 567 (2004); *Smith*, 354 U.S. at 93 n.1.

Section 7623(b)(4) provides that "[a]ny determination regarding an award under paragraph (1), (2), or (3) may, within 30 days of such determination, be appealed to the Tax Court (and the Tax Court shall have jurisdiction with respect to such matter)."[2] Thus, a whistleblower proceeding is commenced under section 7623(b)(4) when (1) the IRS makes a determination regarding an award under section 7623(b)(1), (2), or (3); and (2) a petition is timely filed as to that determination. *See Whistleblower 14106–10W v. Commissioner*, 137 T.C. 183, 186–187 (2011); *Kasper v. Commissioner*, 137 T.C. 37, 41 (2011); *Cooper v. Commissioner*, 135 T.C. 70, 73–74 (2010).

The November 7, 2012, letter contains a determination for purposes of section 7623(b)(4). *See Cooper v. Commissioner*, 135 T.C. at 75–76 (stating that this Court has jurisdiction under section 7623 with regard to a letter not labeled a determination where, as here, the letter stated that the applicant was not entitled to an award and provided an explanation for that conclusion); *see also Kasper v. Commissioner*, 137 T.C. at 41. The fact that the Whistleblower Office said in a letter dated June 11, 2013, that the determination was not definitive does not terminate this Court's jurisdiction. The November 7, 2012, letter contains a determination, and petitioner filed a timely petition invoking our jurisdiction under section 7623(b)(4) with respect to that matter. Our jurisdiction is unaffected by the fact that the Whistleblower Office later told petitioner it was still considering information he provided.

Our conclusion is supported by consideration of rules relating to notices of deficiency. The Court acquires jurisdiction in a deficiency case when the IRS has determined a deficiency and the taxpayer timely files a petition. *See* secs.

[2] Para. (1) of sec. 7623(b) generally requires that the IRS pay an individual 15% to 30% of the collected proceeds where the IRS proceeds with any administrative or judicial action based on certain information furnished by the individual. Para. (2) generally lets the IRS pay an individual up to 10% of the collected proceeds in certain other cases. Para. (3) sets forth rules under which the IRS may reduce an award otherwise payable under para. (1) or (2).

6212(a), 6213(a). It is the determination of a deficiency, rather than the existence of a deficiency, that provides the basis for the Court's jurisdiction. *See, e.g.*, *Hannan v. Commissioner*, 52 T.C. 787, 791 (1969). Thus, even if a determination in a notice of deficiency is erroneous or the Commissioner concedes the determination in full, the notice is generally not rendered void but continues to provide a basis for our jurisdiction. *See, e.g.*, *Charlotte's Office Boutique, Inc. v. Commissioner*, 121 T.C. at 103 (stating that the Commissioner's concession of employment tax issue during a proceeding in this Court did not deprive the Court of jurisdiction over the subject matter underlying that issue); *LTV Corp. v. Commissioner*, 64 T.C. 589 (1975) (stating that the Commissioner's concession of no deficiency for a year did not deprive the Court of jurisdiction over the subject matter of that year); *Cawal v. Commissioner*, T.C. Memo. 1992–444. Similarly, the Court does not lose jurisdiction when the Commissioner wishes to revoke or issues in error a notice of determination in a collection case. *Kim v. Commissioner*, T.C. Memo. 2005–96. [3]

On the basis of the foregoing, we hold that we have jurisdiction, and we will deny respondent's motion to dismiss for lack of jurisdiction.

An appropriate order will be issued.

DANIEL RICHARD BUCZEK, PETITIONER *v.* COMMISSIONER OF INTERNAL REVENUE, RESPONDENT

Docket No. 8512–14L. Filed October 6, 2014.

P timely filed a Form 12153, Request for a Collection Due Process or Equivalent Hearing, with attachments, in response to a final notice of intent to levy to collect P's unpaid income tax liability for 2009. P did not raise any issues specified in

---

[3] In *Whistleblower 22231–124W v. Commissioner*, T.C. Memo. 2014–157, at *12–*13, we said that "[s]ince the [Whistleblower] Office was still investigating * * * [an issue raised in a Whistleblower's claim], it had not yet made 'a final administrative decision regardingpetitioner's whistleblower claim in accordance with the established procedures.'" Our holding in *Whistleblower 22231–124W v. Commissioner* is consistent with our holding herein because in *Whistleblower 22231–124W v. Commissioner* there had not been a determination at the time the petition was filed.

I.R.C. sec. 6330(c)(2) or make any allegations that reasonably indicated he was raising such an issue. The Appeals Office sent P a letter stating that, pursuant to I.R.C. sec. 6330(g), it was disregarding P's hearing request because P's disagreement was frivolous and the IRS Collection Division could proceed with collecting P's unpaid tax liability for 2009. This "disregard letter" resembles the letters that the Appeals Office sent to the taxpayers in *Thornberry v. Commissioner*, 136 T.C. 356 (2011). R filed a motion to dismiss for lack of jurisdiction. R asserts that, contrary to the Court's holding in *Thornberry*, this Court does not have jurisdiction when a disregard letter is issued. R asserts that the holding in *Thornberry* eviscerates I.R.C. sec. 6330(g) and requests that the Court overturn it. We decline to do so. *Held*: The Tax Court has jurisdiction to review the Commissioner's determination as to whether a taxpayer who has sought judicial review under I.R.C. sec. 6330(d)(1) has raised an issue other than issues that have been identified by the Secretary as frivolous or that reflect a desire to delay or impede the administration of Federal tax laws. *Thornberry v. Commissioner*, 136 T.C. 356, followed and clarified. *Held*, *further*, because P did not raise on Form 12153 any issues specified in I.R.C. sec. 6330(c)(2) that may be considered in an administrative hearing, no portion of P's request for a hearing is excluded from R's determination to disregard the entire request and I.R.C. sec. 6330(g) prohibits further judicial review of that determination. *Thornberry v. Commissioner*, 136 T.C. 356, distinguished. *Held*, *further*, because R's determination that the IRS Collection Division could proceed with collecting P's unpaid tax liability for 2009 was not made in response to a proper request for a hearing, i.e., the entire request was properly treated as if it had never been submitted, this Court lacks jurisdiction to review that determination and R's motion to dismiss for lack of jurisdiction will be granted. *Thornberry v. Commissioner*, 136 T.C. 356, distinguished.

Daniel Richard Buczek, pro se.
John M. Janusz, for respondent.

OPINION

DAWSON, *Judge*: This collection case is before the Court on respondent's motion to dismiss for lack of jurisdiction. Petitioner timely filed the petition for review of the determination by the Appeals Office to proceed with levy to collect his unpaid tax assessed for 2009, sent to him in response to his request for a hearing pursuant to sections 6320 and 6330[1] (hearing request).

The determination letter states that, under the authority of section 6330(g), the Appeals Office was disregarding petitioner's entire hearing request because his disagreement is either a position that the Secretary has identified as frivolous or reflects a desire to delay or impede the administration of Federal tax laws, and therefore, his request was being returned to the Internal Revenue Service (IRS) Collection Division and the Collection Division could proceed with collecting the tax. The determination letter resembles the "disregard letters" the Appeals Office issued to the taxpayers in *Thornberry v. Commissioner*, 136 T.C. 356 (2011). This Court held in *Thornberry* that the statements in disregard letters that the IRS collection office could proceed with collection action were determinations for purposes of section 6330(d)(1) and that this Court had jurisdiction to review the Appeals Office's determination that the taxpayer raised only frivolous arguments. Respondent asserts that, contrary to the Court's holding in *Thornberry*, this Court does not have jurisdiction when a disregard letter is issued and that he has made no determination concerning collection action or any other determination that would confer jurisdiction on this Court with respect to petitioner's taxable year 2009. Respondent asserts that *Thornberry* was decided incorrectly in that it eviscerates section 6330(g), which denies judicial review of the portions of a request for an administrative hearing that the Appeals Office determined are frivolous. Therefore, respondent requests that the Court overturn *Thornberry*. We decline to overturn *Thornberry* and explain herein why *Thornberry* neither violates nor eviscerates section 6330(g). The administrative hearing requests that the taxpayers in *Thornberry* submitted are in stark contrast to petitioner's request. A comparison of our review of the section 6330(g) determination with respect to the taxpayers' hearing requests in *Thornberry* with our review of the determination with respect to petitioner's request elucidates the standard we apply in making such a review.

---

[1] Section references are to the Internal Revenue Code of 1986, as amended and in effect at all relevant times.

Background

Petitioner resided in New York when he filed the petition.

On November 13, 2013, respondent sent petitioner a final notice of intent to levy to collect his unpaid Federal income tax and interest assessed for 2009. On November 20, 2013, petitioner returned the notice of intent to levy to the Appeals Office with a timely filed Form 12153, Request for a Collection Due Process or Equivalent Hearing, and seven additional pages. Each page of the notice of intent to levy was stamped "Pursuant to UCC 3–501", "Refused from the cause", "Consent not given", and "Permission DENIED". On the Form 12153 petitioner did not check any of the boxes but wrote "common law hearing" on the line where he could have stated another reason for requesting the hearing. Thus, on the Form 12153 he did not request a collection alternative, he did not assert that he could not pay the tax, he did not request relief under section 6015, and he did not raise any other relevant issue related to the unpaid tax or proposed levy. Nor did he raise any relevant issues in the seven additional pages submitted with the Form 12153.

On January 27, 2014, petitioner and his wife filed the petition in docket No. 1390–14, seeking review of a notice of deficiency for an unspecified year. Attached to the petition were many documents, including a statutory notice of deficiency issued to petitioner's wife for 2011 and several collection notices (i.e., Notice of Levy, Notice of Federal Tax Lien, Final Notice of Intent To Levy and Notice of Your Right to a Hearing, and Notice of Federal Tax Lien Filing and Your Right to a Hearing Under IRC 6320).

On March 12, 2014, the Appeals Office sent petitioner a letter titled "Appeals is disregarding your request for a Collection Due Process and/or Equivalent Hearing". The letter indicates that petitioner did not respond to a January 21, 2014, letter from the Appeals Office requesting that he amend the hearing request to provide a legitimate reason for the hearing or withdraw the request. The disregard letter informed petitioner that, under the authority of section 6330(g), the Appeals Office was disregarding his request for an administrative hearing because it had determined that his disagreement is:

- a "specified frivolous position", identified by the IRS in Notice 2008–14 (for Notice 2008–14, refer to the IRS Internet website at *http://www.irs.gov/newsroom/article/0..id=177519,00.html*); or
- a reason that is not a "specified frivolous position," but is a frivolous reason reflecting a desire to delay or impede federal tax administration; or
- a moral, religious, political, constitutional, conscientious, or similar objection to the imposition or payment of federal taxes that reflects a desire to delay or impede the administration of federal tax laws.

The letter stated that the Appeals Office was returning petitioner's request to the IRS collection office and that "Collection may proceed with collection action as if the hearing request was never submitted."

On March 20, 2014, petitioner and his wife filed, in docket No. 1390–14, a notice of appeals letter dated March 12, 2014 (notice of disregard letter), to which they attached a copy of the March 12, 2014, disregard letter sent to petitioner regarding the collection of his 2009 tax liability. In the order dated April 24, 2014, the Court dismissed petitioner from the case at docket No. 1390–14 for lack of jurisdiction and ordered the notice of disregard letter to be filed, as of March 20, 2014, as an imperfect petition to commence this case regarding the collection of his tax liability for 2009. The Court ordered petitioner to file a proper amended petition on or before May 15, 2014.

On May 5, 2014, petitioner filed the amended petition. On May 16, 2014, petitioner filed a response to the April 24, 2014, order and the "Notice of Judicial Ruling". On June 23 and 27, 2014, petitioner respectively filed the first amended response to the April 24, 2014, order and a status report. In those pleadings, petitioner primarily complains about the conduct of an IRS agent who is not the Appeals officer who reviewed his request and sent him the March 12, 2014, disregard letter. He raises no justiciable issue with regard to the Appeals Office's disregard of his hearing request or its determination to proceed with the collection of his unpaid income tax liability for 2009.

On July 2, 2014, respondent filed the motion to dismiss for lack of jurisdiction.

Discussion

Sections 6320(a)(1) and 6330(a)(1), respectively, require the Commissioner to give a taxpayer written notices when a notice of Federal tax lien is filed upon the taxpayer's property and when the Commissioner intends to levy upon the taxpayer's property. The notices must inform the taxpayer of the right to request a hearing in the Appeals Office (administrative hearing). Secs. 6320(a)(3)(B), 6330(a)(3)(B). In the request for an administrative hearing the taxpayer must state the grounds for the requested hearing. Secs. 6320(b)(1), 6330(b)(1). If a taxpayer makes a timely written request and states the grounds for the requested hearing, he is entitled to a fair hearing conducted by an impartial officer from the Appeals Office. Secs. 6320(b), 6330(b); *Mason v. Commissioner*, 132 T.C. 301, 315 (2009).

During the administrative hearing the taxpayer may raise any relevant issue related to the unpaid tax or proposed collection action, including appropriate spousal defenses, challenges to the appropriateness of collection actions, and collection alternatives. Sec. 6330(c)(2)(A). The taxpayer also may raise challenges to the existence or amount of the underlying tax liability, but only if he/she did not receive a notice of deficiency for that liability or did not otherwise have an opportunity to dispute it. Sec. 6330(c)(2)(B). However, the taxpayer may not properly raise an issue that meets either of the requirements of section 6702(b)(2)(A)(i) or (ii); i.e., is based on a position which the Secretary has identified as frivolous under section 6702(c) or reflects a desire to delay or impede the administration of Federal tax laws. Sec. 6330(c)(4)(B). If the Appeals officer determines that any portion of the taxpayer's hearing request is frivolous, he may treat that portion as if it were never submitted. Sec. 6330(g). Section 6330(g) denies further administrative or judicial review of the portions of a hearing request that the Appeals Office determined are frivolous.

After the administrative hearing is completed, the Appeals Office issues a written notice of determination indicating whether the notice of Federal tax lien should remain in effect and/or whether the proposed levy may proceed. Sec. 6330(c)(3); secs. 301.6320–1(e)(3), Q&A–E8, 301.6330–1(e)(3), Q&A–E8, Proced. & Admin. Regs. A taxpayer may appeal the

Appeals Office determination to the Tax Court within 30 days of the determination; and if an appeal is timely filed, the Court will have jurisdiction with respect to the matter. Sec. 6330(d)(1); sec. 301.6330–1(f)(1), Proced. & Admin. Regs.

We have jurisdiction to determine our jurisdiction. *Cooper v. Commissioner*, 135 T.C. 70 (2010). Our jurisdiction under section 6330(d)(1) depends upon the issuance of a valid notice of determination and a timely petition for review. *Thornberry v. Commissioner*, 136 T.C. at 363; *Sarrell v. Commissioner*, 117 T.C. 122, 125 (2001); *Offiler v. Commissioner*, 114 T.C. 492, 498 (2000). In *Thornberry v. Commissioner*, 136 T.C. at 363–364, the Court held that the Appeals Office statement in the disregard letters that the IRS collection office could proceed with collection action is a determination for purposes of section 6330(d)(1). We observed that section 6703(a) clearly contemplates judicial review with respect to an Appeals Office determination that a request for an administrative hearing under sections 6320 and 6330 is a specified frivolous submission. The Appeals Office determination that a taxpayer's entire hearing request is disregarded because his disagreement is frivolous is essentially a determination that the request is a specified frivolous submission. Indeed, the Appeals Office frequently imposes the civil penalty under section 6702(a) on a taxpayer whose hearing request was disregarded because the Appeals Office determined it was frivolous. *See, e.g., Kurka v. Commissioner*, T.C. Memo. 2014–96. Consequently, while section 6330(g) prohibits judicial review of the portion of a request for an administrative hearing that the Appeals Office determined is frivolous, it does not prohibit judicial review of the determination by the Appeals Office that the request is frivolous and is disregarded. *Thornberry v. Commissioner*, 136 T.C. at 367.

In *Thornberry*, the taxpayers timely requested administrative hearings under sections 6320 and 6330 in response to notices of intent to levy and notices of Federal tax lien filing sent to them with respect to their unpaid tax liabilities, including a section 6702 penalty, for 2000, 2001, 2002, and 2007. They checked almost every box on the Forms 12153, indicating that they requested an installment agreement or an offer-in-compromise as a collection alternative and requested subordination, discharge, or withdrawal of the lien. They set forth additional grounds for their requests in an attachment they downloaded from the Web site of an organization with a history of promoting frivolous arguments and activities that delay or impede the administration of the Federal tax laws. Each attachment listed 23 boilerplate items, of which 21 were checked and 2 were unchecked. Although many of the grounds listed on the attachment did not apply to the taxpayers, in their requests they asserted claims properly allowed under section 6330(c)(2), inter alia that: (1) collection action would place an undue hardship on them and they requested collection alternatives; (2) they qualified for subordination and requested that the notice of lien be withdrawn; (3) they did not receive notices of deficiency for the assessed income taxes or the section 6702 penalty and had not had an opportunity to contest the tax liabilities; and (4) they were requesting reconsideration of the income tax deficiencies and the section 6702 penalty.

In *Thornberry v. Commissioner*, 136 T.C. at 371, we stated that it was improper for the Appeals Office to treat those portions of the taxpayers' requests that set forth legitimate issues as if they were never submitted without explaining how the requests reflected a desire to delay or impede Federal tax administration. Under *Thornberry*, unless the Appeals Office explains how the request reflects a desire to delay or impede Federal tax administration, the legitimate section 6330(c)(2) issues raised in a taxpayer's hearing request must be excluded, and are deemed to be excluded, from any portions of the request that the Appeals Office determined were frivolous. Absent such an explanation, the portions of the hearing request raising otherwise legitimate issues may not be treated as if they were never submitted.

In *Thornberry v. Commissioner*, 136 T.C. at 367–368, we held that this Court has jurisdiction to review the Appeals Office determination that the taxpayer's request for an administrative hearing was entirely frivolous or for purposes of delay and thus properly treated as if it were never submitted. We remanded the case to the Appeals Office for a hearing to consider the taxpayers' challenges to the section 6702 penalty and their requests for collection alternatives, withdrawal of the lien, and section 6015 relief—legitimate issues they properly raised in their hearing requests that are deemed excluded from any portions of the request that the Appeals Office determined were frivolous. Following the remand, the Court entered the decision stipulated by the parties that the taxpayers' income tax liabilities for 2000, 2001, and 2002 were closed as currently uncollectible by reason of economic hardship and the section 6702 penalty for 2007 was abated.

In *Thornberry*, the taxpayers' hearing request, on its face, clearly raised proper issues set forth in section 6330(c)(2)(A) and (B), and the taxpayers raised those issues in the petition they filed in this Court appealing the disregard letter sent by the Appeals Office. By contrast, petitioner's hearing request, which included Form 12153 and the pages attached thereto, does not challenge the appropriateness of the collection action, offer or request any collection alternatives, challenge the existence or amount of the underlying tax liability, or raise any spousal defenses. Nor does it make any assertions that would implicitly raise a legitimate issue; for example, it does not assert that the collection action would cause petitioner undue hardship or that he did not receive a notice of deficiency or otherwise have an opportunity to challenge the underlying tax liability.

Because petitioner did not raise in his hearing request any issues that may be considered in the administrative hearing, there are no issues that are deemed to be excluded from any portions of his request that the Appeals Office determined were frivolous. In accordance with section 6330(g), we make no review of the portions of a request for an administrative hearing that the Appeals Office has determined are frivolous. Moreover, because respondent's determination that the IRS Collection Division could proceed with collecting petitioner's unpaid tax liability for 2009 *was not* made in response to a proper request for a hearing, i.e., the entire request was properly treated as if it had never been submitted, this Court lacks jurisdiction to review respondent's determination that collection may proceed, and therefore respondent's motion to dismiss for lack of jurisdiction will be granted.

In conclusion, the decision entered in *Thornberry* demonstrates the importance of this Court's review of the Appeals Office's determinations under section 6330(g) in protecting taxpayers from determinations that are arbitrary and capricious. Our Opinion today demonstrates that our review does not violate or eviscerate section 6330(g), and we therefore decline respondent's invitation to overturn *Thornberry*.

This case is distinguished from *Thornberry*, and we will grant respondent's motion to dismiss for lack of jurisdiction on the facts presented here.

Accordingly,

An order of dismissal for lack of jurisdiction will be entered.

APPLIED RESEARCH ASSOCIATES, INC. AND AFFILIATE, PETITIONER *v.* COMMISSIONER OF INTERNAL REVENUE, RESPONDENT

Docket No. 21076–11. Filed October 9, 2014.

P, an affiliated group consisting of a qualified personal service corporation A, the parent corporation, and a corporation that is not a qualified personal service corporation, filed consolidated Federal income tax returns for 2006 and 2007. P reported consolidated taxable income for 2006 and 2007, all of which was attributable to A. On the basis that the affiliated group, as a single entity, was not a qualified personal service corporation, P paid tax on the consolidated taxable income of the affiliated group at graduated rates set forth in I.R.C. sec. 11(b)(1). On the basis that each affiliate's status as a qualified personal service corporation is to be examined separately, R determined that the consolidated taxable income of the affiliated group was subject to the I.R.C. sec. 11(b)(2) flat 35% tax rate applicable to qualified personal service corporations. *Held*: Graduated rates set forth in I.R.C. sec. 11(b)(1) should be used to compute the amount of tax to be imposed on the consolidated taxable income of an affiliated group consisting of a qualified personal service corporation and an entity that is not a qualified personal service corporation where the group, as a single entity, is not a personal service corporation.

Kenneth W. Heathington (an officer), for petitioner.

Nancy Wentz Hale and *Beth A. Nunnink*, for respondent.

OPINION

JACOBS, *Judge*: The parties submitted this case fully stipulated pursuant to Rule 122. Applied Research Associates, Inc. (Applied Research), is a corporation organized under the laws of Tennessee. It provides professional engineering and consulting services and is a qualified personal service corporation as defined in section 448(d)(2). During the years involved (2006 and 2007) Applied Research owned all the outstanding stock of Oak Crest Land & Cattle Co., Inc. (Oak Crest), a Texas corporation. During the years involved Oak Crest owned and operated a 400-acre ranch in Texas which owned between 200 and 300 head of cattle. Oak Crest is not a qualified personal service corporation.

Applied Research and Oak Crest constituted an affiliated group during the years involved. The affiliated group timely filed consolidated 2006 and 2007 Federal income tax returns. Applied Research generated taxable income, whereas Oak Crest generated a loss, for each of the years involved. The consolidated return reported taxable income for each of the years involved.

The issue for decision concerns the rate(s) of tax (graduated or a flat 35%) to be used to compute the amount of tax to be imposed by section 11(b) on the consolidated taxable income of an affiliated group consisting of a qualified personal service corporation and an entity that is not a qualified personal service corporation where the group, as a single entity, is not a qualified personal service corporation. For the reasons set forth *infra*, we hold that graduated tax rates should be used.

All Rule references are to the Tax Court Rules of Practice and Procedure, and unless otherwise indicated all section references are to the Internal Revenue Code (Code) as in effect for the years involved. All monetary amounts are rounded to the nearest dollar. At the time the petition was filed, petitioner's principal place of business was in Tennessee, and the parties have stipulated that appeal in this case is to the Court of Appeals for the Sixth Circuit.

Background

During the years involved Dr. Kenneth Heathington owned 50% of the common stock of Applied Research and his wife, Dr. Beth Heathington, held the remaining 50%. Dr. Kenneth Heathington served as president of the corporation, and Dr. Beth Heathington served as its vice president.

Dr. Kenneth Heathington is an engineer licensed in Tennessee, Illinois, Indiana, and Mississippi. During the years involved Dr. Kenneth Heathington provided engineering services to Applied Research, including lectures and consulting services; chaired workshops; wrote reports, books and papers; and provided design work and construction supervision for structures that Applied Research owned. He spent 70% to 75% of his working time doing so, billing 1,143.75 hours in 2006 and 1,296.5 hours in 2007. Dr. Beth Heathington holds a doctorate in education and specializes in literacy. She has written numerous articles and books in that field. During the years involved she provided administrative, financial accounting, and recordkeeping services to Applied Research, spending 45% to 50% of her working time doing so. Applied Research paid the Heathingtons, as well as 12 others, nonemployee compensation for their services. [1]

Dr. Kenneth Heathington was president of Oak Crest and spent between 25% and 30% of his working time farming and ranching. He vaccinated and branded cattle, purchased and trained horses, hired and supervised contractors, and purchased equipment for Oak Crest. Dr. Beth Heathington served as Oak Crest's vice president and spent 50% to 55% of her working time on the job at the ranch. Oak Crest paid nonemployee compensation to four individuals; it paid no money to either Dr. Heathington.

Petitioner's 2006 consolidated Federal income tax return reported the following: [2]

Line item	*Applied Research*	*Oak Crest*	*Consolidated total reported on Form 1120*
Gross receipts	$555,652	$52,030	$607,682
Cost of goods sold	-0-	16,366	16,366
Interest	12,648	2,972	15,621
Gross rents	7,200	2,800	10,000
Form 4797 net gain	-0-	2,000	2,000
Other income	-0-	3	3
Total income	575,500	43,439	618,940
Officers' comp.	50,000	-0-	50,000
Repairs/maintenance	29,156	54,538	83,693
Rents	1,000	2,796	3,796

[1] The parties stipulated that, when looked at as a separate entity, Applied Research was a qualified personal service corporation. *See infra* p. 316. Although both Doctors Heathington received nonemployee compensation from Applied Research, we assume that as officers who received remuneration and who provided substantial services to the corporation, both were employees of Applied Research. *See* sec. 1.448–1T(e)(5)(ii), Temporary Income Tax Regs., 52 Fed. Reg. 22770 (June 16, 1987); sec. 31.3121(d)–1(b), Employment Tax Regs.

[2] Dollar discrepancies for both the 2006 and 2007 tables result from rounding of the monetary amounts to the nearest dollar.

Line item	*Applied Research*	*Oak Crest*	*Consolidated total reported on Form 1120*
Taxes/licenses	15,830	14,229	30,059
Depreciation	9,824	97,162	106,986
Other deductions	186,304	110,542	296,846
Taxable income	283,387	-235,827	47,560

Petitioner's 2007 consolidated Federal income tax return reported the following:

Line item	*Applied Research*	*Oak Crest*	*Consolidated total reported on Form 1120*
Gross receipts	$632,841	$75,918	$708,760
Cost of goods sold	-0-	11,645	11,645
Interest	13,948	3,084	7,033
Gross rents	7,200	-0-	7,200
Total income	653,989	67,358	721,347
Officers' comp.	50,000	-0-	50,000
Repairs/maintenance	43,813	72,935	116,748
Taxes/licenses	12,020	14,229	26,249
Depreciation	78,598	71,377	149,975
Other deductions	204,154	93,442	297,596
Taxable income	265,404	-184,625	80,779

As indicated by the above tables, for each of the years involved the consolidated taxable income reported on petitioner's consolidated Federal income tax return was attributable solely to Applied Research. The affiliated group paid tax on its consolidated taxable income at graduated rates set forth in section 11(b)(1).

On June 9, 2011, respondent issued petitioner a notice of deficiency with respect to 2006 and 2007. Respondent determined that the consolidated taxable income reported on both consolidated returns is subject to the section 11(b)(2) 35% rate applicable to qualified personal service corporation income.

Discussion

I. *Statutory and Regulatory Framework*

For 2006 and 2007 Applied Research and Oak Crest constituted an affiliated group as defined by section 1504(a). Applied Research was the common parent. *See* sec. 1504(a). The affiliated group filed consolidated Federal income tax returns for both years involved as permitted by section 1501.

Section 1503(a) provides that in any case in which a consolidated return is made, the tax shall be determined in accordance with the regulations promulgated under section 1502. Section 1502 provides that the Secretary shall prescribe such regulations as he may deem necessary in order that the tax liability of the affiliated group, and of each of its members, may be computed, assessed, and collected in such manner as to clearly reflect its income tax liability and to prevent avoidance of tax liability. *See also Norwest Corp. & Subs. v. Commissioner*, 111 T.C. 105, 153 (1998); *Woods Inv. Co. v. Commissioner*, 85 T.C. 274, 277 (1985).

Section 1.1502–2, Income Tax Regs., provides that the computation of an affiliated group's tax liability shall be determined by adding together the following categories of tax:

> (a) The tax imposed by section 11 on the consolidated taxable income for such year (see §1.1502–11 for the computation of consolidated taxable income);
>
> (b) The tax imposed by section 541 on the consolidated undistributed personal holding company income;
>
> (c) If paragraph (b) of this section does not apply, the aggregate of the taxes imposed by section 541 on the separate undistributed personal holding company income of the members of the group which are personal holding companies;
>
> (d) If paragraph (b) of this section does not apply, the tax imposed by section 531 on the consolidated accumulated taxable income (see §1.1502–43);
>
> (e) The tax imposed by section 594(a) in lieu of the taxes imposed by section 11 or 1201 on the taxable income of a life insurance department of the common parent of a group which is a mutual savings bank;
>
> (f) The tax imposed by section 802(a) on consolidated life insurance company taxable income;
>
> (g) The tax imposed by section 831(a) on the consolidated insurance company taxable income of the members which are subject to such tax;
>
> (h) The tax imposed by section 1201, instead of the taxes computed under paragraphs (a) and (g) of this section, computed by reference to the net capital gain of the group (see §1.1502–22) (or, for consolidated return years to which §1.1502–22 does not apply, computed by reference to the excess of the consolidated net long-term capital gain over the consolidated net short-term capital loss (see §1.1502–41A for the determination of the consolidated net long-term capital gain and the consolidated net short-term capital loss));
>
> (i) [Reserved]
>
> (j) The tax imposed by section 1333 on war loss recoveries; and
>
> by allowing as a credit against such taxes the investment credit under section 38 (see §1.1502–3) and the foreign tax credit under section 33 (see §1.1502–4). For purposes of this section, the surtax exemption of the group for a consolidated return year is $25,000, or if a lesser amount is allowed under section 1561, such lesser amount. See §1.1561–2(a)(2). For

increase in tax due to the application of section 47, see §1.1502–3(f). For amount of tax surcharge, see section 51 and §1.1502–7.

Consolidated taxable income principally represents the affiliated group's dealings with the outside world after the elimination of intercompany profit and loss. *See First Nat'l Bank in Little Rock v. Commissioner*, 83 T.C. 202, 209 (1984) (citing Bittker & Eustice, Federal Income Taxation of Corporations and Shareholders, par. 15.20, at 15–51 (4th ed. 1979)). Section 1.1502–11, Income Tax Regs., provides that consolidated taxable income is computed by first taking into account the separate taxable income of each member of the group. Each member's separate taxable income is calculated as if the member were a separate corporation, and then certain modifications are made for any intercompany transactions and other items. *First Nat'l Bank in Little Rock v. Commissioner*, 83 T.C. at 207–208; *see* sec. 1.1502–12, Income Tax Regs.

Once the affiliated group calculates its consolidated taxable income, section 1.1502–2(a), Income Tax Regs., directs the affiliated group to apply "[t]he tax imposed by section 11" on that consolidated taxable income. Section 11(a) imposes a tax on the taxable income of every corporation. Section 11(b)(1) provides for graduated rates of tax based on the corporation's taxable income. Section 11(b)(2) imposes a flat 35% tax on the taxable income of a qualified personal service corporation, as defined in section 448(d)(2). [3]

[3] Sec. 448 governs limitations on the use of the cash method of accounting. Sec. 448(a) provides that generally (1) C corporations, (2) partnerships which have a C corporation as a partner, and (3) tax shelters may not compute their taxable income under the cash receipts and disbursements method of accounting. Pursuant to sec. 448(b)(2), qualified personal service corporations are excepted from this general rule.

Sec. 448(d)(2) provides that a corporation is a qualified personal service corporation if (A) substantially all of its activities involve the performance of services in the fields of health, law, engineering, architecture, accounting, actuarial science, performing arts, or consulting (the function test) and (B) substantially all of the stock of the corporation, by value, is held directly, or indirectly through one or more partnerships, S corporations, or qualified personal service corporations not described in sec. 448(a)(2) or (3), by (i) employees performing services for the corporation in connection with the activities involving one of the aforementioned enumerated fields (the ownership test); (ii) retired employees who had performed such services for

Continued

Although for purposes of the imposition of tax, section 11 makes a distinction for entities that are qualified personal service corporations and those that are not, section 1.1502–2(a), Income Tax Regs., does not make such a distinction. Section 1.1502–2, Income Tax Regs., first addressed computation of tax liability in 1966 in T.D. 6894, 1966–2 C.B. 362, 366. At that time, section 11(b) provided that all corporations were subject to graduated tax rates.[4] In 1987 the Revenue Act of 1987 (RA 1987), Pub. L. No. 100–203, sec. 10224(a), 101 Stat. at 1330–412, amended section 11(b) to prevent qualified personal service corporations from reaping the benefits of graduated corporate tax rates. However, section 1.1502–2(a), Income Tax Regs., was not updated to reflect the 1987 amendment to section 11(b). Thus, section 1.1502–2(a), Income Tax Regs., for the years involved, retained the rule that consolidated taxable income is a singular item and does not provide different tax rates for qualified personal service corporations.

II. *Contentions of the Parties*

The parties have stipulated that Applied Research, if considered by itself, was a qualified personal service corporation for both years involved. Further, the parties agree that if examined as a separate entity, Oak Crest was not a qualified personal service corporation for the years involved.

---

the corporation; (iii) the estate of any individual described in the two previous clauses; or (iv) any other person who acquired the stock by reason of the death of any of the aforementioned individuals, but only for the two-year period beginning on the date of the death of that individual.

[4] Before the enactment of the Revenue Act of 1987, Pub. L. No. 100–203, sec. 10224(a), 101 Stat. at 1330–412, sec. 11(b) provided:

SEC. 11. TAX IMPOSED.

(b) AMOUNT OF THE TAX.—The amount of tax imposed by subsection (a) shall be the sum of—

(1) 15 percent of so much of the taxable income as does not exceed $50,000;

(2) 25 percent of so much of the taxable income as exceeds $50,000 but does not exceed $75,000;

(3) 34 percent of so much of the taxable income as exceeds $75,000.

In the case of a corporation with taxable income in excess of $100,000 for any taxable year, the amount of tax determined under the preceding sentence for such taxable year shall be increased by the lesser of (A) 5 percent of such excess, or (B) $11,750.

The parties disagree as to the tax rate to be imposed on the consolidated taxable income of an affiliated group when a qualified personal service corporation and another type of corporation combine to form the affiliated group and file a consolidated income tax return. Respondent asserts that in that situation each member corporation is to be examined separately to determine whether it is a qualified personal service corporation. Respondent further asserts that if at least one member of the affiliated group is determined to be a qualified personal service corporation, the consolidated taxable income of the group is to be split or broken up into separate baskets, one for the income of the qualified personal service corporation and another for the income of the other type of corporation. And, respondent maintains, after doing so, a flat 35% rate is to be applied to the qualified personal service corporation's income and graduated rates are to be applied to the income of the corporation that is not a qualified personal service corporation.

In contrast, petitioner asserts, in essence, that because the consolidated return regulations do not provide for the splitting of an affiliated group's consolidated taxable income after the affiliated group's consolidated taxable income has been calculated, the entire amount of consolidated taxable income of the affiliated group is taxed at graduated rates.

The parties agree that if the affiliated group's consolidated taxable income may not be split into two separate baskets, the entire amount of the consolidated taxable income of the affiliated group is taxed at graduated rates. On the other hand, the parties agree that if the affiliated group's consolidated taxable income can be split into separate baskets, then inasmuch as all of the consolidated taxable income of the affiliated group is attributable to the operations of Applied Research, a qualified personal service corporation, all of petitioner's taxable income is subject to the flat 35% rate.[5]

---

[5] In his brief respondent notes that sec. 1.1502–2(e), Income Tax Regs., imposes a tax on a life insurance department's income without netting it against any losses of the consolidated group. Respondent asserts that this section grants him authority to impose the qualified personal service corporation's tax rate on the entire amount of income attributable to the qualified personal service corporation member without taking into consideration losses suffered by other members of the affiliated group. However,

Continued

III. *Analysis*

The consolidated return regulations are intended to balance what this Court described in *Norwest Corp. & Subs. v. Commissioner*, 111 T.C. at 152, as "two countervailing principles of the law relating to consolidated returns". The first of these principles is that "the purpose of the consolidated return provisions * * * is 'to require taxes to be levied according to the true net income and invested capital resulting from and employed in a single business enterprise, even though it was conducted by means of more than one corporation.'" *First Nat'l Bank in Little Rock v. Commissioner*, 83 T.C. at 209 (quoting *Handy & Hartman v. Burnet*, 284 U.S. 136, 140 (1931)). The contrasting second principle is that "'[e]ach corporation is a separate taxpayer whether it stands alone or is in an affiliated group and files a consolidated return.'" *Wegman's Props., Inc. v. Commissioner*, 78 T.C. 786, 789 (1982) (quoting *Elec. Sensing Prods., Inc. v. Commissioner*, 69 T.C. 276, 281 (1977)); *see also* secs. 1.1502–21A(f), 1.1502–12, Income Tax Regs.

Calculating consolidated taxable income requires an affiliated group to combine its members' separate taxable incomes, as defined in section 1.1502–12, Income Tax Regs., into one unitary amount. *See* sec. 1.1502–11, Income Tax Regs. Section 11, on the other hand, provides different taxing regimes, one for qualified personal service corporations and another for corporations that are not qualified personal service corporations. Thus, the resolution of the issue in this case requires us to decide whether we should (1) treat each member of the affiliated group separately and break the affiliated group's consolidated taxable income into separate baskets: one for the income of the qualified personal service corporation and another for the other corporation or (2) treat the affiliated group as a single entity and not break up the affiliated group's consolidated taxable income into separate baskets.

---

respondent states he took a "more conservative approach in this case to allow the members to net their income before applying the qualified personal service corporation tax rate". Because of respondent's concession, we need not and do not consider netting losses against qualified personal service corporation income.

Respondent asserts that where one member of an affiliated group is a qualified personal service corporation and another is not, the consolidated taxable income of the affiliated group must be broken up into two separate baskets. Respondent argues that section 448 requires that the determination as to whether a corporation is a qualified personal service corporation is to be made at the entity level, not at the level of the affiliated group. Further, respondent posits that the Code provides for treating qualified personal service corporate members of an affiliated group differently from other members. We disagree.

Although section 448(d)(4) provides special rules by which members of an affiliated group may determine their status as a qualified personal service corporation in electing whether to use the cash method of accounting, it provides no illumination as to the rate of tax to be applied to the consolidated taxable income of the entire group. Nor does section 448(d)(4) provide support for the proposition that the consolidated taxable income of an affiliated group is to be broken up into separate baskets.

Respondent maintains that because Applied Research is a qualified personal service corporation, when considered alone, it holds a "special status". Respondent asserts that when a member of an affiliated group has a "special status", the tax applicable to that member is calculated and added to the non-special-status members' tax under section 11. This, respondent claims, is the regime provided by paragraphs (b) through (j) of section 1.1502–2, Income Tax Regs. To support this assertion, respondent cites section 1.1502–2(g), Income Tax Regs., which adds the tax imposed by section 831(a) on consolidated insurance company taxable income to the tax liability of the affiliated group. Respondent posits that just as insurance company income is taxed separately from the affiliated group's consolidated taxable income, qualified personal service corporation income is to be taxed separately from the affiliated group's consolidated taxable income. We disagree.

Paragraphs (b) through (j) of section 1.1502–2, Income Tax Regs., enumerate taxes to be added to an affiliated group's tax liability. Qualified personal service corporate income is not one of the enumerated special types of income. Indeed, far from providing qualified personal service corporations with special status, section 1.1502–2(a), Income Tax Regs., includes the income of qualified personal service corporations in the affiliated group's consolidated taxable income.

Respondent next argues that Applied Research and Oak Crest are, in reality, two separate corporations that have been permitted to file a consolidated return. Respondent analogizes the facts in this case to the facts in *Specialty Rests. Corp. v. Commissioner*, T.C. Memo. 1992–221. In *Specialty Rests. Corp.*, the taxpayer (a parent corporation) incurred startup costs for its subsidiary restaurants. On its tax return, the taxpayer deducted these preopening costs under section 162. We rejected the taxpayer's position, finding that the subsidiaries were separate legal entities. We thus held that the expenses were preopening expenses of the subsidiaries and represented capital contributions by a parent corporation to its subsidiaries.

The facts of *Specialty Rests. Corp.* are distinguishable from those in the instant matter. In rejecting the taxpayer's position, we emphasized that the subsidiaries had not begun operations at the time the expenses were incurred and thus the subsidiaries' expenses were not properly deductible under section 162. In this case, Applied Research and Oak Crest, as members of an affiliated group filing a consolidated return, were operating companies, and respondent has conceded that Applied Research and Oak Crest are permitted to net their incomes and expenses.

Petitioner argues that the affiliated group must be examined as a single, unitary entity for purposes of determining the proper tax rate to be applied to the affiliated group's consolidated taxable income. Petitioner's primary argument is that there is no guidance in the Code, the regulations, or other authority regarding the method of establishing the proper rate or rates of tax on consolidated taxable income where one member, but not all members, of the affiliated group is a qualified personal service corporation. While petitioner is correct that there is no guidance with respect to such a situation, acceptance of petitioner's position is fraught with danger. Section 11(b) was intended to deny the benefits of graduated corporate income tax rates to qualified personal service corporations. *See* RA 1987 sec. 10224(a); H.R. Rept. No. 100–391 (Part 2), at 1097 (1987). Although we can envision circumstances where this intent could be circumvented by petitioner's position, we are nevertheless compelled to find in favor of petitioner.

Our conclusion is bolstered by our holding in *Woods Inv. Co. v. Commissioner*, 85 T.C. 274 (1985). In that matter, the taxpayer filed a consolidated return for itself and its four wholly owned subsidiaries. The subsidiaries used accelerated depreciation as provided by section 1.1502–32, Income Tax Regs. However, when the taxpayer parent sold the subsidiaries, it determined its basis in the subsidiaries' stock using straight-line depreciation as provided by section 312(k). The Commissioner determined that the taxpayer's straight-line depreciation gave it a "double deduction" and reduced the taxpayer's basis in the subsidiaries' stock.

We rejected the Commissioner's position and sustained the taxpayer's basis adjustments. We noted that section 312(k) was enacted after section 1.1502–32, Income Tax Regs., was promulgated; that the Commissioner was aware of the interplay between section 312(k) of the Code and section 1.1502–32, Income Tax Regs.; and that the Commissioner had failed to amend his regulations to reflect his litigating position. *Woods Inv. Co. v. Commissioner*, 85 T.C. at 281. We stated:

> If respondent believes that his regulations and section 312(k) together cause petitioner to receive a "double deduction," then respondent should use his broad power to amend his regulations. *See Henry C. Beck Builders, Inc. v. Commissioner*, 41 T.C. 616, 628 (1964). Since respondent has not taken steps to amend his regulations, we believe his apparent reluctance to use his broad power in this area does not justify judicial interference in what it essentially a legislative and administrative matter. *Henry C. Beck Builders, Inc. v. Commissioner, supra* (Drennen, J., concurring at page 633). [*Id.* at 282.]

See also Gottesman & Co. v. Commissioner, 77 T.C. 1149, 1158 (1981) (refusing to "fill in the gaps" in the regulations with respect to the imposition of accumulated earnings tax on corporations filing consolidated returns).

In computing the proper tax liability of an affiliated group, we begin with section 1.1502–2, Income Tax Regs. Section 1.1502–2(a), Income Tax Regs., does not distinguish between taxable income under section 11(b)(1) and (2), and we find no authority to permit the breakup of an affiliated group's consolidated taxable income into separate baskets. We look to the affiliated group as a whole, i.e., the entity which generated the consolidated taxable income, to determine the characterization of the consolidated taxable income. And in this regard, the parties agree that, when viewed as a whole, Applied Research's affiliated group is not a qualified personal service corporation.

To conclude, we hold that in the situation involved herein, graduated rates set forth in section 11(b)(1) should be applied to the affiliated group's consolidated taxable income. In reaching our holding, we have considered all of the contentions and arguments of the parties that are not discussed herein, and we find them to be either without merit, irrelevant, or moot.

To reflect the foregoing,

Decision will be entered for petitioner.

KENNA TRADING, LLC, JETSTREAM BUSINESS LIMITED, TAX MATTERS PARTNER, ET AL., PETITIONERS[1] *v.* COMMISSIONER OF INTERNAL REVENUE, RESPONDENT

Docket Nos. 7551–08, 7552–08, 7553–08, 7554–08, 7555–08, 7556–08, 7618–08, 7625–08, 9021–08, 9035–08, 9036–08, 9037–08, 9038–08, 9039–08, 9040–08, 9041–08, 9042–08, 9121–08, 9122–08, 9123–08, 9124–08, 9125–08, 9126–08, 9127–08, 9128–08, 14094–08, 16796–08, 19924–08, 19925–08, 13980–09, 13981–09, 13982–09, 13983–09, 27636–09, 30586–09, 671–10.

Filed October 16, 2014.

Brazilian retailers purportedly contributed distressed consumer receivables to a limited liability company, S, treated as

[1] Cases of petitioners listed in the appendix remain consolidated herewith. Other petitioners have settled their cases with respondent, and therefore their cases have been severed since the trial of these cases

a partnership for Federal income tax purposes. S claims carryover bases in these receivables under I.R.C. sec. 723. In 2004 S in turn contributed some of these Brazilian receivables to trading companies and contributed its interest in each trading company to a holding company. S claimed a cost of goods sold for each holding company equal to the basis of the receivables contributed. S then sold an interest in each holding company to an investor. The trading companies claimed bad debt deductions. In 2005 S allegedly contributed more of the Brazilian receivables to main trusts. Each main trust then assigned the receivables to a newly created subtrust. Investors allegedly contributed cash to the main trust in exchange for the beneficial interest in the subtrust. The subtrust claimed a bad debt deduction. Asserting that the subtrusts were, for Federal income tax purposes, grantor trusts, the investors claimed deductions on their tax returns. Mr. Rogers, the creator of the investment program, also invested in such a trust. R disallowed the bad debt deductions, adjusted S' income for 2004 alleging that S inflated its cost of goods sold, determined that S failed to include all items of income in its gross receipts for 2004 and 2005, and disallowed S' business expense deductions. R also determined I.R.C. sec. 6662(h) gross valuation misstatement penalties against S, the trading companies, and Mr. and Mrs. Rogers, I.R.C. sec. 6662(a) accuracy-related penalties on the amounts of S' underpayments due to increased gross receipts for unreported income and the disallowed deductions, and an I.R.C. sec. 6662A listed transaction understatement penalty against S for the 2005 taxable year. *Held*: The Brazilian retailers did not intend to enter into a partnership for Federal income tax purposes. *Held*, *further*, S had a cost basis, not a carryover basis, in the receivables. *Held*, *further*, the transactions in issue lacked economic substance. *Held*, *further*, the trading companies are not entitled to I.R.C. sec. 166 deductions. *Held*, *further*, Mr. and Mrs. Rogers purchased their beneficial interest in the subtrust and are not entitled to a carryover basis. *Held*, *further*, R properly disallowed the Rogerses' claimed I.R.C. sec. 166 deduction. *Held*, *further*, S overstated its cost of goods sold. *Held*, *further*, R correctly adjusted S' income to reflect certain unreported deposits. *Held*, *further*, S is not entitled to the disallowed deductions. *Held*, *further*, S and the trading companies are liable for the I.R.C. sec. 6662(h) gross valuation misstatement penalty. *Held*, *further*, S is liable for an I.R.C. sec. 6662(a) and (b) accuracy-related penalty on the underpayments attributable to the omitted items of income and the disallowed deductions. *Held*, *further*, R's I.R.C. sec. 6662A listed transaction understatement pen-

took place.

alty against S is sustained insofar as related to the income from the trust transactions.

John E. Rogers (an officer), for petitioner Jetstream Business Limited.

John E. Rogers, for petitioners John E. and Frances L. Rogers.

Ronald S. Collins, Jr., *Laurie A. Nasky*, and *Bernard J. Audet, Jr.*, for respondent.

Michael D. Hartigan (an officer), for participating partners in docket Nos. 7552–08, 9039–08, 9121–08, and 13982–09.

WHERRY, *Judge*: In 2003 John Rogers developed, marketed, and sold investments, which also allegedly provided potential tax shelter, whereby investors in a partnership structure could claim partially worthless bad debt deductions under section 166[2] on certain distressed assets formerly owned by a Brazilian retailer. Those transactions did not produce the hoped-for tax benefits for the myriad of reasons outlined in our prior opinions and by the Court of Appeals for the Seventh Circuit. *See Superior Trading, LLC v. Commissioner*, 137 T.C. 70 (2011), *supplemented by* T.C. Memo. 2012–110, *aff'd*, 728 F.3d 676 (7th Cir. 2013). In 2004 Mr. Rogers sold the same shelter, this time using additional distressed assets of other Brazilian retailers. That same year, Congress modified the rules governing the allocation of built-in loss property contributed to a partnership, rendering the partnership flow-through loss-shifting shelter impotent.[3] Undeterred, for various transactions entered into after October 22, 2004, Mr. Rogers selected and used a trust structure to attempt to gain the same tax benefits for himself and various investor-clients.

Respondent has challenged all of the partially worthless bad debt deductions under section 166, for the partnerships[4]

---

[2] All section references are to the Internal Revenue Code of 1986 (Code), as amended and in effect for the tax years at issue, and all Rule references are to the U.S. Tax Court Rules of Practice and Procedure.

[3] The American Jobs Creation Act of 2004 (AJCA), Pub. L. No. 108–357, sec. 833, 118 Stat. at 1589, amended secs. 704, 734, and 743 effective for transactions entered into after October 22, 2004. Sec. 704 as amended provides that in the case of contributions of built-in loss property to a partnership, the built-in loss may be taken into account only by the contributing partner and may not be allocated to a different partner.

[4] Mr. Rogers used limited liability companies in these transactions. In

involved in the 2004 tax year[5] as well as for Mr. Rogers and his wife, Frances Rogers, who claimed a section 166 deduction on their individual tax return for 2005 using the trust variant. We consolidated the Rogerses' case with the partnership cases for the purpose of resolving only the section 166 deduction issue in that case.[6]

Respondent also challenged certain aspects of the 2004 and 2005 partnership returns of Sugarloaf Fund, LLC (Sugarloaf), the common ancestor in the many-branched family tree of partnerships and trusts through which inves-

---

part because they are treated as partnerships for Federal income tax purposes, *see* sec. 301.7701–3(a), Proced. & Admin. Regs., we refer to them as such.

[5] One partnership, Zurichsee Trading, LLC, docket No. 13980–09, claimed a sec. 166 deduction on its 2005 Federal income tax return, and respondent issued a notice of final partnership administrative adjustment (FPAA) for this year.

[6] Mr. Rogers on brief asserts that his wife is entitled to innocent spouse relief. We did not try this issue and do not decide it here. We likewise do not decide whether respondent properly determined penalties against the Rogerses.

Along with Mr. Rogers, Gary R. Fears, petitioner in docket No. 27636–09, invested in the trust structure in 2005. As with the Rogerses' case, we consolidated Mr. Fears' case solely for the purpose of resolving the sec. 166 deduction at issue there. Although Mr. Fears and respondent have entered into a stipulation of settled issues concerning the deficiencies in his case, the secs. 6662(a) and (h) and 6662A penalties allegedly flowing from those deficiencies, which themselves stem from the sec. 166 deduction's disallowance, remain in dispute. Mr. Fears' case remains consolidated for purposes of this Opinion because our redetermination in this partnership-level proceeding of penalties determined against Sugarloaf could potentially affect Mr. Fears, notwithstanding that he held an interest in a lower tier entity. *See* sec. 6226(f); *United States v. Woods*, 571 U.S. ____, ____, 134 S. Ct. 557, 564 (2013) (holding "that TEFRA gives courts in partnership-level proceedings jurisdiction to determine the applicability of any penalty that could result from an adjustment to a partnership item, even if imposing the penalty would also require determining affected or nonpartnership items such as outside basis"). Mr. Fears resides in St. Louis, Missouri, which lies within the jurisdiction of the U.S. Court of Appeals for the Eighth Circuit. Before *Woods*, that Court of Appeals held, in the context of a gross valuation misstatement penalty determined against a sham partnership, that "outside basis is an affected item that must be determined at the partner level" before a penalty determined at the partnership level may be imposed. *See Thompson v. Commissioner*, 729 F.3d 869, 873 (2013), *rev'g and remanding* 137 T.C. 220 (2011). Thus, as stated in our order of May 3, 2013, we intend to return Mr. Fears' case to the general docket after issuance of this Opinion.

tors in Mr. Rogers' shelters claimed tax losses. First, respondent alleges that Sugarloaf overstated its cost of goods sold for 2004 and 2005 on account of inflated tax bases of sold partnership interests. In addition, after concessions, respondent alleges adjustments to Sugarloaf's partnership income due to alleged underreported income of $299,996 and $925,467 for the 2004 and 2005 taxable years, respectively.[7] Respondent also disallowed a number of Sugarloaf's claimed deductions, amounting to $747,069 for the 2004 tax year and $982,436 for the 2005 tax year, as unsubstantiated.

Respondent determined against Sugarloaf for each tax year a section 6662(a) and (h) penalty for a gross valuation misstatement, a section 6662(a) penalty on the amount of the underpayment attributable to each year's disallowed deductions, and a section 6662A penalty for understatements attributable to undisclosed reportable or listed transactions. Against the lower tier partnerships whose cases were tried with Sugarloaf's, respondent determined penalties under section 6662(a) and (h) due to gross valuation misstatements and section 6662(a) and (b)(1), (2), and (3) penalties due to negligence, substantial understatements of income tax, and substantial valuation misstatements.

Jetstream, as tax matters partner for Sugarloaf and each of the other partnerships whose cases we consolidated with Sugarloaf's for trial, petitioned this Court for readjustment of partnership items and redetermination of penalties.[8]

In this Opinion, we resolve: (1) whether Jetstream and the Brazilian retailers formed a bona fide partnership for Federal income tax purposes for purposes of servicing and collecting distressed consumer receivables owed to the retailers; (2) whether the Brazilian retailers made valid contributions of the receivables to the purported partnership under section 721; (3) whether the retailers' claimed contributions to and subsequent redemptions from Sugarloaf should be collapsed

[7] Respondent and Jetstream Business Limited (Jetstream), Sugarloaf's tax matters partner, entered into a stipulation of settled issues reducing the unreported income from $1,549,692 for 2004 and $1,227,467 for 2005 to the amounts stated above.

[8] Jetstream was represented in this litigation by its officer, Mr. Rogers, who also represented himself and his wife in their consolidated individual tax case. Throughout this Opinion, we frequently refer to petitioners, whether jointly or individually, simply as Mr. Rogers.

into a single transaction and treated as a sale of the receivables, such that the receivables had a cost basis under section 1012 rather than a carryover basis under section 723; (4) whether the 2004 partnership transactions had economic substance; (5) whether the 2004 partnership transactions satisfied the statutory prerequisites for a section 166 deduction; (6) whether the 2005 trust transactions should be collapsed into sales or lacked economic substance, such that Mr. and Mrs. Rogers' trust investment would not entitle them to a section 166 deduction for 2005; (7) whether Sugarloaf understated gross income for the 2004 and 2005 tax years; (8) whether Sugarloaf is entitled to various deductions for the 2004 and 2005 tax years; (9) whether Sugarloaf and the other partnerships are liable for section 6662(a) penalties; and (10) whether Sugarloaf is liable for the section 6662A penalty.

We hold for respondent on all issues. [9]

FINDINGS OF FACT

The parties' stipulation of facts, supplemental stipulation of facts, and second supplemental stipulation of facts, all with the facts found from the accompanying exhibits, are incorporated herein by this reference, as are all stipulations of settled issues filed in various of these consolidated cases. [10] The parties have stipulated that venue for appeal would be the Court of Appeals for the Seventh Circuit.

I. *The Mastermind: John E. Rogers*

The central individual in these cases is John Rogers. During the years at issue Mr. Rogers was a partner at the Chicago-based law firm Seyfarth Shaw. As we have previously found, Mr. Rogers

---

[9] With regard to Sugarloaf, our analyses and holdings as to questions (1)–(5) represent alternative reasons, all of which, when applied, result in the same ultimate tax result. Similarly, with regard to the trust shelter, we offer alternative analyses and holdings on question (6).

[10] Petitioners objected to a number of the stipulations and stipulated exhibits on the grounds of relevance. According to Fed. R. Evid. R. 401: "Evidence is relevant if: (a) it has any tendency to make a fact more or less probable than it would be without the evidence; and (b) the fact is of consequence in determining the action." We find the stipulations and stipulated exhibits relevant and consequently overrule petitioners' objections.

> started his professional career in 1969 at the now-dissolved accounting firm Arthur Andersen, where he rose through the ranks to eventually become an equity partner. [Mr.] Rogers left Arthur Andersen in 1991 and went to work for a startup medical device company called Reddy Laboratories. The venture failed after the Food and Drug Administration denied the company's application for a license. In 1992 [Mr.] Rogers joined FMC Corp., a $5 billion company with operations in over 100 countries. [Mr.] Rogers served as FMC Corp.'s director of taxes and assistant treasurer through 1997.
>
> In 1998 [Mr.] Rogers became an equity partner in Altheimer & Gray, a full-service law firm headquartered in Chicago, Illinois, with offices in Eastern Europe. Altheimer & Gray dissolved in 2003, and [Mr.] Rogers joined the Seyfarth Shaw, LLP (Seyfarth Shaw), law firm in July of that year. * * * [Mr.] Rogers left Seyfarth at the end of May 2008, when he opened his own firm, Rogers & Associates.
>
> [*Superior Trading, LLC v. Commissioner*, 137 T.C. at 75.]

Mr. Rogers during or before 2003 conceived a plan that he contended would successfully invest in and manage distressed retail consumer receivables overseas and remit the proceeds to the United States. He used a tiered partnership structure in 2003 and most of 2004 and a tiered trust structure in 2005, 2006, and 2007 to sell interests to individual investors. Mr. Rogers contended the business would profit through aggressive collection efforts, translation gain from currency speculation, and a planned initial public offering. The first step under this plan was for Brazilian retailers to "contribute" receivables to a limited liability entity controlled by Mr. Rogers, which, for U.S. tax purposes, would accede to the tax basis of the retailers in the consumer debt.

In 2003 he used a limited liability company called Warwick Trading, LLC, to purchase receivables from Lojas Arapua, S.A. (Arapua), a Brazilian retailer of household appliances and consumer electronics. In 2004 he used a different limited liability company, Sugarloaf, to which two other Brazilian retailers, Globex Utilidades, S.A. (Globex), and Companhia Brasileira de Distribuição (CBD), also "contributed" distressed accounts receivable for interests in that company. In 2004 Sugarloaf contributed a tranche of those assets to other limited liability companies (trading companies). Sugarloaf then contributed most or all of its interest in the trading companies to yet other limited liability companies (holding companies). In 2005 Sugarloaf "contributed" assets to trusts (main trusts), which each created another trust (subtrust). The main trust assigned the beneficial interests of the receivables in the subtrust to an investor who contributed money to the main trust. In both years Sugarloaf and the trading companies entered loan management and servicing agreements with a British Virgin Islands company called Multicred Investments Limited and/or a Brazilian company called Multicred Investimentos Limitada. Renato Mazzucchelli and Jennifer Dowek were both intimately involved in the management and operation if not also the ownership of these companies. While the parties dispute the significance of these two companies and Mr. Rogers alleges that the British Virgin Islands company engaged in some sort of scheme to defraud, such a dispute is irrelevant to these cases, and we find that for practical purposes the companies are the same and refer to them interchangeably as Multicred.

Mr. Rogers formed Sugarloaf through entities he owned and controlled. He was the sole owner of an S corporation, Portfolio Properties, Inc. (PPI), which owned Jetstream, at that time a British Virgin Islands company. On April 17, 2003, Mr. Rogers, through Jetstream, formed Sugarloaf, a Delaware limited liability company. According to the operating agreement, Jetstream was the initial manager. On July 23, 2003, Mr. Rogers sent an engagement letter to Mr. Mazzucchelli as “Managing Member” of Sugarloaf by which Sugarloaf agreed to retain Seyfarth Shaw as its legal counsel. In August Mr. Rogers represented to Seyfarth Shaw that the owners of Sugarloaf were Mr. Mazzucchelli and Ms. Dowek. He never disclosed Jetstream’s ownership, which was 100% at that time.

II. *The Receivables: The Brazilian Connection*

A. *Arapua*

On July 1, 2004, Sugarloaf and Arapua entered into a contribution agreement by which Arapua agreed to “contribute” distressed consumer receivables with an outstanding balance of R$37,765,501 to Sugarloaf in exchange for a 99% membership interest.[11] Sugarloaf later disposed of these receivables

[11] When we refer to receivables of the three Brazilian retailers, we refer to checks written by consumers for products. Brazilian companies at the time generally lacked sufficient purchase-with-financing installment sales

Continued

in a transaction not necessarily at issue in these cases. Mr. Rogers signed this contribution agreement as manager of Sugarloaf.

B. *Globex*

In July 2004 Sugarloaf entered into a contribution agreement with Globex, a consumer-goods retailer doing business under the name Ponto Frio. According to the contribution agreement, Globex contributed receivables with an outstanding balance of R$219,087,756.03 in exchange for a 99% membership interest in Sugarloaf. Mr. Rogers signed this agreement as manager of Sugarloaf.[12]

The parties provided three versions of the contribution agreement: a Portuguese version, a certified English translation of that version, and the English version provided by Mr. Rogers. A cursory comparison of the certified English translation and Mr. Rogers' version reveals that Mr. Rogers' and the Portuguese versions are not reliable translations of one another. One difference is that, according to the certified English translation, Sugarloaf represented that it "is aware that, for purposes of Brazilian law, taxes were lowered for accounting and tax purposes for the majority of the tax credits of most objects of this instrument, although it had not been lowered for the purpose of American law." The version

facilities and in lieu thereof had the practice of extending credit to consumers whereby the consumer would write a series of postdated checks and the retailer would deposit those checks on the appropriate day. The receivables in these cases are distressed, meaning that they are past due. The average age of the sampled receivables as of the date of contribution to Sugarloaf was 5.2 years in the case of CBD and 6.6 years in the case of Globex. The contributed receivables' value in Brazilian reais was not stated in the CBD contribution agreement but was to be provided in a schedule I to the agreement. However, no schedule I was attached to the translated version of the agreement Mr. Rogers placed in evidence and submitted to the Court. The same was true of the translated Globex contribution agreement offered by Mr. Rogers, discussed *infra* p. 331.

[12] According to the Arapua contribution agreement, Arapua already owned 99% of Sugarloaf. The transfer of a 99% interest to Globex is a mathematical impossibility. And, as discussed *infra* pp. 332–334, CBD entered a contribution agreement whereby it ostensibly received a 17% membership interest. Mr. Rogers contends that the subsequent contribution agreements merely diluted the previous ownership. But these numbers cannot be reconciled, and they support our finding, *see infra* pp. 351–353, that the parties did not intend to form a partnership.

provided by Mr. Rogers lacks identical or even analogous language.

Mr. Rogers' version of the contribution agreement purported to have attached an exhibit A which set forth all of the receivables contributed. The certified English translation included an annex I, which stated in part: "The data related to the Credits are recorded on a CD–Rom delivered in this act by GLOBEX to the Fund [Sugarloaf]". The parties stipulated that neither exhibit A nor the media referenced in annex I were attached to the agreements.

One of the individuals promoting the shelter for Mr. Rogers, Michael Hartigan, sent money in 2004 to Multicred, which passed on a portion of that money to Globex as indicated in a January 5, 2005, email from Ms. Dowek to Mr. Rogers. These payments were, in Mr. Rogers' own words, "constructive distributions from Warwick or Sugarloaf." In 2005 Mr. Hartigan sent money received from the investors, less his fees, directly to the credit of the trusts.[13]

At some point, Globex requested a partial redemption of its membership interest. Initially Globex requested a 13.24% partial redemption and apparently later requested a larger or complete redemption. In the spring of 2006 Ms. Dowek sent two emails to Mr. Rogers telling him that Globex needed documentation showing the sale of its interest in Sugarloaf. On December 15, 2006, Mr. Rogers wired $300,000 to a bank account in the name of Globalstores, S.A. A week or so later, Ms. Dowek wrote the following to Mr. Rogers: "Bought more from Globex . . . Global Store . . . so please send $650K instead of $350K." Mr. Rogers agreed and on December 28, 2006, wired an additional $650,000 to the account of Globalstores, S.A. Further correspondence between Mr. Rogers and the various parties involved in these transactions demonstrates an intent to redeem Globex out of Sugarloaf.

In April 2007 Mr. Rogers expressed concerns to Multicred that Globex never transferred the distressed assets to Sugarloaf. He asked Multicred for proof of a transfer before 2006, which was when collections on the Globex receivables began. The parties stipulated that Globex retained custody of the receivables until at least March 28, 2007.

---

[13] *See infra* pp. 342–344.

C. *CBD*

In the fall of 2004 Sugarloaf and Multicred were negotiating the acquisition of receivables from another Brazilian retailer, CBD, a large supermarket chain in Brazil which operated some stores under the brand name Pão de Açúcar.[14] Early drafts of agreements from Multicred indicate that as of August 3, 2004, Sugarloaf and CBD intended to enter into a purchase-sale agreement. On October 1, 2004, Sugarloaf and Multicred entered into a contribution agreement with CBD. Once again, there are several versions of this contribution agreement: one copy in Portuguese, a certified English translation of the Portuguese version, and an English-language version provided by Mr. Rogers. While, from their cover pages, the Portuguese version and Mr. Rogers' version appear to be translations of one another, a cursory examination of the format of the body of the agreement in each version quickly reveals that they are not accurate translations.

The certified English translation only confirms that Mr. Rogers' version and the Portuguese version are different documents. The certified translation and Mr. Rogers' version both state that CBD received a 17% membership interest in Sugarloaf in exchange for a contribution of receivables contracts. Mr. Rogers' version indicates that the subject receivables contracts are listed in schedule I, which itself refers to an attached "diskette" (although apparently Mr. Rogers never received a copy), while the certified translation includes an annex I which references a contemporaneously delivered CD–ROM and provides a detailed key to the data supposedly contained thereon. Mr. Rogers' version and the certified translation both state that the receivables had an outstanding balance of R$154,630,651.15. Only the certified translation, however, discloses that the *value* of these receivables was R$1,855,568. Further, according to the certified translation, the Portuguese document is an agreement between CBD, Sugarloaf (with Mr. Rogers signing as manager), and Multicred (with Mr. Mazzucchelli signing on its behalf). Mr. Rogers' version, however, is an agreement between only CBD and Sugarloaf, with Mr. Rogers again

[14] The parties often refer to CBD as CBD/PDA or PDA. For convenience, we use CBD.

signing as manager. Finally, Mr. Rogers' version contains a representation by CBD that it had not taken action with respect to the receivables that would constitute a charge-off under section 166. The certified translation contains no such representation.

Sugarloaf, CBD, and Multicred entered the contribution agreement with the understanding that CBD would be redeemed out for cash shortly. On December 22, 2004, Sugarloaf loaned Multicred $800,000 pursuant to a promissory note. According to an October 21, 2007, email from Mr. Rogers: "The $800,000 was used to redeem out PDA."[15] Multicred then purchased CBD's 17% interest in Sugarloaf for R$1,855,568 on December 29, 2004. On October 14, 2005, Multicred assigned its interest in Sugarloaf to an entity called Sugarloaf Investimentos Limitada (Sugarloaf Limitada), which was owned by Sugarloaf and controlled by Mr. Rogers, in exchange for Sugarloaf Limitada's assumption of the obligations to Sugarloaf under the $800,000 promissory note. Sugarloaf, through Mr. Rogers, was a party to this agreement. On September 22, 2006, Sugarloaf Limitada sold the 17% interest in Sugarloaf back to Sugarloaf, and it paid off three-quarters of the promissory note. Mr. Rogers signed this agreement on behalf of both Sugarloaf and Sugarloaf Limitada. Sugarloaf Limitada paid the remaining balance due on the note in 2007. The Sugarloaf purchase agreement refers to these transactions as "stage" or "stages".

In addition, the record contains hints that a shadow investment group may have been involved in the purchase of the CBD receivables. An email from Ms. Dowek says: "[W]e will have four or five investors purchasing their [CBD's] interest and * * * Multicred will act as agent for them." Additional documents implicate an entity named Sugarloaf Overseas, Ltd. (Sugarloaf Overseas), in this shadow investment group; it received $1 million from Sugarloaf as payment for assets on or about February 26, 2006. Mr. Rogers repeatedly denied knowing Sugarloaf Overseas and claimed that he could remember no reason why Sugarloaf would have made the $1 million transfer. We do not credit his testimony and believe that Mr. Rogers knew, at the time, what Sugarloaf Overseas

[15] PDA and CBD are one and the same. *See supra* note 14.

was and also what its role was, however murky to us, in the CBD buyout.

D. *Collections*

As mentioned, collections on the Globex receivables did not begin until 2006 at the earliest. As for the other receivables, Multicred did not have collection data available for 2004. Mr. Rogers therefore used R$2,656, or about USD$1,000, as the collections reported for each investor in 2004.

E. *Valuation and Performance*

Sugarloaf received valuations for the CBD and the Globex receivables from Financial Management Control, Ltda. (FMC). Both these letters were dated October 1, 2004, but the parties stipulated that Sugarloaf did not receive the letters until 2007. The letters are almost identical. The FMC letter for Globex opined that the fair market value of the receivables, which had an average age of six to seven years and average balance of R$500, was 6% of the notional face value amount. FMC concluded that the CBD receivables had an average age of three years and average balance of R$300 and were also worth 6% of the notional face value amount. These appraisal letters bear a remarkable similarity to an appraisal letter written by a company called Lourenço Assessoria e Recuperadora de Crédito Ltda. (LARC) for Warwick. The LARC appraisal letter purported to appraise Arapua receivables at, again, 6% of the notional face value amount.

At the trial and without objection, respondent offered John D. Finnerty as an expert in valuation of fixed income investments. The Court accepted Dr. Finnerty as such an expert and received his report into evidence. Dr. Finnerty used a discounted cashflow method which took into account similar assets, expected net cashflow, and the collection expenses at the time of acquisition. He concluded that the Globex receivables had a fair market value of at most 0.5% of the notional face value amount and that the CBD receivables had a fair market value of at most 0.8% of the notional face value amount.

Dr. Finnerty also dismissed the FMC valuations as being internally inconsistent and containing flawed reasoning. For example, the FMC valuations purport to use the comparables method, the replacement method, and the discounted cashflow method to arrive at the 6% figure. But the letters state that the comparables method yields a 2% to 4% valuation and the replacement method yields a 2% valuation for the CBD receivables and a 3% valuation for the Globex receivables. The letters do not discuss a specific value determined using the discounted cashflow method and why such a method would result in higher valuations. So, it is not clear how FMC arrived at the 6% valuations. Furthermore, the FMC letters purport to affirm the discounted cashflow analysis provided by Multicred without mentioning what valuation that method yields. Finally, FMC fails to explain why it gave identical valuations to two sets of receivables despite significantly different characteristics, such as the age and average balance per account of the receivables. The Court is left to assume that the $200 higher average balance of the Globex receivables exactly balanced out the fact that their average age was three to four years older than the CBD receivables so that each group was worth 6% of face.

At trial and without objection, the Court accepted respondent's witness Martin D. Hanan as an expert in business valuation and received his report into evidence. Mr. Hanan's extensive report opined as to the expected and actual pretax and after-tax rates of return from the investments at issue in these cases. He reviewed the amounts paid by investors, the collections allegedly made, and other data. He concluded that an after-tax rate of return was positive only because of the tax benefit afforded by the section 166 deduction. Mr. Hanan concluded that the exorbitant fees and the exchange rate at the time of the origination of the receivables contributed heavily to the negative pretax rates of return. Only Mr. Hartigan's investment, on his own behalf, stood a chance of realizing a profit because Mr. Hartigan waived his own fee. Mr. Hannan concluded that a reasonable investor would not have invested in this transaction but for the tax benefit. The Court does note that Mr. Hannan's analysis assumes a constant exchange rate of 2.00 Brazilian reais to the U.S. dollar. Mr. Rogers with some reasonable basis for his conclusions believed the Brazilian real was undervalued and would appreciate vis-a-vis the dollar within a reasonable investment period. Investors may have thought likewise.

F. *Other Problems With the Receivables*

At trial and without objection, the Court accepted respondent's witness Sergio Tostes as an expert in Brazilian commercial taxation law. Mr. Tostes reported that the contribution agreement between Globex and Sugarloaf was illicit under Brazilian law because it purported to assign a 99% interest in Sugarloaf to Globex. According to Mr. Tostes, because Arapua already owned a 99% interest, the Globex contribution agreement was legally impossible. Mr. Tostes opined that the CBD agreement is similarly invalid under Brazilian law.

III. *The 2004 Partnership Structure: Your DAD's Tax Shelter*

The 2004 partnership shelters essentially mirror the Distressed Asset/Debt or "DAD" shelter structure we described in *Superior Trading, LLC v. Commissioner*, 137 T.C. at 71–73.

A. *The Typical Structure*

Mr. Rogers typically structured the 2004 shelters as follows. Jetstream and Sugarloaf would create a trading company, an Illinois limited liability company, with Jetstream contributing a nominal amount of cash (e.g., $1,500) for a 1% membership interest and Sugarloaf contributing distressed assets. The contribution agreement between Sugarloaf and the trading company would state that Sugarloaf was contributing a portfolio of notes. The contribution agreement would also state that exhibit A would set forth the notes contributed, but this exhibit was never prepared for any of the 2004 transactions.[16]

Jetstream and Sugarloaf would then form a holding company, also an Illinois limited liability company, with Jetstream contributing a nominal amount of cash for a 1% interest and Sugarloaf contributing a 99% interest in a trading company in exchange for a 99% interest. Next,

[16] In its reply brief at 114, Jetstream states: "The schedules were prepared and were provided to IRS [Internal Revenue Service] auditors. Mazzucchelli retained the original version." This contention directly contradicts paragraph 147 of the parties' trial stipulation, which states in part: "Exhibit A to the Contribution Agreements between Sugarloaf and each trading company was never prepared." To the extent that Jetstream's objection requests to be relieved of the stipulation, we reject that request.

Sugarloaf would sell its 99% interest or, in some cases, a 98% interest, in the holding company to an investor.[17] Two individuals marketed the Sugarloaf transactions for Mr. Rogers, Mr. Thomas Agresti and Mr. Hartigan. The investor would pay a percentage of the U.S. dollar notional amount of the receivables, and the size of that percentage depended on whether the investor purchased the interest through Mr. Hartigan or Mr. Agresti. Jetstream would retain a 1% interest in each trading company and each holding company and would act as tax matters partner for both companies. Sugarloaf would retain a 1% interest in each trading company and for the most part in each holding company. Numerous iterations of this sequence took place.

The investors' contribution agreements incorrectly stated the value of the outstanding balance of the receivables contributed. For instance, the Bielersee contribution agreement states that Sugarloaf contributed assets with an outstanding balance of R$2,500,000. But, on its Form 1065, U.S. Return of Partnership Income, Bielersee reported a section 166 loss of $2,425,000, or 97% of $2,500,000. That amount, in Brazilian currency, would be greater than R$2,500,000. In any event, the amount contributed to the partnership depended on the size of the tax deduction the investor sought.

Generally, Mr. Agresti's clients paid 8% of the U.S. dollar notional amount, while Mr. Hartigan's clients paid 15%. Of those amounts, between 4% and 5% went to Sugarloaf or PPI as the purchase price of the receivables. Another 2% to 3% represented an amount retained by Sugarloaf for professional and operating expenses. Mr. Rogers gave discounts to his two promoters. Mr. Hartigan paid only 1.75% to Sugarloaf to buy into the shelter, and Mr. Agresti paid 4%. Like the percentage paid, the source of the receivables also depended on

[17] It is not always clear how much of an interest Sugarloaf retained in a particular holding company. The parties stipulated that Sugarloaf retained "for the most part, a 1% interest in each holding company." Jetstream, on brief, contends that "Sugarloaf retained no interest in a holding company." The documentary evidence is similarly contradictory. For example, in the case of Bielersee Trading, LLC (Bielersee), Sugarloaf purported to contribute a 98% interest in Bielersee to Alber Fund, LLC (Alber), in exchange for a 99% membership interest in Alber. Sugarloaf then purported to sell its entire 99% interest in Alber to the investor, RD3J, Ltd.

whose client the investor was. For Mr. Agresti's clients, Sugarloaf contributed CBD receivables. For Mr. Hartigan's clients, Sugarloaf used Globex receivables.

The formation of R B Taylor Trading, LLC (R B Taylor), is an exception from the general pattern. The documents indicate that Warwick, on July 17, 2004, contributed the receivables to R B Taylor in exchange for membership interests; that Warwick, on July 18, 2004, contributed 98% of R B Taylor to a holding company, Chipping Wood Fund, LLC; and that Warwick then sold 99% of the holding company on July 26, 2004, to the investors, Russell and Betsy Taylor. R B Taylor claimed a section 166 bad debt loss of $11,640,000 in 2004. A document purporting to be an inventory of receivables transferred to and owned by R B Taylor lists Globex receivables, which Warwick did not have. The investor was a client of Mr. Hartigan's. We find that, to the extent there was a partnership formed, Sugarloaf, not Warwick, was the initial contributing entity.[18]

In addition to a contribution agreement, each investor also had to enter into a subscription agreement. This agreement allowed the investor to establish sufficient tax basis in the partnership interest to claim the deduction flowing from the anticipated section 166 bad debt charge-off. The amounts of the subscription agreements were generally the same as the U.S. dollar notional amounts of the receivables less any purchase price paid. Some investors used promissory notes in favor of Sugarloaf to obtain the necessary tax basis in their partnership interests.

B. *The Music Stops*

In October 2004 Congress passed the American Jobs Creation Act of 2004 (AJCA), Pub. L. No. 108–357 sec. 833, 118 Stat. at 1589, which sharply curtailed the tax benefits of the partnership structure used by Mr. Rogers and Sugarloaf in 2004 by amending sections 704, 734, and 743. The relevant provisions had an effective date of October 20, 2004. Mr. Rogers determined that if an investor signed a letter of intent to purchase a partnership interest before that date,

[18] We are disappointed that the parties did not provide the Court with a complete rather than a partial copy of R B Taylor's 2004 partnership return, which could have assisted the Court with this finding of fact.

the partner would still be entitled to deduct the built-in losses from subsequently contributed receivables. In addition, if a potential investor signed a letter of intent but then backed out of the deal, Mr. Rogers determined that a new investor could be substituted for the original investor despite not having signed a letter of intent before the effective date of the AJCA.

C. *The Underlying Investors*

Most of the individual investors in these partnerships have settled the underlying tax liability issues. In some cases the investors filed notices of election to participate under section 6226(c) and Rule 245(b) in the Tax Court cases for the trading companies in which they indirectly invested. Most of these investors have settled and have entered into stipulations of settlement with respondent.[19] But these stipulations settle these trading company cases only as to the distributive shares of the settling partners. Furthermore, Mr. Hartigan remains an officer for participating partners in four cases. At trial, Mr. Rogers, Mr. Hartigan, and respondent disagreed as to the proper tax matters partner of Knight Trading, LLC, docket No. 9121–08. We asked the parties to submit status reports on this subject, and only respondent submitted the requested report. Mr. Hartigan did not produce any documentation showing that Paragon Fund, LLC, replaced Jetstream as the tax matters partner of Knight Trading, and in the absence of other evidence, Jetstream is the proper tax matters partner.

In addition, Windmere Fund, LLC, as tax matters partner for Ironwood Trading, LLC, docket No. 19925–08, and respondent have entered into a stipulation of settled issues as to Windmere Fund's partnership items. Jetstream initially filed the petition on behalf of Ironwood Trading. Windmere

[19] Respondent and the following participating partners entered into stipulations of settled issues: Robert Greer, participating partner in docket No. 7555–08; Joel R. Baker, participating partner in docket No. 7625–08; Russell C. Taylor, participating partner in docket No. 9038–08; Mark Herbert, participating partner in docket No. 9124–08; Michael Koretsky, participating partner in docket No. 19924–08; and Thomas Turner, participating partner in docket No. 13980–09.

was subsequently substituted as the tax matters partner.[20] Because Jetstream initially filed the petition and retains a 1% interest in Ironwood, we treat Jetstream as a participating partner in these cases. Likewise, respondent and Arrowhead Fund, LLC, as tax matters partner for Murtensee Trading, LLC, docket No. 9040–08,[21] entered a stipulation of settled issues as to Arrowhead Fund's partnership items. Again, Jetstream was the tax matters partner at the time the petition was filed, and we treat Jetstream as a participating partner in these cases.

Finally, two participating investors have not yet settled: Jonathan Greer, participating as the ultimate investor in Grey Stone Trading, LLC, docket No. 7556–08, and Scott Ray, participating as the ultimate investor in Thornhill Trading, LLC, docket No. 9021–08. They did not appear at trial and have waived any right to participate therein.

D. *Returns and Adjustments*

In 2004, Sugarloaf entered into at least 30 investment deals using the tiered partnership structure described above and distressed assets from Globex and CBD. The trading companies in these deals all filed Forms 1065, which were prepared by an employee of Mr. Rogers, Jonathan Gabel, and signed by Mr. Rogers, and all claimed section 166 deductions. Respondent issued FPAAs in these cases denying the following deductions:

Partnership name	*Bad debt deduction sec. 166*
Bielersee Trading, LLC	$2,425,000
Bodensee Fund, LLC	4,850,000
Connemara Trading Group, LLC	485,000
Cumnor Group, LLC	1,940,000
Davis Fund, LLC	1,660,000
Dent-Blanche Fund, LLC	1,067,000
Essex Fund, LLC	1,940,000
Grey Stone Trading, LLC	485,000

[20] Participating partner Lancer A. Barton represents that he is Ironwood Trading's majority member through one or more pass-through entities, including Windmere, in which he holds at least a majority interest.

[21] Participating partner Christopher H. Brown represents that he is Murtensee Trading's majority member through one or more pass-through entities, including Arrowhead, in which he holds at least a majority interest.

Partnership name	*Bad debt deduction sec. 166*
Grand-Combin Fund, LLC	1,455,000
Harlan Fund, LLC	1,455,000
Ironwood Trading, LLC	970,000
Kenna Trading, LLC	970,000
Knight Trading, LLC	4,365,000
Lakeview Trading, LLC	1,670,000
Larkspur Trading, LLC	970,000
Lyman Trading, LLC	4,850,000
Monte Rosa Trading, LLC	1,940,000
Murtensee Trading, LLC	3,977,000
Northgate Trading, LLC	970,000
Ofenpass Fund, LLC	2,910,000
Remington Trading, LLC	7,275,000
Ridgeway Trading, LLC	485,000
Riversedge Fund, LLC	2,910,000
Saddlebrook Trading, LLC	4,850,000
Suten Fund, LLC	2,910,000
R B Taylor Trading, LLC	11,640,000
Thornhill Trading LLC	485,000
Turnberry Trading LLC	824,500
Warner Fund, LLC	2,260,000
Zugersee Trading, LLC	3,880,000
Zurichsee Trading, LLC	2,538,000
Total	81,411,500

Most trading companies claimed the deduction for 2004. Riversedge Fund, LLC (Riversedge), claimed a $450,000 deduction for 2004 and a $2,460,000 deduction for 2005. [22] Zurichsee Trading, LLC, claimed the deduction for 2005. Zugersee Trading, LLC, claimed a $3,200,000 deduction for 2004 and a $680,000 deduction for 2005. Warner Fund, LLC, claimed a $2,260,000 deduction for 2005. [23]

In most cases, the trading company claimed a deduction equal to 97% of the U.S. dollar notional value of the receivables. In other cases, the investor requested that a smaller deduction be used for that tax year. Respondent timely issued notices of final partnership administrative adjustment (FPAA) to all trading companies disallowing their claimed section 166 losses. Respondent also adjusted to zero deduc-

[22] We note that Riversedge's 2005 tax return is not in the record. We instead rely on the FPAA issued for that year.

[23] Warner Fund, LLC, also claimed a $650,000 deduction on its 2004 tax return. Jetstream's petition for that year, docket No. 19542–08, was dismissed as untimely.

tions claimed for amortization expenses and collection expenses. Petitioners in these partnership cases timely filed petitions for review of the partnership adjustments.[24]

IV. *The 2005 Trust Structure: DAD 2.0*

Because Congress in late 2004 essentially eviscerated Mr. Rogers' 2004 shelter structure, Mr. Rogers moved toward a similar structure that purported to use trusts to reach the same end result. In this structure, two Illinois common law business trusts, a main trust and a subtrust, replaced the holding company and the trading company.

A. *The Typical Structure*

When an investor agreed to purchase the shelter, Sugarloaf would form a main trust with Mr. Rogers as trustee and Sugarloaf as the initial grantor and beneficiary. Each trust would have its own bank account controlled by Mr. Rogers. Sugarloaf would then contribute receivables through a contribution agreement between Mr. Rogers, as trustee of the main trust, and Sugarloaf. The contribution agreement would include a schedule A stating: "See CD Rom disk attached hereto describing the issuer name, date of issuance, outstanding amount and other relevant data." No such media would be attached.

The investor would purchase a beneficial interest in the main trust. Sugarloaf and Mr. Rogers would then create a subtrust, allocate the receivables to the subtrust, and designate the investor as the beneficiary. The investor would also receive a Series 2005–A Beneficial Interest Certificate granting a 100% interest in the rights to the receivables in the trust.

Investors in the trust structure usually paid between 5% and 6% of the notional value of the receivables, which was also the tax basis eventually claimed, plus fees charged by the promoters to obtain their subtrust interests.[25] The purchase money went into the main trust's bank account, but

[24] Jetstream, through its "Director", Mr. Rogers, filed petitions for them as their tax matters partner.

[25] For the 2005 transactions, the investors appear to have paid approximately 5% of the notional value of the receivables plus other fees. Other evidence in the record suggests that for transactions in subsequent tax years, the purchase price was 6%.

over the course of 2005, 2006, and 2007, these amounts were essentially transferred to Sugarloaf. Even though the purchase money went into the bank account Mr. Rogers established for the main trust, the parties to the transaction viewed the transaction as a purchase and not a contribution of money to a trust account. For example, most investors signed an Agreement for Purchase of Trust Beneficial Interest. The compliance booklets, which investors received and signed, cast the transaction as a purchase of a beneficial interest in the main trust.

The investors, pursuant to the agreements creating the subtrusts, had the power to transfer the certificates of beneficial ownership. The only apparent restriction was that an investor had to give notice to the trustee. Furthermore, an investor could at any time choose to revoke and terminate the subtrust in which that investor had acquired an interest. During the revocation and termination, the investor was entitled to direct the disposition of the subtrust assets.

Mr. Rogers prepared and filed for each main trust and each subtrust a Form 1041, U.S. Income Tax Return for Estates and Trusts. The returns indicated that each subtrust was a grantor trust and attached Grantor Information Statements. These statements indicated that the investors were the grantors and listed amounts for collection income, collection expenses, fiduciary expenses, legal expenses, and section 166 deductions. The main trusts' returns indicated that the investors were the beneficiaries and reported no gains or losses.

Respondent issued notices of deficiency to the subtrust investors. Some of these investors petitioned the Court for redetermination. We consolidated some of those cases for trial at the same time as the partnership and Sugarloaf cases. All but Mr. and Mrs. Rogers and Gary R. Fears[26] have settled with respondent, and we have since severed those other individual tax cases from this group.

B. *Sterling Ridge Trust*

Mr. and Mrs. Rogers invested in the Sterling Ridge 2005–A Subtrust through an S corporation wholly owned by Mrs. Rogers, Sterling Ridge, Inc. Mr. Rogers was president of

[26] *See supra* note 6.

Sterling Ridge. Sugarloaf contributed receivables to Sterling Ridge 2005 Trust with a claimed tax basis of $5 million. Sterling Ridge 2005 Trust allocated these receivables to the Sterling Ridge 2005–A Subtrust. Sterling Ridge, Inc., purchased the beneficial interest in Sterling Ridge 2005–A Subtrust for $150,000. Sterling Ridge, Inc., sent the purchase money to the Heritage Bank account of the Sterling Ridge 2005 Trust. Over the course of December 2005 $95,500 was withdrawn from this bank account.

Mr. Rogers filed Forms 1041 for the main trust and the subtrust for the tax years 2005 and 2006. On the subtrust's 2005 Form 1041, he attached a Grantor Information Statement stating that Sterling Ridge, Inc., was the grantor. This statement also listed collection income of $1,518, collection expenses of $304, a fiduciary expense of $1,000, a legal expense of $1,000, and a section 166 expense of $4,850,000. On its 2006 Form 1041, the subtrust reported collecting $39,232 of income and a collection expense of $19,616.

Sterling Ridge, Inc., on its 2005 Form 1120S, U.S. Income Tax Return for an S Corporation, prepared by Mr. Rogers, reported a loss of $3,282,119 almost entirely attributable to the $4,850,000 section 166 deduction.[27] Mr. and Mrs. Rogers reported this loss on their 2005 tax return, which they both signed. Respondent timely issued a notice of deficiency for 2005 disallowing, among other determinations, the section 166 deduction that flowed through from Sterling Ridge. Mr. and Mrs. Rogers timely petitioned this Court for redetermination.

V. *The Section 166 Deduction: Aggregate and Arbitrary*

At no point did the participants in these transactions conduct any kind of study as to which of the receivables should be written down. The individual receivables were not charged off individually. Mr. Gabel's handwritten notes after a 2005 meeting in Brazil reflect the reality that Multicred lacked the resources to conduct a writeoff study. At one point, statistical

[27] Sterling Ridge did not report the collection expense or the fiduciary expense from the 2005 Grantor Information Statement, and it is not clear whether the legal expense and the collection income were included on its return.

sampling was discussed, but such a sampling was never done.

VI. *The Hub: Searching for Sugarloaf*

A. *Uncertain Ownership*

Evidence as to the purported owners of Sugarloaf is contradictory. The three principal sources all provide conflicting information. First, contribution agreements suggest that Jetstream owns a 1% interest in Sugarloaf, Arapua owns a 99% interest in Sugarloaf, Globex owns a 99% interest in Sugarloaf, and CBD owns a 17% interest in Sugarloaf. Second, Sugarloaf's Quickbooks balance sheet for 2003 lists Barnard, CITCO NV, Mr. Rogers, and Teviot as having equity interests in Sugarloaf.[28] The 2004 yearend balance sheet shows the same equity owners. The 2005 yearend balance sheet reflects that the following entities and persons owned equity in Sugarloaf: Barnard, CITCO NV, Mr. Rogers, Multicred, Sugarloaf Overseas, and Teviot. Mr. Rogers testified that Barnard, CITCO NV, and Teviot all made equity investments in Sugarloaf. He also stated that the balance sheets, with the 2005 yearend balance sheet time-stamped October 2006, reflected only equity deposits that had been recorded up to that point and that the equity portion of the balance sheets was irrelevant. Third and finally, Schedules K–1, Partner's Share of Income, Deductions, Credits, etc., filed with Sugarloaf's 2004 and 2005 tax returns claimed that Jetstream was a 1% capital and 0.1% profit and loss owner, Warwick a 1% capital and 0.1% profit and loss owner, CBD a 49% capital and 49.9% profit and loss owner, and Globex a 49% capital and 49.9% profit and loss owner.

Additional evidence provides no clarity. With respect to Teviot and Barnard, a May 3, 2005, email from Mr. Mazzucchelli to Mr. Rogers lists investors in Sugarloaf. These investors were Andrew Barnard for $100,000, Teviot Investments, Ltd., for $100,000, and Warwick for $100,000. Sugarloaf's bank accounts show wire transfer deposits in

[28] According to Mr. Rogers, Teviot is Teviot Investments, Ltd., a company related to Mr. Mazzuchelli, and Barnard is Mr. Mazzuchelli's father-in-law. Somewhat surprisingly, the voluminous record in these cases affords no meaningful information about CITCO NV.

December 2004 from Teviot and Barnard in the amounts of $200,000 and $99,995, respectively.

A fax from Ms. Dowek to Mr. Rogers suggests that Sugarloaf Overseas was due $950,000 on behalf of a PDA Investor Group for acquisition of notes. Emails among the parties suggest that Teviot and Barnard were involved, along with Multicred and Mr. Rogers, in the purchase of the CBD assets. Mr. Rogers also states that Sugarloaf Overseas received a $1 million payment for the sale of CBD receivables having a $47,500,000 notional face value.

B. *Adjustments to Income*

Respondent used the specific item method to reconstruct Sugarloaf's income for the 2004 and 2005 tax years through a bank deposits analysis. The only deposits remaining in dispute for the 2004 tax year are:

Date	*Source*	*Amount*
12/1/2004	Teviot Investments Ltd.	$200,000
12/20/2004	Andrew A. Barnard	99,995
Total		299,995

Mr. Rogers testified that these amounts represented equity investments. He also testified that Mr. Mazzucchelli approached him in 2010 demanding repayment of money Mr. Barnard sent to Sugarloaf.

Respondent also alleges that the following deposits in 2005 constitute gross income to Sugarloaf:

Date	*Description*[1]	*Amount*
7/28/05	Unknown—deposit from PPI	$72,000
9/28/05	Multicred	49,982
11/10/05	Unknown—deposit from PPI	60,000
11/29/05	Kevin Walzter	100,000
11/30/05	Unknown—Sterling Ridge	87,500
12/7/05	M–D Medical Services	24,000
12/14/05	Betacom Inc.	180,000
12/19/05	Sugarloaf Overseas	249,985
12/23/05	Orchard Financial Group, LLC	60,000
12/29/05	Capital Preservation Services	12,000
12/30/05	CO Trust	30,000

Date	*Description*[1]	*Amount*
Total		925,467

[1] The Description column is gleaned from the bank statements. Where the bank statements are missing or not helpful, we use "unknown" followed by, for demonstrative purposes, the description or source as listed in Sugarloaf's Quickbooks reconciliation. This is not a finding that these are necessarily the sources of the deposits because we do not believe the Quickbooks data alone is a sufficiently reliable indicator of Sugarloaf's items of income and loss.

With respect to the July 28, 2005, $72,000 deposit, the parties provided a customer receipt evidencing a deposit in that amount, but it does not otherwise identify a source. Also in the record are handwritten notes stating that the July Sugarloaf bank statement is missing and purporting to show that the $72,000 deposit was from "JER". The Sugarloaf Quickbooks bank account reconciliation records the deposit as a deposit from "PPI a/c".

The September 28, 2005, $49,982 deposit is reflected on Sugarloaf's bank statement as a wire transfer from Multicred. The Quickbooks reconciliation also records this amount as a deposit from Multicred.

The bank account statement for Sugarloaf does not list any detail beyond "deposit" for the $60,000 November 10, 2005, deposit. The Quickbooks reconciliation describes this deposit as a deposit from PPI and/or Mr. Rogers.

The bank account statement describes the $100,000 November 29, 2005, deposit as a wire transfer from Kevin Waltzer. The Quickbooks reconciliation describes this deposit as "Customer Deposits/Retainers".

The bank account statement lists no detail beyond "deposit" for the $87,500 November 30, 2005, deposit. The Quickbooks reconciliation describes the deposit as a deposit from Sterling Ridge.

The bank account statement describes the December 7, 2005, $24,000 deposit as a wire transfer from "M–D Medical Services". The Quickbooks reconciliation describes this deposit as "Customer Deposits/Retainers".

The bank account statement describes the December 14, 2005, $180,000 deposit as a wire transfer from "Betacom Incorporated". The wire transfer information sheet lists a reference of "Betacom 2005 Trust". The Quickbooks reconciliation describes this deposit as "Customer Deposits/ Retainers".

The bank account statement describes the December 19, 2005, $249,985 deposit as a wire transfer from Sugarloaf Overseas. The Quickbooks reconciliation does not describe this deposit in any meaningful way but does indicate it is a deposit from Sugarloaf Overseas.

The bank account statement describes the December 23, 2005, $60,000 deposit as a wire transfer from Orchard Financial Group LLC. The wire transfer information sheet lists a reference of "30000 - Lance Barton 2005 Fund 30000 - Brad Black 2005 Fund". The Quickbooks reconciliation describes this deposit as "Deposits from Barton (30,000) and Black (30,000)".

The bank account statement describes the December 29, 2005, $12,000 deposit as a wire transfer from Capital Preservation Services. The wire transfer information sheet lists the same as well as a reference to "CPS 2005 Trust". The Quickbooks reconciliation describes this deposit as "Customer Deposits/ Retainers".

The bank account statement describes the December 30, 2005, $30,000 deposit as a wire transfer from CO Trust. The Quickbooks reconciliation describes this deposit as from CO Trust and contains Mr. Rogers' initials.

C. *Adjustments to COGS*

In the FPAA respondent also adjusted Sugarloaf's reported cost of goods sold. On its 2004 tax return, Sugarloaf reported a cost of goods sold of $122,950,000. Sugarloaf claimed a cost of goods sold for each holding company it sold to an investor and took the position that the cost of goods sold was equal to the claimed adjusted basis in the contributed receivables. [29]

D. *Disallowed Deductions*

Sugarloaf claimed on its 2004 and 2005 tax returns the following miscellaneous deductions:

[29] The total of the claimed adjusted bases of the receivables in the companies at issue in these cases is $102,950,000. This amount does not include three transactions which are not part of these cases, for which the total claimed adjusted basis is $20 million.

Deduction	*2004*	*2005*
Legal & professional fees	$218,530	$345,743
Management fees	80,000	290,000
Consulting fees	430,000	78,312
Amortization	86	400
Meals & entertainment	280	---
Accounting	18,120	27,229
Bank charges	53	73
Computer services	---	2,000
Office expense	---	2,679
Trust expense	---	236,000
Total	747,069	982,436

Respondent disallowed all deductions. Petitioner provided Quickbooks account records and canceled checks purporting to substantiate the expenses.

OPINION

Because this Opinion disposes of 10 discrete issues, *see supra* pp. 326–327, we first offer a road map for the reader. We begin with the big picture. In Part I we focus on Sugarloaf, analyzing (1) whether it constitutes a bona fide partnership for Federal income tax purposes, (2) whether the Brazilian retailers made valid contributions to it under section 721, (3) whether the step transaction doctrine should be applied to collapse those claimed contributions and the retailers' subsequent redemptions into sales, such that the receivables had a cost basis under section 1012 rather than a carryover basis under section 723, (4) whether the 2004 partnership transactions had economic substance, and (5) whether the statutory prerequisites for a section 166 deduction were satisfied. We then turn in Part II to (6) whether Mr. and Mrs. Rogers' trust investment entitles them to a section 166 deduction for 2005, applying the analysis of Part I to the trust structure in which the Rogerses invested. With respect to Sugarloaf and the trust structure, we present our analyses and holdings in the alternative.

We then turn to the details. In Part III we consider (7) whether Sugarloaf understated gross income and/or (8) is entitled to various deductions for the 2004 and 2005 tax years. In Part IV, we resolve (9) whether Sugarloaf and the other partnerships are liable for the section 6662(a) penalties, and (10) whether Sugarloaf is liable for the section 6662A penalty.

I. *Superior Trading Revisited*

Section 723 states the general rule that the basis of property a partner contributes to a partnership is a carryover tax basis, which is the same adjusted basis as it had in the hands of the contributing partner, increased by any gain recognized by the contributing partner under section 721(b).

Petitioners contend that the distressed, unpaid Brazilian receivables contributed to Sugarloaf had the same tax basis in the United States as they had in the hands of the Brazilian retailers and that section 723 preserved the built-in losses inherent in those receivables. Under their theory, section 723 continued to operate upon and governed the subsequent contribution of the receivables to the trading companies. Petitioners allege that under section 722, Sugarloaf had a basis in each trading company equal to the basis it had in the receivables. When Sugarloaf contributed the trading company to the holding company, petitioners contend that Sugarloaf again, under section 722, obtained a tax basis in its interest in the holding company equal to its tax basis in the trading company. Here petitioners contend that tax basis was equal to the tax basis in the underlying receivables. And when Sugarloaf sold the holding company, it sold it for a fraction of its adjusted tax basis, resulting in a cost of goods sold much higher than the purchase price.

The investors, when they bought their interests in the holding companies, each took a cost basis. But they then inflated their bases in their partnership interests through contributions of cash, notes, or other property to the holding companies. Thus, when a trading company claimed the section 166 deduction, the investor could claim a corresponding flowthrough deduction up to the full amount of his or her basis in the holding company partnership.

As this recounting of petitioners' theory illustrates, the whole shelter revolves around the initial contribution of the receivables and the shifting of the built-in loss from the tax-indifferent Brazilian retailer to the tax-sensitive United States taxpayer/investor. Up until October 22, 2004, such shifting was theoretically possible because the inside basis adjustment of section 743(b) was required only if the partnership filed an election under section 754. Section 704(c)(1)(C) now requires allocation of built-in losses to the partner contributing the built-in loss property, and only to that partner. A section 743(b) basis adjustment is now mandatory upon any transfer of a partnership interest in a partnership with a substantial built-in loss. In short, the partnership version of the transaction as originally structured by Mr. Rogers clearly no longer worked after October 22, 2004, even according to Mr. Rogers' interpretation of the law; thus, Mr. Rogers substituted his trust structure. We add the caveat concerning Mr. Rogers' interpretation of the law because, for all of the reasons we articulated in *Superior Trading*, his structures were conceptually flawed, very clearly never worked, and in any event were never fully implemented in accordance with Mr. Rogers' design.

Respondent attacks the 2004 partnership transactions using a variety of analytical tools. He unscrews the partnership itself, taking the position that Sugarloaf was not a valid partnership because the parties did not intend to enter into a partnership nor did the alleged "contributions" of receivables ever properly occur. He next saws through all the steps undertaken by the parties and collapses them into simple sales and purchases of receivables. Using the heaviest hammer in the toolbox, he then smashes the entire transaction as lacking economic substance. Finally, large-scale demolition completed, he pries apart the section 166 deduction piece by piece, contending that petitioners failed to prove they satisfied the requisite statutory elements.

A. *Still Not a Valid Partnership*

As an initial matter, we ask whether the retailers and Jetstream formed a partnership. "Whether a valid partnership exists for purposes of Federal tax law is governed by Federal law. *See Commissioner v. Culbertson*, 337 U.S. 733, 737 (1949)." *Superior Trading, LLC v. Commissioner*, 137 T.C. at 81. The Supreme Court directs us to ask "'whether the partners really and truly intended to join together for the purpose of carrying on the business and sharing in the profits and losses or both.'" *Commissioner v. Culbertson*, 337 U.S. at 741 (quoting *Commissioner v. Tower*, 327 U.S. 280, 287 (1946)). The question is one of fact. *Id.* at 742.

Section 301.7701–3(a), Proced. & Admin. Regs., allows "[a]n eligible entity with at least two members * * * [to] elect to be classified as * * * an association * * * or a partnership". If no election is made, the regulations by default treat an eligible two-or-more-member entity as a partnership. Sec. 301.7701–3(b)(i), Proced. & Admin. Regs. These so-called check-the-box regulations do not supersede *Culbertson* insofar as the putative members must still come together to form an entity. *See, e.g., Superior Trading, LLC v. Commissioner*, 728 F.3d at 680 (applying the tests of *Culbertson* and *Tower*). And we do not believe or find that Jetstream, Globex, Arapua, and/or CBD came together to form a partnership.

Nothing in the record convinces us that Jetstream, Globex, and CBD intended to join together for the purposes of carrying on a debt collection business. Everything in the record convinces us that Globex and CBD had every intention of dumping their distressed receivables and that Jetstream intended to sell a tax shelter.

Among many other indicators, the math in the contribution agreements between Sugarloaf and Arapua, CBD, and Globex just does not add up. According to these agreements, the three Brazilian retailers own a collective 215% interest in Sugarloaf. Mr. Rogers would have us believe that with every new contribution agreement, the membership interests of the current members were diluted to make room for the new member. But he provides no contemporaneous acknowledgment or assent from the members of such dilution of their membership interests nor other corroborating evidence.

Their arithmetical flaws aside, the contribution agreements highlight a second indicator that no partnership was formed: They directly conflict with other evidence in the record as to who Sugarloaf's purported partners even were. Arapua, CBD, and Globex executed contribution agreements suggesting that Jetstream was Sugarloaf's only other partner. Sugarloaf's 2004 and 2005 tax returns identify Jetstream, CBD, and Globex as partners but exclude Arapua and include Warwick. And Mr. Rogers testified that there are at least three other equity partners in Sugarloaf whose capital interests do not appear on Sugarloaf's tax returns. There is not a scrap of documentation of these supposed capital interests outside of Quickbooks balance sheets, corroborated only by Mr. Rogers' self-serving testimony.

Parties genuinely embarking on a joint business endeavor with the intent of sharing in its profits and losses would not accept such ambiguity regarding their respective proportions and with whom they would be sharing those profits and losses. These issues in Sugarloaf's formation are alone enough for us to conclude that, as a factual matter—and as was true in *Superior Trading*—the parties never intended to join together in the conduct of a business. But we need not and do not stop there.

B. *Poorly Disguised Sales*

Like the transactions with the partnerships, the transactions with the Brazilian retailers in these cases suffer the same infirmity as the transactions in *Superior Trading*; namely, Mr. Rogers has once again failed to adequately and convincingly rebut persuasive evidence of redemptions.[30] Both Globex and CBD received cash distributions in redemption of their interests within two years of their alleged contributions of property to Sugarloaf.

Generally contributions of property by partners to a partnership do not trigger gain or loss recognition. Sec. 721(a). But in some situations the direct or indirect transfer of money or other property to a partner that is related to a direct or indirect transfer of money to the partnership can be recharacterized as a sale or exchange of property. Sec. 707(a)(2)(B). The basic test to determine whether the transfers constitute a sale of property is whether, considering all the facts and circumstances, "(i) [t]he transfer of money or other consideration would not have been made but for the transfer of property; and (ii) [i]n cases in which the transfers are not made simultaneously, the subsequent transfer is not dependent on the entrepreneurial risks of partnership operations." Sec. 1.707–3(b)(1), Income Tax Regs. The regulations instruct us to consider a number of facts and circumstances in determining whether the transaction constitutes a sale. *Id.* subpara. (2).

[30] There is also a significant question whether the purported transactions ever occurred given the apparent failure to properly identify the receivables being transferred, to notify the makers, and to otherwise comply with Brazilian law.

The regulations governing disguised sales also contain a two-year presumption. *Id.* para. (c). Distributions within two years of a contribution give rise to a presumption that the transaction is a disguised sale. *Id.* Distributions more than two years after the contribution give rise to a presumption that the transaction is not a disguised sale. *Id.* Petitioners here bear the burden of rebutting the former presumption. *See Superior Trading, LLC v. Commissioner*, 738 F.3d at 681.

With respect to Globex, as Mr. Hartigan signed up investors and received the purchase price, he forwarded some of the money to Multicred. Multicred used a portion of this money to redeem Globex. These initial payments took place in 2004 and thus trigger the two-year presumption in favor of a sale.[31] Petitioners did nothing to rebut this presumption, and it is only strengthened by the undated letter in which Globex requests a redemption.

Furthermore, Mr. Rogers sent additional money to the account of Globalstores, which we believe to be related to Globex, in 2006. The evidence surrounding these 2006 payments shows that Mr. Rogers believed that he had already paid Globex. It is possible that these 2006 payments were for the purchase of additional receivables. Either way, petitioners introduced no evidence sufficient to rebut the disguised-sale presumption raised by Mr. Hartigan's payments to Globex via Multicred in 2004. Therefore, Sugarloaf, to the extent it was a partnership, had only a cost basis in the Globex receivables. Because of the opaque manner of the redemption, Sugarloaf lacks clear records of what it paid for

[31] Mr. Rogers and Mr. Hartigan spent a significant portion of the trial disputing who paid what, when, and why. Mr. Rogers evidently believes, or at least would have us believe, that Mr. Hartigan embezzled the money paid by the investors and due to Sugarloaf. Mr. Hartigan says that, pursuant to Mr. Rogers' instructions, he sent the money to Multicred. Respondent, to the extent he wanted to get embroiled in this dispute, states these disagreements amount to finger-pointing possibly stemming from Mr. Hartigan's 10% fees. Ultimately, the evidence shows that Mr. Rogers instructed Mr. Hartigan to send portions of the payments Mr. Hartigan collected from investors and owed to Sugarloaf, to Multicred, as constructive distributions from Sugarloaf. To us, the intent to distribute the cash in 2004 is sufficient to invoke the disguised-sale rule. At the very least, it is near-conclusive proof that the transfer of the receivables would not have been made but for the promise of near-contemporaneous cash payments.

the receivables and so has not established that its basis was greater than zero.

With respect to CBD, we also find that the two-year presumption in favor of a disguised sale applies. While the transactions here were slightly more complex, the weight of the evidence reflects an indirect transfer of money to CBD in exchange for a direct transfer of assets. The purported transfer of assets took place as early as the date of the contribution agreement, October 1, 2004. CBD received money for its partnership interest by the end of December 2004. As with the Globex receivables, petitioners have not presented evidence sufficient to overcome the presumption under the disguised-sale regulations that the transaction should be treated as a sale. Therefore, in Sugarloaf's hands, the CBD receivables, like the Globex receivables, had only a cost basis.

C. *Retracing Our Steps*

Once again echoing *Superior Trading*, we also believe that the transactions at issue here should be collapsed to reflect their true economic substance: a sale of receivables from the retailers to Sugarloaf. The true substance of a transaction rather than its nominal form governs its Federal tax treatment. *Superior Trading, LLC v. Commissioner*, 137 T.C. at 88; *see also Commissioner v. Court Holding Co.*, 324 U.S. 331, 334 (1945). One tool that this Court, like others, uses to drill down to the substance of a transaction is the step transaction doctrine. *See Gordon v. Commissioner*, 85 T.C. 309, 324 (1985) ("[F]ormally separate steps in an integrated and interdependent series that is focused on a particular end result will not be afforded independent significance in situations in which an isolated examination of the steps will not lead to a determination reflecting the actual overall result of the series of steps."). In deciding whether to invoke this doctrine, courts generally look to one of three alternative tests: the binding commitment test, the end result test, or the interdependence test. *Superior Trading, LLC v. Commissioner*, 137 T.C. at 88.

The binding commitment test is the most restrictive and asks whether there was a binding commitment at the time of the first step to take the subsequent steps. *Commissioner v. Gordon*, 391 U.S. 83, 96 (1968). This test "is seldom used and is applicable only where a substantial period of time has passed between the steps that are subject to scrutiny." *Andantech LLC v. Commissioner*, T.C. Memo. 2002–97, slip op. at 70, *aff'd in part, remanded in part*, 331 F.3d 972 (D.C. Cir. 2003); *see also McDonald's Rests. of Ill., Inc. v. Commissioner*, 688 F.2d 520, 525 (7th Cir. 1982) (stating that the test "was formulated to deal with the characterization of a transaction that in fact spanned several tax years"), *rev'g* 76 T.C. 972 (1981). The transactions in question took place within two months at the shortest and, if we look only at Mr. Rogers' 2006 payment to Globex and disregard the contemporaneous payments by Mr. Hartigan, two years at the longest. This is not a situation where the transactions spanned several years, and it is unclear whether the binding commitment test should apply. *See Superior Trading, LLC v. Commissioner*, 137 T.C. at 89 (citing *Associated Wholesale Grocers, Inc. v. United States*, 927 F.2d 1517, 1522 n.6 (10th Cir. 1991), for the same proposition).

The end result test looks to the subjective intent of the parties and asks "whether the formally separate steps are prearranged components of a composite transaction intended from the outset to arrive at a specific end result." *Id.*; *see also McDonald's Rests. of Ill., Inc. v. Commissioner*, 688 F.2d at 524. In these cases, Mr. Rogers intended from the outset to import the foreign losses into the United States to obtain tax benefits. He could not have done so without the alleged partnership contributions and subsequent distributions—otherwise he would lose the tax basis and would be unable to allocate the built-in losses to the investors.

While no one from Globex or CBD testified as to the intent of the Brazilian retailers, our disguised-sale analysis above supports the conclusion that they intended from day one to obtain cash for their assets independent of any entrepreneurial risk of a debt collection business. In fact, the parties underwent transactional contortions to avoid the appearance of a redemption. In the case of CBD, the parties used a series of middlemen and loan documents. In the case of Globex, Mr. Rogers and Mr. Hartigan sent the money to Globex through Multicred. In both cases the end result is the same: The Brazilian retailers received cash, and Sugarloaf acquired receivables with, in its view, built-in tax losses. The end result test allows and encourages us to collapse the contribution of receivables to Sugarloaf and its subsequent distributions of money and to treat the transactions as sales.

The same holds true when we apply the interdependence test, which asks "whether 'the steps are so interdependent that the legal relations created by one transaction would have been fruitless without a completion of the series.'" *Penrod v. Commissioner*, 88 T.C. 1415, 1430 (1987) (quoting *Redding v. Commissioner*, 630 F.2d 1169, 1177 (7th Cir. 1980), *rev'g on other grounds* 71 T.C. 597 (1979)). The steps in the transactions among Sugarloaf, the retailers, and the intermediaries who funneled cash to the retailers wholly lack valid and independent economic or business purposes, which represents the heart of the inquiry under the interdependence test. *Superior Trading, LLC v. Commissioner*, 137 T.C. at 90. Petitioners cannot explain the redemption of the Brazilian retailers except to claim any payments were participation payments due to Sugarloaf's securitization of the receivables. This feeble explanation—much like Mr. Rogers' claims that when he used the word "redeemed" in contemporaneous documents he was using the term loosely, and that he used the term "purchase" as a term of art—do not persuade us that the cash payments to the retailers served any purpose other than redeeming their purported partnership interests. We find no economic or business purpose for the Brazilian retailers' entry into and exit from Sugarloaf. These transactions' only purpose was to facilitate the always-intended writeoff of the receivables' built-in losses and their allocation to the United States tax shelter investors.

Thus, we collapse the steps undertaken by Mr. Rogers, the retailers, and the intermediaries. The proper characterization of the "stepped" transaction is as a sale of the receivables from the retailers to Sugarloaf. Hence, Sugarloaf's basis in the receivables would be a cost basis. With respect to CBD, the evidence shows that the money sent to CBD through middlemen was $800,000. Thus, Sugarloaf took a basis in the CBD receivables of $800,000. As discussed *infra* pp. 359–360, this finding does not allow the trading company petitioners a section 166 deduction because they failed to prove that they meet the requirements of section 166.

The evidence with respect to Globex is less clear. Globex clearly received money from both Mr. Hartigan, via Multicred, in 2004 and again from Mr. Rogers in 2006, but petitioners were unable to substantiate these payments in any meaningful manner. Evidence suggests that Mr. Rogers sent Globex $950,000 in 2006, but its not clear whether this payment was solely duplicative of payments by Mr. Hartigan or whether a portion of it was for a new batch of receivables. Either way, it is not enough for us to accurately determine Sugarloaf's cost basis. Consequently, petitioners having failed to carry their burden of establishing basis, Sugarloaf had a zero basis in the Globex receivables.

D. *Sham on You*

A general principle of Federal income taxation is that while a taxpayer has a right to conduct transactions in a manner that minimizes or outright avoids Federal income tax, *Gregory v. Helvering*, 293 U.S. 465, 469 (1935), the taxpayer does not have a right to use forms or structures lacking economic substance to avoid taxation, *Zmuda v. Commissioner*, 79 T.C. 714, 719, *aff'd*, 731 F.2d 1417 (9th Cir. 1984). In such a case, "[s]ubstance prevails over form." *Superior Trading, LLC v. Commissioner*, 728 F.3d at 680. This doctrine is as applicable in the trust context, *Paulson v. Commissioner*, 992 F.2d 789, 790 (8th Cir. 1993), *aff'g* T.C. Memo. 1991–508, as it is in the partnership context, *Superior Trading, LLC v. Commissioner*, 728 F.3d at 680.

The Court of Appeals for the Seventh Circuit, addressing a transaction almost identical to the 2004 partnership transactions in these cases, said: "There is not even a colorable basis for the tax shelter that * * * [Mr. Rogers] created and the * * * [parties] implemented." *Id.* at 682. Affirming this Court's decision for the Commissioner, the Court of Appeals held that the Sugarloaf-type entity in that case was a sham partnership and "entitled to none of the benefits that the Internal Revenue Code bestows on partnerships." *Id.* at 681. The Court of Appeals concluded that "[n]o joint business goal motivated the creation of Warwick", the Sugarloaf-type entity, and that a redemption by Warwick of the Brazilian retailer created the presumption of a sale, which the taxpayers did not rebut. *Id.* at 680–681. The only differences in these cases are that two different Brazilian retailers were used, and the redemption of these retailers occurred in a slightly different manner. But for all practical purposes, the transactions are the same. Consequently, under the Court of

Appeals for the Seventh Circuit's logic and ours, Sugarloaf must also be a sham partnership not entitled to the benefits of the Federal income tax laws.

E. *Statutory Noncompliance*

The loss deductions ultimately claimed by the partnerships and by Mr. and Mrs. Rogers rested on the claim that the receivables were bad debts. Section 166(a) provides:

> SEC. 166(a). GENERAL RULE.—
>
> (1) WHOLLY WORTHLESS DEBTS.—There shall be allowed as a deduction any debt which becomes worthless within the taxable year.
>
> (2) PARTIALLY WORTHLESS DEBTS.—When satisfied that a debt is recoverable only in part, the Secretary may allow such debt, in an amount not in excess of the part charged off within the taxable year, as a deduction.

The amount of the deduction is limited to the taxpayer's adjusted basis. Sec. 166(b). The Code does not permit noncorporate taxpayers to take ordinary income deductions under section 166 for wholly or partially worthless nonbusiness debt, requiring that they instead treat such worthlessness as a capital loss. Sec. 166(d)(1). Nonbusiness debt is "debt other than—(A) a debt created or acquired (as the case may be) in connection with a trade or business of the taxpayer; or (B) a debt the loss from the worthlessness of which is incurred in the taxpayer's trade or business." Sec. 166(d)(2). The taxpayer must establish the amount of the debt that is worthless. Sec. 1.166–3(a)(2)(ii), Income Tax Regs.

Respondent distills the above requirements into four elements: (1) a charge-off for a partially worthless debt, (2) proof of a trade or business, (3) proof of worthlessness, and (4) proof of basis in the debt. We agree with this characterization and also agree with respondent that petitioners have not carried their burden of proof with respect to any of these elements.

First, the partnerships and the trusts, as far as we can tell, did not keep reliable, if any, financial books or records, particularly as to the specific receivables purchased and which ones should be charged off. Instead a blanket 97% of all receivables was used for charge-off purposes. Thus, petitioners failed to properly show that they charged off the portion of the debt claimed as a deduction.

Second, petitioners failed to show that they acquired the receivables in connection with a trade or business. The trading companies and the trusts did not operate as trades or businesses. They merely operated as conduits for losses imported into the U.S. tax system. With one exception, there is no evidence that any of the investors entered into these relationships with the expectation of economic profit independent of the tax results.[32] In addition, in the case of the Globex receivables, it is likely that the collection efforts (the only purported business activity with which Sugarloaf and the other partnerships were connected) did not even begin until a considerable time after the receivables were acquired.

Third, petitioners failed to prove worthlessness. Evidence in the record reflects that petitioners and Multicred could not conduct an analysis of the individual debts. And petitioners provided no statistical study or other analysis of which debts or types of debts were worthless. The fact that every trading company and trust claimed a deduction of 97% across the board undercuts any claim that the companies truly analyzed the assets' value.[33]

Fourth, petitioners failed to prove they ever had bases in the receivables equal to the deductions claimed. For the reasons discussed above, petitioners had at most cost bases.

In summary, petitioners have not carried their burden of proving their entitlement to the claimed section 166 deductions. Respondent correctly disallowed these deductions in full.

II. *Superior Trading With a Twist of Trust*

The substantive analysis above applies equally to the 2004 and 2005 tax year transactions, in particular the trans-

---

[32] The one exception is Christopher Heath Brown, an investor who questioned Mr. Rogers as to when he would see results. Mr. Rogers essentially rebuffed Dr. Brown, saying that he should be happy with the tax losses, and Dr. Brown did not complain again.

[33] Petitioners' only argument on the worthlessness issue, presented in their answering brief, is: "97% built-in loss was chosen as that was the rate of bad debt reserve provided by Arapua against the balance sheet gross historic cost of the receivables. A partial worthlessness percentage against CBD and Globex receivables could have been less [or more] than the 97% used in the case of Arapua." Far from carrying petitioners' burden of proof, this argument amounts to additional evidence that the 97% worthlessness claim was an arbitrary number.

actions involving Sterling Ridge that underlay the Rogerses' claimed section 166 deduction for 2005. The Brazilian retailers' "contributions" to Sugarloaf failed to preserve the retailers' built-in losses in the receivables because no valid partnership was formed, or alternatively because the "contributions" were in fact disguised sales. Accordingly, there was no, or next to no, section 166 deduction for the subtrusts formed in 2005 to claim.

Yet even leaving aside the fundamental flaws in the transfer of assets at the Sugarloaf level, which necessarily limit built-in losses in the assets of the trusts, the step transaction doctrine discussed *supra* pp. 355–358 applies to collapse the steps in the trust transactions into sales of receivables from Sugarloaf to the main trusts.

The steps of the 2005 transactions can be summarized as follows. Mr. Rogers formed a main trust in the name of an investor. He then caused Sugarloaf to "contribute" receivables to the main trust, formed a subtrust under that main trust, and assigned the receivables to the subtrust. The investor "contributed" cash (and/or promissory notes) to the main trust's bank account, which was controlled by Mr. Rogers, and received in exchange a beneficial interest in the receivables in the subtrust. The investor, by the terms of the various documents, was entitled to take direct ownership of those receivables. Sugarloaf, over the course of months, drained the main trust bank account under the guise of maintenance payments or other payments.

Applying the end result test, the overall objective of these transactions was for Mr. Rogers to sell, and for the investors to purchase, tax losses. Achieving this objective entailed transferring the receivables to the investor in a manner that would preserve the receivables' tax bases in the hands of the Brazilian retailers while obtaining cash from the investors. Because of the AJCA, the partnership structure was no longer viable, so Mr. Rogers employed a trust structure instead. The parties clearly intended that the transaction generate tax losses well in excess of the investors' economic outlays. Applying the interdependence test, no independent business or economic purpose existed for the convoluted trust structure. The creation of the main and subtrusts would be fruitless without the eventual flowthrough of the section 166 deductions. Thus, we have no qualms about collapsing the steps of the trust transactions. Sterling Ridge's investment in the 2005 trust transaction was no more than a purchase of receivables from Sugarloaf. Thus, Sterling Ridge was entitled to only a cost basis.

Our foregoing conclusions regarding the collapse of the trust transactions into sales of receivables and the basis problems at the Sugarloaf level would each alone suffice to disallow the Rogerses' claimed section 166 deduction for 2005. But the 2005 trust structure fails at a more fundamental level, and lest Mr. Rogers' faulty template persist as a trap for the unwary, we proceed to explain why.

The 2005 trust transactions were close cousins of the 2004 partnership transactions. Because built-in losses could no longer be shifted within a partnership, while the Code contained no analogous limitation for trusts, Mr. Rogers hoped that the receivables would have a carryover basis upon contribution to a trust without the relationship between the investor and Sugarloaf turning into a partnership. *See* sec. 1015. After those receivables had been allocated to a subtrust and an investor designated as its beneficiary, the investor would be the subtrust's beneficiary and grantor, by virtue of the investor's cash "contribution" to the main trust. Because the terms of the various trust documents entitled the investor to take direct ownership of the subtrust assets, Mr. Rogers reasoned that the subtrust would be a grantor trust. In a grantor trust, the person treated as the grantor includes in his or her Federal taxable income, as computed on the tax return, the trust's items of income, deduction, and credits against tax. *See* sec. 671. Hence, the investor could partake in the receivables' built-in losses.

Mr. Rogers also hoped that the main and subtrusts would qualify as trusts under the check-the-box regulations. *See* sec. 301.7701–4, Proced. & Admin. Regs. But Federal law determines how an entity organized under State law is taxed. *Moline Props., Inc. v. Commissioner*, 319 U.S. 436, 438–439 (1943). Whether an arrangement is a trust generally depends on whether "the purpose of the arrangement is to vest in trustees responsibility for the protection and conservation of property for beneficiaries who cannot share in the discharge of this responsibility and, therefore, are not associates in a joint enterprise for the conduct of business for profit." Sec. 301.7701–4(a), Proced. & Admin. Regs.; *see also*

Morrissey v. Commissioner, 296 U.S. 344, 357, 359–360 (1935) (discussing the difference between an ordinary trust and a business trust). The "business trust" label "will not change the real character of the organization if the organization is more properly classified as a business entity under § 301.7701–2." Sec. 301.7701–4(b), Proced. & Admin. Regs.[34]

As a purely factual matter, the purpose of the trust arrangements was not "to vest in trustees responsibility for the protection and conservation of property for beneficiaries who cannot share in the discharge of this responsibility". *See* sec. 301.7701–4(a), Proced. & Admin. Regs. The purpose of the main trust and the subtrust was merely to transfer tax losses from one party to another party. The parties did not intend to protect and conserve the receivables, as the absence of assignment and collection documentation demonstrates. That the trusts wrote off most of the receivables within weeks or months of their formation reveals for the fiction that it is the proposition that the trustee here protected and conserved the trusts' assets. Therefore, neither the main trusts nor the subtrusts appear to be trusts for Federal income tax purposes. Nor can we properly classify them as "business trusts", given that they did not operate "to provide a medium for the conduct of a business and sharing its gains." *See Morrissey v. Commissioner*, 296 U.S. at 357.

Because these entities were not trusts for the purposes of Federal income tax law, we are left to determine what hap-

---

[34] Mr. Rogers calls his trusts Illinois business trusts. Such entities, under State law, are not partnerships. *Schumann-Heink v. Folsom*, 159 N.E. 250, 252 (Ill. 1927) (discussing a Massachusetts business trust). A business trust can be a trust "'where the owners of a business, or of shares in a business corporation, transfer the property of the business, or all or a large part of the stock, to trustees for themselves.'" *Hanley v. Kusper*, 337 N.E.2d 1, 6 (Ill. 1975) (quoting G. Bogert, The Law of Trusts and Trustees, sec. 270.40, at 347 (2d ed. 1964)).

Sec. 301.7701–4(b), Proced. & Admin. Regs., merely restates the general principle that labels used by taxpayers are not conclusive. *See Frank Lyon Co. v. United States*, 435 U.S. 561, 583–584 (1978); *see also Hutchinson v. Commissioner*, 47 T.C. 680, 686 (1967) ("'Mere forms of instruments, of course, and the use of words 'trust' and 'trustee' cannot be depended upon in determining whether or not a trust is in reality created. The transaction itself must be scrutinized.'" (quoting *Morsman v. Commissioner*, 90 F.2d 18, 23 (8th Cir. 1937), *aff'g* 33 B.T.A. 800 (1935))). We look beyond Mr. Rogers' labels.

pened. Usually, such an entity with two or more members would, by default, be considered a partnership. Sec. 301.7701–2, Proced. & Admin. Regs. But there was no more intent for the investor and Sugarloaf to join together to conduct a debt-collection business than there was for Sugarloaf and the Brazilian retailers to join together in such a business. *See Commissioner v. Culbertson*, 337 U.S. at 742; *supra* pp. 351–353. Therefore, we are left in a situation analogous to that with the Brazilian retailers and Sugarloaf. The investor exchanged cash for receivables, which were intended to generate tax losses. We note that even if we were to find that the trust investor and Sugarloaf entered into a partnership, the AJCA would prevent the shifting of losses away from a contributing partner, and the disguised sales rules of section 707 would also come into play.

Under both the step transaction doctrine and the rules governing trusts, neither the Sterling Ridge Trust nor its subtrust was a trust for Federal income tax purposes. Rather, Sterling Ridge as a stand-alone entity purchased the receivables from Sugarloaf.

Finally, as we concluded with Sugarloaf, we find that the Sterling Ridge Trust and subtrust lacked economic substance and were shams. Sterling Ridge Trust and subtrust were not trusts for the purposes of Federal income tax law. The parties did not intend for the trustee to preserve and conserve the assets for the beneficiaries. Consequently, Mr. and Mrs. Rogers were entitled to none of the Federal income tax benefits of the trust structure. *See Superior Trading, LLC v. Commissioner*, 728 F.3d at 681 ("'An entity without economic substance, whether a sham partnership or a sham trust, is a sham either way and hence is not recognized for federal tax law purposes.'" (quoting *Sparkman v. Commissioner*, 509 F.3d 1149, 1156 n.6 (9th Cir. 2007), *aff'g* T.C. Memo. 2005–136)).

For the foregoing reasons, we conclude that respondent properly disallowed the Rogerses' claimed section 166 deduction for 2005.

III. *The Devil's in the Details*

Respondent determined that Sugarloaf greatly overstated its cost of goods sold on its partnership return by taking the position that its cost of goods sold was equal to its claimed carryover basis in the "contributed" receivables. We agree. For the reasons stated above, Sugarloaf failed to prove that it had a basis in the Globex receivables and failed to prove it had a basis greater than $800,000 in the CBD receivables. At most, therefore, Sugarloaf proved a basis of $800,000 in the partnership interests it sold. Sugarloaf is entitled to a cost of goods sold of only $800,000.[35]

With respect to the deductions respondent disallowed, Sugarloaf is not entitled to them. Deductions are "a matter of legislative grace", and taxpayers bear the burden of proving that they are entitled to any deduction. Rule 142(a); *INDOPCO, Inc. v. Commissioner*, 503 U.S. 79, 84 (1992). Taxpayers must identify each deduction, show they meet all requirements, and substantiate all items underlying claimed deductions. Sec. 6001; *Roberts v. Commissioner*, 62 T.C. 834, 836–837 (1974). Section 162(a) allows a deduction for all ordinary and necessary business expenses paid or incurred in connection with a trade or business. But "expenditures made in an attempt to obtain abusive tax shelter benefits are not ordinary and necessary business expenses or otherwise deductible under section 162(a)." *Gerdau Macsteel, Inc. v. Commissioner*, 139 T.C. 67, 182 (2012). The transactions in question were tax shelters, and Sugarloaf's claimed expenditures were made in an attempt to obtain abusive tax shelter benefits.[36]

[35] We note that while "economic substance is a prerequisite to the application of any Code provision allowing deductions," *Lerman v. Commissioner*, 939 F.2d 44, 52 (3d Cir. 1991), *aff'g* T.C. Memo. 1988–570, cost of goods sold is not a deduction, *see Azimzadeh v. Commissioner*, T.C. Memo. 2013–169, at *12-*13 (citing *Metra Chem. Corp. v. Commissioner*, 88 T.C. 654, 661 (1987)).

[36] Furthermore, Jetstream, through Mr. Rogers, failed to substantiate items underlying Sugarloaf's deductions. The record includes only a Quickbooks transaction record for most expenses and canceled checks drawn on Sugarloaf's bank account to Mr. Gabel and to Seyfarth Shaw. Sugarloaf's records are generally unreliable, and we do not accept the Quickbooks records as sufficient substantiation. While Mr. Gabel testified that he provided services to Sugarloaf during the years at issue, we have no invoices or other proof, including testimony, of the extent of his services. Mr. Rogers failed to provide evidence as to the nature and extent of the services provided by Seyfarth Shaw. Because of the confusing flows of money among the investors, Seyfarth Shaw, Sugarloaf, and various other

Continued

Respondent also determined that Sugarloaf understated its gross income based upon a bank deposits analysis. Petitioner Jetstream disputes certain deposits for both 2004 and 2005 and accordingly bears the burden of proving that respondent's inclusion of these deposits in Sugarloaf's income is incorrect. *See DiLeo v. Commissioner*, 96 T.C. 858, 869 (1991), *aff'd*, 959 F.2d 16 (2d Cir. 1992).

With respect to the two disputed deposits in 2004, Mr. Rogers claims that both were equity contributions to Sugarloaf. Unfortunately, Mr. Rogers provides no evidence other than his self-serving testimony and a balance sheet. Mr. Rogers disavows the accuracy of the balance sheet with respect to some entries, but expects us to accept it as accurate with respect to others.[37] We decline to do so. In addition, his testimony conflicts with the tax returns filed by Sugarloaf. He did not provide contribution agreements or other indicia of an equity investment by the depositing individuals. Thus, we cannot conclude that these payments were equity contributions. Mr. Rogers did not provide any other explanation for these deposits, and he did not carry Jetstream's burden of proof that these deposits were other than income to Sugarloaf.

With respect to the disputed 2005 deposits, Mr. Rogers claims these deposits are either capital contributions (equity deposits) or amounts transferred to Sugarloaf that should have been deposited directly into trust accounts (trust deposits). As with the 2004 deposits, we reject Mr. Rogers' position. He introduced no evidence, other than self-serving testimony and Quickbooks records, that the equity deposits were in fact equity contributions. As to the July 28, November 10, and November 30, 2005, deposits, Sugarloaf's Quickbooks entries indicate these deposits were from PPI funds or, in the case of the November 30 deposit, Sterling Ridge. But, there is no corroborating evidence that these

entities, and in light of the lack of a factual basis on which to make estimates, we decline to estimate the extent of services, and hence we bear heavily on Sugarloaf's inexactitude. *See Williams v. United States*, 245 F.2d 559, 560 (5th Cir. 1957); *Cohan v. Commissioner*, 39 F.2d 540, 543–544 (2d Cir. 1930); *Vanicek v. Commissioner*, 85 T.C. 731, 742–743 (1985).

[37] On brief, Mr. Rogers contends that the amounts shown as equity interests for Multicred and Sugarloaf Overseas are loans, not equity investments.

deposits actually came from PPI, and frankly, we do not find Mr. Rogers' testimony or the Quickbooks entries credible. With respect to the alleged Sterling Ridge deposit, we have no way of knowing whether the deposit came from Sterling Ridge, Inc., or the Sterling Ridge Trust, if it even came from either of these sources.

With respect to the alleged Multicred equity deposit, we have rejected petitioner's contention that Multicred was a partner in Sugarloaf and likewise reject its contention that this deposit was an equity contribution. The Quickbooks entries alone are insufficient to prove these deposits were equity investments. *Cf. Olive v. Commissioner*, 139 T.C. 19, 32–33 (2012) (holding that general ledgers by themselves are insufficient to substantiate items underlying a taxpayer's claimed deductions); *Ohana v. Commissioner*, T.C. Memo. 2014–83, at *21 (finding Quickbooks records of expenses a summary of the taxpayer's assertions, which, when uncorroborated, are not enough to substantiate items underlying the taxpayer's claimed deductions).

While the names of the transferors are consistent with those of trust investors, Mr. Rogers has nonetheless failed to convince us that the trust deposits are anything but income to Sugarloaf. First, we have no evidence that these amounts were ever transferred to the trust bank accounts. Second, and conclusively here, we found that in these 2005 transactions, the investors each purchased a tranche of receivables from Sugarloaf, making the money paid into the trust accounts income to Sugarloaf under section 1001. So, regardless of whether the 2005 investors' payments went into the trust accounts or directly to Sugarloaf, those amounts were still income to Sugarloaf.[38]

[38] We note that respondent has determined only that the six trust deposits actually deposited into Sugarloaf's bank account constitute income. Under our findings, all payments by the trust investors would constitute income to Sugarloaf, less fees retained by the promoters. We will not question respondent's magnanimity.

IV. *In the Penalty Box*[39]

A. *Section 6662*

Respondent determined penalties against all of the partnerships in these consolidated cases—that is, for Sugarloaf and for each of the trading companies. He determined that the partnerships were liable for the gross valuation misstatement penalty under section 6662(h) on portions of their underpayments attributable to misstatements of their respective bases in the receivables. Respondent also determined that Sugarloaf is liable for the accuracy-related penalty for negligence or, in the alternative, substantial understatements of income tax on portions of its underpayments attributable to its additional income and the disallowed deductions. He bears the burden of production with respect to these accuracy-related penalties, but petitioners bear the burden of proof if respondent meets his burden of production. *See Higbee v. Commissioner*, 116 T.C. 438, 446–447 (2001).

Section 6662(a) and (b)(3) provides for a 20% penalty to be imposed on the portion of an underpayment of tax required to be shown on a return that is attributable to a substantial valuation misstatement. As relevant here, for returns filed after August 17, 2006, a substantial valuation misstatement occurs when "the value of any property (or the adjusted basis of any property) claimed on any return of tax imposed by chapter 1 is 150 percent or more of the amount determined to be the correct amount of such valuation or adjusted basis (as the case may be)". Sec. 6662(e)(1)(A). For returns filed on or before August 16, 2006, the percentage was 200% instead of 150%. Pension Protection Act of 2006, Pub. L. No. 109–280, sec. 1219(a)(1)(A), (e), 120 Stat. at 1083, 1085. Section 6662(h) increases this penalty to 40% if the value or adjusted basis claimed on the return is 200% or more of the actual value or adjusted basis. For returns filed on or before August 16, 2006, the 40% penalty applies if the value or adjusted basis is 400% or more of the actual basis or value. *Id.* sec. 1219(a)(2)(A). A regulation clarifies that, when the actual value or basis is zero, that value is considered 400% or more

[39] We do not here redetermine the penalties determined against Mr. and Mrs. Rogers and Mr. Fears with respect to their Forms 1040, U.S. Individual Income Tax Return. *See supra* note 6.

of the correct amount. Sec. 1.6662–5(g), Income Tax Regs. Petitioners do not challenge application of this regulation. *See United States v. Woods*, 571 U.S. ___, ___, 134 S. Ct. 557, 566 n.4 (2013) (noting the inherent mathematical problem of dividing a number by zero).

In these cases, respondent has met his burden of production. The Globex receivables had a zero basis, and the partnerships with those receivables grossly overstated their bases in those receivables. For the CBD receivables, which had a total combined basis of $800,000, the partnerships (including two not at issue here) reported a total adjusted basis of $48,600,000. Assuming that each partnership received a tranche of receivables with a basis equal to its pro rata share of the $800,000 aggregate basis, each partnership overstated its basis by far more than 400%. Furthermore, Sugarloaf's aggregate claimed adjusted basis in the partnership interests it sold was far more than 400% of the actual adjusted basis, which we found to be, in total, $800,000.

An accuracy-related penalty will not be imposed "with respect to any portion of an underpayment if it is shown that there was a reasonable cause for such portion and that the taxpayer acted in good faith". Sec. 6664(c)(1). When determining whether a partnership had reasonable cause and acted in good faith, we look to the general partner. *Superior Trading, LLC v. Commissioner*, 137 T.C. at 91. During the years at issue Jetstream was the managing member of Sugarloaf and each of the trading companies. We do not believe Mr. Rogers when he claims that Mr. Mazzucchelli was the manager of Sugarloaf. We think that claim, along with the engagement letter between Sugarloaf and Seyfarth Shaw, a poorly veiled attempt to get around the conflict of interest inherent in having Mr. Rogers' law firm represent a limited liability company controlled, through its tax matters partner, Jetstream, by Mr. Rogers. Mr. Rogers, through Jetstream, was the only individual with the authority to act on behalf of Sugarloaf and the trading companies, and it is his conduct that is relevant for determining whether we should sustain the determined accuracy-related penalties.

As was the case in *Superior Trading*, Mr. "Rogers' knowledge and experience should have put him on notice that the tax benefits sought by the form of the transactions would not be forthcoming and that these transactions would be recharacterized and stepped together to reveal their true substance." *Id.* at 92. We reject his contention that he reasonably relied on the advice of tax professionals. *See Neonatology Assocs., P.A. v. Commissioner*, 115 T.C. 43, 99 (2000) (establishing a three-factor test for determining whether reliance on tax professionals may be reasonable cause), *aff'd*, 299 F.3d 221 (3d Cir. 2002). Mr. Rogers' assertions on brief that he relied upon outside professionals lack even a smidgen of evidentiary foundation other than his own testimony.

Petitioners have not borne their burden of proof under section 6664(c) with respect to any of the partnerships, and we therefore hold that the section 6662(a) and (h) penalty applies. To be clear, this penalty applies against the trading companies, for overstating their bases in the receivables, as well as to Sugarloaf. In Sugarloaf's case, it not only overstated its basis in the receivables but also overstated its basis in the trading companies that it subsequently sold, resulting in a grossly overstated cost of goods sold.

Further, we find that an accuracy-related penalty of 20% applies to the portions of the undepayments attributable to Sugarloaf's omissions from gross income and disallowed deductions. A section 6662(a) penalty applies to portions of an underpayment of tax due to negligence or disregard of rules and regulations or to a substantial understatement of income tax if the amount of the understatement exceeds the greater of $5,000, $10,000 in the case of a corporation, or 10% of the tax required to be shown on the return. Sec. 6662(b)(1) and (2).

We conclude that respondent has met his burden of production with respect to the penalty for negligence or disregard of rules and regulations. Petitioners failed to substantiate the items underlying their deductions and provide a reasoned and convincing explanation for the deposits. Their recordkeeping appears to have been scanty to nonexistent, and noncontemporaneous beyond a Quickbooks log, which we did not find credible and will not rely on. The cashflows to and from Sugarloaf are confusing, and Mr. Rogers' failure to keep records of the alleged contributions to capital and to explain contemporaneous document equity ownership totaling up to 215% is negligent at best. Furthermore, for the same reasons discussed above, Mr. Rogers has fallen well short of his burden of proving reasonable cause and good faith.

B. *Section 6662A*

Respondent also seeks to impose a section 6662A penalty on Sugarloaf for its 2004 and 2005 tax years. Section 6662A imposes a 20% penalty on understatements due to reportable transactions or listed transactions. Sec. 6662A(a), (b)(2). This penalty increases to 30% if the taxpayer does not adequately disclose the transaction. Sec. 6662A(c).

For the same reasons discussed below with respect to the 2005 tax year, we find that respondent has satisfied his burden of production as to this penalty for 2004. However, the section 6662A penalty does not apply with respect to the portion of an understatement on which a gross valuation misstatement penalty is imposed. Sec. 6662A(e)(2)(B). We have imposed the gross valuation misstatement penalty on the portions of the 2004 understatement of Sugarloaf that would be subject to the section 6662A penalty, so that penalty does not apply to any amount for Sugarloaf's 2004 tax year.

As for Sugarloaf's 2005 tax year, respondent wants us to apply the section 6662A penalty to "any understatement attributable to adjustments to Sugarloaf's tax characterization of the DAT [distressed asset trust] transaction in 2005". Respondent contends that the DAT transaction is a listed transaction, and Sugarloaf did not disclose it.

Section 6662A(d) refers us to section 6707A(c)(2) for the definition of a listed transaction. The Code defines a listed transaction as a tax avoidance transaction identified by the Internal Revenue Service (IRS) and points us to the regulations under section 6011. Sec. 6707A(c)(2). The regulations define a listed transaction as the same as or substantially similar to any transaction identified by the IRS as such in a "notice, regulation, or other form of published guidance". Sec. 1.6011–4(b)(2), Income Tax Regs. A substantially similar transaction is "either factually similar or based on the same or similar tax strategy." Sec. 1.6011–4(c)(4), Income Tax Regs.

In these cases, no one disputes that the trust transactions are substantially similar to the transaction identified in

Notice 2008–34, 2008–1 C.B. 645.[40] Generally, the IRS requires a taxpayer to disclose listed transactions on a statement attached to the taxpayer's return. Sec. 1.6011–4(e)(1), Income Tax Regs. In these cases, the IRS issued the notice on March 24, 2008, well after Sugarloaf filed its 2005 tax return on October 14, 2006. The regulations in effect for the tax years at issue covered just such a situation, requiring the taxpayer to file a disclosure statement "as an attachment to the taxpayer's tax return next filed after the date the transaction is listed". Sec. 1.6011–4(e)(2)(i), Income Tax Regs. Neither Sugarloaf nor its tax matters partner filed such a disclosure statement. Section 6664(d)(1) provides a reasonable cause and good faith defense to the section 6662A penalty, but only if the transaction is disclosed. Thus, the 30% penalty applies to the portion of Sugarloaf's 2005 understatement that stems from the trust transactions to the extent the understatement is not already subject to the 40% section 6662(h) gross valuation misstatement penalty. *See* sec. 6662A(e)(2)(B).

V. *Conclusion*

Contrary to Mr. Rogers' contentions throughout these cases, the 2004 partnership structures did not materially

---

[40] Mr. Rogers, on Sugarloaf's behalf, contends that Notice 2008–34, 2008–1 C.B. 645, is invalid as a violation of Executive Order 12866, 3 C.F.R. 638 (1994). He believes that Notice 2008–34, *supra*, is a significant regulatory action, and that under Executive Order 12866 the Office of Management and Budget (OMB) must review proposed significant regulatory action. Because OMB did not do so, Mr. Rogers argues the notice is invalid. In so arguing, he ignores section 10 of the executive order, which states:

> Nothing in this Executive order shall affect any otherwise available judicial review of agency action. This Executive order is intended only to improve the internal management of the Federal Government and does not create any right or benefit, substantive or procedural, enforceable at law or equity by a party against the United States, its agencies or instrumentalities, its officers or employees, or any other person. [Exec. Order No. 12866, 3 C.F.R. at 649.]

Mr. Rogers cannot challenge Notice 2008–34, *supra*, as not in compliance with the executive order. *See Blak Invs. v. Commissioner*, 133 T.C. 431, 447 (2009) (rejecting for the same reason a taxpayer's challenge to temporary regulations under Executive Order 12866), *supplemented by* T.C. Memo. 2012–273.

differ from the 2003 structures at issue in *Superior Trading, LLC*. Like Arapua in *Superior Trading, LLC*, the Brazilian retailers in these cases were also redeemed out of the parent partnership (in that case, Warwick), resulting in a deemed sale of the receivables to Sugarloaf. And Mr. Rogers provided no convincing evidence that the structure in these cases had any objective independent of the shifting of losses from a tax-indifferent party to a tax-motivated party.

The 2005 trust transactions differed little from the 2004 transactions. They suffer from the same fatal flaws as the 2004 transactions—namely, the planned and near-contemporaneous redemption of the Brazilian retailers. Further, the form of the transaction, when appropriately stepped together, consists of a sale of receivables to the investors. We treat it as such. In addition, the 2005 trust transaction was devoid of economic substance, and we will therefore issue an order stating that Mr. and Mrs. Rogers are not entitled to the section 166 deduction they claimed on their 2005 tax return.

This Opinion makes abundantly clear that neither the 2004 partnership transaction nor the 2005 trust transaction works, and we have discussed myriad reasons why not. These reasons constitute "alternative holdings, each by itself sufficient to sustain respondent's adjustments". *Superior Trading, LLC v. Commissioner*, T.C. Memo. 2012–110, slip op. at 7.

Moreover, Jetstream, through Mr. Rogers, failed to successfully carry its burden of proof with respect to any of Sugarloaf's claimed deductions on its 2004 and 2005 tax returns. Mr. Rogers similarly failed to provide convincing explanations for the challenged gross receipts in Sugarloaf's 2004 and 2005 tax years.

Sugarloaf is liable for the 40% gross valuation misstatement penalty for the 2004 tax year for overstating the bases of its interests in the holding companies sold to investors. The remaining partnerships in these cases are likewise liable for the 40% gross valuation misstatement penalty for overstating their bases in the receivables. Sugarloaf is further liable for a 20% accuracy-related penalty under section 6662(a) and (b)(1) for the portions of the underpayments due to the disallowed deductions for the 2004 and 2005 tax years and the amounts of income omitted from its 2004 and 2005 tax returns. Sugarloaf is also liable for a 30%

penalty under section 6662A for the reportable transaction understatement attributable to the 2005 trust structure.

The Court has considered all of the parties' contentions, arguments, requests, and statements. To the extent not discussed herein, the Court concludes that they are moot, irrelevant, or without merit.[41]

Appropriate orders will be issued at docket Nos. 27636–09 and 30586–09, decision will be entered under Rule 155 in docket No. 671–10, and decisions will be entered for respondent in all other cases.

APPENDIX

Kenna Trading, LLC, Jetstream Business Limited, Tax Matters Partner, docket No. 7551–08; Connemara Trading Group, LLC, Jetstream Business Limited, Tax Matters Partner, docket No. 7552–08; Zugersee Trading, LLC, Jetstream Business Limited, Tax Matters Partner, docket No. 7553–08; Bielersee Trading, LLC, Jetstream Business Limited, Tax Matters Partner, docket No. 7554–08; Ridgeway Fund, LLC, Jetstream Business Limited, Tax Matters Partner, docket No. 7555–08; Grey Stone Trading, LLC, Jetstream Business Limited, Tax Matters Partner, docket No. 7556–08; Turnberry Trading, LLC, Jetstream Business Limited, Tax Matters Partner, docket No. 7618–08; Northgate Trading, LLC, Jetstream Business Limited, Tax Matters Partner, docket No. 7625–08; Thornhill Trading, LLC, Jetstream Business Limited, Tax Matters Partner, docket No. 9021–08; Saddlebrook Trading, LLC, Jetstream Business Limited, Tax Matters Partner, docket No. 9035–08; Suten Fund, LLC, Jetstream Business Limited, Tax Matters Partner, docket No. 9036–08; Remington Trading, LLC, Jetstream Business Limited, Tax Matters Partner, docket No.

[41] For instance, we find Mr. Rogers' contention that respondent's failure to audit the subtrusts' returns is fatal to be without merit. Likewise, respondent's statement in his answer in docket No. 671–10 that he prepared the answer without benefit of the administrative file does not render the determined deficiency arbitrary and capricious. Finally, we reject Mr. Rogers' claim to a deduction for Sugarloaf for income reported by Warwick on its 2003 tax return but purportedly never received.

9037–08; R B Taylor Trading, LLC, Jetstream Business Limited, Tax Matters Partner, docket No. 9038–08; Riversedge Fund, LLC, Jetstream Business Limited, Tax Matters Partner, docket No. 9039–08; Murtensee Trading, LLC, Arrowhead Fund, LLC, Tax Matters Partner, docket No. 9040–08; Monte Rosa Fund, LLC, Jetstream Business Limited, Tax Matters Partner, docket No. 9041–08; Ofenpass Fund, LLC, Jetstream Business Limited, Tax Matters Partner, docket No. 9042–08; Knight Trading, LLC, Jetstream Business Limited, Tax Matters Partner, docket No. 9121–08; Essex Fund, LLC, Jetstream Business Limited, Tax Matters Partner, docket No. 9122–08; Lyman Trading, LLC, Jetstream Business Limited, Tax Matters Partner, docket No. 9123–08; Dent-Blanche Fund, LLC, Jetstream Business Limited, Tax Matters Partner, docket No. 9124–08; Harlan Fund, LLC, Jetstream Business Limited, Tax Matters Partner, docket No. 9125–08; Grand-Combin Fund, LLC, Jetstream Business Limited, Tax Matters Partner, docket No. 9126–08; Larkspur Trading, LLC, Jetstream Business Limited, Tax Matters Partner, docket No. 9127–08; Lakeview Trading, LLC, Jetstream Business Limited, Tax Matters Partner, docket No. 9128–08; Davis Fund, LLC, Jetstream Business Limited, Tax Matters Partner, docket No. 14094–08; Cumnor Trading, LLC, Jetstream Business Limited, Tax Matters Partner, docket No. 16796–08; Bodensee Fund, LLC, Jetstream Business Limited, Tax Matters Partner, docket No. 19924–08; Ironwood Trading, LLC, Windmere Fund, LLC, Tax Matters Partner, docket No. 19925–08; Zurichsee Trading, LLC, Jetstream Business Limited, Tax Matters Partner, docket No. 13980–09; Zugersee Trading, LLC, Jetstream Business Limited, Tax Matters Partner, docket No. 13981–09; Warner Fund, LLC, Jetstream Business Limited, Tax Matters Partner, docket No. 13982–09; Riversedge Fund, LLC, Jetstream Business Limited, Tax Matters Partner, docket No. 13983–09; Gary R. Fears, docket No. 27636–09; John E. Rogers & Frances L. Rogers, docket No. 30586–09; Sugarloaf Fund, LLC, Jetstream Business Limited, Tax Matters Partner, docket No. 671–10.

VIVIAN L. RADER, ET AL.,[1] PETITIONERS v. COMMISSIONER OF INTERNAL REVENUE, RESPONDENT

Docket Nos. 11409–11, 11476–11, 27722–11. Filed October 29, 2014.

Ps failed to file returns for 2003–06 and 2008 (years in issue). The IRS examining agent, using the bank deposits method and information returns issued in connection with payments to P–H or to both Ps, reconstructed Ps' income for the years in issue and determined tax deficiencies and additions to tax under I.R.C. secs. 6651(a)(1) and (2) and 6654, which he incorporated on substitutes for returns (SFRs) for each P for 2003–06 and an SFR for P–H for 2008. The SFRs constituted the basis for the notices of deficiency issued to Ps. R filed amendments to answer in docket Nos. 11409–11 and 11476–11 in which he changed the erroneous selection of "single" filing status on the 2003–06 SFRs for each P to "married filing separate", thereby increasing the tax deficiencies and additions to tax for each of those years, as set forth on attachments to the amendments to answer. During the trial, the parties stipulated that any and all deficiencies and additions to tax arising therefrom would be imposed on P–H alone. Among the items of income that Ps received in 2006 were proceeds from two sales of Colorado real property that were subjected to 10% withholding by the escrow agent pursuant to I.R.C. sec. 1445(a), which applies to dispositions of U.S. real property interests by foreign persons and gives rise to a credit under I.R.C. sec. 33. Ps failed to furnish the payor with a taxpayer identification number or a certification that Ps were not foreign persons, which would have exempted them from I.R.C. sec. 1445(a) withholding pursuant to I.R.C. sec. 1445(b)(2). Ps attack the sufficiency of the SFRs, argue that the 2006 tax deficiency must be offset by the tax withheld under I.R.C. sec. 1445(a), raise a frivolous Fifth Amendment claim against having to testify at trial concerning their nonfiling of returns for the years in issue, and contest R's imposition of additions to tax under I.R.C. secs. 6651(a)(1) and (2) and 6654.

1. *Held*: P–H is liable for the income tax deficiencies that R determined for the years in issue and set forth on the SFRs, as revised by the amendments to answer.

2. *Held*, *further*, P–W is not entitled to a refund of any portion of the tax withheld from the proceeds of the 2006 real property sales because the deemed filing date of P–W's refund claim (the Feb. 11, 2011, notice of deficiency mailing date)

[1] Cases of the following petitioner are consolidated herewith: Steven R. Rader, docket Nos. 11476–11 and 27722–11.

was more than two years after the overpayment (deemed to have occurred on the Apr. 15, 2007, due date of P–W's 2006 return). *See* I.R.C. secs. 6511(b)(2)(B), 6512(b)(3)(B); *Healer v. Commissioner*, 115 T.C. 316 (2000).

3. *Held, further*, the amounts withheld from the proceeds of Ps' 2006 sales of real property gave rise to an I.R.C. sec. 33 credit, which, pursuant to I.R.C. sec. 6211(b)(1), may not be taken into account in determining P–H's 2006 tax deficiency.

4. *Held, further*, Ps' Fifth Amendment claim is rejected.

5. *Held, further*, P–H is liable for the additions to tax under I.R.C. secs. 6651(a)(1) and (2) and 6654 except that, because the attachments to the amendments to answer did not constitute amended SFRs, i.e., they did not set forth amounts "shown as tax on any return" within the meaning of I.R.C. sec. 6651(a)(2), the I.R.C. sec. 6651(a)(2) addition to tax for the years in issue must be based upon the tax liabilities shown on the original SFRs, not upon the larger tax liabilities set forth in the amendments to answer.

6. *Held, further*, P–H is subject to sanction under I.R.C. sec. 6673(a)(1) for procedures instituted primarily for delay, etc.

Vivian L. Rader and Steven R. Rader, pro sese.

Thomas G. Hodel, *Matthew A. Houtsma*, *Luke D. Ortner*, and *Robert A. Varra*, for respondent.

HALPERN, *Judge*: These consolidated cases involve the following determinations of deficiencies in and additions to petitioners' 2003–06 and petitioner Steven R. Rader's 2008 Federal income tax:[2]

		Additions to tax		
Year	*Deficiency*	*Sec. 6651(a)(1)*	*Sec. 6651(a)(2)* [1]	*Sec. 6654(a)*
2003	$139,964	$29,804	---	---
2004	136,414	30,693	---	$3,909
2005	144,511	32,515	---	5,797
2006	212,648	47,846	---	10,063
2008	7,859	1,768	$1,061	253

[1] With respect to the sec. 6651(a)(2) addition to tax for 2003–06, the notices of deficiency for those years state: "The amount of the addition to tax cannot be determined at this time, but an addition to tax of 0.5 percent will be imposed for each month, or fraction thereof, of nonpayment, up to 25 percent, based on the liability shown on this report." Respondent included

[2] Unless otherwise indicated, all section references are to the Internal Revenue Code of 1986, as amended and in effect for the years in issue, and all Rule references are to the Tax Court Rules of Practice and Procedure. We round all dollar amounts to the nearest dollar.

the omitted amounts in his pretrial memorandum, which the Court received on May 22, 2013, after the maximum 50-month period for additions to tax under sec. 6651(a)(2) had run its course for petitioners' 2003–06 tax years. Those amounts were $33,116 for 2003, $34,104 for 2004, $36,128 for 2005, and $48,909 for 2006. Those same amounts were included as sec. 6651(a)(2) additions to tax in the 2003–06 substitutes for returns that respondent prepared pursuant to sec. 6020(b) and which constituted the basis for the notices of deficiency pertaining to those years. Respondent does not explain the seemingly contrary statement in the notices that those amounts could not yet be determined.

Respondent issued identical notices of deficiency (notices) for 2003–06 to each petitioner on February 11, 2011, on the grounds that he was unable "to determine which of the petitioners received the income during * * * [2003–06]" and he did not want to be "whipsawed" (i.e., lose the case because he attributed the income to the wrong taxpayer). At the conclusion of the trial, however, respondent conceded that any tax deficiencies that the Court might determine and any additions to tax and penalties, "to the extent that they follow the deficiencies" that the Court might impose, would be attributed to Mr. Rader, and no tax deficiencies, additions to tax, or penalties would be attributed to petitioner Vivian L. Rader. Thus, all tax deficiencies, additions to tax and penalties at issue herein are directed to Mr. Rader (petitioner).

In his petitions, petitioner states his intention to "contest" the notices, thus, in effect, assigning error to respondent's determinations.

On June 6, 2013, we issued an order granting respondent's motions (1) for leave to file amendments to answer in docket Nos. 11409–11 and 11476–11, which involve petitioners' 2003–06 taxable years, and (2) to consolidate for trial, briefing, and opinion, all three cases. In his amendments to answer, respondent acknowledged that the notices for 2003–06 erroneously determined the deficiency amounts and additions to tax on the basis of an assumed "single" filing status for each petitioner rather than a "married filing separate" filing status (appropriate because petitioners were married during those years). Correcting for that error, in his amendments to answer respondent increased his proposed deficiency amounts and additions to tax for 2003–06 as follows:

		Additions to tax		
Year	*Deficiency*	*Sec. 6651(a)(1)*	*Sec. 6651(a)(2)*	*Sec. 6654(a)*
2003	$146,235	$31,215	$34,684	---
2004	142,828	32,136	35,707	$4,093
2005	151,072	33,991	37,768	6,060
2006	219,412	49,368	54,853	10,383

At the conclusion of the trial, the Court, on its own motion, invoked the application of section 6673(a)(1), which, as pertinent, empowers the Court to sanction a taxpayer for instituting or maintaining a proceeding primarily for delay or for maintaining a frivolous or groundless position.

Except for the increases in the deficiency amounts and additions to tax, petitioners bear the burden of proof. *See* Rule 142(a).[3]

FINDINGS OF FACT

At the time the petitions were filed, petitioners resided in Colorado.

During the years in issue, petitioner was a self-employed plumber, paid by his customers for plumbing services he provided to them. Petitioner did not file Federal income tax returns for the years in issue, and, therefore, he failed to report any income from his plumbing business or any other income attributable to those years. One of respondent's revenue agents began an examination of petitioner's failures to file for the years in issue. After verifying that petitioner had been issued (1) a plumbing license in 1995, which remained in active status as of December 31, 2008, and (2) multiple plumbing permits during 2003–06, the revenue agent acquired and analyzed petitioner's bank records for 2003–06 to determine deposits that might have represented unre-

[3] Petitioners have not invoked sec. 7491(a), which shifts the burden of proof to the Commissioner in certain situations. In any event, sec. 7491(a) is inapplicable herein because petitioners have failed to introduce credible evidence that respondent's adjustments were in error, *see* sec. 7491(a)(1), nor have they shown that they have satisfied the preconditions for its application, *see* sec. 7491(a)(2). Moreover, the revenue agent's ability to establish that petitioner was a plumber and made substantial bank deposits during the years in issue, *see* discussion *infra*, satisfied the requirement to establish "some reasonable foundation" for the deficiency, *see, e.g.*, *Erickson v. Commissioner*, 937 F.2d 1548, 1551 (10th Cir. 1991), *aff'g* T.C. Memo. 1989–552.

ported income. For 2008, he examined information-return documents filed by customers paying petitioner, as reported under petitioner's Social Security number, in order to establish his reportable gross income from his plumbing business for 2008. In reconstructing petitioner's reportable gross income from his plumbing business for 2003–06, the examining agent subtracted from the gross deposits listed in the bank statements loans, transfers, and other amounts that would not constitute income. On the basis of his bank deposits analysis for 2003–06 and the information returns for 2008, respondent concluded that petitioner's income from his plumbing business was \$351,449, \$387,714, \$420,818, and \$577,811 for 2003–06, respectively, and at least \$34,174 for 2008. In addition, respondent determined that petitioner received additional income in the form of a "title wire transfer" of \$137,477 in 2003, a "limited international funds check" of \$1,500 in 2004, and "Colorado land title checks" totaling \$66,352 representing the net proceeds from the sale of two parcels of real property in 2006, all of which he treated as long-term capital gain.

In connection with the two 2006 payments, the payor withheld and paid to the IRS \$25,000 from one and \$2,500 from the other, which represented 10% of the gross proceeds from the sale of each parcel. The withholdings were made and reported by the title company as escrow agent (presumably on behalf of the purchasers) on a Form 8288–A, Statement of Withholding on Dispositions by Foreign Persons of U.S. Real Property Interests, a form used pursuant to regulations under section 1445(a). *See* sec. 1.1445–1(c)(1), Income Tax Regs. Although petitioners were not foreign persons subject to section 1445, it appears that the title company felt it necessary to withhold in accordance with that section because petitioners, as transferors, failed to furnish either a certification of non-foreign-person status or a taxpayer identification number (TIN), as required by section 1445(b)(2) and section 1.1445–2(b)(2)(i), Income Tax Regs., for exemption from withholding. See also the instructions for Form 8288, U.S. Withholding Tax Return for Dispositions by Foreign Persons of U.S. Real Property Interests, to which the Form 8288–A must be attached.

Petitioners have failed to furnish evidence of entitlement to any deductions offsetting the foregoing items of income.

On the basis of his reconstruction of petitioner's income, as aforesaid, respondent prepared substitutes for returns (SFRs) for the years in issue, consisting, in each case, of a Form 13496, IRC Section 6020(b) Certification, signed by the IRS revenue agent who prepared the SFR, a Form 4549–A, Income Tax Discrepancy Adjustments,[4] and a Form 886–A, Explanations of Items. Those SFRs incorporated the above-described adjustments to income and the tax liabilities and additions to tax set forth in the notices. Exhibit A attached to respondent's amendments to answer in docket Nos. 11409–11 and 11476–11, in order to reflect petitioners' filing status as "married filing separate" (rather than "single") consists of revised Forms 4549–A and Forms 5278, Statement—Income Tax Changes, both of which incorporate the increased amounts resulting from that change in filing status.

OPINION

I. *Tax Deficiencies*

A. *Introduction*

Petitioners do not directly dispute respondent's adjustments to petitioner's income during the years in issue as reflected in the SFRs, and, indeed, petitioner's admission at trial that he earned income from his plumbing business and the evidence of his real estate sales sufficiently link him to income-producing activities that support respondent's adjustments. Instead, petitioners attack the sufficiency of the SFRs on technical grounds and, thus, attack indirectly the contents thereof. They also allege that the tax deficiency for 2006 must be offset by the taxes withheld and paid to the IRS on their real estate sales, and they raise a Fifth Amendment (to the United States Constitution) objection.[5]

[4] The 2008 SFR included a Form 4549, Income Tax Examination Changes, rather than a Form 4549–A.

[5] Petitioners also raise evidentiary objections and continue to argue that the notice addressed to Mrs. Rader is invalid because she had no income for the years in issue. The evidentiary objections were overruled at trial and the dispute with respect to Mrs. Rader's liability is moot because, as noted *supra*, respondent conceded at trial that any deficiences and additions to tax and penalties related thereto will be attributed solely to petitioner.

B. *Sufficiency of the SFRs*

Essentially, petitioners argue that the SFRs are invalid because they fail "to cite a deficiency statute and/or a tax statute from which a deficiency and penalties could arise." They also cite the fact that the SFRs were not attached to what petitioners refer to as a "nearly blank SFR 1040" that petitioners believe (from IRS transcripts) "was filed, processed and posted to" petitioners' account "three years prior to the dates on the alleged certifications."

To constitute a section 6020(b) SFR, "the return must be subscribed, it must contain sufficient information from which to compute the taxpayer's tax liability, and the return form and any attachments must purport to be a 'return'." *Spurlock v. Commissioner*, T.C. Memo. 2003–124, 2003 WL 1987156, at *10. The SFRs that respondent filed on petitioners' behalf each consisted of an IRC Section 6020(b) Certification (Form 13496), the income tax examination changes (either Form 4549–A or Form 4549), and an explanation of the changes (Form 886–A). That combination of documents is sufficient to constitute a valid SFR under section 6020(b). *See Gleason v. Commissioner*, T.C. Memo. 2011–154, 2011 WL 2600917, at *12. There is no requirement that a valid SFR include a Form 1040, U.S. Individual Income Tax Return, executed on behalf of the taxpayer. *See id.*; *see also Nix v. Commissioner*, T.C. Memo. 2012–304, at *13–*14, *aff'd*, 553 Fed. Appx. 960 (11th Cir. 2014); *Holloway v. Commissioner*, T.C. Memo. 2012–137, 2012 WL 1727685, at *2; sec. 301.6020–1(b)(2), Proced. & Admin. Regs. Moreover, respondent had the right under section 6020(b) to elect married filing separately status for petitioners rather than joint filing status. *See Smalldridge v. Commissioner*, 804 F.2d 125, 127–128 (10th Cir. 1986), *aff'g* T.C. Memo. 1984–434; *Conovitz v. Commissioner*, T.C. Memo. 1980–22, 1980 Tax Ct. Memo LEXIS 567, at *12.[6] In these cases, respondent elected that status by

---

[6] The Court of Appeals for the Tenth Circuit in *Smalldridge v. Commissioner*, 804 F.2d 125, 127–128 (10th Cir. 1986), *aff'g* T.C. Memo. 1984–434, held that the Commissioner's election of married filing separately status on an SFR was binding where, as in that case, the married taxpayers' right to elect joint filing status had expired pursuant to sec. 6013(b)(2)(B) (now sec. 6013(b)(2)(A)), which prohibits married taxpayers from electing joint filing status more than three years after the initial due date of their return. In *Millsap v. Commissioner*, 91 T.C. 926 (1988), however, we re-

way of amendments to answer rather than in connection with the preparation of petitioners' 2003–06 SFRs. The change in filing status resulted in an increase in the tax deficiencies and additions to tax set forth in the notice for 2003–06.[7]

The SFRs executed by respondent pursuant to section 6020(b) were valid SFRs.

C. *Petitioners' Right to an Offset*

In their brief, petitioners ask for a finding that "there exists a failure on * * * [respondent's] part * * * to recognize receipt of a substantial payment from the closing on the sale of a piece of property." Although it is styled as a request for a proposed finding of fact, we interpret petitioners' request as their argument that they are entitled to an offset for the amounts withheld from the proceeds of their 2006 real estate sales and remitted to respondent.

Respondent acknowledges that $25,000 and $2,500 were withheld from the proceeds of the two real estate sales, respectively, and that those amounts were remitted to the IRS Service Center in Philadelphia. After noting the "peculiarities" of applying a withholding regime directed at foreign sellers of U.S. real property interests to petitioners, who were Colorado residents, respondent argues that (1) because "the withholding credit is not a factor in determining a tax deficiency", we are without jurisdiction to

---

jected the court's reasoning in *Smalldridge*, overruled or rejected several of our precedents, two of which were cited with approval by the court in *Smalldridge*, and held that the sec. 6013(b)(2) limitations on electing joint filing status are not a bar to married taxpayers' right to elect joint filing status at any time after the Commissioner's election of married filing separately status in preparing an SFR for the taxpayers. *See Millsap v. Commissioner*, 91 T.C. at 936–938. Petitioners have not attempted to elect joint filing status. Therefore, *Millsap* is inapplicable in these cases. Moreover, even if petitioners had attempted to elect joint filing status, we would be required to reject the attempt pursuant to *Golsen v. Commissioner*, 54 T.C. 742 (1970), *aff'd*, 445 F.2d 985 (10th Cir. 1971), because of the likelihood that any appeal of these cases would be to the Court of Appeals for the Tenth Circuit, which decided *Smalldridge*. *See Millsap v. Commissioner*, 91 T.C. at 937 n.23 ("In accord with our holding in *Golsen* * * * we will follow *Smalldridge* * * * in all cases appealable to the 10th Circuit.").

[7] As discussed *infra*, because the amendments to answer do not incorporate corrected or amended SFRs for 2003–06, we must reject respondent's increases in the sec. 6651(a)(2) addition to tax for those years.

consider it, citing *Forrest v. Commissioner*, T.C. Memo. 2011–4, 2011 WL 13626, discussed *infra*, and (2) even if Mrs. Rader were entitled to a credit for the withholding applied to her, we could not treat that withholding as a refundable overpayment under section 6512(b)(1) because the notice mailing date, February 11, 2011, which constitutes the deemed filing date of Mrs. Rader's refund claim for 2006, was more than two years after the overpayment, deemed, pursuant to section 6513(b)(1), to have occurred on April 15, 2007, the due date of her 2006 return. *See* secs. 6512(b)(3)(B), 6511(b)(2)(B); *see also Commissioner v. Lundy*, 516 U.S. 235, 247–250 (1996); *Healer v. Commissioner*, 115 T.C. 316, 319–323 (2000).

We agree with respondent that we may not order a refund of the deemed overpayment to Mrs. Rader for her share of the amount withheld from the proceeds of the 2006 real estate sales.[8] In *Lundy*, the Supreme Court applied the two-year lookback (to date of payment) rule of section 6511(b)(2)(B) (rather than the three-year lookback (to date of return filing) rule of section 6511(b)(2)(A)) under circumstances in which the taxpayer filed a return after issuance of the notice of deficiency, and, in *Healer*, we followed *Lundy* and rejected the taxpayer's argument that an SFR constituted a return filed by the taxpayer for purposes of section 6511. Thus, the 2006 SFR that respondent executed on Mrs. Rader's behalf on January 21, 2011, did not give her three years from that date in which to assert a refund claim for 2006 pursuant to section 6511(b)(2)(A).

We also agree with respondent that we may not offset petitioner's 2006 tax deficiency by the amount of the withheld taxes, but not for the reasons stated by respondent.

In *Forrest*, the Commissioner sought to increase a taxpayer's deficiency by the amount of Federal income taxes withheld by the State of California and claimed as a credit by the taxpayer from a 2005 settlement payment (on account of the termination of an employment-related lawsuit) that the parties agreed was not includible in the taxpayer's

[8] We reject, however, respondent's argument that Mrs. Rader is entitled to no credit simply because she stated that none of the sales proceeds were hers. The record indicates that she and petitioner were coowners of the properties, and the title company issued a Form 8288–A to each of them.

income until 2006. Thus, the credit for the withheld taxes claimed by the taxpayer for 2005 constituted an overstated credit. In considering the Commissioner's claim with respect to the withheld taxes we stated:

> Under section 6211(b)(1) a deficiency is determined "without regard to payment on account of estimated tax, without regard to the credit under section 31". Section 31 generally allows the taxpayer to claim a credit for Federal income tax withheld from wages for that taxable year. The amount of an overstated credit may be summarily assessed and is not subject to deficiency procedures. * * * [*Forrest v. Commissioner*, 2011 WL 13626, at *3.]

We then concluded: "Since the [section 31] withholding credit issue is not a factor in determining the tax deficiency, we have no jurisdiction to consider it and therefore may not decide whether petitioner is entitled to a Federal income tax withholding credit * * * for the 2005 tax year." *Id.*

In pertinent part, section 6211(a), which provides the general definition of a "deficiency", states:

> SEC. 6211. DEFINITION OF DEFICIENCY.
>
> (a) IN GENERAL.—For purposes of this title in the case of income * * * taxes imposed by subtitle[] A * * * the term "deficiency" means the amount by which the tax imposed by subtitle A * * * exceeds the excess of—
>
> (1) the sum of
>
> (A) the amount shown as the tax by the taxpayer upon his return, if a return was made by the taxpayer and an amount was shown as the tax by the taxpayer thereon, plus
>
> (B) the amounts previously assessed (or collected without assessment) as a deficiency, over—
>
> (2) the amount of rebates, as defined in subsection (b)(2), made.

In its entirety, section 6211(b)(1), upon which our decision in *Forrest* was based, provides:

> SEC. 6211(b). RULES FOR APPLICATION OF SUBSECTION (a).—For purposes of this section—
>
> (1) The tax imposed by subtitle A and the tax shown on the return shall both be determined without regard to payment on account of estimated tax, without regard to the credit under section 31, without regard to the credit under section 33, and without regard to any credits resulting from the collection of amounts assessed under section 6851 or 6852 (relating to termination assessments).

Thus, only the taxes, credits, etc., listed in section 6211(b)(1), i.e., estimated tax payments, the section 31 and section 33 credits, and "credits resulting from the collection of amounts assessed under section 6851 or 6852", are to be disregarded in determining the amount of any deficiency under section 6211(a).

Petitioners were subjected to income tax withholding under section 1445, applicable to payments to foreign persons on the sale of U.S. real property interests. Withholding under section 1445 does not give rise to a section 31 credit. That is because it does not constitute an "amount withheld as tax under chapter 24 [sections 3401–3406]". *See* sec. 31(a)(1). In reaching that conclusion, we note that the withholding from the proceeds of petitioners' 2006 real property sales, even though prompted, in part, by petitioners' failure to supply the title company payor with a TIN, did not constitute backup withholding under section 3406 because neither of those sales involved a "reportable payment" under section 3406(b)(1)(A) and (B) and (3). Therefore, *Forrest*, which involved a section 31 credit, is inapposite and not controlling.

We conclude, however, that, although the section 1445 withholding herein was applied to U.S. rather than foreign persons, (i.e., nonresident alien individuals, *see* sec. 1.1445–2(b)(2)(i), Income Tax Regs. (flush language)), it gave rise to a section 33 credit. Therefore, pursuant to section 6211(b)(1), we must disregard it in determining petitioner's 2006 deficiency.

Section 33 provides a credit for "the amount of tax withheld at source under subchapter A of chapter 3 (relating to withholding of tax on nonresident aliens and on foreign corporations)." Subchapter A of chapter 3 encompasses section 1445. Section 1445(a) generally provides that "in the case of any disposition of a United States real property interest * * *, the transferee shall * * * withhold a tax equal to 10 percent of the amount realized on the disposition." Section 1445(b) provides a list of exemptions from the section 1445(a) withholding requirement. Section 1445(b)(2) generally provides such an exemption "if the transferor furnishes to the transferee an affidavit by the transferor stating, under penalty of perjury, the transferor's United States * * * [TIN] and that the transferor is not a foreign person." *See also* sec. 1.1445–2(b)(2)(i), Income Tax Regs. (to the same effect). It is clear on the face of the Forms 8288–A issued by the title company payor that it did not have a TIN for petitioners, and petitioners have failed to demonstrate that they furnished to the title company either a TIN or the affidavit/certification of non-foreign-person status required by section 1445(b)(2) and the regulations thereunder. Moreover, although section 1.1445–2(b)(1), Income Tax Regs., states that section 1445 and the regulations thereunder "do not impose any obligation upon a transferee to obtain a certification from the transferor" and that "a transferee may instead rely upon other means to ascertain the non-foreign status of the transferor", it appears that the title company was unwilling to pursue that option and risk becoming liable for the nonwithheld tax pursuant to section 1.1445–1(e), Income Tax Regs., should its ascertainment of non-foreign-person status prove to be incorrect. *See* sec. 1.1445–2(b)(1), Income Tax Regs. (last sentence of first paragraph).

Thus, rightly or wrongly, the title company payor withheld tax pursuant to section 1445(a), thereby giving rise to petitioners' right to a section 33 credit. Because section 6211(b)(1) specifically excludes the section 33 credit from the deficiency computation, we agree with respondent and hold that the withheld taxes at issue herein are not to be taken into consideration in determining petitioner's 2006 deficiency.[9]

D. *Petitioners' Fifth Amendment Objection*

During the trial, petitioner was asked whether he had filed a return for 2003. Among petitioner's grounds for initially refusing to answer that question was his invoking of his right, under the Fifth Amendment, not to "be compelled in any criminal case to be a witness against himself". U.S. Const. amend. V. Mrs. Rader, who testified as to the issue, attempted to justify petitioner's assertion of a Fifth Amendment privilege on the ground that the agent assigned to their case appeared to be connected to the IRS Criminal Investiga-

[9] Also exempt from the requirement to withhold under sec. 1445(a) are sales of U.S. real property interests for $300,000 or less if "the property is acquired by the transferee for use by him as a residence". *See* sec. 1445(b)(5); sec. 1.1445–2(d)(1), Income Tax Regs. Petitioners' 2006 real property sales were for $250,000 and $25,000, respectively. The record is silent regarding the buyers' intended use of the properties, and we can only assume that the title company payor did not avail itself of the sec. 1445(b)(5) exemption either because (1) the buyers did not intend to use the properties as a residence or (2) it was not aware of the exemption.

tion Division (CID). Therefore, his request to examine petitioners' books and records and make a "visual examination" of petitioners' premises implied "that there was some kind of criminal investigation going on." We concluded that petitioner had not "shown a well founded fear of prosecution", overruled his Fifth Amendment claim, and compelled him to answer the question, whereupon he acknowledged that he had not filed returns for any of the years in issue.

On brief, petitioner reiterates his claim of Fifth Amendment protection and, impliedly, criticizes the Court for rejecting that claim at trial, in what we can only assume is an effort to have his admissions of nonfiling stricken from the record. What that would accomplish is a mystery as there is no evidence in the record on which to base a finding that petitioner did file a return for any of the years in issue, nor does petitioner claim that he filed a return for any of those years.

In any event, we hereby affirm our rejection at trial of petitioner's Fifth Amendment claim. There is no evidence that petitioner was actually under criminal investigation for any of the years in issue. In order for an individual to validly claim the privilege against self-incrimination, there must be a "real and appreciable danger" from "substantial hazards of self incrimination", and the individual must have "reasonable cause to apprehend (such) danger from a direct answer to questions posed to him." *United States v. Neff*, 615 F.2d 1235, 1239 (9th Cir. 1980) (internal quotation marks and citations omitted); *see also United States v. Schmidt*, 816 F.2d 1477, 1481 (10th Cir. 1987) (stating that the risk of incrimination resulting from compelled testimony must be "substantial and real, not merely trifling or imaginary" (internal quotation marks omitted)). Petitioner's apprehension of criminal liability, upon the basis of an unconfirmed suspicion that the examining agent was somehow connected with CID, even if genuine, does not, in the context of a civil audit examination with no actual threat of a criminal investigation, meet the foregoing standard. "The fifth amendment privilege cannot be used as a method of evading payment of lawful taxes." *Edelson v. Commissioner*, 829 F.2d 828, 832 (9th Cir. 1987), *aff'g* T.C. Memo. 1986–223.

E. *Conclusion*

Petitioner is liable for the income tax deficiencies that respondent determined for the years in issue.

II. *Additions to Tax*

A. *Introduction*

Respondent determined that petitioner is liable for additions to tax pursuant to sections 6651(a)(1) and (2) and 6654. Respondent has the burden of production with respect to those additions to tax. *See* sec. 7491(c). To meet that burden, respondent must produce evidence showing that the additions to tax are appropriate. *See id.*; *Higbee v. Commissioner*, 116 T.C. 438, 446 (2001). Once respondent satisfies that burden, petitioner has the burden of proof with respect to exculpatory factors such as reasonable cause, *see Higbee v. Commissioner*, 116 T.C. at 446–447, except that respondent bears the overall burden of proof with respect to his increases in the additions to tax, *see* Rule 142(a); *Arnold v. Commissioner*, T.C. Memo. 2003–259, 2003 WL 22053838, at *4, i.e., respondent must prove that there were not exculpatory factors.

B. *Respondent's Section 6651(a)(1) and (2) and 6654 Determinations*

Section 6651(a)(1) provides for an addition to tax in the event a taxpayer fails to file a timely return (determined with regard to any extension of time for filing), unless it is shown that such failure is due to reasonable cause and not due to willful neglect. The amount of the addition is equal to 5% of the amount required to be shown as tax on the delinquent return for each month or fraction thereof during which the return remains delinquent, up to a maximum addition of 25% for returns more than four months delinquent.

Section 6651(a)(2) provides for an addition to tax for failure to timely pay "the amount shown as tax on any return specified in paragraph (1)" unless the taxpayer establishes that the failure was due to reasonable cause and not willful neglect. The addition is calculated as 0.5% of the amount shown as tax on the return but not paid, with an additional 0.5% for each month or fraction thereof during which the failure to pay continues, up to a maximum of 25%.

Id. The amount of the addition to tax under section 6651(a)(2) reduces the addition to tax under section 6651(a)(1) for any month for which both additions to tax apply. *See* sec. 6651(c)(1). Pursuant to section 6651(g)(2), SFRs prepared by the Commissioner under section 6020(b) are treated as taxpayer returns for purposes of determining the addition to tax under section 6651(a)(2).

Section 6654(a) and (b) provides for an addition to tax in the event of an underpayment of a required installment of individual estimated tax. Each required installment of estimated tax is equal to 25% of the "required annual payment", which, in turn, is equal to the lesser of (1) "90 percent of the tax shown on the return for the taxable year (or, if no return is filed, 90 percent of the tax for such year)", or (2) if the individual filed a return for the immediately preceding year, 100% of the tax shown on that return. Sec. 6654(d)(1)(A) and (B). Except in very limited circumstances not applicable herein, *see* sec. 6654(e)(3)(B), section 6654 provides no exception for reasonable cause or lack of willful neglect.

It is undisputed that petitioner failed to (1) file returns, (2) discharge his tax liabilities, or (3) pay any estimated tax for the years in issue. Thus, respondent has satisfied his burden of production, under section 7491(c), with respect to his imposition of additions to tax under sections 6651(a)(1) and (2) and 6654.

Petitioners offer only meritless arguments against respondent's imposition of additions to tax; e.g., in opposition to imposition of the section 6651(a)(1) addition to tax, that nothing "he has read in his research of the law states he is required to file a return"; that the SFRs were not valid returns "showing an amount due and unpaid" that could constitute a basis for imposition of the section 6651(a)(2) addition to tax; and that "[n]othing on the * * * [notice] demonstrates the computation of an 'income' tax upon which * * * [the section 6654] penalty is based." Petitioner's first argument ignores section 6012(a), pursuant to which he was required to file returns for the years in issue; his second argument is belied by the fact that the SFRs meet all of the requirements, discussed *supra*, for a valid return; and his third argument is belied by the notices themselves, which do, in fact, compute income tax deficiencies for the years in issue. We will not painstakingly further address petitioner's assertions "with somber reasoning and copious citation of precedent; to do so might suggest that these arguments have some colorable merit." *Crain v. Commissioner*, 737 F.2d 1417, 1417 (5th Cir. 1984); *see also Wnuck v. Commissioner*, 136 T.C. 498, 501–505 (2011). Moreover, the complete absence of evidence of exculpatory factors and petitioner's exclusive reliance on frivolous arguments as justification for his nonfiling of returns and nonpayment of tax support a finding that respondent has satisfied his burden of proof to show that no such factors exist, thereby justifying his increases in the additions to tax.

We will sustain respondent's imposition of additions to tax under sections 6651(a)(1) and (2) and 6654 for the years in issue. We conclude, however, that respondent has overstated the addition to tax under section 6651(a)(2) for 2003–06 by the amount of the increases in that addition to tax as set forth in respondent's amendments to answer.

As stated *supra*, section 6651(a)(2) imposes an addition to tax for failure to timely pay the amount shown as tax on a return, and section 6651(g)(2), in effect, states that SFRs are to be treated as taxpayer returns for purposes of determining the section 6651(a)(2) addition to tax. The notice for 2003–06 properly bases the section 6651(a)(2) additions to tax for 2003–06 on the amounts of tax shown on the 2003–06 SFRs. Respondent's amendments to answer with respect to petitioner's 2003–06 tax years, whereby he elects married filing separately filing status for petitioner, increases both petitioner's tax deficiencies for those years and the proposed additions to tax, which are based upon the increased tax deficiencies. All of those increased amounts are computed on attachments to the amendments to answer, which attachments consist of a new Form 4549–A, a Form 5278, and computations of the various penalty amounts and of petitioner's self-employment tax for 2003–06. Respondent has failed to attach to his amendments to answer a Form 13496 for any of the years covered by the amendments to answer. The Form 13496, in pertinent part, states: "The officer of the IRS identified below, authorized by Delegation Order 182, certifies the attached pages constitute a valid return under section 6020(b)." The attachments to the amendments to answer satisfy one of the requirements of *Gleason*, *Spurluck*, and section 301.6020–1(b)(2), Proced. & Admin. Regs., for a valid return, i.e., that it "contain[ ] sufficient information from which to compute * * * [petitioner's] tax liability". However, without their having been subscribed to or certified by an authorized Internal Revenue Officer or employee, under those same authorities, the attachments do not "purport[ ] to be", and do not constitute, a section 6020(b) return for any of the 2003–06 tax years. Therefore, we sustain the section 6651(a)(2) additions to tax set forth in the notice for 2003–06 and reject the increases to those amounts set forth in respondent's amendments to answer.

III. *Section 6673(a)(1) Penalty*

As noted *supra*, at the conclusion of the trial the Court, on its own motion, invoked the application of section 6673(a)(1).

In pertinent part, section 6673(a)(1) provides a penalty of up to $25,000 if the taxpayer has instituted or maintained proceedings before the Tax Court primarily for delay or the taxpayer's position in the proceeding is frivolous or groundless. "The purpose of section 6673 is to compel taxpayers to think and to conform their conduct to settled principles before they file returns and litigate." *Takaba v. Commissioner*, 119 T.C. 285, 295 (2002). "A taxpayer's position is frivolous if it is contrary to established law and unsupported by a reasoned, colorable argument for change in the law." *Goff v. Commissioner*, 135 T.C. 231, 237 (2010).

Petitioner makes no principled defense of his failure to (1) file returns or pay tax for the years in issue with respect to the substantial earnings from his plumbing business or (2) report and pay tax on his capital gains from the 2006 real property sales. Nor would he cooperate with respondent in reconstructing the income from his plumbing business. Rather, petitioner makes groundless arguments attacking the SFRs and the notices and makes unwarranted assertions of Fifth Amendment rights. Petitioner's meritless arguments are frivolous within the foregoing definition of that term. Moreover, petitioner's testimony during the trial and arguments on brief are consistent with an intent to delay the collection of income taxes due and owing. *See Winslow v. Commissioner*, 139 T.C. 270, 276 (2012). On that basis we hereby impose on petitioner a penalty under section 6673(a)(1) of $10,000. [10]

Decision will be entered for petitioner in docket No. 11409–11, and appropriate decisions will be entered in docket Nos. 11476–11 and 27722–11.

ROBERT LIPPOLIS, PETITIONER *v.* COMMISSIONER OF INTERNAL REVENUE, RESPONDENT

Docket No. 18172–12W. Filed November 20, 2014.

R collected $844,746 of tax from the target as a result of an audit performed in response to P's whistleblower claim. By letter to P, R said an award under I.R.C. sec. 7623(a) equal to 15% of the amount collected had been approved. Thereafter, P commenced this whistleblower proceeding pursuant to I.R.C. sec. 7623(b)(4). I.R.C. sec. 7623(b)(5)(B) provides that an award shall not be made under I.R.C. sec. 7623(b) unless more than $2 million is in dispute in the action ($2 million requirement). R moved to dismiss for lack of jurisdiction and in that motion contends that P does not meet the $2 million requirement. *Held*: The $2 million requirement is an affirmative defense and is not jurisdictional. We will deny R's motion and allow time for R to file an appropriate motion for leave to amend the answer.

Thomas C. Pliske, for petitioner.
Ashley M. Bender, for respondent.

OPINION

COLVIN, *Judge*: Petitioner commenced this whistleblower proceeding pursuant to section 7623(b)(4). [1]

---

[10] We acknowledge that petitioner's claim of offset for the taxes withheld from the proceeds of the 2006 real property sales, although unsustainable, is not frivolous. That has no bearing upon, and does not justify, however, the frivolous nature of petitioners' overall position in these cases. After all, the fact that a broken clock tells the correct time twice each day does not alter the fact that it is broken.

[1] Unless otherwise indicated, section references are to the Internal Revenue Code in effect at all relevant times, and Rule references are to the Tax Court Rules of Practice and Procedure. We round monetary amounts to the nearest dollar.

Section 7623(b)(5) bars the making of an award under section 7623(b) unless more than $2 million is in dispute in the action ($2 million requirement). Respondent filed a motion to dismiss for lack of jurisdiction in which respondent contends that petitioner does not meet the $2 million requirement. For reasons discussed below we will deny respondent's motion.

Neither party requested a hearing, and we conclude that none is necessary to decide respondent's motion. For purposes of deciding respondent's motion, we consider the undisputed information contained in the pleadings, respondent's motion and documents attached to his motion, and petitioner's response.

Background

Petitioner resided in New York when he filed the petition. Petitioner filed a whistleblower claim which the Internal Revenue Service (IRS) Whistleblower Office received on August 24, 2007. In the claim petitioner alleged, inter alia, that an individual taxpayer and certain flowthrough entities in which the individual taxpayer had a majority interest had underreported income on their Federal income tax returns.

After reviewing the claim, the Whistleblower Office sent the case to the IRS Examination Division, which examined the target's returns. Later, the Commissioner assessed and collected from the individual taxpayer (and from his estate) tax and interest of $844,746.

The Examination Division prepared a Form 11369, Confidential Evaluation Report on Claim for Award, and returned that form and the examination file to the Whistleblower Office. The Whistleblower Office concluded that petitioner was not eligible for an award under section 7623(b) pursuant to subsection (b)(5) but was eligible for an award under subsection (a) of $126,712 (i.e., 15% of the amount the IRS had collected from the target).

On June 12, 2012, the Whistleblower Office sent petitioner a letter (June 12, 2012, letter) which stated, in part, that "[w]e have approved an award under I.R.C. section 7623(a) in the amount of $126,711.85 based on your Form 211, Application for Reward for Original Information dated August 8, 2007. This award represents full payment of your claim."

Discussion

A. *Tax Court Whistleblower Jurisdiction*

The Tax Court may exercise jurisdiction only to the extent provided by Congress. *See* sec. 7442; *Breman v. Commissioner*, 66 T.C. 61, 66 (1976); *see also*, *e.g.*, Rules 13, 340(b). We nevertheless have jurisdiction to decide whether we have jurisdiction. *SECC Corp. v. Commissioner*, 142 T.C. 225, 229 (2014); *Hambrick v. Commissioner*, 118 T.C. 348 (2002); *Pyo v. Commissioner*, 83 T.C. 626, 632 (1984); *Kluger v. Commissioner*, 83 T.C. 309, 314 (1984).

The Tax Court's jurisdiction over whistleblower cases is provided by section 7623(b)(4). Paragraph (4) in pertinent part provides that "[a]ny determination regarding any award under paragraph (1), (2), or (3) may, within 30 days of such determination, be appealed to the Tax Court (and the Tax Court shall have jurisdiction with respect to such matter)."

Section 7623(b)(1) provides for mandatory awards if certain requirements are met. More specifically, section 7623(b)(1) provides:

> SEC. 7623(b). AWARDS TO WHISTLEBLOWERS.—
>
> (1) IN GENERAL.— If the Secretary proceeds with any administrative or judicial action described in * * * [section 7623](a) based on information brought to the Secretary's attention by an individual, such individual shall, subject to paragraph (2), receive as an award at least 15 percent but not more than 30 percent of the collected proceeds (including penalties, interest, additions to tax, and additional amounts) resulting from the action (including any related actions) or from any settlement in response to such action. The determination of the amount of such award by the Whistleblower Office shall depend upon the extent to which the individual substantially contributed to such action.

Section 7623(b)(5)(B) provides in relevant part that "[section 7623(b)] shall apply with respect to any action * * * if the tax, penalties, interest, additions to tax, and additional amounts in dispute exceed $2,000,000". The phrase "any action" refers to "any administrative or judicial action" with which the Secretary "proceeds" based on information provided by a whistleblower under section 7623. *See* sec. 7623(a) and (b)(1).

B. *Respondent's Motion*

In the motion respondent points out that the June 12, 2012, letter (1) states the Whistleblower Office had approved an award under section 7623(a) and (2) makes no reference to section 7623(b).[2] In the motion respondent also (1) contends that petitioner is not entitled to an award under section 7623(b) (and thus the Court lacks jurisdiction) because petitioner does not meet the $2 million requirement, and (2) acknowledges that section 7623(b)(5)(B) itself is not "jurisdictional in character".

C. *Whether the $2 Million Requirement Is Jurisdictional*

In considering whether to grant respondent's motion we will decide (1) whether section 7623(b)(5)(B) is jurisdictional or is an affirmative defense, and if the latter, (2) what procedures apply to our consideration of the $2 million limit.

The Supreme Court has "endeavored in recent years to 'bring some discipline' to the use of the term 'jurisdictional' ", cautioning courts not to "lightly attach those 'drastic' consequences to limits Congress has enacted." *See Gonzalez v. Thaler*, 565 U.S. ___, ___, 132 S. Ct. 641, 648 (2012). Recognizing that "[j]urisdictional rules may * * * result in the waste of judicial resources and may unfairly prejudice litigants", *see Henderson ex rel. Henderson v. Shinseki*, 562 U.S. 428, 434 (2011), the Supreme Court has created a "readily administrable bright line" rule for courts to use in deciding whether a statutory provision affects a court's jurisdiction, *see Arbaugh v. Y & H Corp.*, 546 U.S. 500, 503, 516 (2006); *see also Gonzalez*, 565 U.S. at ___, 132 S. Ct. at 648; *Henderson*, 562 U.S. at 435. Specifically, courts are to review whether Congress " 'clearly states that a threshold limitation on a statute's scope shall count as jurisdictional' * * * [b]ut when 'Congress does not rank a statutory limitation on cov-

[2] The letter from the Whistleblower Office does not refer to sec. 7623(b), but the phrase in the letter "[t]his award represents full payment of your claim" obviously denies petitioner's claim under that subsection. Denying a whistleblower's claim under sec. 7623(b) without saying so does not deprive this Court of jurisdiction. *Cooper v. Commissioner*, 135 T.C. 70 (2010) (holding a Whistleblower Office letter constituted a determination where it stated that an award determination could not be made under sec. 7623(b)).

erage as jurisdictional, courts should treat the restriction as nonjurisdictional' [in character]." *Gonzalez*, 565 U.S. at ___, 132 S. Ct. at 648 (quoting *Arbaugh*, 546 U.S. at 515, 516); *Henderson*, 562 U.S. at 436. Moreover, the "jurisdictional analysis must focus on the 'legal character' of the requirement, * * * which * * * [may be] discerned by looking to the condition's text, context, and relevant historical treatment". *Reed Elsevier, Inc. v. Muchnick*, 559 U.S. 154, 166 (2010) (citation omitted). The Supreme Court has stated that this approach "is suited to capture Congress' likely intent and also provides helpful guidance for courts and litigants, who will be 'duly instructed' regarding a rule's nature." *Henderson*, 562 U.S. at 436.

Available indicators of congressional intent are not sufficient to support the conclusion that section 7623(b)(5)(B) is jurisdictional. The text of section 7623(b)(5)(B) does not clearly indicate that Congress intended this provision to serve as a jurisdictional bar. *See Henderson*, 562 U.S. at 438. Rather, an entirely separate provision, section 7623(b)(4), provides that this Court has jurisdiction over "the matter" that is the subject of any determination regarding an award under section 7623(b)(1), (2), or (3). The fact that the two provisions are close together is not dispositive. *See Gonzalez*, 565 U.S. at ___, 132 S. Ct. at 651 ("Mere proximity will not turn a rule that speaks in nonjurisdictional terms into a jurisdictional hurdle."). The legislative history sheds no light on the question whether section 7623(b)(5) is jurisdictional. It is noteworthy that when Congress has chosen to place an amount in controversy as a jurisdictional bar on a Federal court's authority to review a matter, it has done so expressly. *See* 16 U.S.C. sec. 814 (2012) ("[The] United States district courts shall only have jurisdiction of cases when the amount claimed by the owner of the property to be condemned exceeds $3,000[.]"); 22 U.S.C. sec. 6713 (2012) ("The district courts of the United States shall have original jurisdiction, concurrent with the United States Court of Federal Claims, of any civil action or claim described in subparagraph (A) that does not exceed $10,000."); 28 U.S.C. sec. 1332(a) (2012) ("The district courts shall have original jurisdiction of all civil actions where the matter in controversy exceeds the sum or value of $75,000[.]"); *id.* sec. 1346 ("The district courts shall have original jurisdiction, concurrent with the

United States Court of Federal Claims, of * * * [a]ny other civil action or claim against the United States, not exceeding $10,000 in amount[.]"). In sum, we conclude that section 7623(b)(5)(B) is not a jurisdictional requirement. [3]

D. *Whether Section 7623(b) Is an Affirmative Defense*

We next decide whether section 7623(b)(5) creates an affirmative defense that must be pleaded in the answer and proved by the Commissioner [4] or whether it is an element of petitioner's case and must be pleaded in the petition and proved by petitioner. Neither party included in the pleadings any allegations relating to the $2 million requirement.

An affirmative defense is an "assertion of facts and arguments that, if true, will defeat the * * * [cause of action], even if all the allegations in the complaint are true." Black's Law Dictionary 482 (9th ed. 2009); *see also Saks v. Franklin Covey Co.*, 316 F.3d 337, 350 (2d Cir. 2003). Rule 39 provides a nonexhaustive list of affirmative defenses a party may raise in this Court, including res judicata, collateral estoppel, estoppel, waiver, duress, fraud, and the statute of limitations. In deciding whether a statute provides an affirmative defense, courts often consider practicality and fairness. [5] *See*

---

[3] In a recent opinion we recognized that the parties disputed certain aspects of sec. 7623(b)(5), but we concluded that it was not necessary to reach that issue. *Whistleblower 22231–12W v. Commissioner*, T.C. Memo. 2014–157, at *17.

[4] Rule 39, Pleading Special Matters, provides that "[a] party shall set forth in the party's pleading any matter constituting an avoidance or affirmative defense, including res judicata, collateral estoppel, estoppel, waiver, duress, fraud, and the statute of limitations. A mere denial in a responsive pleading will not be sufficient to raise any such issue." Paragraph (b) of Rule 36, Answer, provides in pertinent part that "the answer shall contain a clear and concise statement of every ground, together with the facts in support thereof on which the Commissioner relies and has the burden of proof."

[5] In their commentary discussing the categorization of affirmative defenses, Wright and Miller state:

> "Fairness" probably should be viewed as a shorthand expression reflecting the judgment that all or most of the relevant information on a particular element of a claim is within the control of one party or that one party has a unique nexus with the issue in question and therefore that party should bear the burden of affirmatively raising the matter. [5 Charles Alan Wright & Arthur R. Miller, Federal Practice and Procedure sec. 1271, at 603 (3d ed. 2004).]

Hernandez-Miranda v. Empresas Diaz Masso, Inc., 651 F.3d 167, 176 (1st Cir. 2011); *Ray v. Kertes*, 285 F.3d 287, 295 (3d Cir. 2002); *Ingraham v. United States*, 808 F.2d 1075, 1078–1079 (5th Cir. 1987); *Jicarilla Apache Tribe v. Andrus*, 687 F.2d 1324, 1336 (10th Cir. 1982).

Since 1867 the Secretary has had the discretionary authority to pay awards to persons who provide information to the Commissioner that aids in detecting underpayments of tax. Act of Mar. 2, 1867, ch. 169, sec. 7, 14 Stat. at 473 (codified by ch. 11, sec. 3463, 35 Rev. Stat. 686 (1873–74)). In 2006 Congress enacted section 7623(b) to encourage tax whistleblowers to provide information regarding persons who underpay tax or violate the internal revenue laws. *See Cooper v. Commissioner*, 135 T.C. 70, 73 (2010). Section 7623(b)(4) provides this Court with jurisdiction over any determination made by the Secretary regarding an award under section 7623(b)(1), (2), or (3). Section 7623(b)(1) provides for mandatory rather than discretionary awards if certain requirements are met. *See supra* p. 395.

In assigning pleading obligations and the burden of proof for the $2 million requirement, it is helpful to consider the nature of the information that would show whether that requirement has been met. In the motion respondent contended that the "amount in dispute" in this "action" is $844,746, i.e., the amount assessed and collected from the target after consideration of petitioner's whistleblower claim. In a supplement to the motion respondent contends that "the 'amount in dispute' * * * is the maximum total of tax, penalties, interest, additions to tax, and additional amounts that could have resulted from the action(s) with which the IRS proceeded based on the information provided, if the formal positions taken by the IRS had been sustained."[6] Petitioner

See also Ray v. Kertes, 285 F.3d 287, 295 (3d Cir. 2002).

[6] Regulations first effective after the events in question here provide as follows: "[T]he term *amount in dispute* means the greater of the maximum total of tax, penalties, interest, additions to tax, and additional amounts that resulted from the action(s) with which the IRS proceeded based on the information provided, or the maximum total of such amounts that were stated in formal positions taken by the IRS in the action(s)". *See* sec. 301.7623–2(e)(2), Proced. & Admin. Regs. The regulations are effective and apply to information submitted on or after August 12, 2014, and to claims

Continued

contends that applying respondent's standard would be difficult or impossible because respondent has not provided sufficient information, particularly regarding the audit of the target, showing whether the dispute was for more than $2 million. As a result, according to petitioner, whistleblowers may have no basis for identifying an amount in dispute different from the amount assessed and collected. We need not decide what constitutes the "amount in dispute" at this time.

The Commissioner generally should have easy access to all of the records or documents that would show whether the amount in dispute in "the action", i.e., "any administrative or judicial action", sec. 7623(b)(1), initiated against the target as a result of the whistleblower claim exceeds $2 million. Those documents may not be available to the whistleblower and may constitute confidential taxpayer information of the target. It would be unduly burdensome to require the whistleblower to provide or perhaps even to know of the existence of those records. We conclude that section 7623(b)(5)(B) is an affirmative defense and that the Commissioner bears the burden of proof on this issue. *See* Rule 142;[7] *Ray*, 285 F.3d at 295; *see also ITSI T.V. Prods., Inc. v. Agric. Ass'ns*, 3 F.3d 1289, 1292 (9th Cir. 1993) ("'When the true facts relating to a disputed issue lie peculiarly within the knowledge of' one party, the burden of proof may properly be assigned to that party[.]" (quoting *United States v. Hays*, 369 F.2d 671, 676 (9th Cir. 1966))); *Drexel Burnham Lambart Grp., Inc. v. Galadari*, 777 F.2d 877, 880 (2d Cir. 1985) ("The party asserting an affirmative defense usually has the burden of proving it * * * [and] [t]his rule has particular cogency where the facts in support of the defense are peculiarly within the knowledge of the party asserting it." (Citations omitted.)); *Adler v. Commissioner*, 85 T.C. 535, 540 (1985); *Farmers Feed Co. v. Commissioner*, 10 B.T.A. 1069, 1075–1076 (1928) (determining the Commissioner had the burden

---

for award under sec. 7623(b) that are open as of August 12, 2014. Sec. 301.7623–2(f), Proced. & Admin. Regs.

[7] Paragraph (a)(1) of Rule 142, Burden of Proof, provides: "(a) General: (1) The burden of proof shall be upon the petitioner, except as otherwise provided by statute or determined by the Court; and except that, in respect of any new matter, increases in deficiency, and affirmative defenses, pleaded in the answer, it shall be upon the respondent. As to affirmative defenses, see Rule 39."

of proving an exception to the statute of limitations because that information was within his, and not the taxpayer's, realm of knowledge).

E. *Conclusion*

We will deny respondent's motion to dismiss for lack of jurisdiction. Rule 41, Amended and Supplemental Pleadings, provides that "leave [to amend a pleading] shall be given freely when justice so requires", and that "[a] motion for leave to amend a pleading shall state the reasons for the amendment and shall be accompanied by the proposed amendment." We will issue an order allowing respondent 60 days to file a motion for leave to amend the answer to raise the section 7623(b)(5)(B) affirmative defense and to include allegations of fact supporting the amendment to the answer. If the Court grants respondent's motion to amend raising the section 7623(b)(5)(B) affirmative defense, petitioner will have 45 days from the date of service of the amendment to answer to file a reply or 30 days from that date within which to move with respect to the amendment to answer. *See* Rule 37.

To reflect the foregoing,

An appropriate order will be issued.

RSW ENTERPRISES, INC., PETITIONER *v.* COMMISSIONER OF INTERNAL REVENUE, RESPONDENT

KEY LIME INVESTMENTS, INC., PETITIONER *v.* COMMISSIONER OF INTERNAL REVENUE, RESPONDENT

Docket Nos. 14820–11R, 14821–11R. Filed November 26, 2014.

Ps, domestic corporations, each established a retirement plan and received a favorable determination letter from the IRS regarding the plan's qualified status under I.R.C. sec. 401(a). The IRS later revoked the plans' qualified status on the basis that each plan failed to satisfy the coverage requirements of I.R.C. secs. 401(a)(3) and 410(b) and also failed to satisfy the minimum participation requirements of I.R.C. sec. 401(a)(26). Ps petitioned requesting declaratory judgments that the plans' qualified status should not have been revoked. R seeks summary judgment in his favor. *Held*: R's motion for summary judgment will be denied because genuine disputes of material fact remain. *Held, further*, the Court is not limited to considering the administrative record alone in a proceeding concerning a revocation where the parties disagree as to whether the administrative record contains all the relevant facts and as to whether those facts are in dispute.

June Waage (an officer), for petitioners.
Shawn P. Nowlan, for respondent.

OPINION

BUCH, *Judge*: Petitioners are before the Court seeking declaratory judgments as to the revocation of their retirement plans' qualified status under section 401.[1] After initially issuing favorable determinations, the IRS issued subsequent revocation letters stating that the plans did not qualify under section 401(a) because the plans did not meet the coverage requirements of sections 401(a)(3) and 410(b) and also failed to satisfy the minimum participation requirements of section 401(a)(26). Respondent filed a motion for summary judgment and a supporting memorandum. Petitioners oppose the motion and filed a response and a supporting memorandum. After viewing the facts in the light most favorable to petitioners as the nonmoving parties, we will deny respondent's motion because genuine disputes of material fact still remain.

Background

The following facts are not in dispute and are stated solely for the purpose of deciding respondent's motion for summary judgment. These are not findings of fact for this case. *See Estate of Roski v. Commissioner*, 128 T.C. 113, 115 (2007); *see also Estate of Kahn v. Commissioner*, 125 T.C. 227, 228 (2005) (citing Fed. R. Civ. P. 52(a) and *Lakewood Assocs. v. Commissioner*, T.C. Memo. 1995–552).

Scott and June Waage were husband and wife at all relevant times, and either one or both of them were involved in all of the relevant entities. Mr. Waage was the sole shareholder, CEO/president, chief financial officer, and secretary of the Waage Law Firm from its incorporation until its dis-

[1] Unless otherwise indicated, all section references are to the Internal Revenue Code in effect at all relevant times, and all Rule references are to the Tax Court Rules of Practice and Procedure.

solution after the years in issue. The Waage Law Firm employed tax attorneys, certified public accountants, actuaries, paralegals, and accountants. The Waage Law Firm provided a section 401(k) plan for its employees. From 2001 through 2007 the section 401(k) plan offered coverage to between 10 and 31 eligible employees.

RSW Enterprises, Inc., is a California corporation organized in June 1999. Ms. Waage is the president, secretary, and chief financial officer, and Mr. Waage is the vice president. RSW provided real estate and marketing services to the Waage Law Firm. All of RSW's stock is owned by the RSW Irrevocable Trust, U.T.D. Ms. Waage, as the settlor of the RSW Irrevocable Trust, transferred the stock into the trust, the beneficiaries of which are the siblings of Ms. Waage. Ms. Waage's sister is the trustee.

RSW adopted the RSW Enterprises, Inc. Defined Benefit Pension Plan (RSW plan). The IRS issued a favorable determination letter dated August 27, 2002, regarding the RSW plan. During each year in issue RSW contributed money to the RSW plan and deducted the contributed amount on its return. During those years Mr. and Ms. Waage were the only plan participants.

Key Lime Investments, Inc., is a Nevada corporation organized in December 2001. Ms. Waage is the president, secretary, and chief financial officer, and Mr. Waage is the vice president. Key Lime licensed intellectual property to the Waage Law Firm. All of Key Lime's stock is owned by the Key Lime Irrevocable Trust, U.T.D. Ms. Waage, as the settlor of the Key Lime Irrevocable Trust, transferred the stock into the trust, the beneficiaries of which are the siblings of Ms. Waage. Ms. Waage's sister is the trustee.

Key Lime adopted the Key Lime, Inc. 412(i) Defined Benefit Pension Plan (Key Lime plan). The IRS issued a favorable determination letter dated August 27, 2004, regarding the Key Lime plan. During each year in issue Key Lime contributed money to the Key Lime plan and deducted the contributed amount on its return. During those years Mr. and Mrs. Waage were the only plan participants.

The IRS issued revocation letters regarding both the RSW plan and the Key Lime plan. On April 5, 2011, the IRS mailed RSW a final revocation letter notifying it that the RSW plan did not meet the qualification requirements of section 401(a) for the plan year ending June 30, 2002, and all subsequent plan years. The IRS issued a similar letter on the same day to Key Lime notifying it that the Key Lime plan did not meet the qualification requirements of section 401(a) for the plan year ending November 30, 2002, and all subsequent plan years. In essence, the IRS asserts that the Waages are the true owners of both RSW and Key Lime and that because Mr. Waage owns the Waage Law Firm, all three entities are all part of the same controlled group. The IRS also asserts that RSW, Key Lime, and the Waage Law Firm are part of the same affiliated service group because the Waages own RSW and Key Lime and a significant portion of RSW's and Key Lime's business is the performance of services for the Waage Law Firm. Accordingly, because the Waages were the only participants in the RSW plan and the Key Lime plan and the plans were not offered to the employees of the Waage Law Firm, the plans were no longer qualified under section 401(a). Both RSW and Key Lime, while maintaining their principal places of business in California, petitioned this Court. These cases were later consolidated.

Discussion

I. *Summary Judgment*

The purpose of summary judgment is to avoid unnecessary and expensive trials. *Fla. Peach Corp. v. Commissioner*, 90 T.C. 678, 681 (1988). However, summary judgment is not a substitute for trial, and it should not be invoked in proceedings where there are disputed facts. *Shiosaki v. Commissioner*, 61 T.C. 861, 862 (1974). Summary judgment may be granted "if the pleadings, answers to interrogatories, depositions, admissions, and any other acceptable materials, together with the affidavits or declarations, if any, show that there is no genuine dispute as to any material fact and that a decision may be rendered as a matter of law." Rule 121(b).

The party moving for summary judgment bears the burden of demonstrating that a genuine dispute does not exist as to any material fact. *Sundstrand Corp. v. Commissioner*, 98 T.C. 518, 520 (1992), *aff'd*, 17 F.3d 965 (7th Cir. 1994). Because the moving party bears this burden, any factual inferences will be treated in a manner that is most favorable to the nonmoving party. *Dahlstrom v. Commissioner*, 85 T.C. 812, 821 (1985). While the burden falls on the moving party, the nonmoving party "may not rest upon the mere allegations or denials of such party's pleading, but such party's response * * * must set forth specific facts showing that there is a genuine dispute for trial." Rule 121(d). The question of whether there is a dispute for trial in this declaratory judgment proceeding concerning a plan revocation is further complicated by another issue: whether we can go beyond the administrative record.

II. *Tax Court Jurisdiction*

Section 401(a) provides the requirements that must be met for a trust forming part of a stock bonus, pension, or profit-sharing plan to be eligible for favorable tax treatment. This Court has jurisdiction to issue a declaratory judgment with respect to a determination by the Secretary regarding the initial or continuing qualification of a retirement plan under section 401(a). Sec. 7476(a). A determination relating to a continuing qualification includes a revocation. *Id.*

Both parties point us to Rule 217. Rule 217(b)(2) provides that resolution by summary judgment may be appropriate in actions for declaratory judgment. And respondent argues that summary judgment is appropriate because our review is limited to the administrative record. Respondent cites *Stepnowski v. Commissioner*, 124 T.C. 198 (2005), *aff'd*, 456 F.3d 320 (3d Cir. 2006), as support for the proposition that we are limited to the administrative record; however, respondent's position is contradicted by our Rules, which provide that disposition of an action for declaratory judgment involving a revocation "may be made on the basis of the administrative record alone *only* where the parties agree that such record contains all the relevant facts and that such facts are not in dispute." Rule 217(a) (emphasis added). Because *Stepnowski* did not involve a revocation, it is not controlling here.

In *Stepnowski*, a corporation requested a determination letter after amending its plan to comply with a change in the law. The corporation received a favorable determination, but a plan participant petitioned this Court in response to the favorable determination because that participant believed that the amendment was an impermissible cutback. Although the parties stipulated to the administrative record, the plan participant sought to conduct additional discovery. In discussing the Court's rationale in denying the request, the Court stated:

> The legislative history of section 7476 makes clear that Congress did not expect the Court to conduct a trial de novo in declaratory judgment actions arising under that section, no matter whether that action arose with respect to the initial qualification or the continuing qualification of a retirement plan. See *Tamko Asphalt Prods., Inc. v. Commissioner*, 658 F.2d 735, 738–739 (10th Cir. 1981), affg. 71 T.C. 824 (1979); H. Rept. 93–807, at 108 (1974), 1974–3 C.B. (Supp.) 236, 343; S. Rept. 93–383, at 114 (1973), 1974–3 C.B. (Supp.) 80, 193; see also *Wenzel v. Commissioner*, * * * [707 F.2d 694, 696 (2d Cir. 1983), *aff'g* T.C. Memo. 1982–595]. Therefore, discovery or introduction of extrinsic evidence in such cases is inconsistent with the legislative intent that such cases be resolved without a trial based solely on the materials contained in the administrative record. * * * [*Stepnowski v. Commissioner*, 124 T.C. at 206.]

Consistent with *Stepnowski*, absent good cause (for example, when the administrative record is incomplete) we limit ourselves to the administrative record in cases involving the initial qualification of a retirement plan or the initial qualification or classification of an exempt organization, private foundation, or private operating foundation. Rule 217(a). While the presumption in those cases is that we are limited to the administrative record, the presumption contemplated by our Rule is the opposite in the case of a revocation. In cases involving a revocation, we are limited to the administrative record "only where the parties agree that such record contains all the relevant facts and that such facts are not in dispute." *Id.* When promulgating this Rule, we went so far as to highlight the distinction in our notes to the Rule, stating:

> The distinction in treatment under this Rule for cases involving a revocation results from the difference in processing of such cases by the Internal Revenue Service, which usually bases its determination of revocation on its own investigation rather than by accepting the facts asserted by the applicant and which go into the administrative record in other cases. * * * [Rule 217(a) note, 68 T.C. 1048.]

We made this distinction because "[i]n those cases, there may be unresolved factual disputes". Rule 213(b) note, 68 T.C.

1045. "A trial, therefore, may be necessary to resolve these factual disputes." Rule 213(a) note, 68 T.C. 1043.

In short, a revocation case typically involves an audit and likely involves fact disputes, as is the case here. And because this case involves a revocation, we presumptively can go beyond the administrative record. *Cf. Animal Prot. Inst., Inc. v. United States*, 1978 U.S. Ct. Cl. LEXIS 804, 1978 WL 4201 (Ct. Cl. 1978); *Partners in Charity, Inc. v. Commissioner*, 141 T.C. 151, 161–162 (2013).

Neither *Stepnowski* nor the cases it cites fall within this latter rule for the simple reason that they do not involve plan revocations. As discussed above, in *Stepnowski*, the plan was held by the IRS to continue to qualify; it did not involve a revocation. Likewise, in *Wenzel v. Commissioner*, 707 F.2d at 695, the plan participants challenged the IRS' favorable determination as to the plan's continuing qualification after a merger; it did not involve a revocation. *Tamko Asphalt Prods., Inc. v. Commissioner*, 658 F.2d at 736–739, involved an initial determination that the plan at issue did not qualify. In short, neither *Stepnowski* nor the cases it relied upon addressed the question of a plan revocation.

The instant cases present a revocation, the situation in which Rule 217(a) contemplates going beyond the administrative record. RSW and Key Lime argue that the Waage Law Firm, RSW, and Key Lime are not one controlled group because the Waages did not own the stock of RSW and Key Lime because the trusts owned the stock. Respondent counters that the trusts are shams and the Waages are the true owners of RSW and Key Lime. RSW and Key Lime further argue that they are not an affiliated service group with the Waage Law Firm because they did not perform the necessary activities to be considered part of such a group and because the record does not support such a finding. Again, respondent disagrees.

Although RSW and Key Lime do not dispute the genuineness of the items in the administrative record, they maintain that the administrative record contains facts that are conflicting and in dispute. Further, respondent's own motion states that respondent lacks evidence regarding the actions of the trustee and the stock transfers. The filings from RSW and Key Lime indicate that such evidence is available.

Nothing in our Rules precludes RSW and Key Lime from producing this evidence or using it at trial.

Accordingly, when viewing factual inferences in the light most favorable to RSW and Key Lime as the nonmoving parties, we find that genuine disputes of material fact exist. The parties argue about the meaning of Rule 217. We hold that under that Rule, we are not limited to the administrative record in this proceeding concerning plan revocations because the parties do not agree that the administrative record contains all of the relevant facts and that those facts are not in dispute.

To reflect the foregoing,

An appropriate order will be issued denying respondent's motion.

PROCEEDINGS DISPOSED OF UPON MEMORANDUM OPINIONS

T.C. Memo.	*Name*
2014–155	Adell, Franklin Z., Estate, Kevin R. Adell, Temporary Co-Personal Representative
2014–211	Akey, Terry Gene
2014–149	Amazon.com, Inc. & Subsidiaries
2014–245	Amazon.com, Inc. & Subsidiaries
2014–216	Anderson, Robert B. and Cheri L.
2014–233	Annuzzi, Mel A. and Jean L.
2014–249	Austin, Larry J.
2014–176	Bailon-Rivas, Azucena
2014–197	Barone, Daren J. and Colleen R.
2014–256	Bennett, Hamlet C.
2014–152	Bergdale, Micah J.
2014–201	Boyd, Douglas J. and Karen B.
2014–227	Brinkley, Brian K.
2014–167	Brown, Bassett H. and Marcela M.
2014–178	Bruce, Charles T. and Mary A.
2014–239	Budish, James B.
2014–177	Bunch, Delbert M. and Ernestine L.
2014–217	Burrell, Jacqueline D.
2014–185	Bussen, Brian and Apryl
2014–142	Carter, Russell L.
2014–196	Caudle, Dora E.
2014–189	Cavallaro, Patricia, Donor
2014–189	Cavallaro, William, Donor
2014–207	Central Motorplex, Inc.
2014–151	Chapel, Dawn Shannon
2014–248	Clifford, Anthony E.
2014–226	Copeland, Charles and Arlene
2014–181	Cortes, Harold and Julie
2014–186	Cosentino, Garey A. and Jo-Ann
2014–156	Crawford, Marcus Octavious
2014–202	Crile, Susan
2014–139	Cropper, James
2014–179	Crosswhite, Leon Mac
2014–208	Cullifer, Richard H., Transferee
2014–200	Cunningham, Brian R.
2014–147	Davis, Patrick A.
2014–215	Day, David Franklin and Ronda Ching
2014–238	Demeter, Andrea Rae and Jeffrey A. Demeter, Intervenor
2014–136	Dickinson, Ronald R. and Shirley F.
2014–135	Dilani, Dorsaye
2014–168	Doonis, Misty S.
2014–176	Duarte, Eladio
2014–221	Engstrom, Lipscomb & Lack, APC
2014–237	Evans, William D. and Caroline F.
2014–241	Filzer, Paul Neil
2014–219	Fisher, R. Jean
2014–148	Gardner, Raymond E. and Sherry N.
2014–146	Giant Eagle, Inc.
2014–229	Grace Foundation
2014–180	Green, Jerry Wayne and Ramona Kaye
2014–171	Hall, Blonde Grayson, Deceased, Neal Hall, Administrator
2014–170	Hammernik, Brian
2014–240	Hart, Joshua T., Intervenor
2014–214	Hauptman, Bruce A.
2014–192	Hendricks, Anthony J.
2014–134	Hill, John Lewis
2014–250	Hillman, Steven Edward
2014–246	Hosie, Spencer and Diane Rice
2014–212	Howell, Stephen Hunt
2014–135	Hume, Michael
2014–132	Hunter, Colin B., and Alexia Gilmore
2014–164	Hunter, Harrison R.
2014–160	Jackson, Dellward R. and Judith N.
2014–187	James A. Walker, P.A.
2014–240	Johnson, Lindsay M.
2014–205	Kalapodis, Gust and Frances L.
2014–153	Kanofsky, Alvin Sheldon
2014–145	Kaye, Keith Lee
2014–228	Kernan, Eugene J.
2014–236	Kiley, Patricia D.

T.C. Memo.	*Name*
2014–234	Kirkpatrick, Ronald L., Sr.
2014–247	Kupersmit, Harold
2014–137	Lacy-Thompson, Charles and Laura
2014–183	Lang, Patricia L.
2014–210	Langert, Scott M.
2014–195	Larkin, Maryann and Thomas
2014–198	Le Beau, Charles Paul
2014–222	Lozano, Jose M., Intervenor
2014–209	Lundy, Douglas W. and Renitta H.
2014–182	Mantor, Torgeir, Tax Matters Partner
2014–194	May, Howard E. and Judith A., Estate, Marcia M. May, Personal Representative
2014–257	McClellan, Oliver Barr and Cecile Williams
2014–150	McCullar, Janet
2014–163	McElroy, Michael J. and Ruth M.
2014–161	McMahon-Zarlengo, Linda
2014–165	McQuate, Robert S. and Linda S.
2014–259	Milligan, Patricia
2014–220	Moses, C. Lynn
2014–258	Mottahedeh, Peymon and April
2014–251	Muncy, Leroy
2014–191	Mylander, Howard W. and Jacquelyn L.
2014–199	Nguyen, Binh and Nhat K.
2014–213	Odujinrin, Wole, a.k.a. Oluwole Olumide Odujinrin
2014–229	Ohendalski, R.S., Trustee
2014–243	Palomares, Teresa, a.k.a. Teresa Garcia
2014–255	Pansier, Gary Lee and Joan Renee
2014–151	Peery, Joseph
2014–231	Perry, Janetta Lee
2014–235	Powell, James Clement and Lucy Hamrick
2014–253	Price, Raymond, III, and Lynn M.
2014–224	Puentes, Lourdes
2014–218	Reinhart, Kim
2014–230	Reisner, Edward M.
2014–143	Robertson, Keith
2014–141	Rogers, John E. and Francis L.
2014–252	Rosenthal, Jay

T.C. Memo.	*Name*
2014–193	Roudakov, Vladimir
2014–242	Safakish, Amir
2014–244	Salmonson, Christopher
2014–188	Salzer, Donald Thomas
2014–174	Sanchez, Hector
2014–223	Sanchez, Joseph
2014–161	Sandin-Zarlengo, Merilyn H.
2014–162	Savoy, Gregory Scott
2014–159	Schmidt, Leroy S. and Connie M.
2014–138	Schumann, Douglas D.
2014–225	Securitas Holdings, Inc. and Subsidiaries
2014–173	Shi, Zhengnan
2014–203	Smith, Thad Deshawn
2014–201	Suder, Eric G., et al.
2014–172	Swiggart, Michael
2014–140	Synergy Environmental, Inc.
2014–154	Thompson, Randall J. and Karen G.
2014–166	Triola, Robert and Nancy V.
2014–206	Tsai, Stephen, Intervenor
2014–144	Valteau, Harris, Koenig and Mayer
2014–236	Van Malssen, Mark A.
2014–184	Vanney Associates, Inc.
2014–222	Varela, Elizabeth
2014–182	VisionMonitor Software, LLC
2014–169	Wade, Charles E. and Betty G.
2014–133	Waltner, Steven T. and Sarah V.
2014–206	Wang, Irene K.
2014–197	Watkins, Gregory S. and Linda
2014–230	Weintraub, Manda K.
2014–204	Wheeler, Gerald Wayne
2014–157	Whistleblower 22231–12W
2014–158	Williams, Scott Wesley and Michaele Anna
2014–254	Wodack, Rose A.
2014–190	Work, Virgil V., Jr.,
2014–232	Worth, Donald Kenneth and Marie Ann
2014–232	Worth, Frank Kenneth, a.k.a. Frank K. Worth, a.k.a. Frank Worth and Helen Laura, a.k.a. Helen L. Worth, a.k.a. Helen Worth
2014–175	Wright, Terry L. and Cheryl A.
2014–161	Zarlengo, Marco

ISBN 978-0-16-092876-5
90000
9 780160 928765